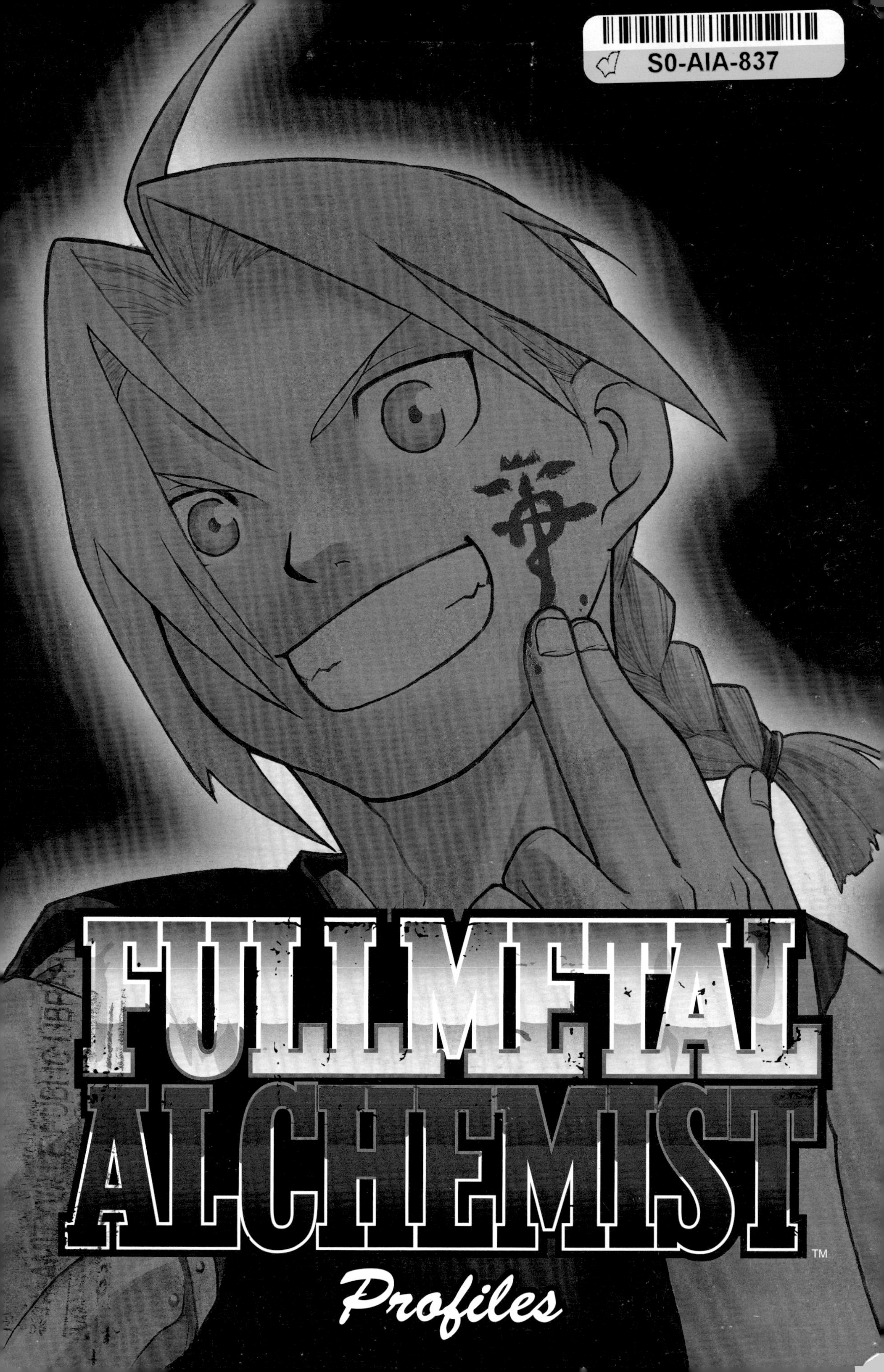
FULLMETAL ALCHEMIST™
Profiles

Hiromu Arakawa's Artistic Secrets

Wanna know how Arakawa puts together *Fullmetal Alchemist*? Here's a step-by-step using the November 2003 cover for *Monthly Shonen Gangan*. We'll look at how the artist develops her work for a specific project and gets the incredible final drawing.

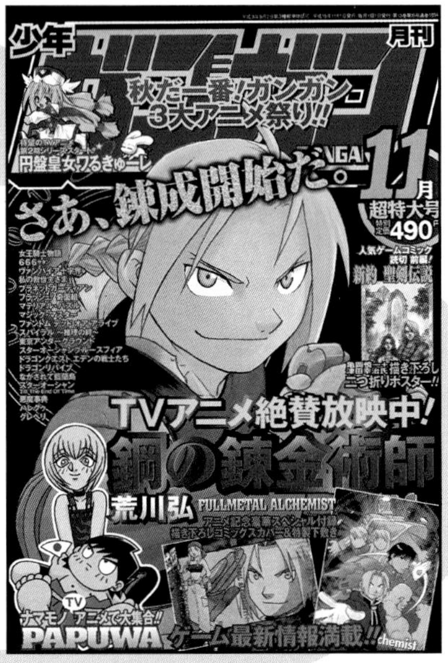
少年
月刊
秋だ一番!ガンガン3大アニメ祭り!!
円盤皇女ワるきゅーレ
さあ、錬成開始だ。
11月
超特大号
490円
TVアニメ絶賛放映中!
鋼の錬金術師
荒川弘
FULLMETAL ALCHEMIST
PARUWA
ゲーム最新情報満載!!

The finished cover used a black background to set off the extra artwork that was displayed in a subtle alchemical transmutation circle motif.

Step 1:

Rough Sketch

After a brief discussion with the editor of the magazine, Arakawa-sensei lays down a rough sketch that is designed to fit exactly where the magazine editor needs it. There are also various notes that have been made on the side of the sketch.

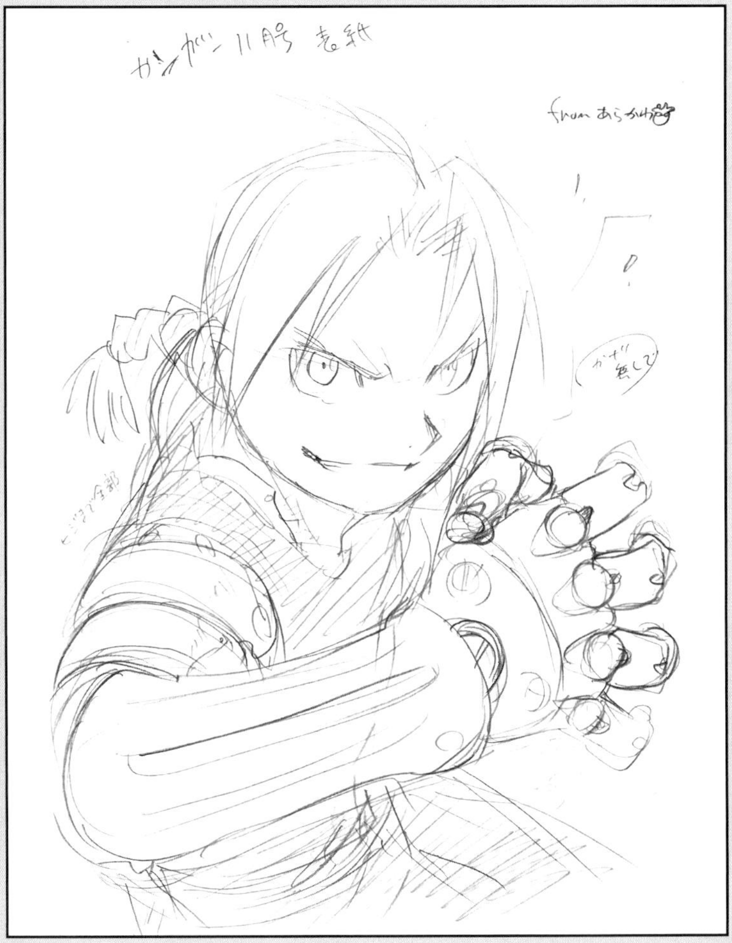
ガンガン 11月号 表紙

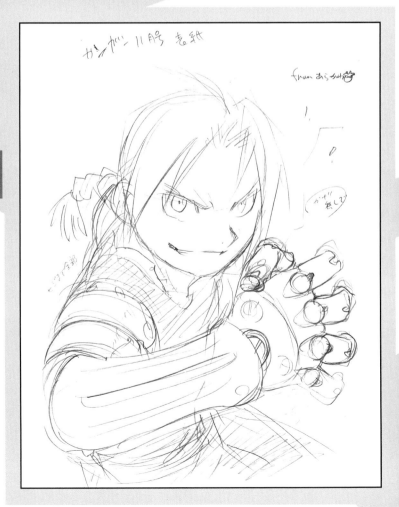

Revealed!!

Step 2:
Final Sketch

Using a regular pencil, Arakawa-sensei finalizes the sketch by erasing any unnecessary lines. When it's cleaned up, the drawing is copied onto thick paper to prepare for the next step…

Completed!

Step 3:
Applying Color

Color is applied in layers. The more detailed the image, the more layers (in this case, the most layers are used for Ed's auto-mail arm). For this particular drawing, the mediums are Liquitex mixed with Copic markers.

The Second Anniversary of *Fullmetal Alchemist*

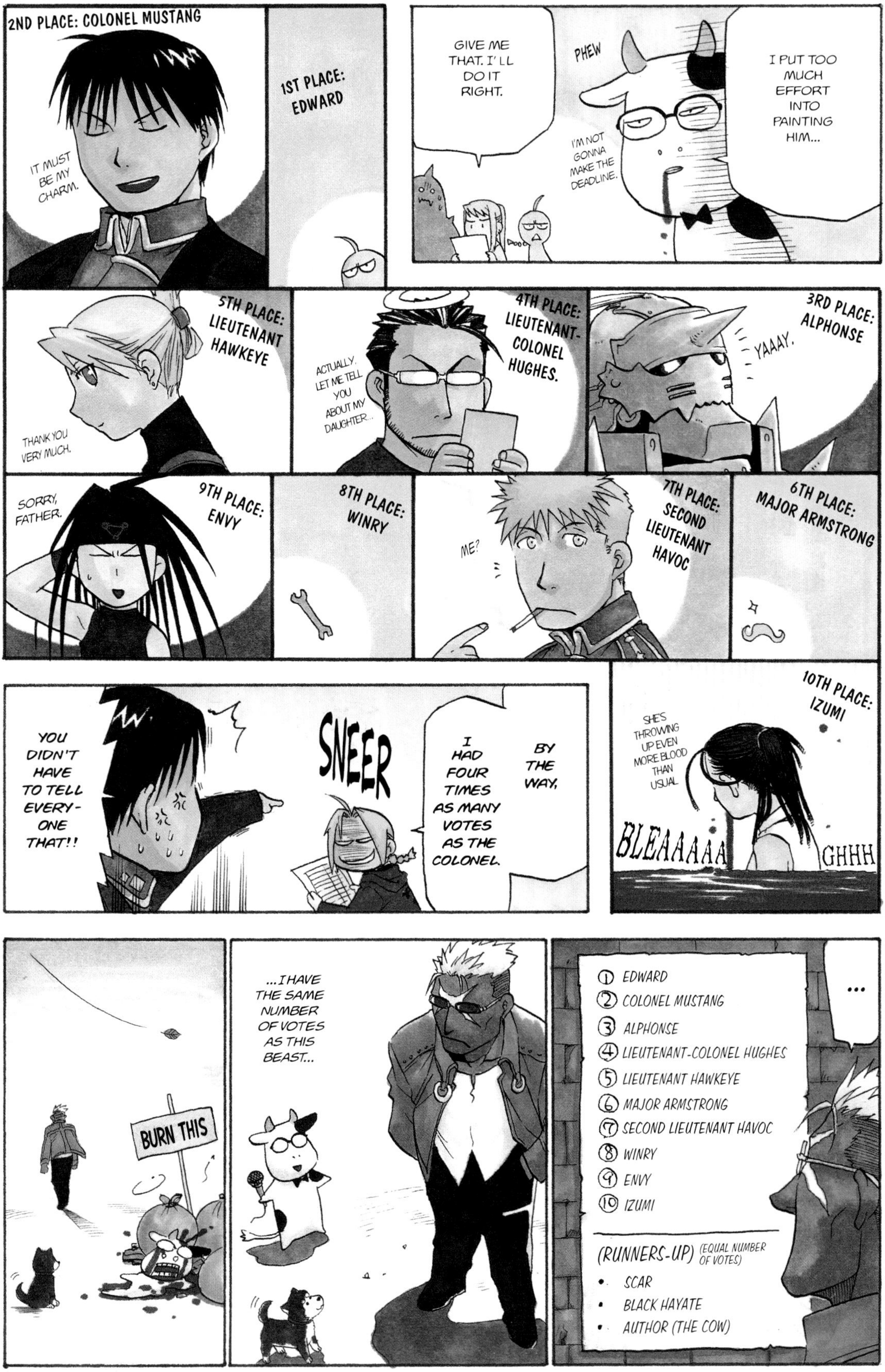
I PUT TOO MUCH EFFORT INTO PAINTING HIM...
I'M NOT GONNA MAKE THE DEADLINE.
PHEW
GIVE ME THAT. I'LL DO IT RIGHT.
1ST PLACE: EDWARD
2ND PLACE: COLONEL MUSTANG
IT MUST BE MY CHARM.
3RD PLACE: ALPHONSE
YAAAY.
4TH PLACE: LIEUTENANT-COLONEL HUGHES.
ACTUALLY, LET ME TELL YOU ABOUT MY DAUGHTER...
5TH PLACE: LIEUTENANT HAWKEYE
THANK YOU VERY MUCH.
6TH PLACE: MAJOR ARMSTRONG
7TH PLACE: SECOND LIEUTENANT HAVOC
ME?
8TH PLACE: WINRY
9TH PLACE: ENVY
SORRY, FATHER.
10TH PLACE: IZUMI
SHE'S THROWING UP EVEN MORE BLOOD THAN USUAL
BLEAAAAAAGHHH
BY THE WAY,
I HAD FOUR TIMES AS MANY VOTES AS THE COLONEL.
SNEER
YOU DIDN'T HAVE TO TELL EVERY-ONE THAT!!
...
① EDWARD
② COLONEL MUSTANG
③ ALPHONSE
④ LIEUTENANT-COLONEL HUGHES
⑤ LIEUTENANT HAWKEYE
⑥ MAJOR ARMSTRONG
⑦ SECOND LIEUTENANT HAVOC
⑧ WINRY
⑨ ENVY
⑩ IZUMI
(RUNNERS-UP) (EQUAL NUMBER OF VOTES)
• SCAR
• BLACK HAYATE
• AUTHOR (THE COW)
...I HAVE THE SAME NUMBER OF VOTES AS THIS BEAST...
BURN THIS

Popularity Poll Results!!

Read from here.

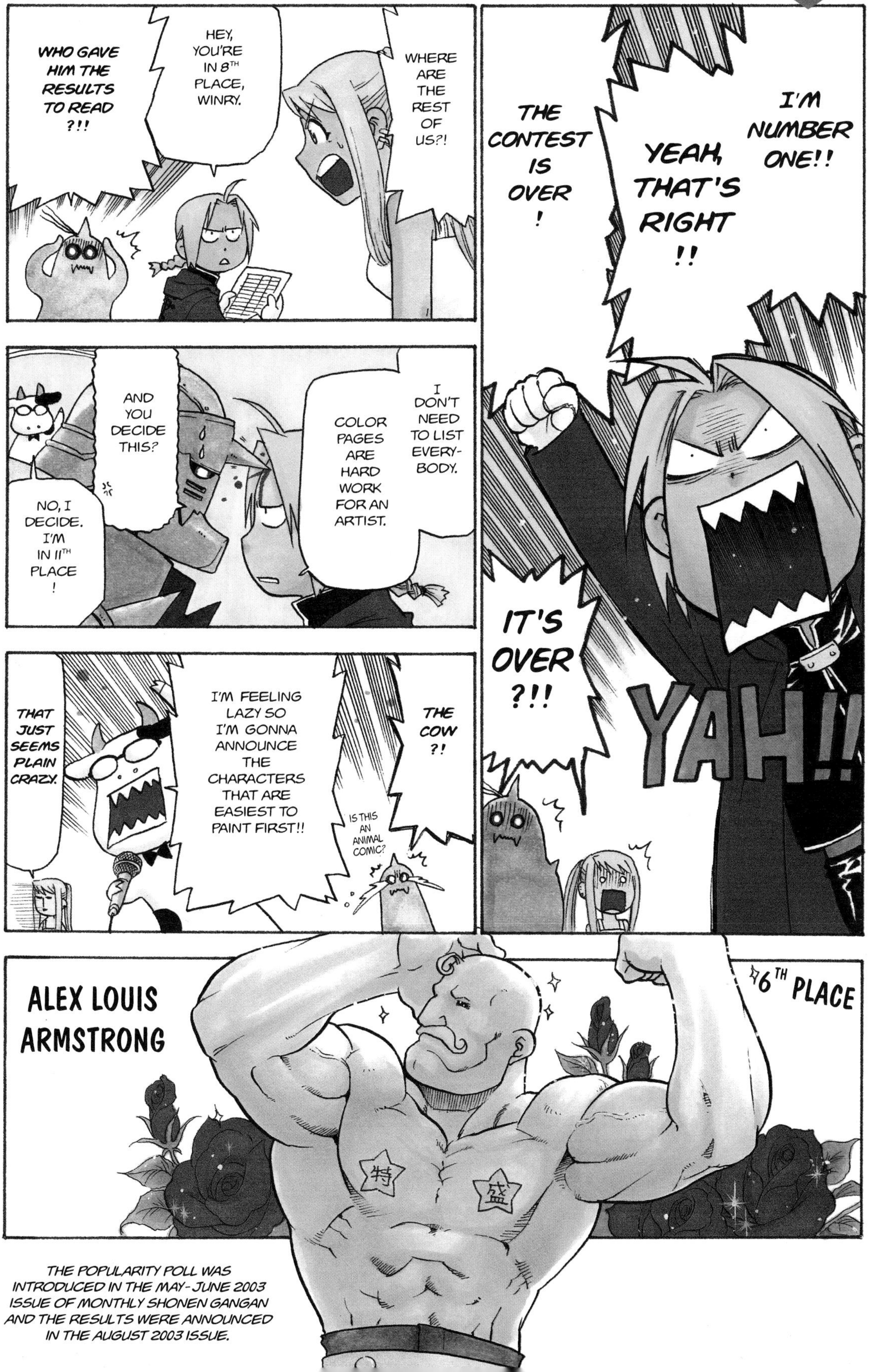

I'M NUMBER ONE!!
YEAH, THAT'S RIGHT!!
THE CONTEST IS OVER!
IT'S OVER?!!
YAH!!
WHERE ARE THE REST OF US?!
HEY, YOU'RE IN 8TH PLACE, WINRY.
WHO GAVE HIM THE RESULTS TO READ?!!
I DON'T NEED TO LIST EVERYBODY.
COLOR PAGES ARE HARD WORK FOR AN ARTIST.
AND YOU DECIDE THIS?
NO, I DECIDE. I'M IN 11TH PLACE!
THE COW?!
IS THIS AN ANIMAL COMIC?
I'M FEELING LAZY SO I'M GONNA ANNOUNCE THE CHARACTERS THAT ARE EASIEST TO PAINT FIRST!!
THAT JUST SEEMS PLAIN CRAZY.
6TH PLACE
ALEX LOUIS ARMSTRONG
特
盛
THE POPULARITY POLL WAS INTRODUCED IN THE MAY-JUNE 2003 ISSUE OF MONTHLY SHONEN GANGAN AND THE RESULTS WERE ANNOUNCED IN THE AUGUST 2003 ISSUE.

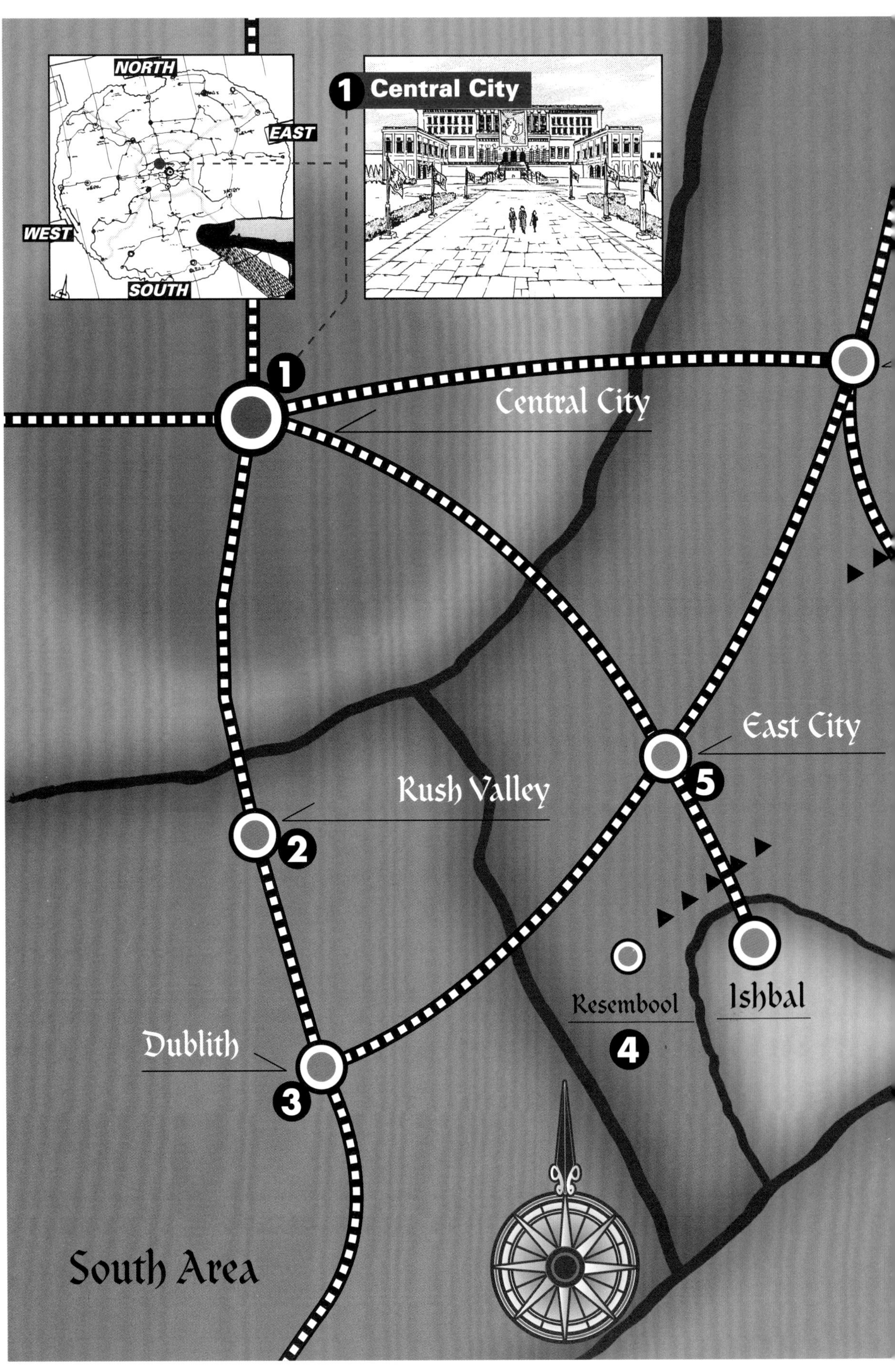
NORTH
EAST
WEST
SOUTH
1 Central City
1 Central City
East City
5
Rush Valley
2
Resembool
4
Ishbal
Dublith
3
South Area

Elric Brothers' Visual Travelogue World Map

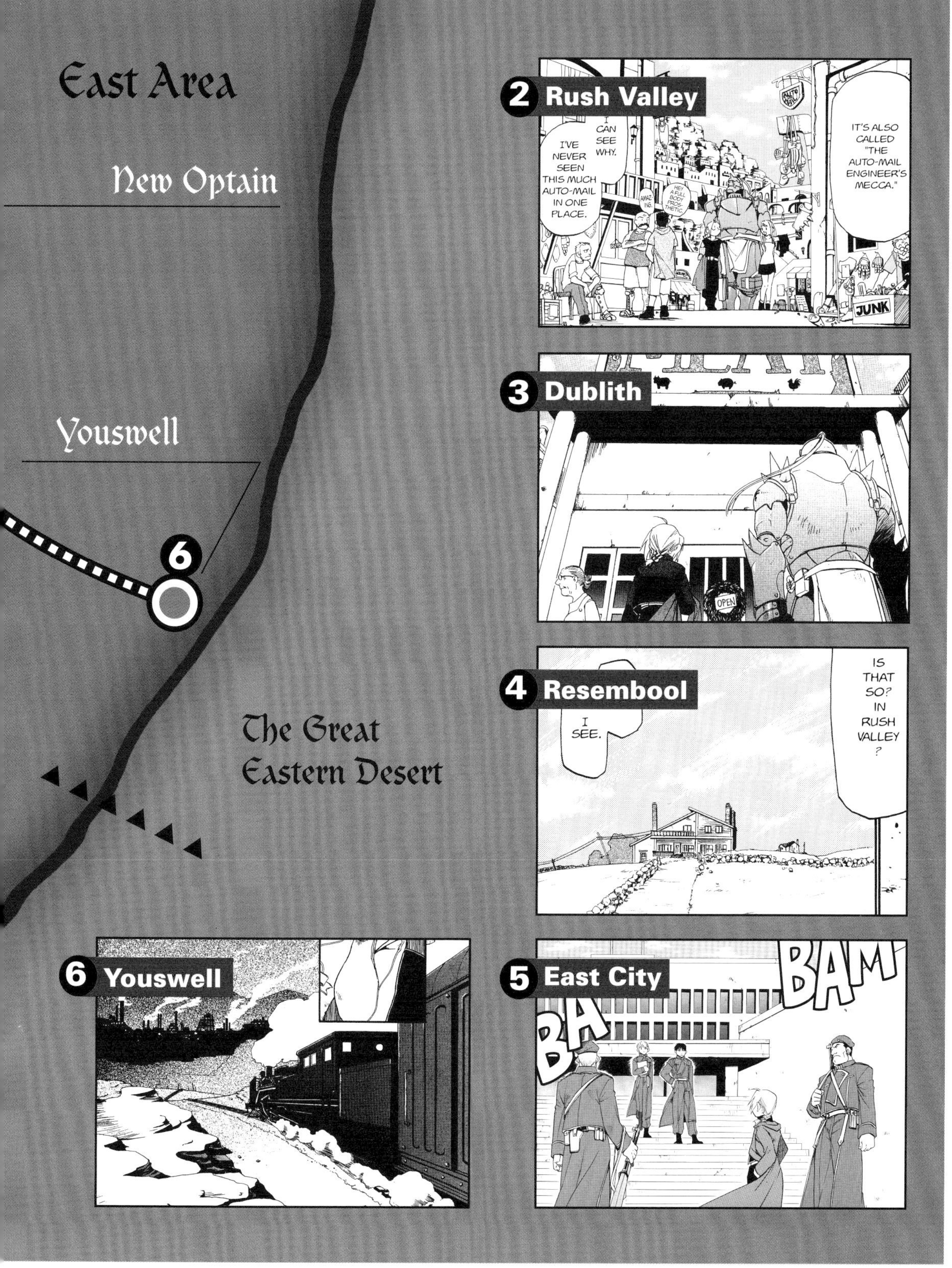
East Area
New Optain
Youswell
6
The Great Eastern Desert
2 Rush Valley
IT'S ALSO CALLED "THE AUTO-MAIL ENGINEER'S MECCA."
I CAN SEE WHY.
I'VE NEVER SEEN THIS MUCH AUTO-MAIL IN ONE PLACE.
HEY, A FULL BODY PROS-THETIC.
AMAZ-ING.
JUNK
3 Dublith
OPEN
4 Resembool
IS THAT SO? IN RUSH VALLEY?
I SEE.
5 East City
BAM
BA
6 Youswell

Fullmetal Alchemist
Final Character Sketches

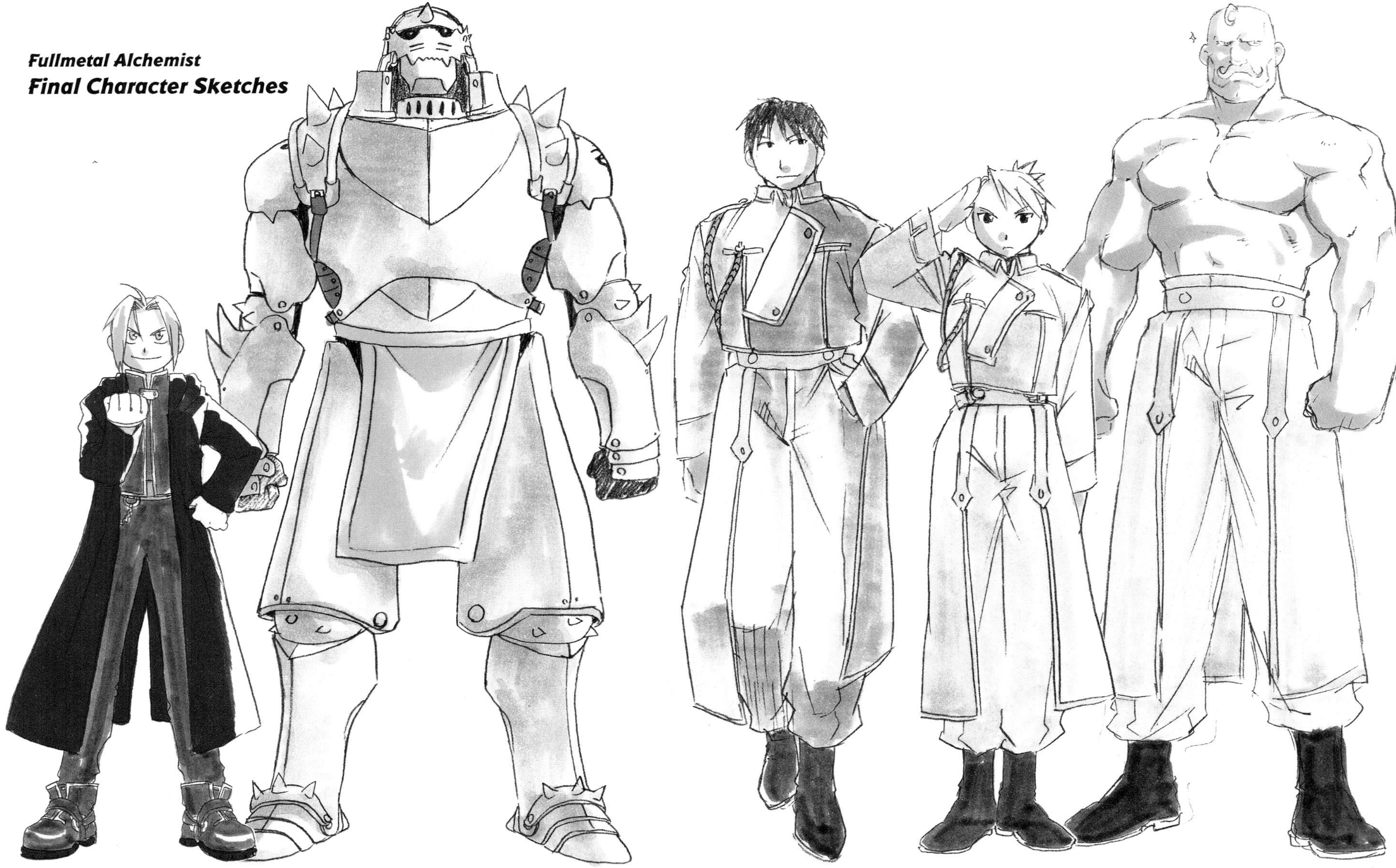

Edward Elric

Alphonse Elric

Roy Mustang

Riza Hawkeye

Alex Louis Armstrong

Fullmetal Alchemist Profiles

Contents

鋼の錬金術師
Fullmetal Alchemist Profiles

Original concept by
Hiromu Arakawa

Translation/Akira Watanabe
Lettering/Wayne Truman
Design/Hidemi Sahara, Casey Dillon
Editor/Joel Enos
Series Editor/Jason Thompson

Managing Editor/Masumi Washington
Director of Production/Noboru Watanabe
Vice President of Publishing/Alvin Lu
Sr. Director of Acquisitions/Rika Inouye
Vice President of Sales & Marketing/Liza Coppola
Publisher/Hyoe Narita

FULLMETAL ALCHEMIST PERFECT GUIDE BOOK

Published by
VIZ Media, LLC
295 Bay Street
San Francisco, CA 94133

Printed in the U.S.A.

First printing, June 2006

www.viz.com
store.viz.com

CHARACTER GUIDE

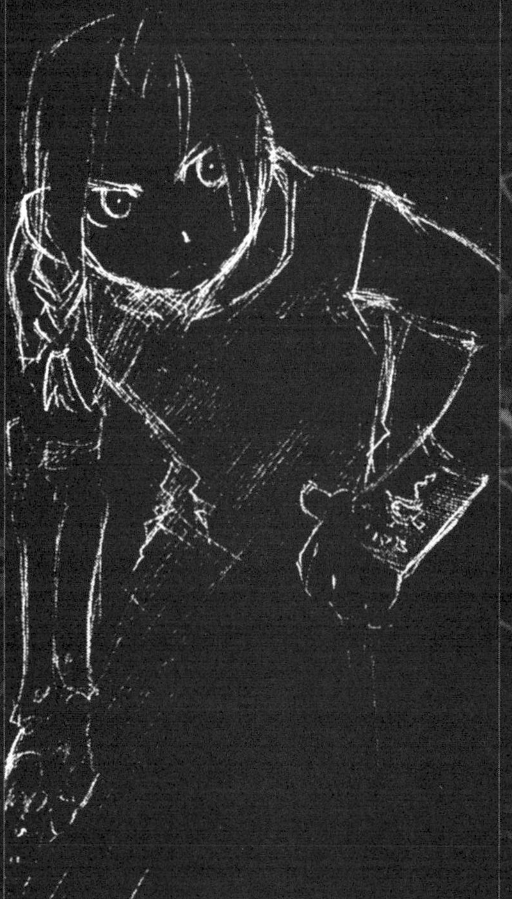

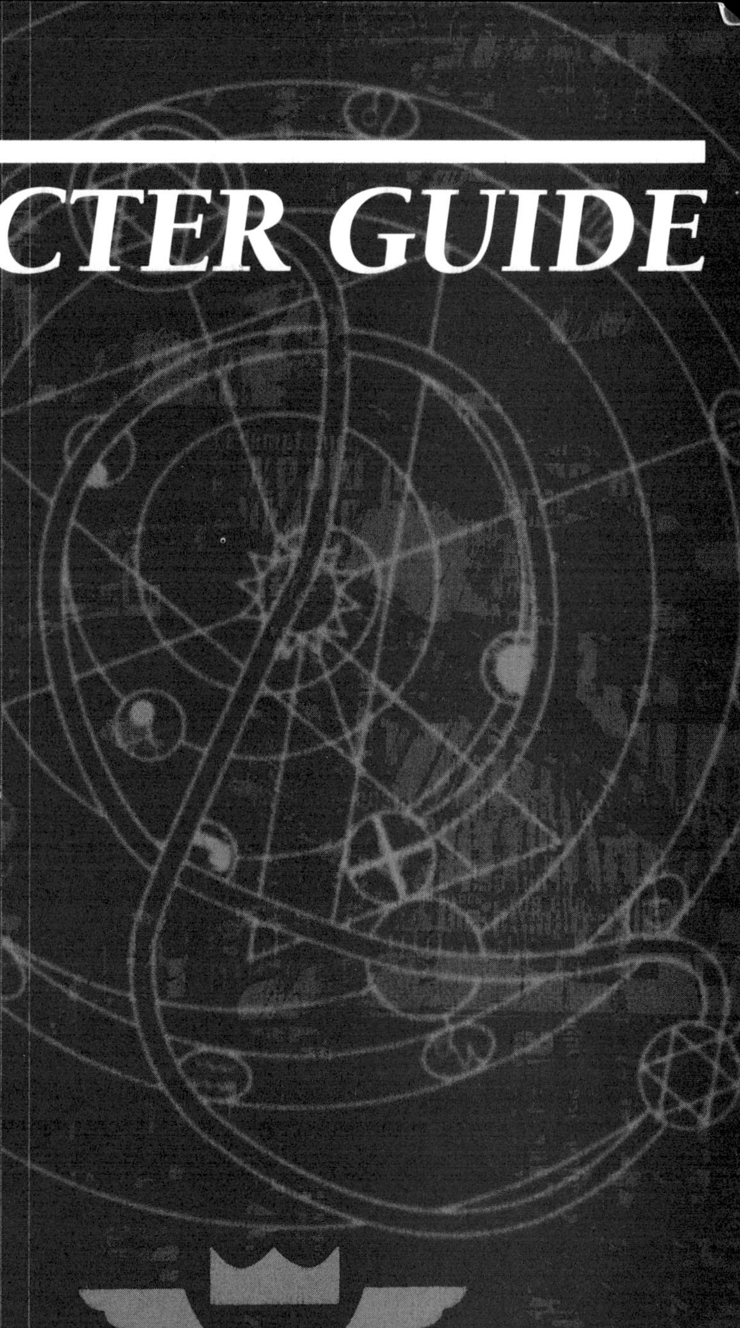

FULLMETAL ALCHEMIST

EDWARD ELRIC

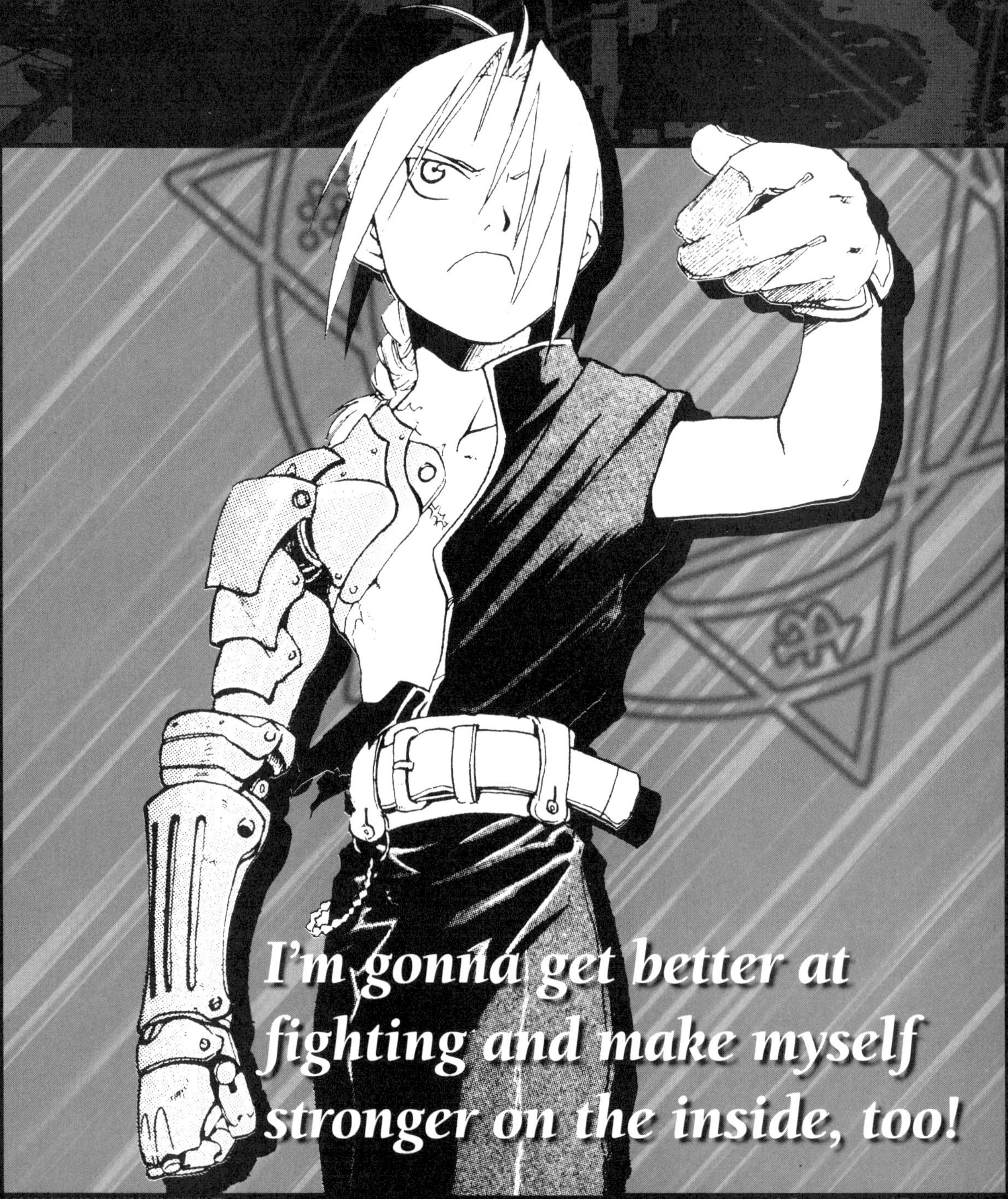
I'm gonna get better at fighting and make myself stronger on the inside, too!

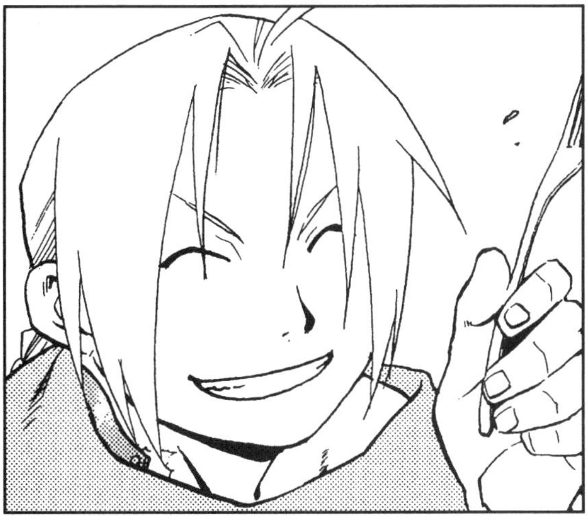

A rare moment of relaxation at the Rockbell house.

Not Your Average 15-Year-Old

Edward Elric is a child genius who was granted a state alchemist license at the tender age of 12. Edward puts up a brave front, but on the inside he's a caring soul with a mission: to transfer his brother's soul from the metal armor it now inhabits back into his flesh and blood body. He hopes to get his own arm and leg back in the process. To do that, the brothers must find the mythical Philosopher's Stone.

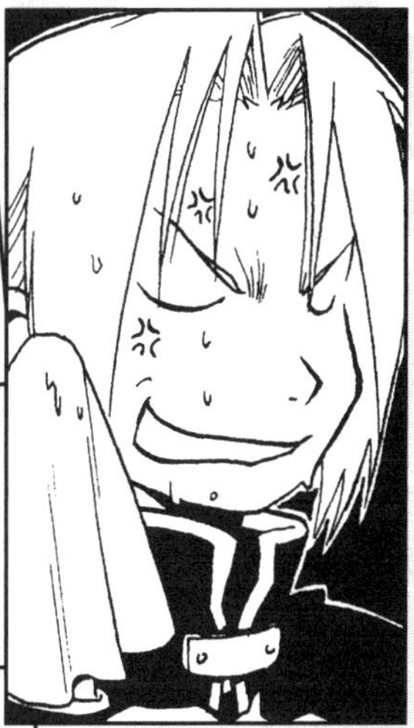

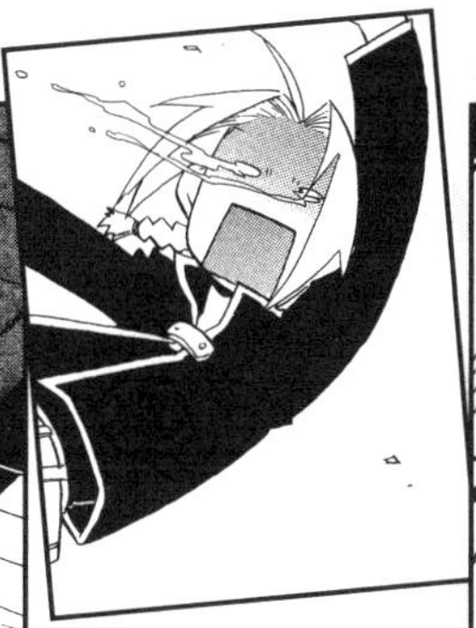

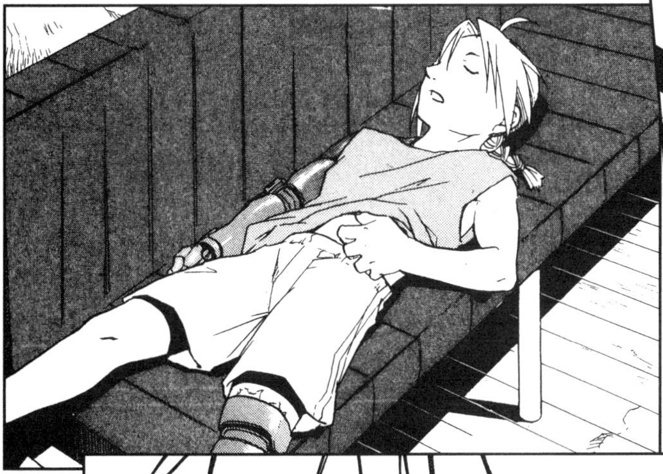

The kid's got range: witness the many moods of Edward Elric.

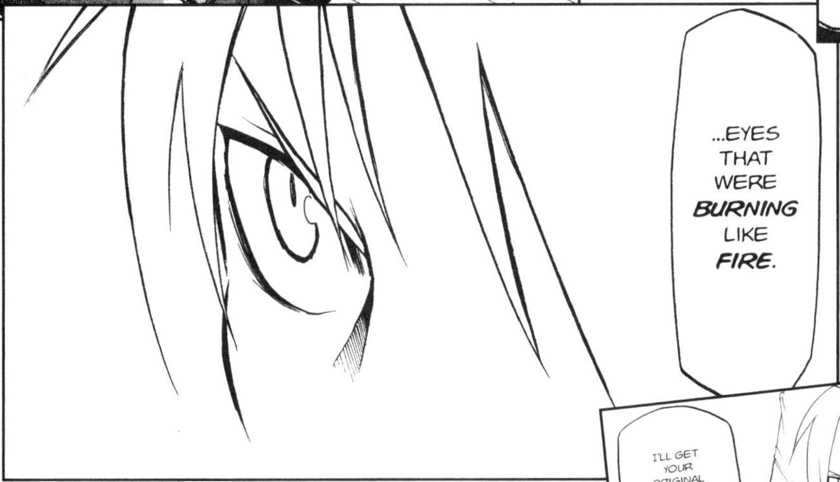
...EYES THAT WERE ***BURNING*** LIKE ***FIRE.***

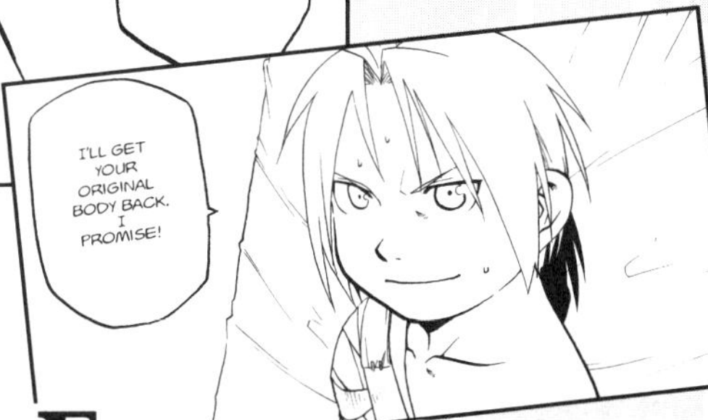
I'LL GET YOUR ORIGINAL BODY BACK. I PROMISE!

Like a phoenix from the flames, Edward Elric rises from tragedy burning with an even stronger determination to reach his final goal.

An Unguarded Expression

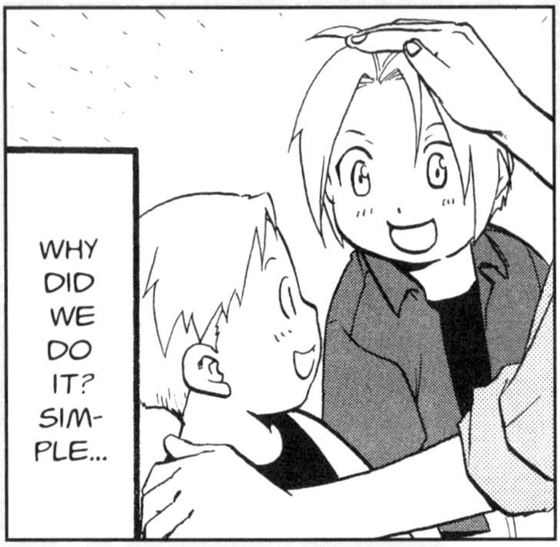
WHY DID WE DO IT? SIMPLE...

The boys initially started practicing alchemy to please their mother.

Fullmetal Steel Prosthetics

When his right arm and left leg were replaced by auto-mail, Ed obtained his state alchemist's license and was given the alias "Fullmetal." While some know him as the Fullmetal Alchemist, others call him the "military's dog" as he has gone against the alchemist's credo of "for the people" in order to obtain his license and to achieve his ultimate goal, to restore his brother's body and to repair his own.

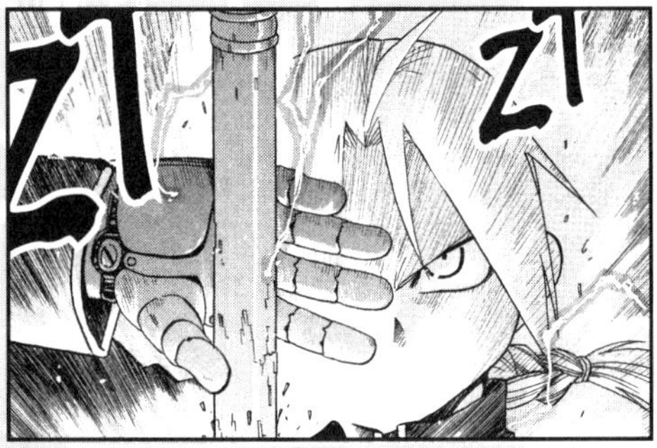
ZI
ZI

During the state alchemist's license test Ed transmuted a spear which he then aimed at the Führer President's throat.

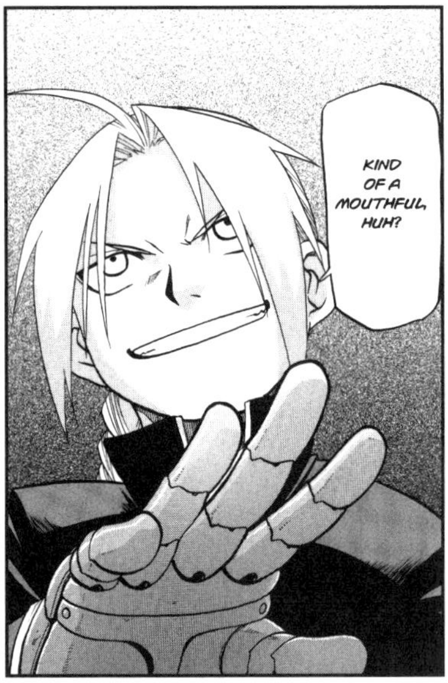
KIND OF A MOUTHFUL, HUH?

Mom gave us praise. That was all it took for us to dive headlong into studying alchemy.

Fullmetal Arm

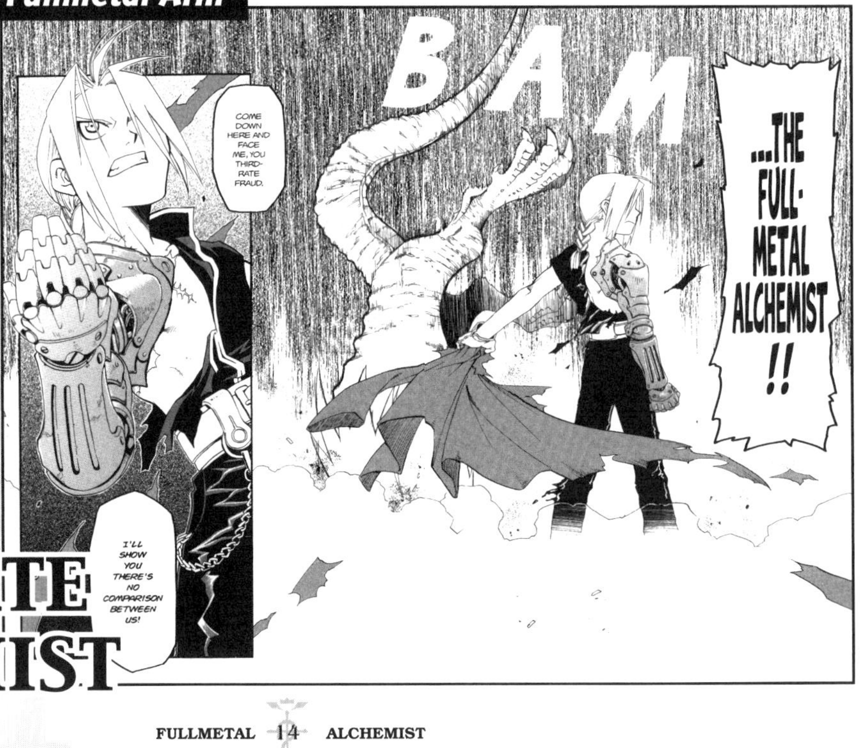
BAM
...THE FULL-METAL ALCHEMIST!!
COME DOWN HERE AND FACE ME, YOU THIRD-RATE FRAUD.
I'LL SHOW YOU THERE'S NO COMPARISON BETWEEN US!

THE STATE ALCHEMIST

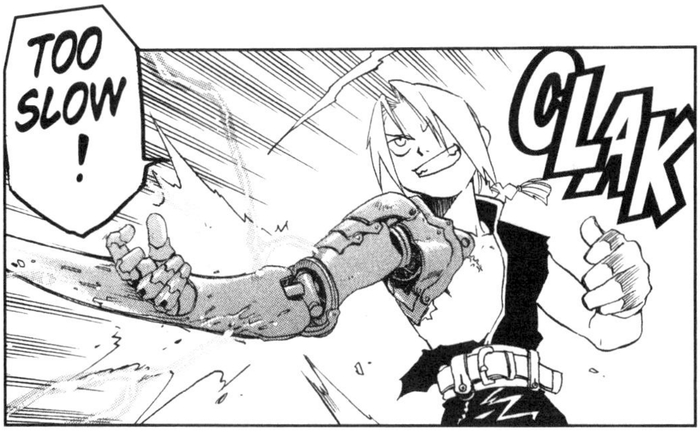
TOO SLOW!
CLAK

Manipulating Matter

Edward Elric can change the shape of anything he transmutes, no matter how large. All he needs is enough material to make an equivalent exchange.

ALCHEMY

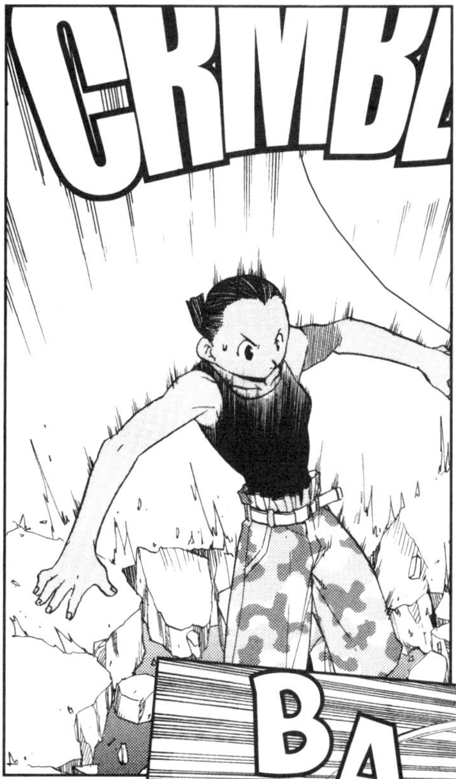
CRMBL

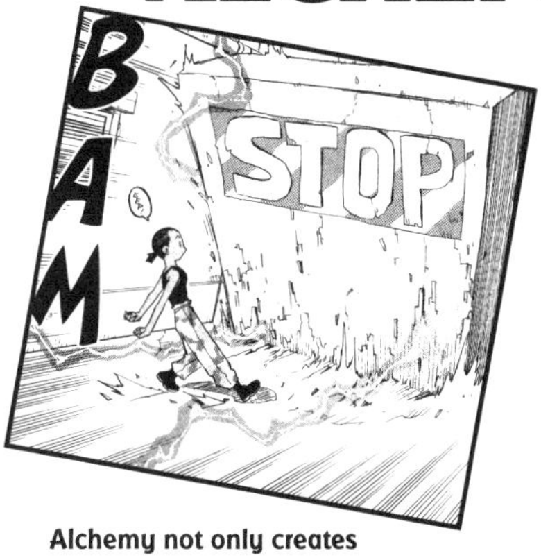
BAM
STOP

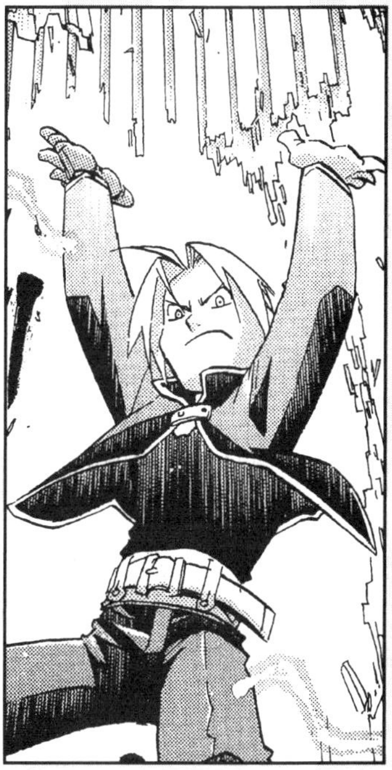

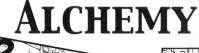

Alchemy not only creates matter, it can also change the density of any substance.

MARTIAL ARTS

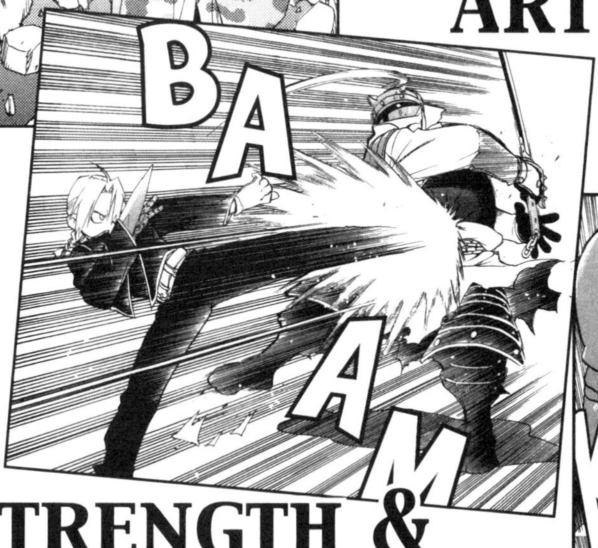
BAAM

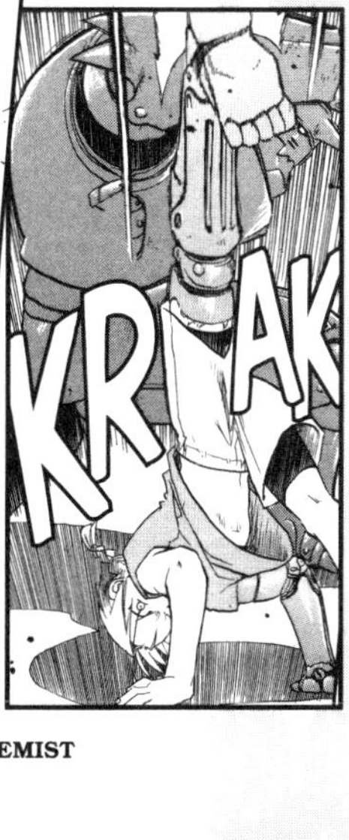
KRAK

Daily Training

Master teacher Izumi Curtis taught the Elric brothers martial arts. They keep in practice by sparring with each other.

STRENGTH & TECHNIQUE

Consequences of Sin

When they were still young, the Elric brothers trespassed into God's domain by daring to conduct a human transmutation. The punishment for their sin was great. Ed lost his left leg and his younger brother Al lost his entire body. In exchange for his right arm, Ed managed to transmute Al's soul into a suit of armor, literally making him a man of steel. Ed has devoted his entire life to putting his brother back into a human body.

IF THAT'S TRUE, I WONDER IF WE CAN BRING MOM BACK.

The Elric brothers ventured into dangerous territory when they broke the rules of alchemy and tried to bring their dead mother back to life.

SNK KRK

SKK

I'll get your original body back. I promise!

OKAY!

LET'S DO IT, AL.

The mistakes of their youth haunt the brothers to this day.

GIVE HIM BACK!!

HE'S THE ONLY FAMILY I HAVE!!

Preparing for the Worst

THERE IS SOMETHING THAT I HAVE TO DO.

SIN

GENTLE HEART

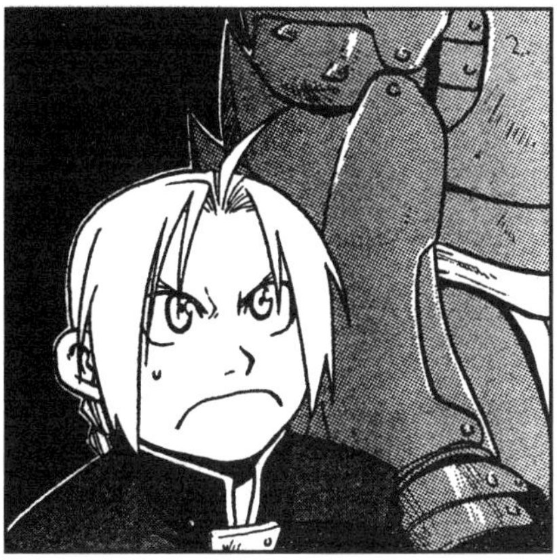

Izumi & Winry

Although the boys have turned their backs on their past, even burning down their childhood home to make sure they can never return, they still have strong ties to a few people. In particular, two women have become very important to the boys after the loss of their mother. At times, their alchemy teacher, Izumi, is more of a parent than an instructor. Winry, the auto-mail engineer, is a childhood friend of Edward's who keeps his artificial limbs in top working order.

TEACHER

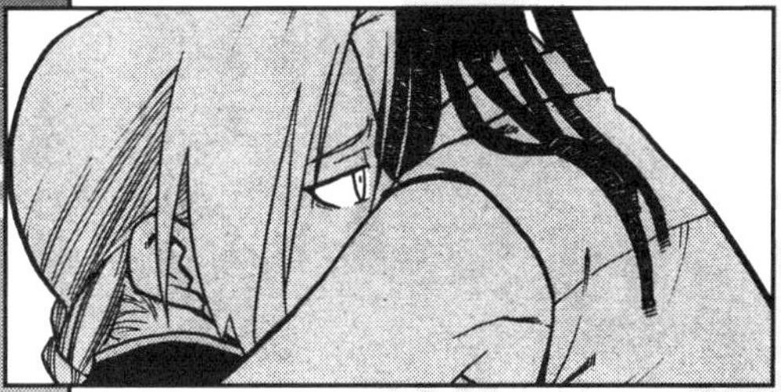

Izumi may be harsh at times, but she is pure of heart and cares deeply for the Elric brothers.

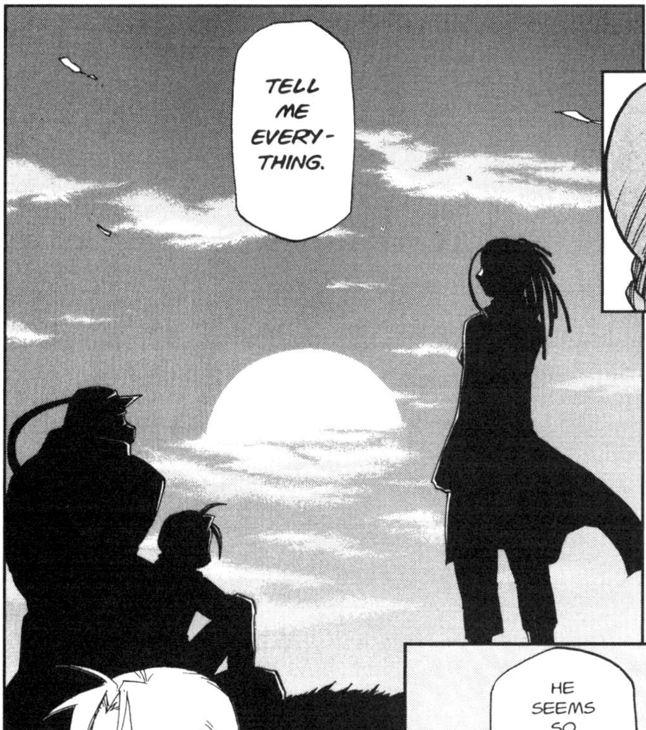
TELL ME EVERY-THING.

CHILDHOOD FRIEND

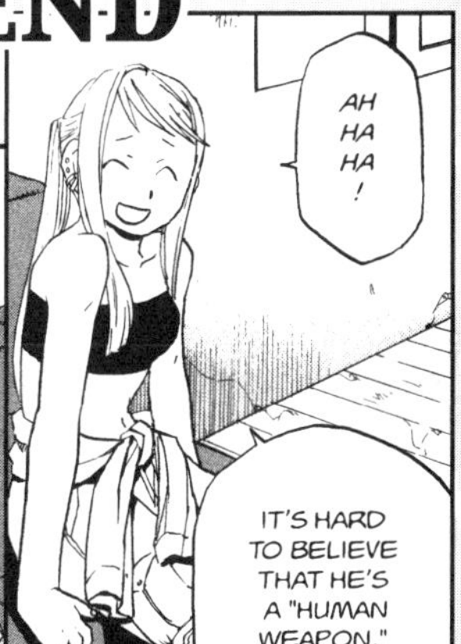
AH HA HA!
IT'S HARD TO BELIEVE THAT HE'S A "HUMAN WEAPON." AFTER ALL, WE'RE THE SAME AGE AND HE'S SO TINY!

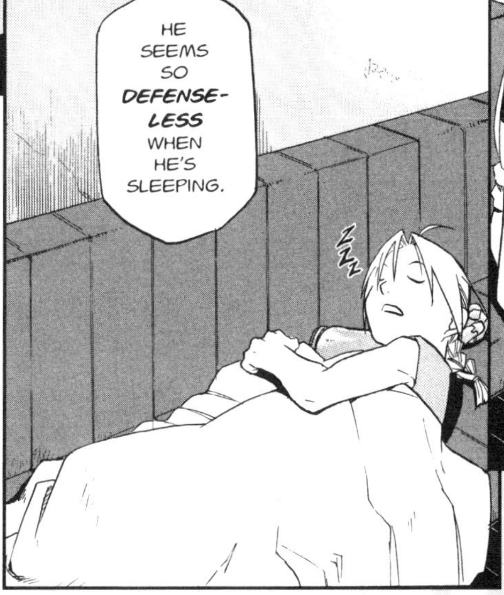
HE SEEMS SO ***DEFENSE-LESS*** WHEN HE'S SLEEPING.

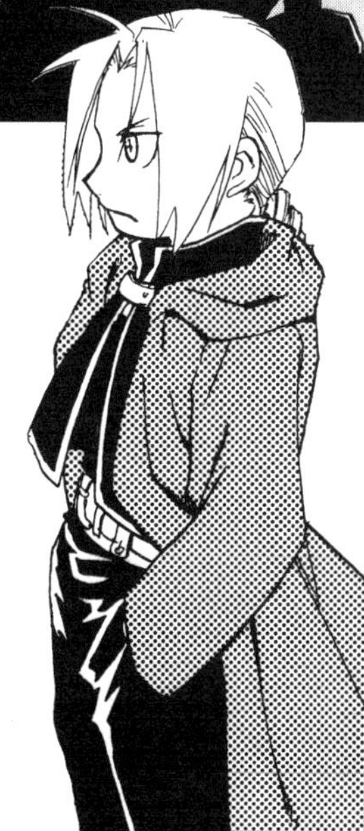

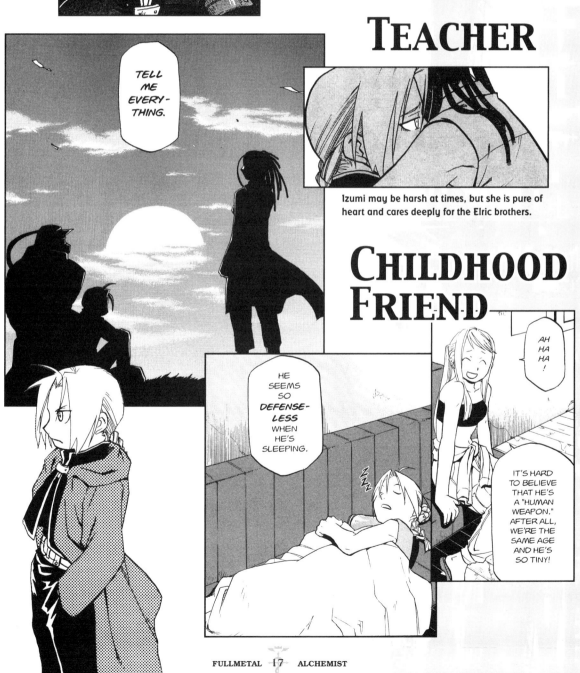

ALPHONSE ELRIC

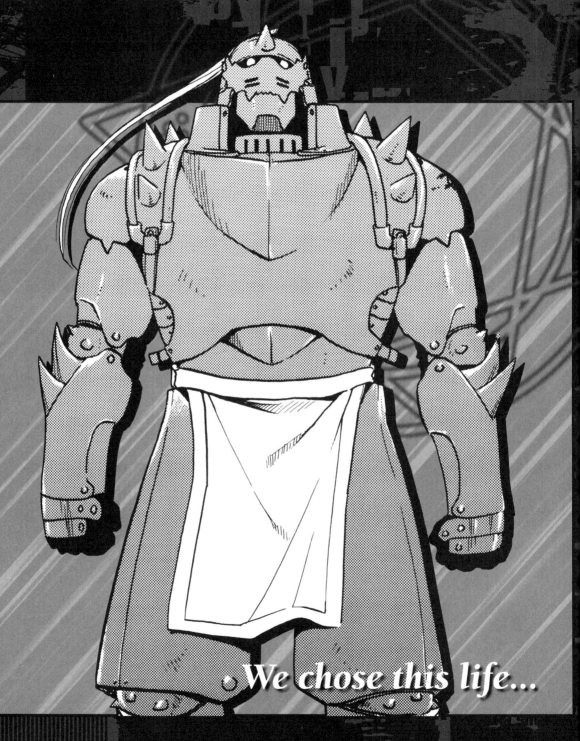

We chose this life...

MILD-MANNERED MONSTER

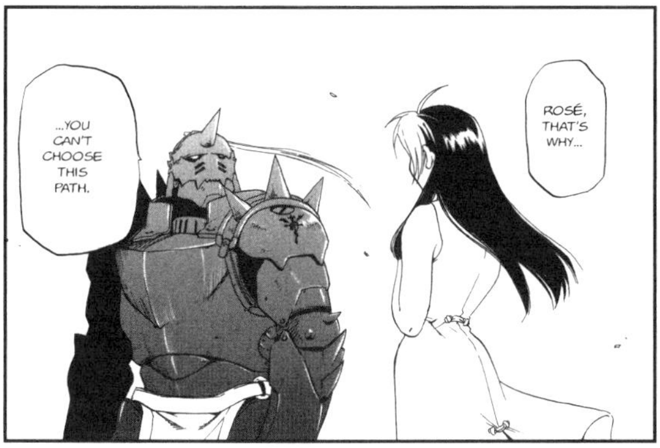
ROSÉ, THAT'S WHY...
...YOU CAN'T CHOOSE THIS PATH.

Even though he's been through a lot himself, Al is extremely sensitive to other people's feelings.

Gentle Soul Encased in Steel

That armor is hollow inside. Alphonse Elric has only a soul and no physical body. Four years ago, he lost his body as equivalent exchange for human transmutation. The only reason he is alive at all is that his older brother Edward, in desperation, bound Al's soul to a suit of armor. Al understands his brother better than anyone else does and at times plays the part of guardian to his big brother, calming the hotheaded Ed down when his emotions get him out of control.

AGE: 14

Though at times he doubts it will happen, Alphonse is hopeful that he and Ed will someday be completely human again.

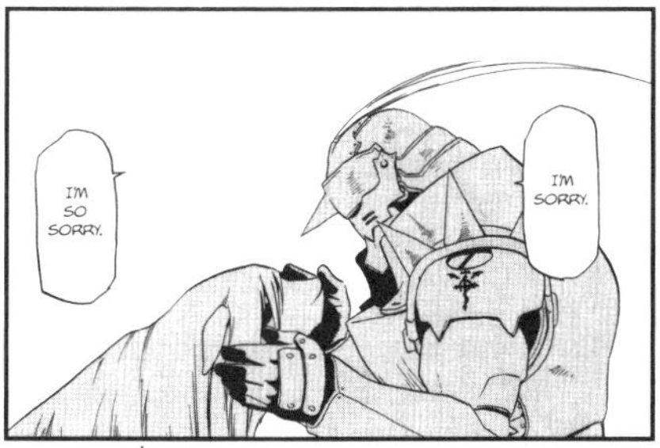
I'M SORRY.
I'M SO SORRY.

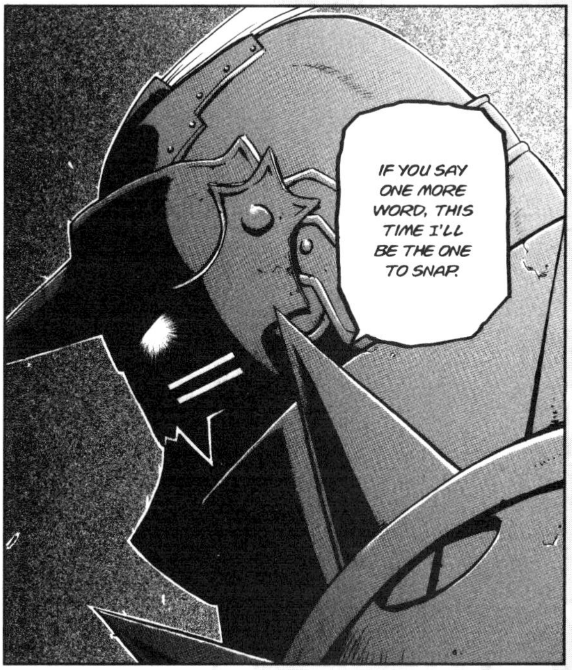
IF YOU SAY ONE MORE WORD, THIS TIME I'LL BE THE ONE TO SNAP.

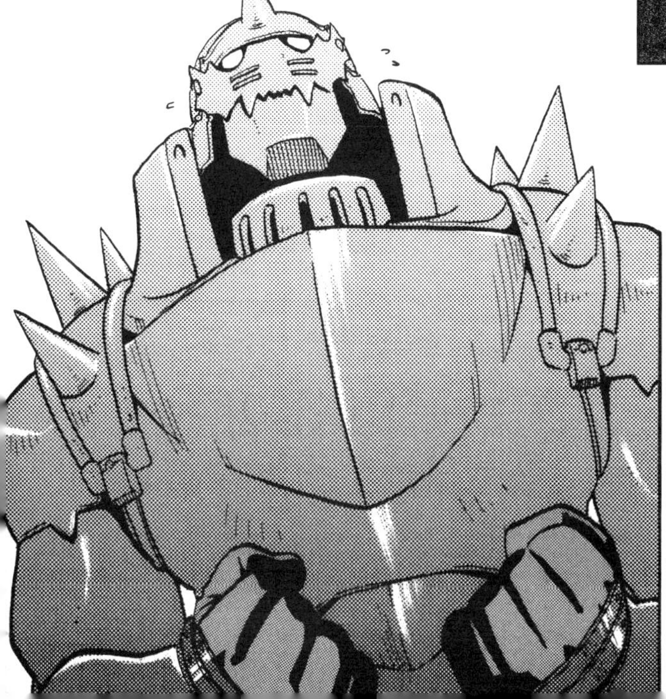

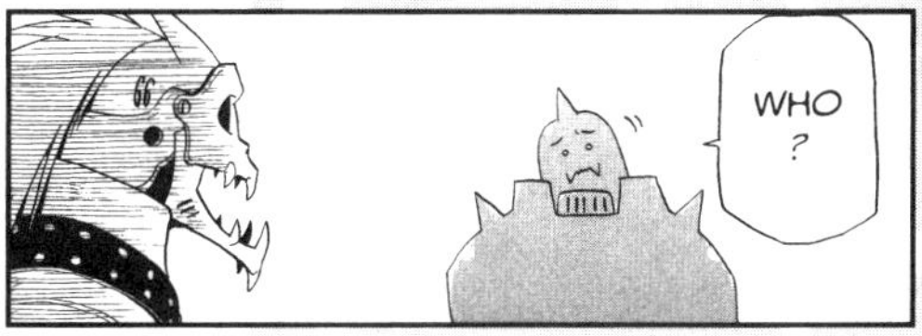
WHO ?

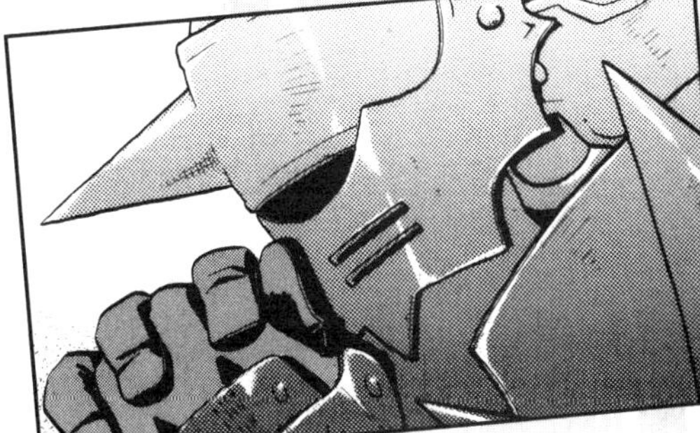

Speed & Skill

Because he has to use a transmutation circle, Al's alchemy is slightly slower than Ed's. But his skill is top notch. And his martial arts prowess surpasses Ed's. Because his body is made of armor ordinary attacks and even bullets are easily deflected, and he never gets tired.

SKRIK
DO

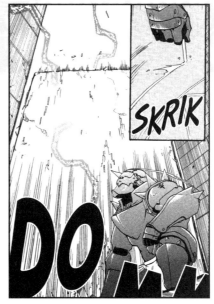

Al's clever approach perfectly complements his older brother's straightforward personality. Because they both care about each other more than they do about themselves, when they are together they are even more powerful.

ALCHEMY

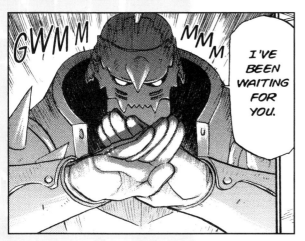

BZT
FZT

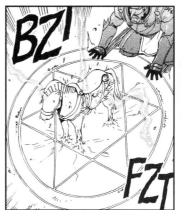

Al's alchemy is more refined than Ed's. His attention to detail is meticulous.

GWMM
MMM
I'VE BEEN WAITING FOR YOU.

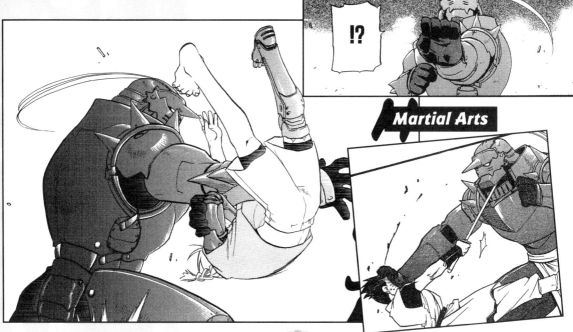

Martial Arts

!?

PURE OF HEART

Before the Binding...

When Al was young, he became absorbed in alchemical research because he wanted to resurrect his mother. All he wanted to do was live happily with his mother again. But the human transmutation ended in failure. Not only did he not get his mother back, his body was taken as an equivalent exchange. Al and his brother have been on a journey to regain their former bodies ever since.

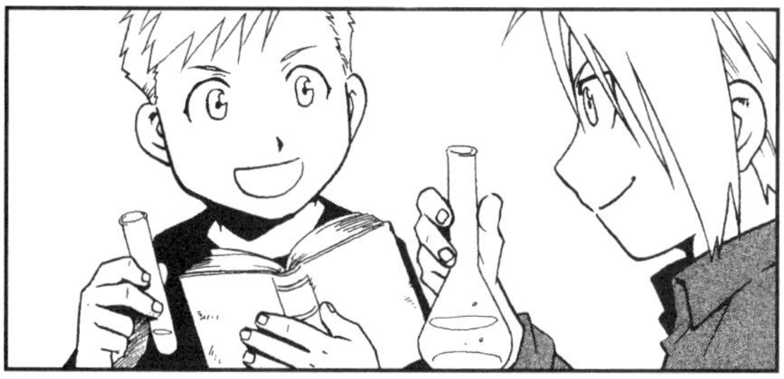

Their mother's passion for alchemy inspired the boys to study the art.

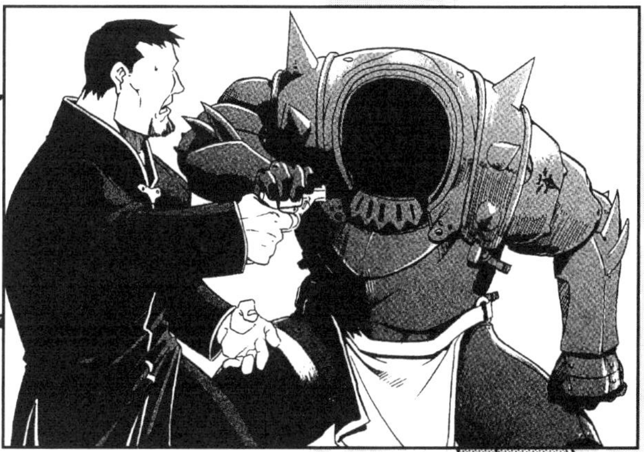

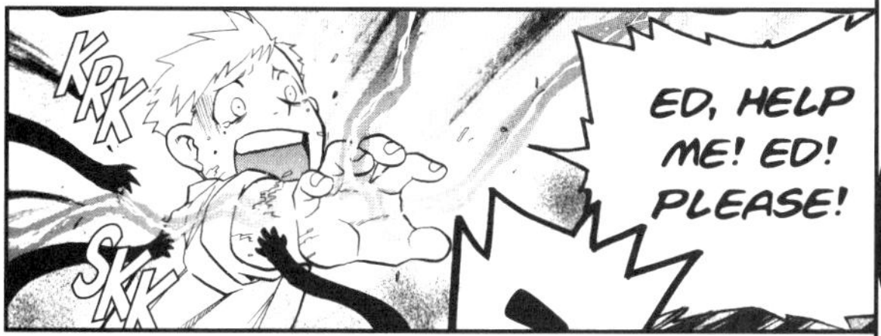
KRK
SKK
ED, HELP ME! ED! PLEASE!

In the end, it was that very love for his mother that cost Al his human form.

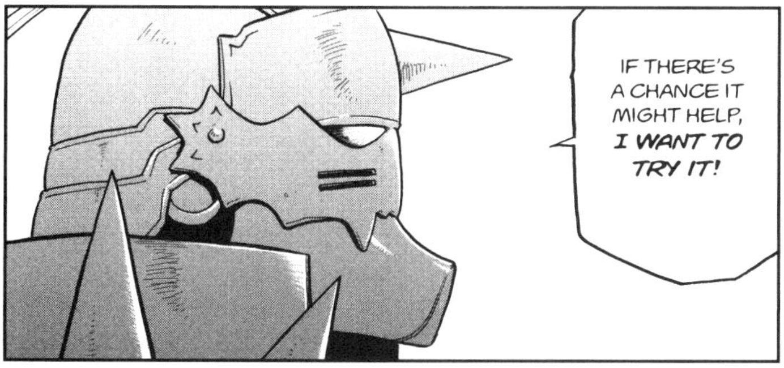
IF THERE'S A CHANCE IT MIGHT HELP, I WANT TO TRY IT!

Al remembers no details of the fateful day he was wrenched from his flesh-and-blood form. The secret to restoring his body may be lost with those memories...

I want to get my old body back...I want to go back to being HUMAN.

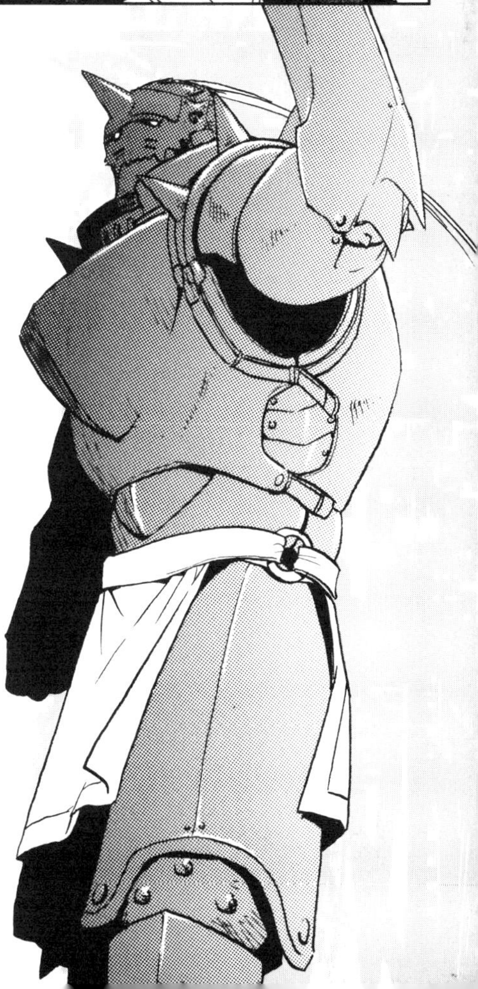

Shadow of Doubt

Number 66's words stung Al's heart like a thorn. "Were all my memories created by someone?" One day as he struggled all alone with his doubt without being able to confide in anyone, a casual comment from Ed sent Al's emotions over the edge. But he finally came to his senses, realizing that the brotherly brawls and the desire to return to his original body had to be undeniable evidence of real memories and emotions.

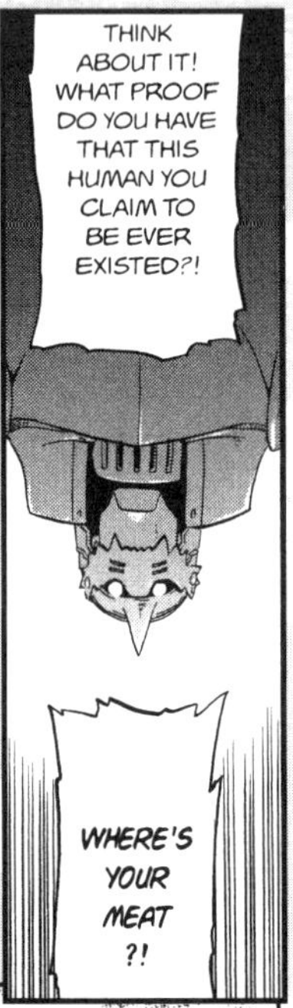
THINK ABOUT IT! WHAT PROOF DO YOU HAVE THAT THIS HUMAN YOU CLAIM TO BE EVER EXISTED?!
WHERE'S YOUR MEAT ?!

Alphonse trusts his big brother, but found it harder to believe in anything after he began to doubt his own memories of childhood.

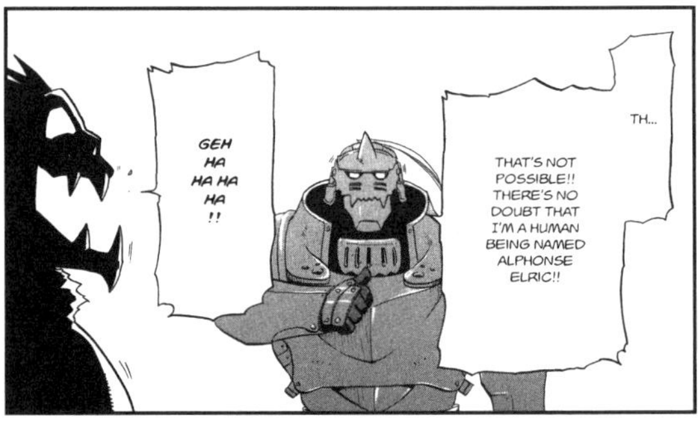
TH...
THAT'S NOT POSSIBLE!! THERE'S NO DOUBT THAT I'M A HUMAN BEING NAMED ALPHONSE ELRIC!!
GEH HA HA HA HA !!

Could it be true? Is all Al knows a lie?

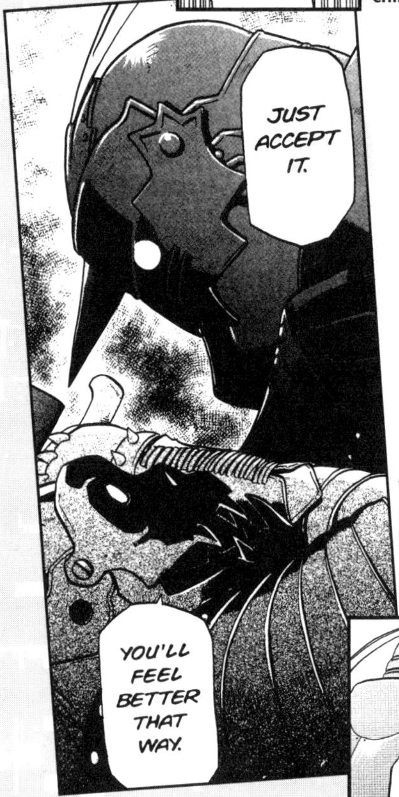
JUST ACCEPT IT.
YOU'LL FEEL BETTER THAT WAY.

What if your personality and memories were all fabricated by your "big brother"?

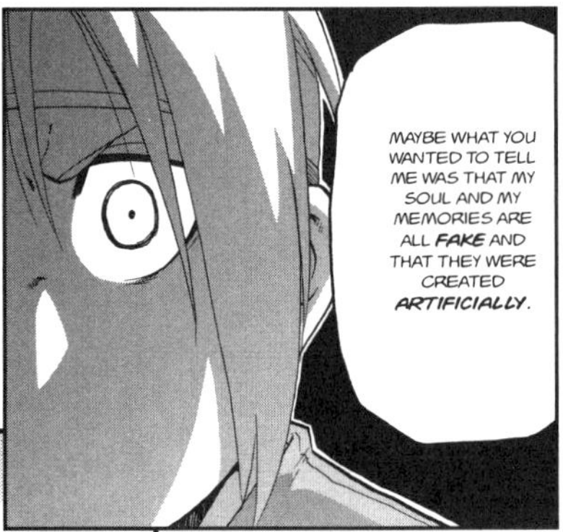
MAYBE WHAT YOU WANTED TO TELL ME WAS THAT MY SOUL AND MY MEMORIES ARE ALL FAKE AND THAT THEY WERE CREATED ARTIFICIALLY.

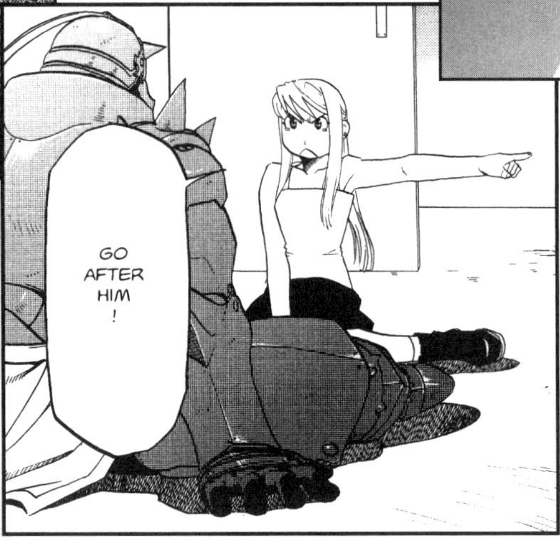
GO AFTER HIM !

Doubt brought more doubt and Al's feelings became trapped in darkness with no way out.

FAMILY

Strong Allies

Whether it was the time Al spent training with his teacher Izumi or when he committed the ultimate sin of human transmutation, he and his brother always moved toward the same goal. Consequently, Al wants to protect Ed no matter what, and Ed feels the same about Alphonse. As the two brothers travel together, the bond between them gets stronger each day. Izumi is also more than just a teacher to Al. To him she is a strict yet emotionally accepting, motherly presence in his life.

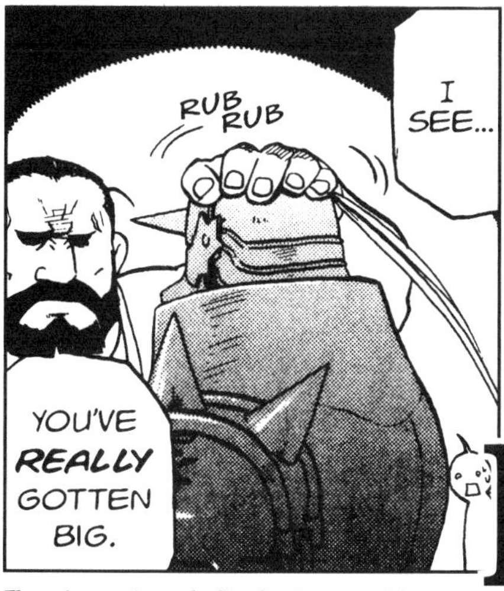
I SEE...
RUB RUB
YOU'VE REALLY GOTTEN BIG.

The wise and gentle Sig Curtis treats Al like an ordinary 14-year-old boy.

HOME

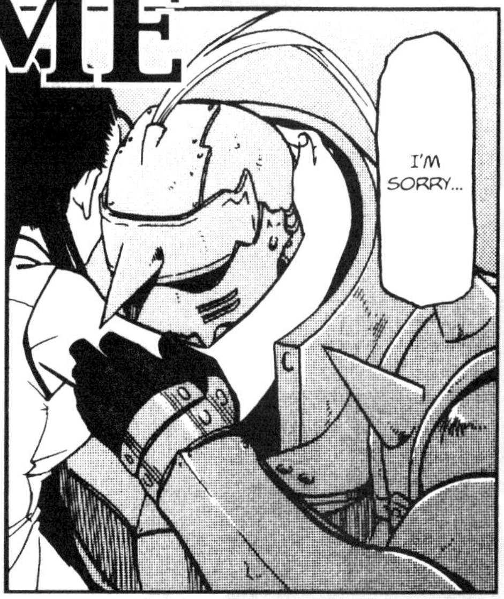
I'M SORRY...

Izumi knows the severity of the sin committed by the brothers. She understands their pain and embraces them without restraint.

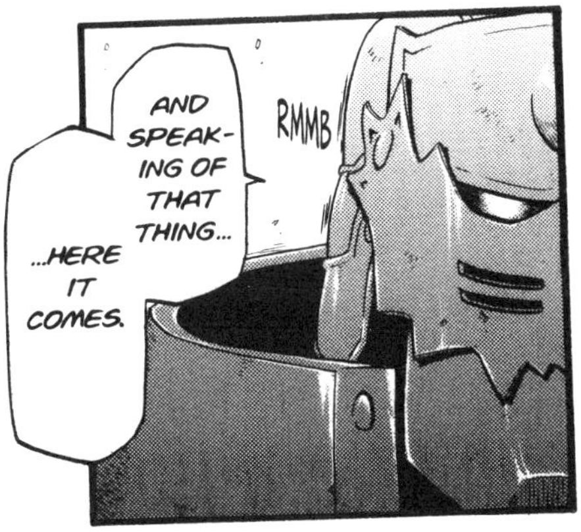
RMMB
AND SPEAKING OF THAT THING...
...HERE IT COMES.

The brothers both love and fear Izumi.

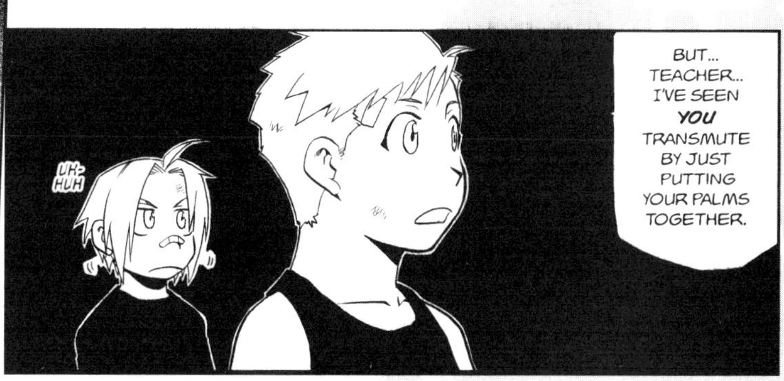
BUT... TEACHER... I'VE SEEN YOU TRANSMUTE BY JUST PUTTING YOUR PALMS TOGETHER.
UH-HUH

As a team, the Elric brothers have yet to be defeated.

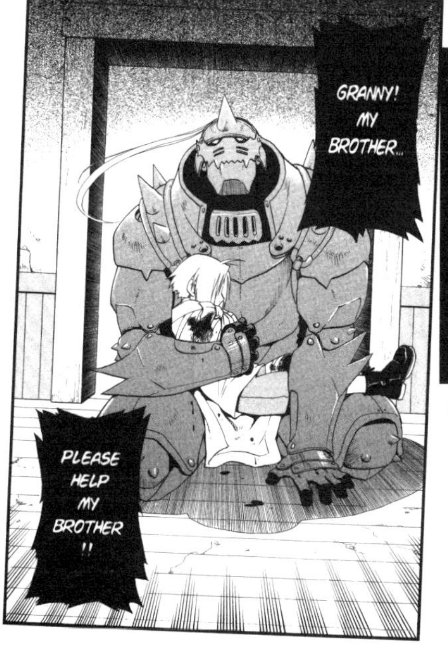
GRANNY! MY BROTHER...
PLEASE HELP MY BROTHER !!

BROTHERS

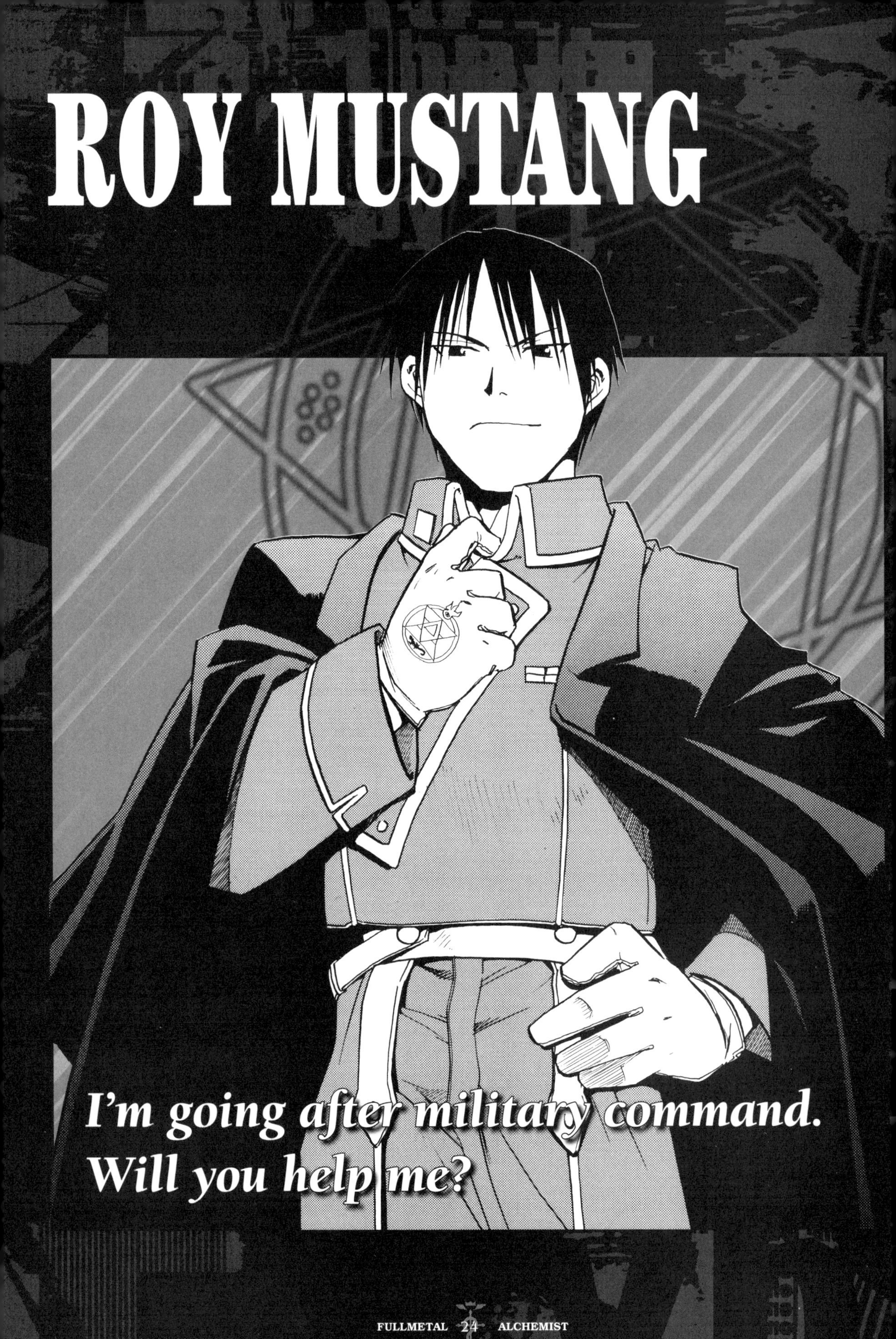
ROY MUSTANG
I'm going after military command.
Will you help me?

POWER

Ambition Incarnate

Roy Mustang is the colonel who is in charge of the eastern military headquarters. He is also the Flame Alchemist and can control fire at will. Mustang, who was promoted to a position in Central headquarters with exceptional speed, is extremely cunning. Although he performs his duties with efficiency, he conceals a secret desire to become the supreme leader of the military.

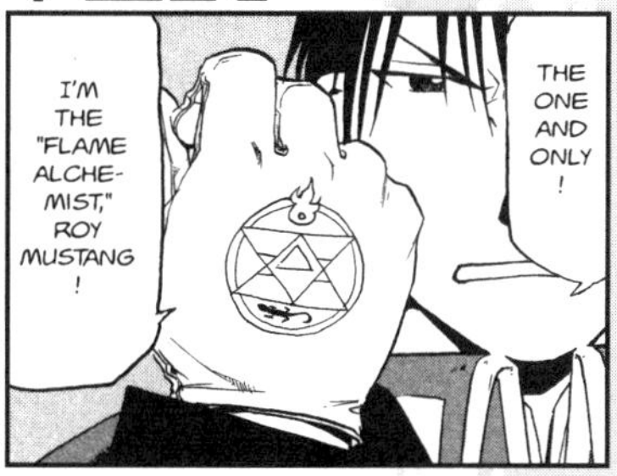
THE ONE AND ONLY !
I'M THE "FLAME ALCHEMIST," ROY MUSTANG !

Roy's alchemical prowess is nearly unmatched.

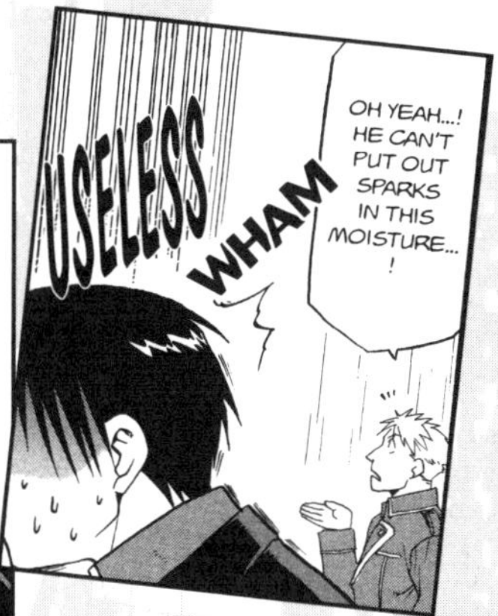
OH YEAH...! HE CAN'T PUT OUT SPARKS IN THIS MOISTURE... !
WHAM
USELESS

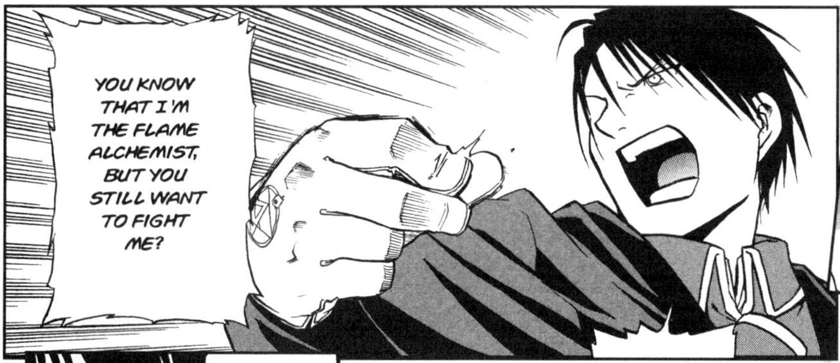
YOU KNOW THAT I'M THE FLAME ALCHEMIST, BUT YOU STILL WANT TO FIGHT ME?

THE FLAME ALCHEMIST

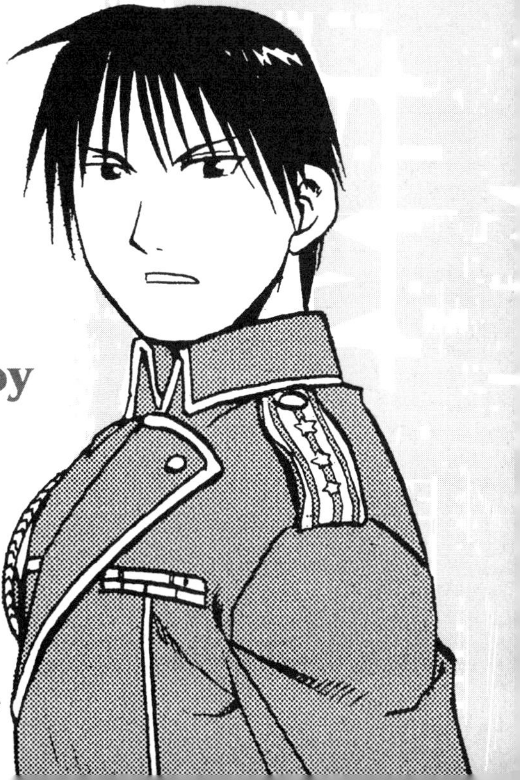

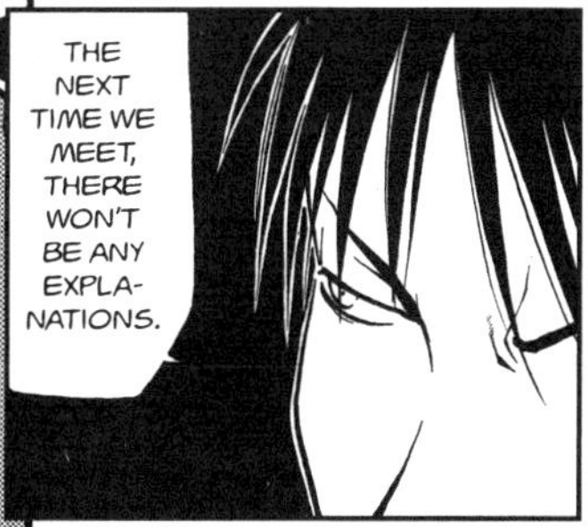
THE NEXT TIME WE MEET, THERE WON'T BE ANY EXPLANATIONS.

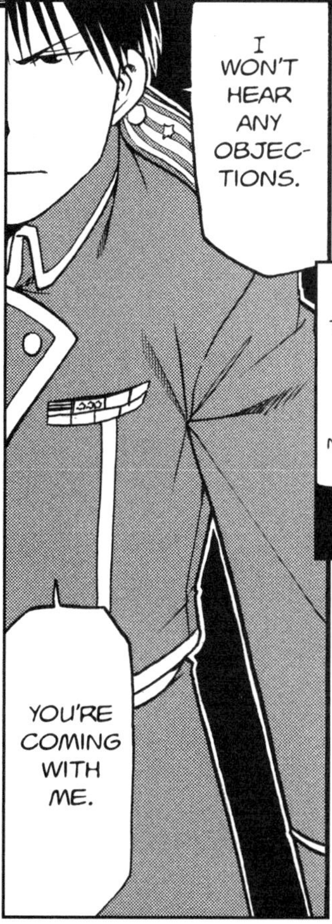
I WON'T HEAR ANY OBJECTIONS.
YOU'RE COMING WITH ME.

I will destroy them all.

MAES HUGHES

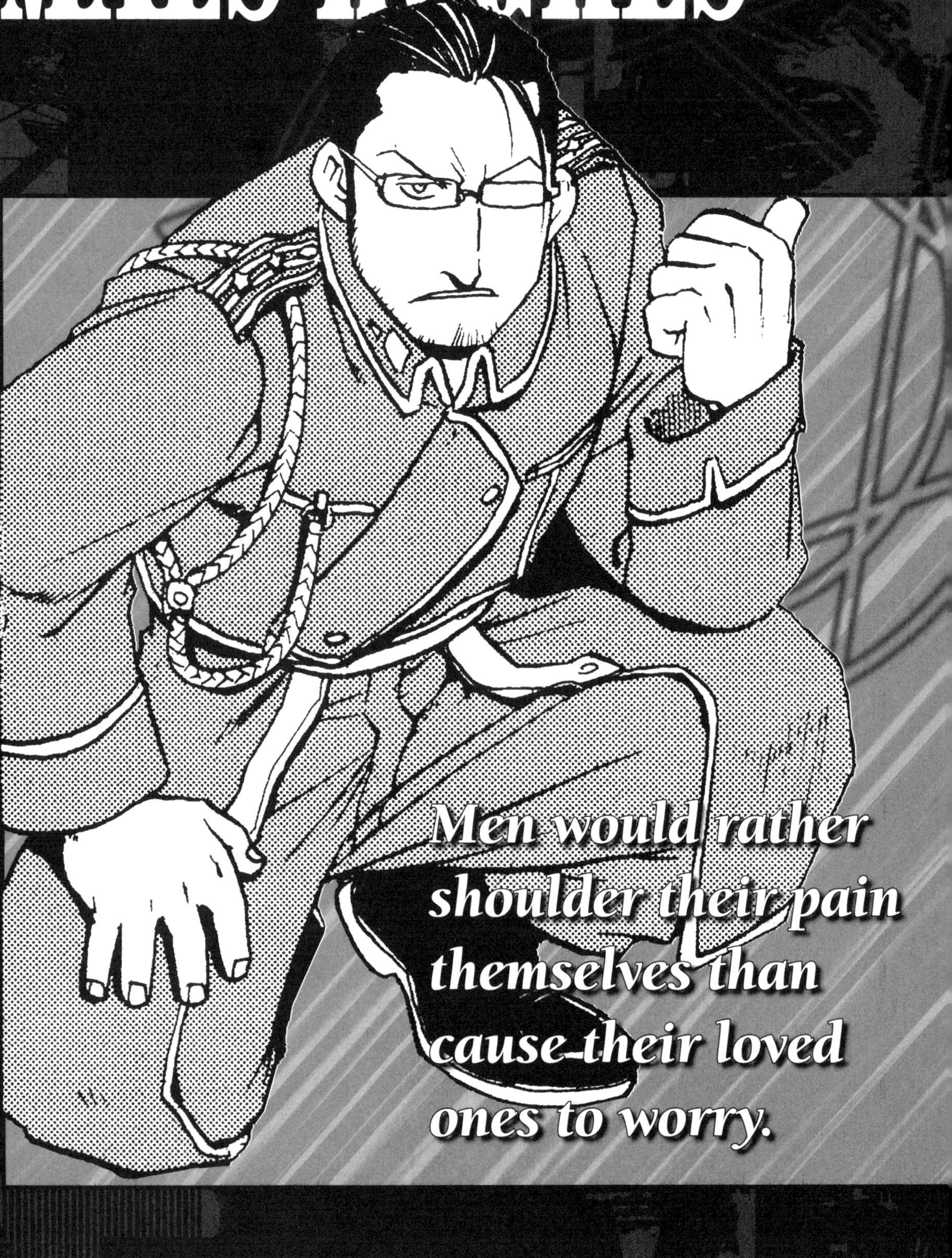
Men would rather shoulder their pain themselves than cause their loved ones to worry.

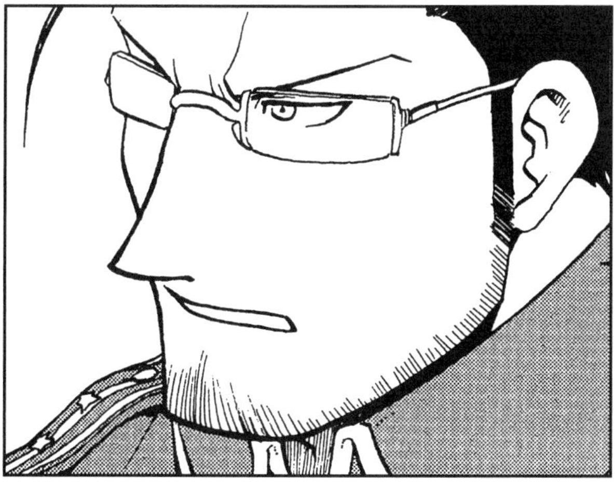

Inner Strength

Maes Hughes loves his family more than anything else in the world and brags about them constantly. His easygoing personality is like a breath of fresh air within the military headquarters, where too often a feeling of impending chaos lingers. On the other hand, Hughes the soldier shows an intelligence that is almost unmatched and was the first person to notice the unusual activities that were taking place within military headquarters.

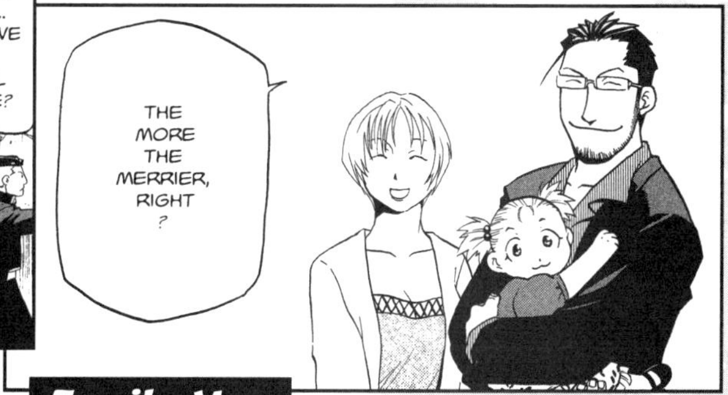
THE MORE THE MERRIER, RIGHT?

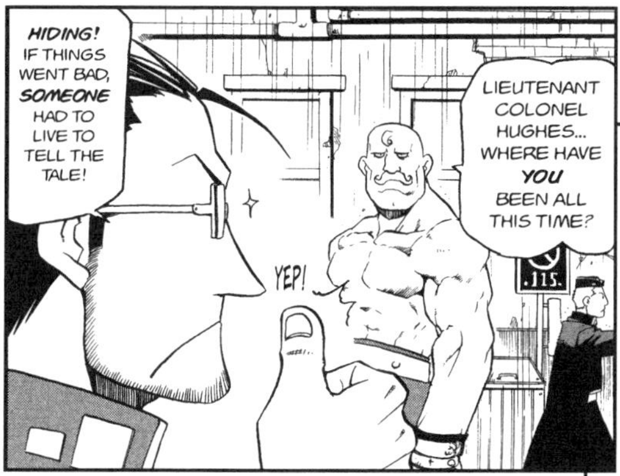
LIEUTENANT COLONEL HUGHES... WHERE HAVE YOU BEEN ALL THIS TIME?
HIDING! IF THINGS WENT BAD, SOMEONE HAD TO LIVE TO TELL THE TALE!
YEP!

Family Man

KNOWLEDGE & COURAGE

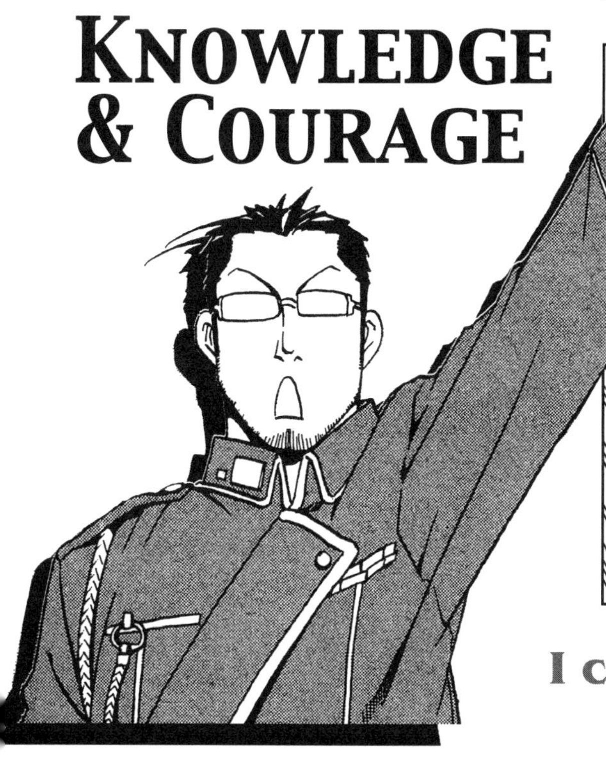

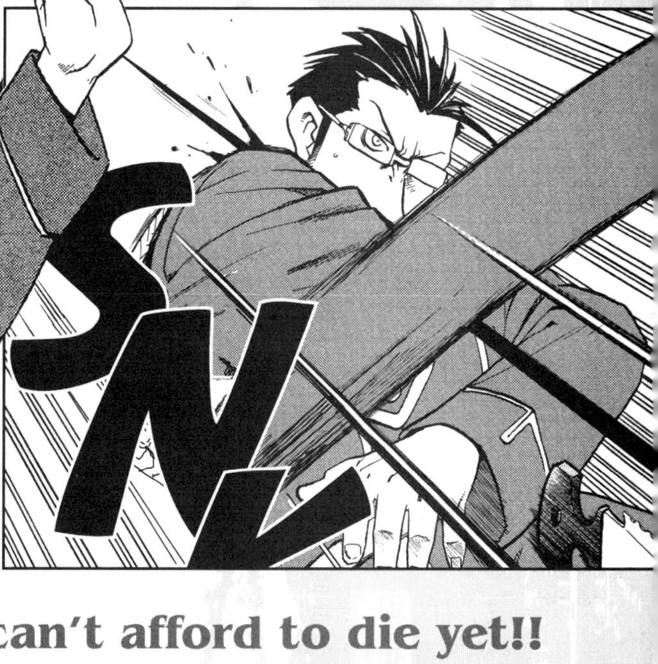

I can't afford to die yet!!

ALEX LOUIS ARMSTRONG

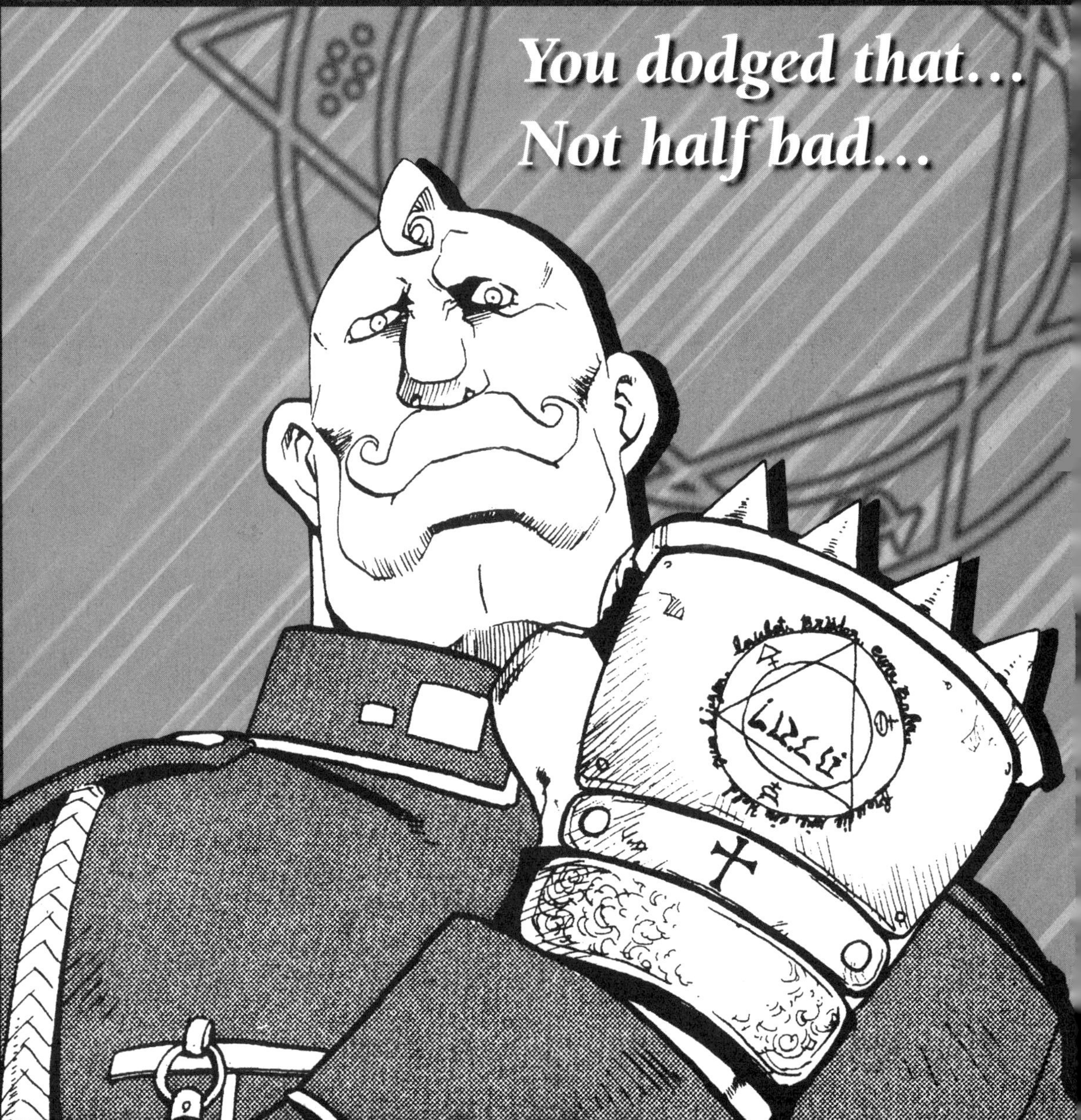
You dodged that...
Not half bad...

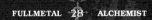

THE STRONG ARM ALCHEMIST

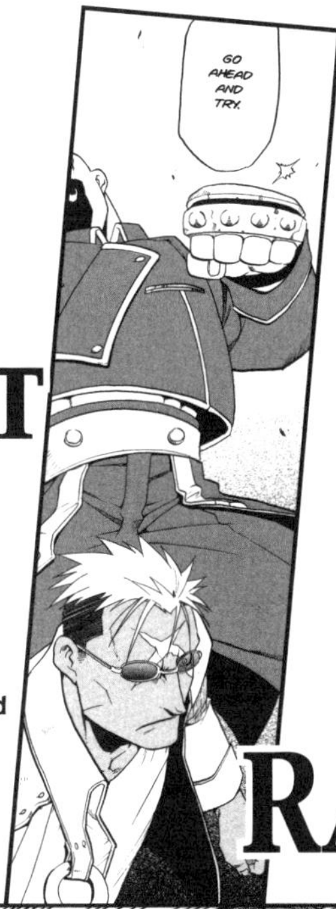
GO AHEAD AND TRY.

When the revenge-crazed Scar corners Ed and the others, Maj. Armstrong comes to their rescue.

Big Man, Big Heart

Major Armstrong is an alchemist who specializes in raw power. The gauntlets he wears can break apart boulders or crack open the ground, thus making him known as the Strong Arm Alchemist. On the other hand he is quite emotional and cries easily. The secret to his uniqueness lies in the dual sides of his personality, as well as in his haircut and moustache!

RAW POWER

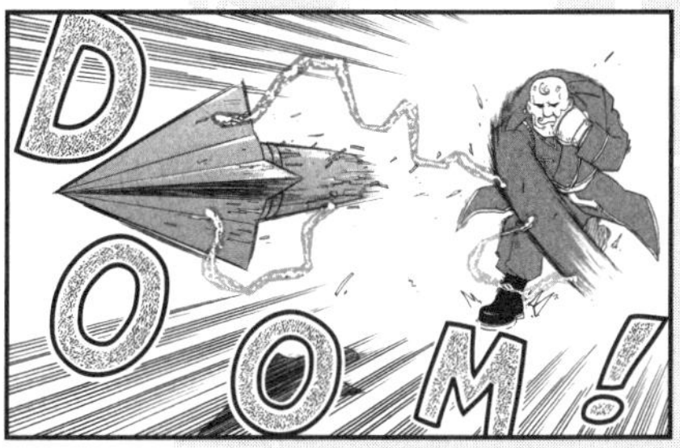
DOOOM!

The Spear is an alchemical technique that's been passed down for generations in the Armstrong family.

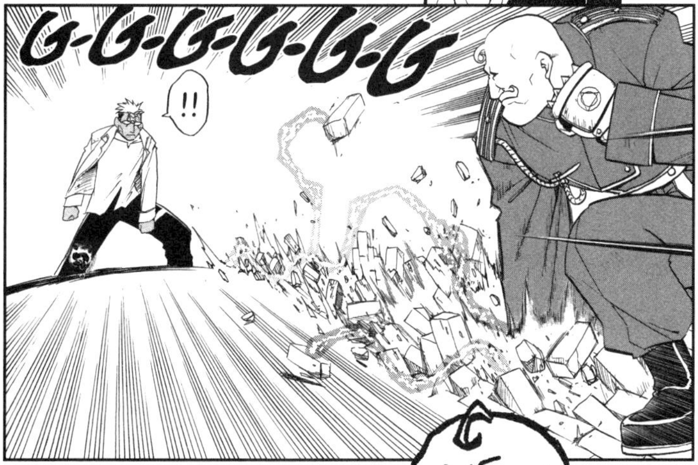
G-G-G-G-G-G
!!

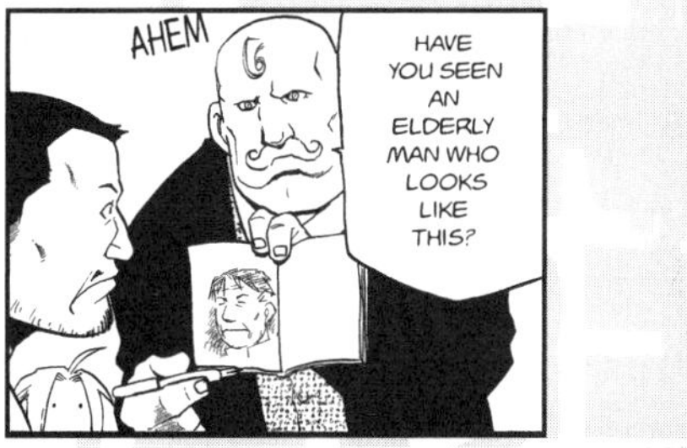
AHEM
HAVE YOU SEEN AN ELDERLY MAN WHO LOOKS LIKE THIS?

Apparently being an artist runs in the Armstrong family as well...

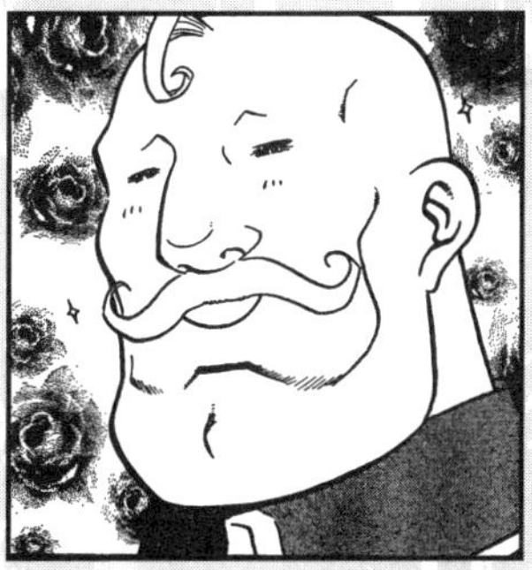

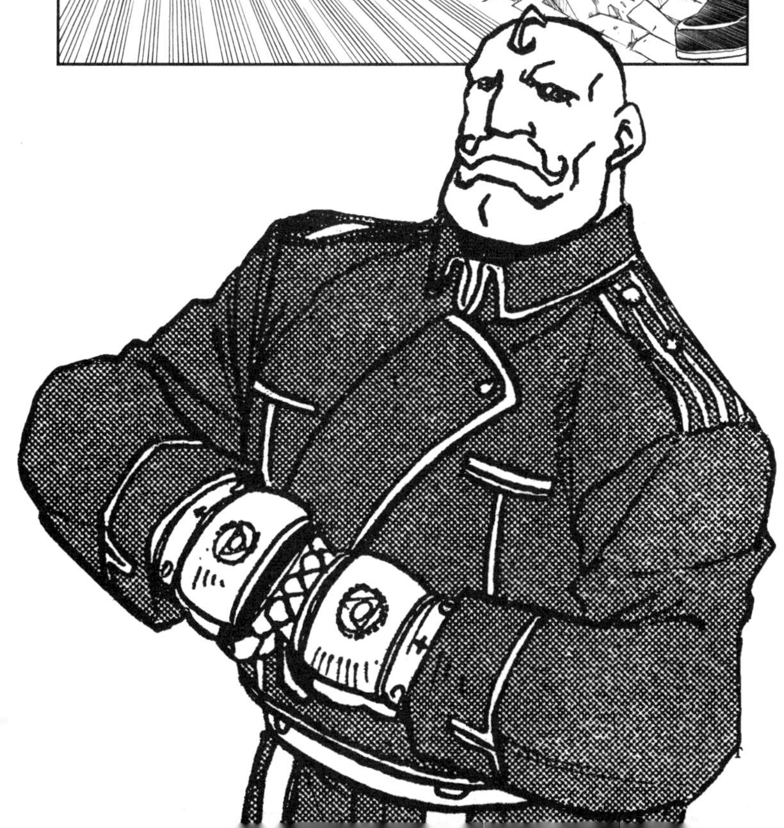

HONESTY

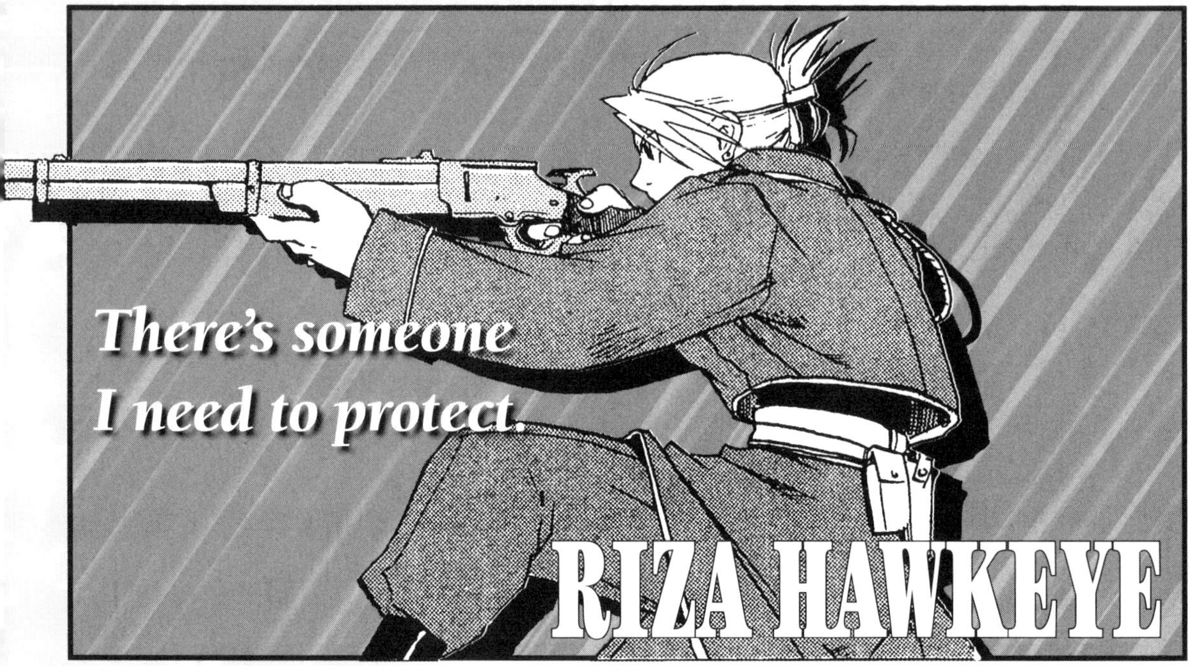
There's someone I need to protect.
RIZA HAWKEYE

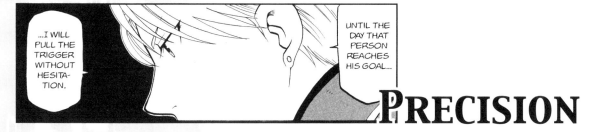

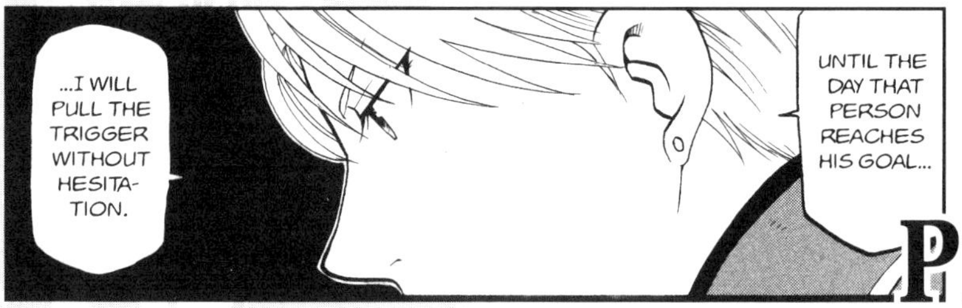
UNTIL THE DAY THAT PERSON REACHES HIS GOAL...
...I WILL PULL THE TRIGGER WITHOUT HESITATION.

PRECISION

I cannot reveal that to you. Not now.

Hidden Agenda

As Colonel Mustang's trusted right hand, Lieutenant Hawkeye is always nearby. Her cool, self-possessed demeanor and direct actions earn her both the respect and fear of those around her. Her skill with guns is good enough to have earned her a position as the colonel's bodyguard. The reason she joined the military is her steadfast desire to protect a certain man.

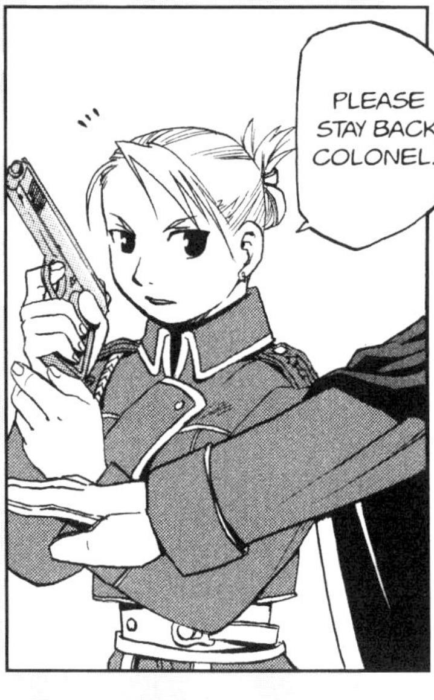
PLEASE STAY BACK, COLONEL...

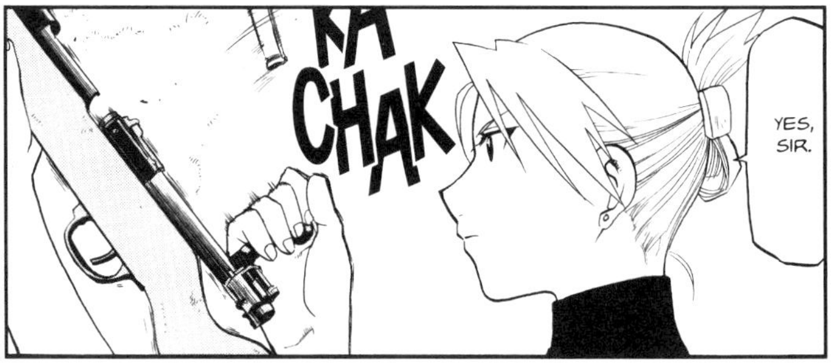
KA CHAK
YES, SIR.

JEAN HAVOC

Although 2nd Lt. Havoc's breezy countenance is seen as a negative trait by his superiors, it wins him points with his subordinates. His dangling cigarette is his trademark.

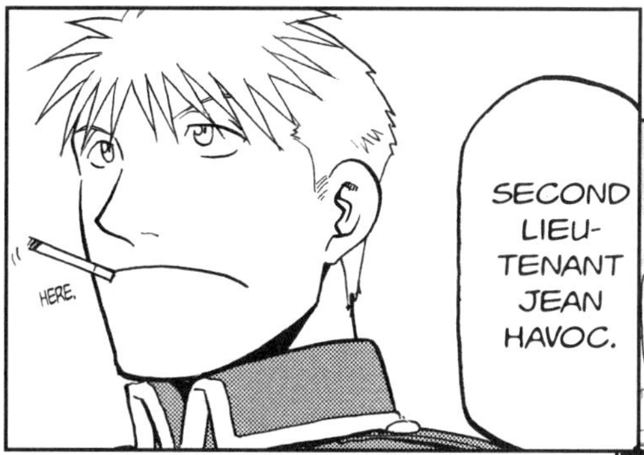
SECOND LIEU-TENANT JEAN HAVOC.
HERE.

Trust

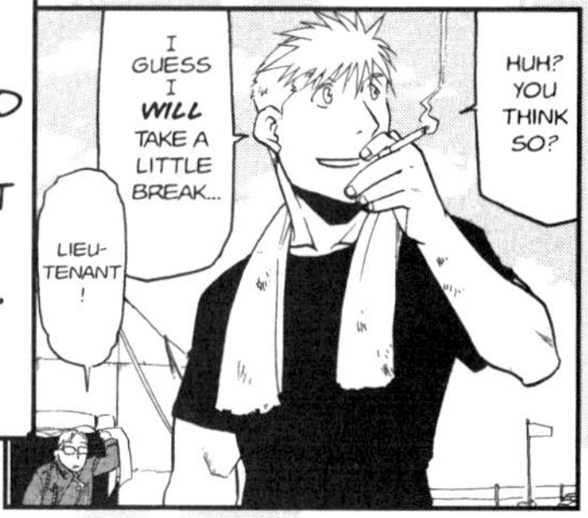
HUH? YOU THINK SO?
I GUESS I *WILL* TAKE A LITTLE BREAK...
LIEU-TENANT!

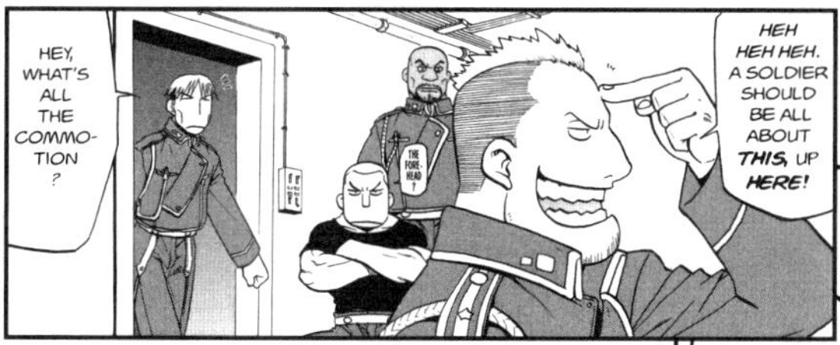
HEH HEH HEH. A SOLDIER SHOULD BE ALL ABOUT *THIS*, UP *HERE!*
THE FORE-HEAD!
HEY, WHAT'S ALL THE COMMO-TION?

Preparation

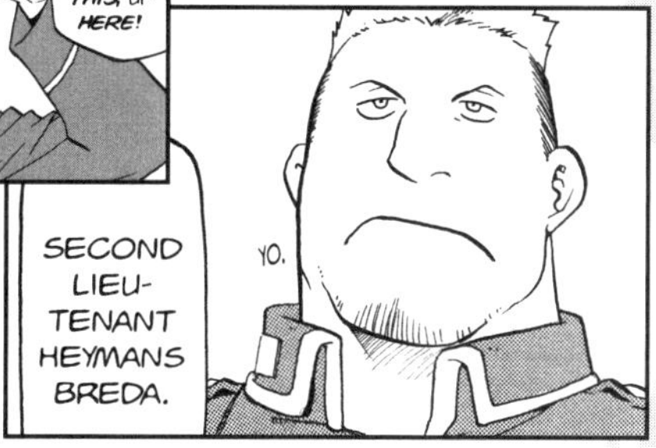
YO.
SECOND LIEU-TENANT HEYMANS BREDA.

HEYMANS BREDA

Despite his powerful appearance 2nd Lt. Breda is skilled at intelligent planning. He also simply cannot stand dogs.

Cool as a cucumber, Warrant Officer Falman is gifted with an encyclopedic knowledge of just about *everything*.

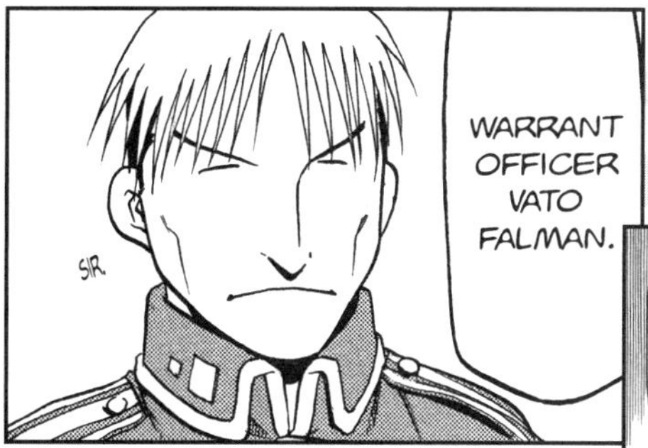
WARRANT OFFICER VATO FALMAN.
SIR.

Smarts

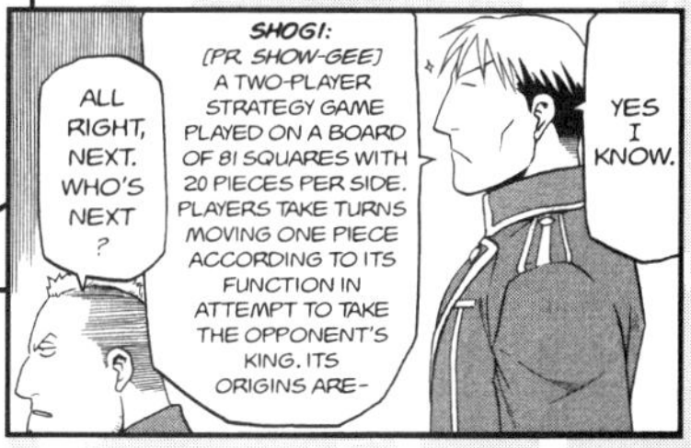
YES I KNOW.
SHOGI: [PR. SHOW-GEE] A TWO-PLAYER STRATEGY GAME PLAYED ON A BOARD OF 81 SQUARES WITH 20 PIECES PER SIDE. PLAYERS TAKE TURNS MOVING ONE PIECE ACCORDING TO ITS FUNCTION IN ATTEMPT TO TAKE THE OPPONENT'S KING. ITS ORIGINS ARE–
ALL RIGHT, NEXT. WHO'S NEXT?

VATO FALMAN

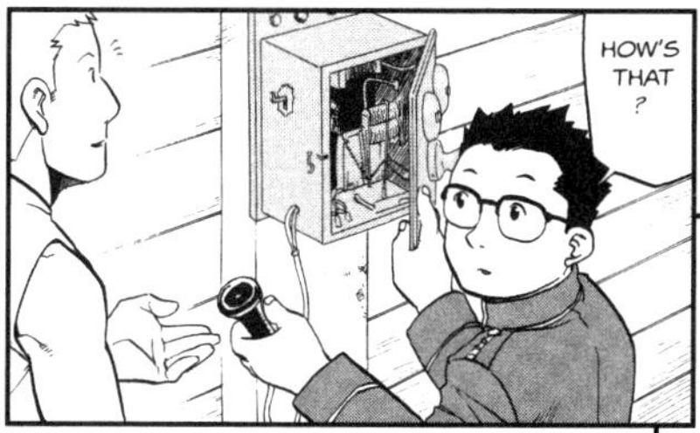
HOW'S THAT?

Techie

KAIN FUERY

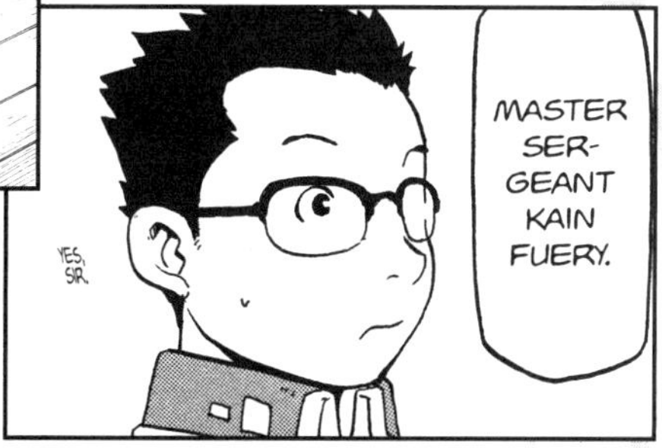
MASTER SER-GEANT KAIN FUERY.
YES, SIR.

Gentle-hearted Master Sgt. Fuery excels at repairing communication radios and just about anything else on the base that ticks, clicks or clinks.

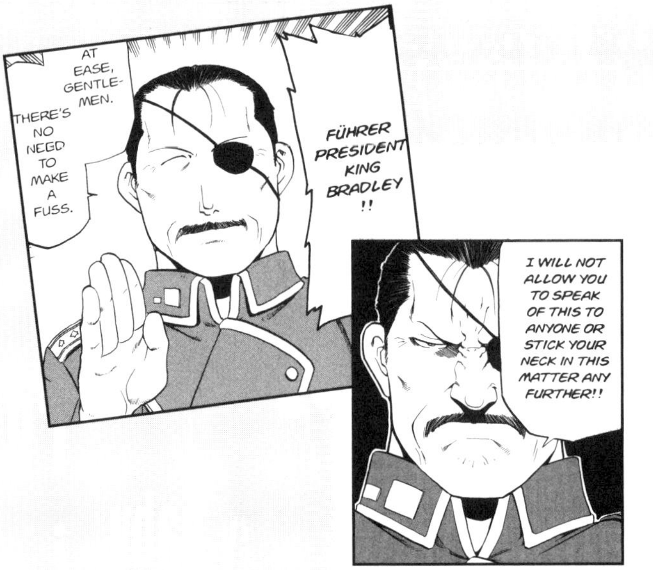
FÜHRER PRESIDENT KING BRADLEY!!
AT EASE, GENTLEMEN. THERE'S NO NEED TO MAKE A FUSS.
I WILL NOT ALLOW YOU TO SPEAK OF THIS TO ANYONE OR STICK YOUR NECK IN THIS MATTER ANY FURTHER!!

FÜHRER PRESIDENT KING BRADLEY

Supreme Commander

Fast as lightning with a blade, stunning even Edward Elric with his skills as a swordsman, the Supreme Commander of the military hides his true nature behind a shining public persona.

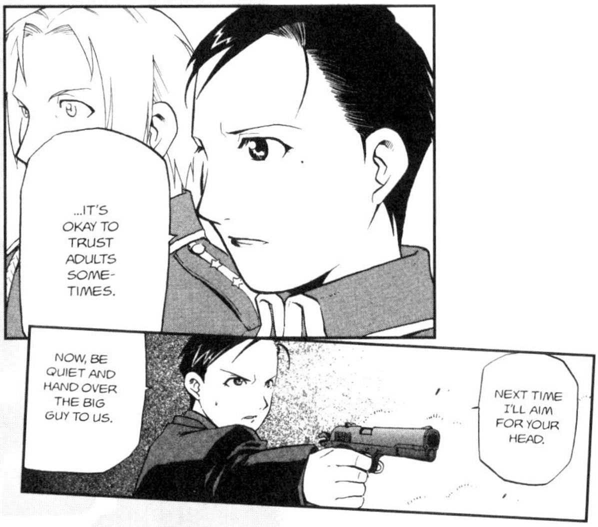
...IT'S OKAY TO TRUST ADULTS SOMETIMES.
NEXT TIME I'LL AIM FOR YOUR HEAD.
NOW, BE QUIET AND HAND OVER THE BIG GUY TO US.

MARIA ROSS

Many Faceted

Second Lt. Ross is dedicated to her job, sometimes at the expense of her own personality. She can be tough or timid depending on which side of her personality is more in control at any given time.

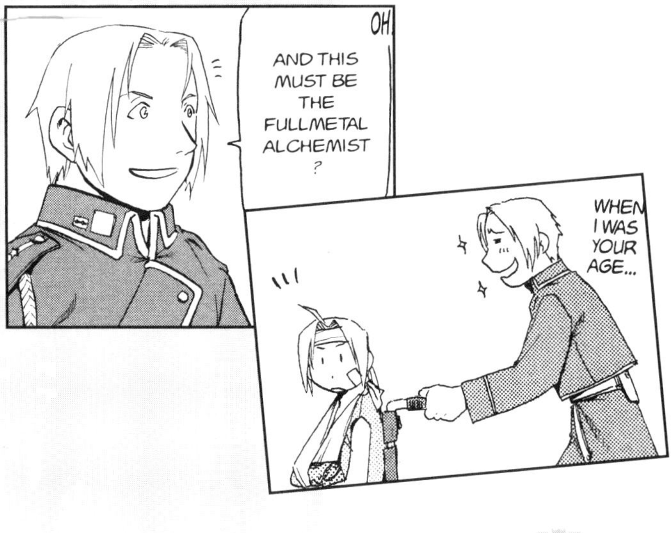
OH!
AND THIS MUST BE THE FULLMETAL ALCHEMIST?
WHEN I WAS YOUR AGE...

DENNY BROSH

Peacekeeper

Sergeant Brosh is just one of those guys that everyone wants to be around. His aura of calm helps keep his fellow soldiers mellowed out even when the going gets rough.

YOKI

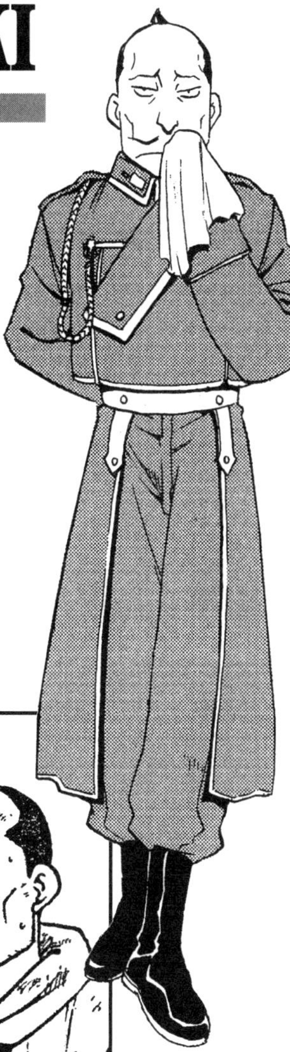

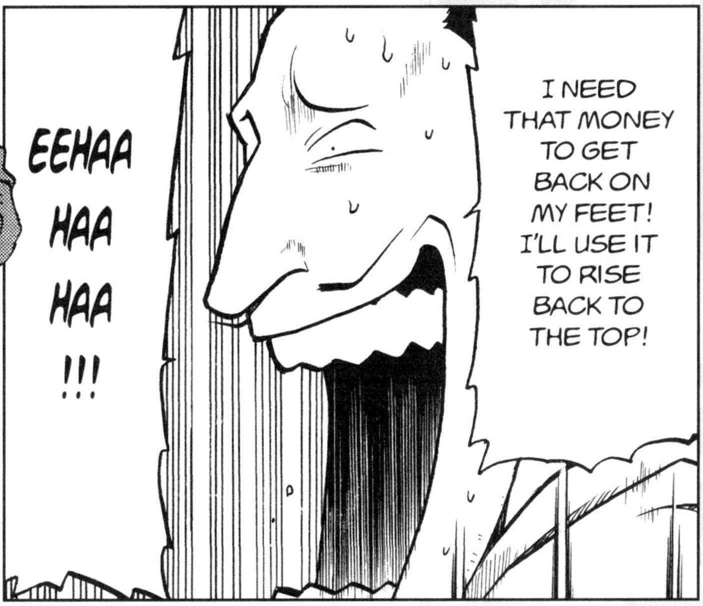
I NEED THAT MONEY TO GET BACK ON MY FEET! I'LL USE IT TO RISE BACK TO THE TOP!
EEHAA HAA HAA !!!

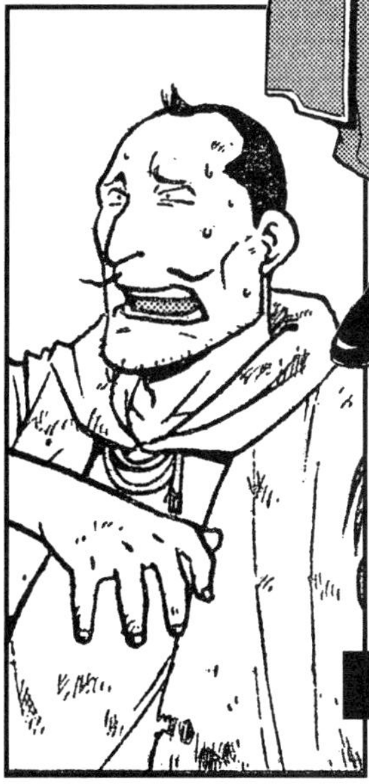

Greed

Sh-shut up! You people lost the war! It's over! I'm not like you at all!

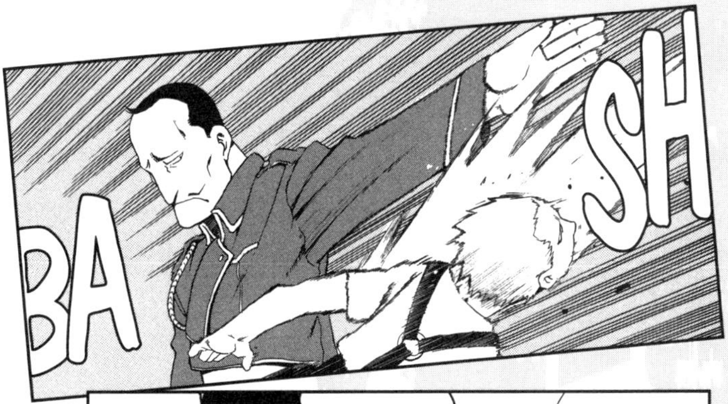
SH
BA

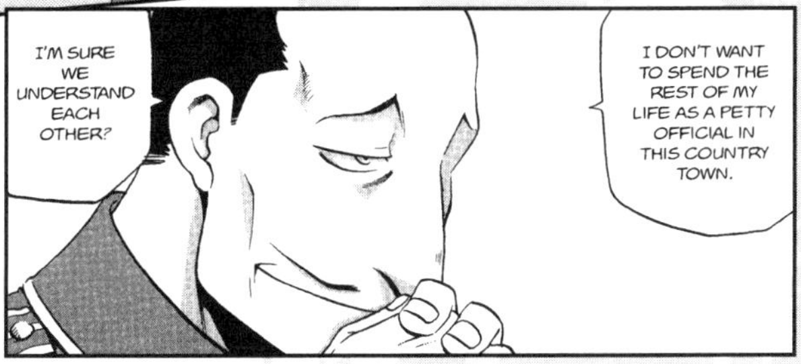
I DON'T WANT TO SPEND THE REST OF MY LIFE AS A PETTY OFFICIAL IN THIS COUNTRY TOWN.
I'M SURE WE UNDERSTAND EACH OTHER?

Destroyed by Desire

Lieutenant Yoki is only concerned with money, position and fame. For his own career advancement he will even entrap those people that helped him when he was in need. Yoki has no sense of humanity or justice whatsoever. The only quality that he could justifiably be proud of is the tenaciousness that motivates him to strive for the top even after failing so miserably.

IZUMI & SIG CURTIS

If anything happens to that boy...I won't hesitate to destroy you.

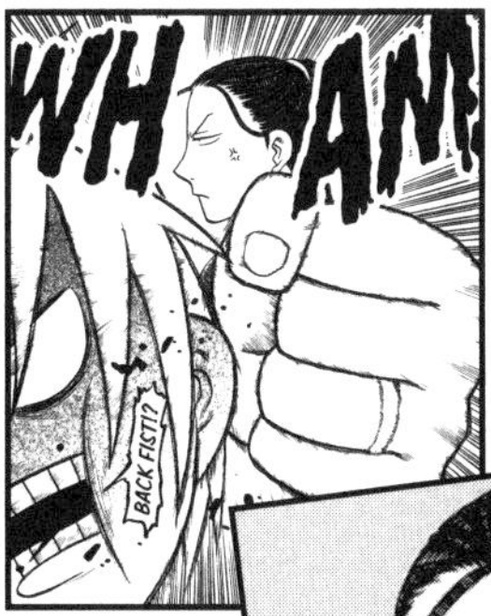
WHAM
BACK FIST!?

Teacher

Though her methods are often confusing, Izumi Curtis has taught the Elric Brothers well. Desperately ill, she hides her pain to give Ed and Al the skills they will need to survive and to fulfill their mission. Her gentle giant husband, Sig, not only watches over his sick wife, he also helps take care of the young Elric brothers.

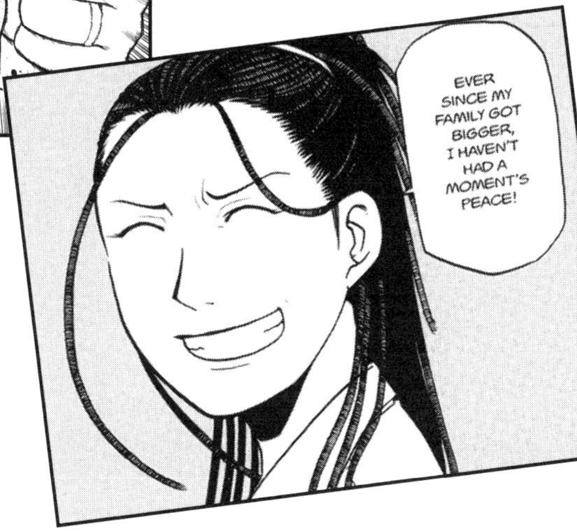
EVER SINCE MY FAMILY GOT BIGGER, I HAVEN'T HAD A MOMENT'S PEACE!

Beastly Beauty & Gentle Giant

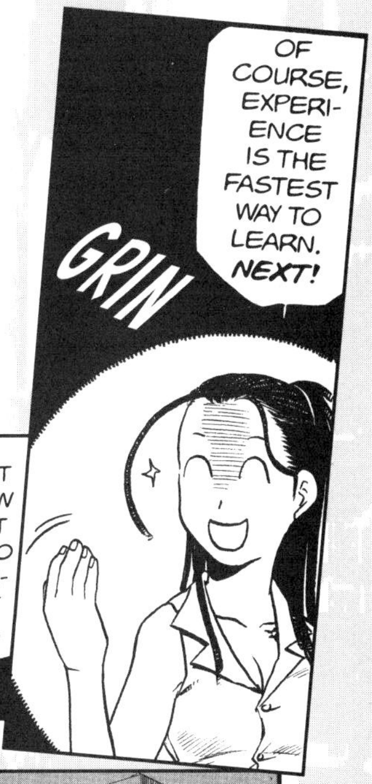
OF COURSE, EXPERI- ENCE IS THE FASTEST WAY TO LEARN. NEXT!
GRIN

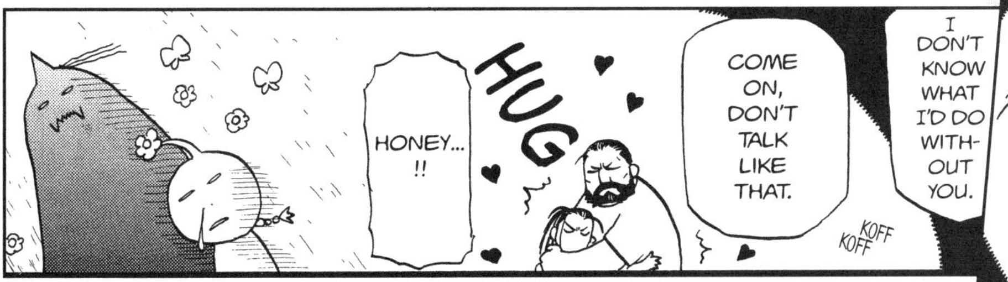
I DON'T KNOW WHAT I'D DO WITH- OUT YOU.
KOFF KOFF
COME ON, DON'T TALK LIKE THAT.
HUG
HONEY... !!

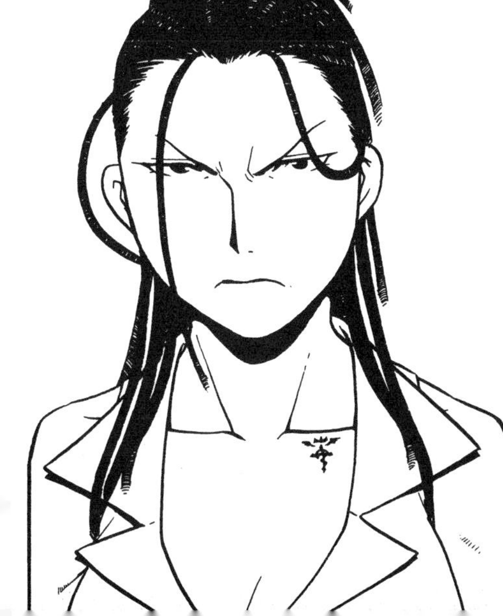

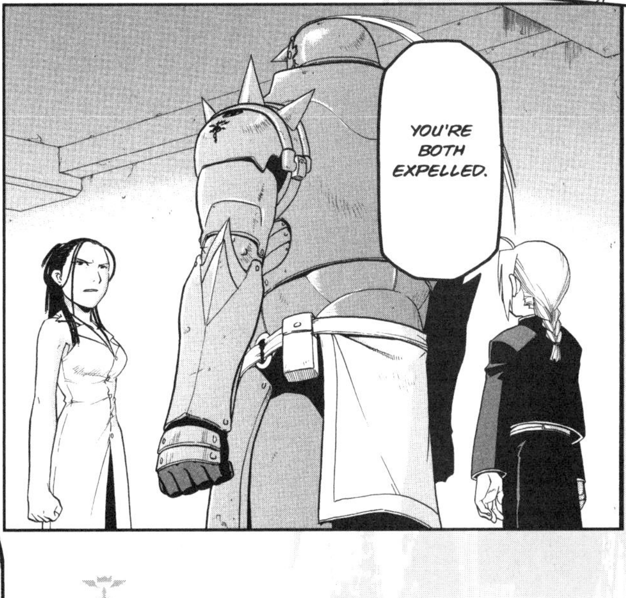
YOU'RE BOTH EXPELLED.

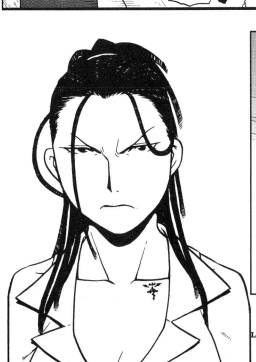

WINRY ROCKBELL

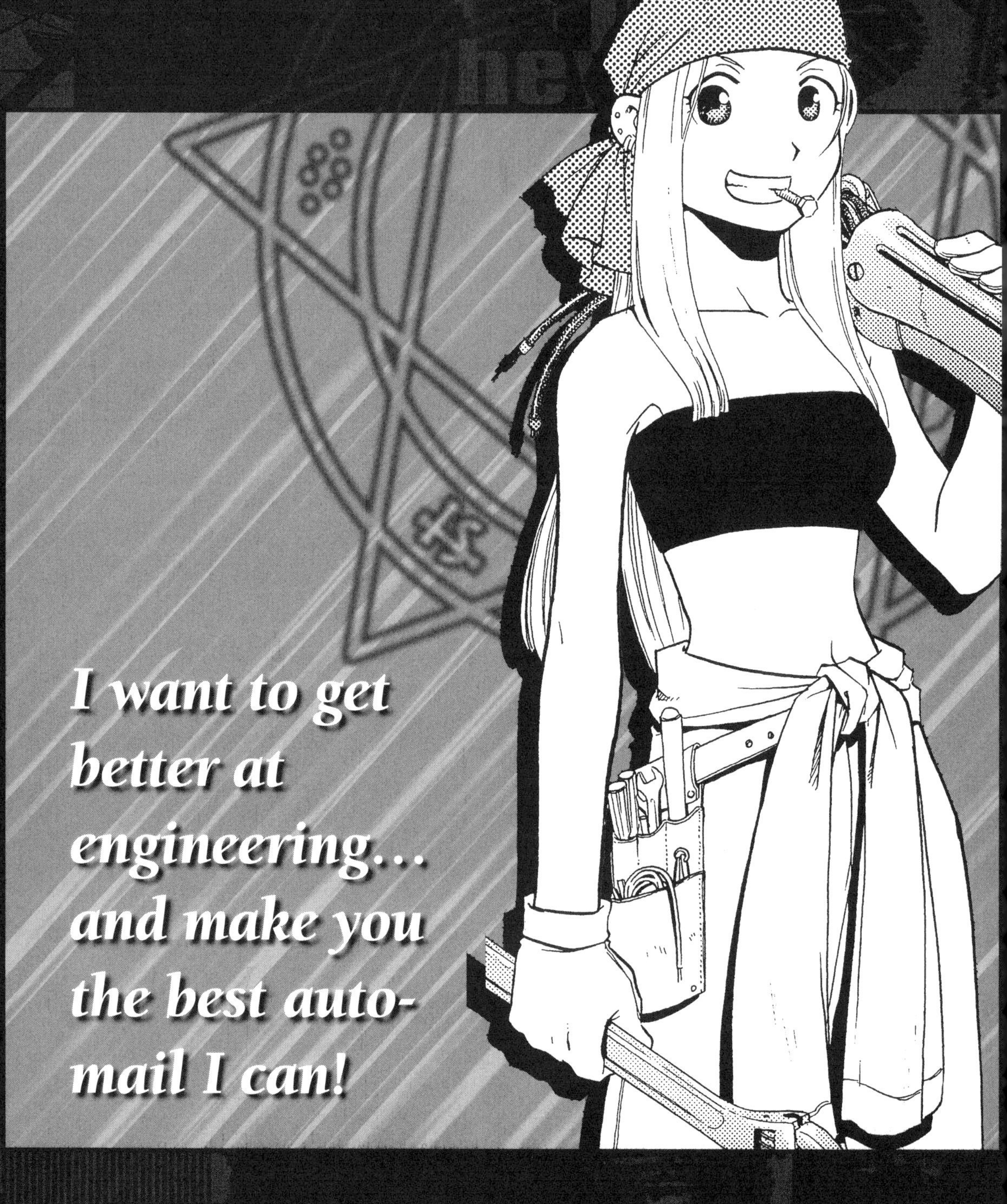
I want to get better at engineering... and make you the best auto-mail I can!

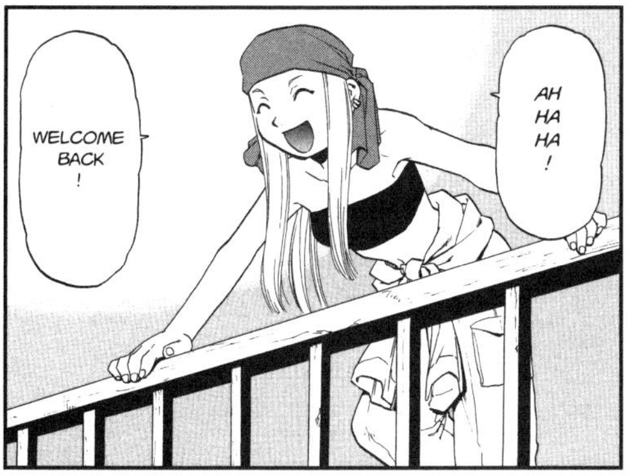
AH HA HA!
WELCOME BACK!

Auto-Mail Whiz-Kid

This cheerful girl is Winry, Ed's auto-mail engineer. She is completely absorbed in the world of auto-mail and could definitely be considered a mech otaku. Winry has no other interest besides constantly improving Ed's auto-mail. Although she lost both of her parents in the Ishbalan civil war, she never allows her sadness to show and lives happily with her grandmother.

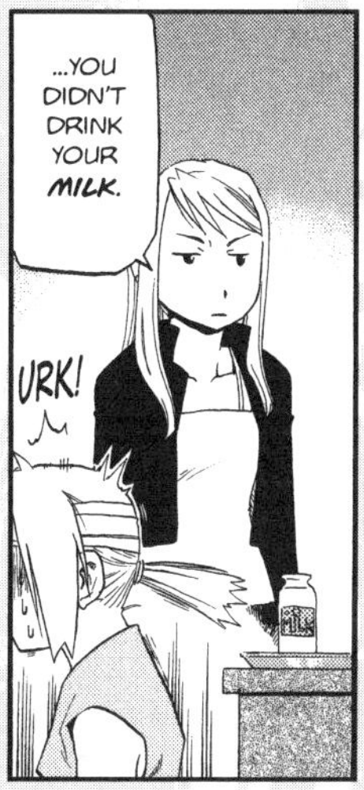
...YOU DIDN'T DRINK YOUR MILK.
URK!

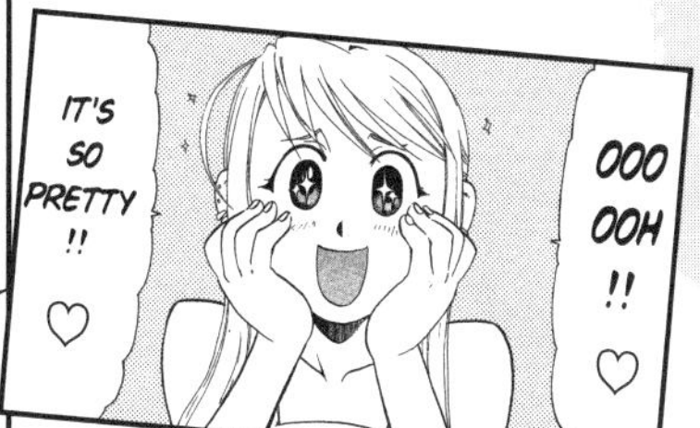
OOOOOH!! ♡
IT'S SO PRETTY!! ♡

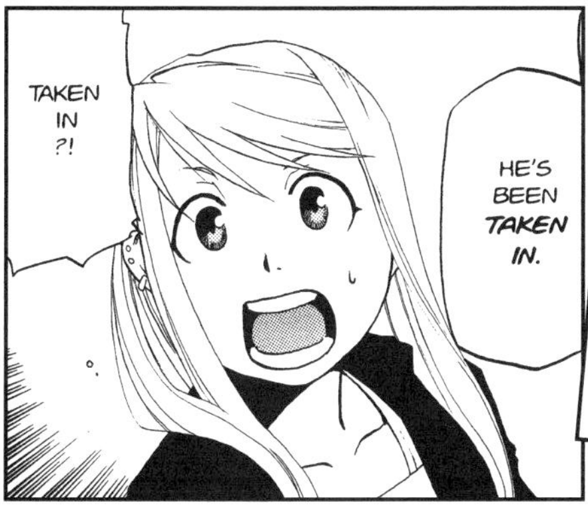
HE'S BEEN TAKEN IN.
TAKEN IN?!

I've never seen auto-mail like that before!!

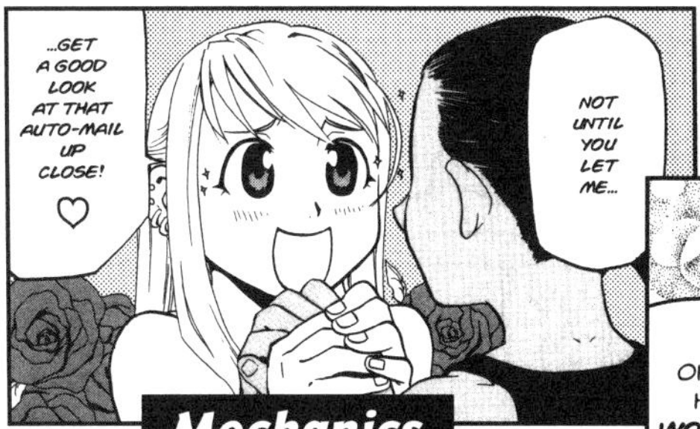
NOT UNTIL YOU LET ME...
...GET A GOOD LOOK AT THAT AUTO-MAIL UP CLOSE! ♡

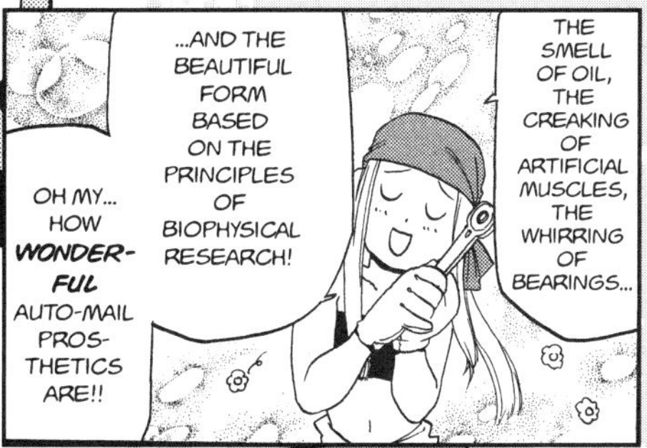
THE SMELL OF OIL, THE CREAKING OF ARTIFICIAL MUSCLES, THE WHIRRING OF BEARINGS...
...AND THE BEAUTIFUL FORM BASED ON THE PRINCIPLES OF BIOPHYSICAL RESEARCH!
OH MY... HOW WONDERFUL AUTO-MAIL PROSTHETICS ARE!!

Mechanics Otaku

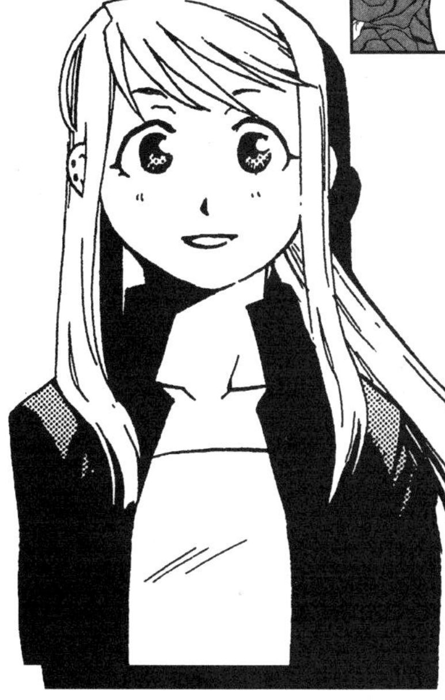

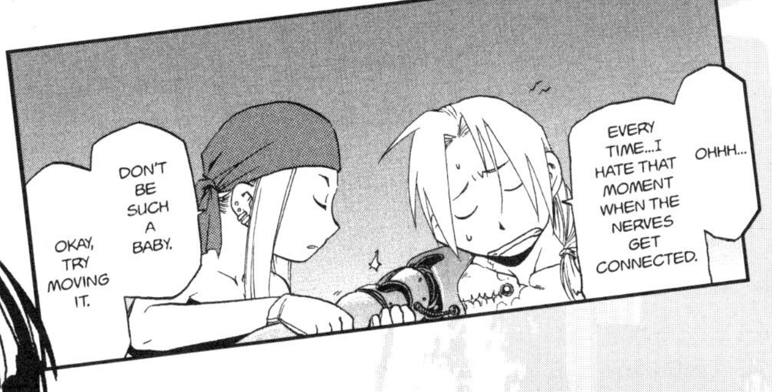
OHHH...
EVERY TIME...I HATE THAT MOMENT WHEN THE NERVES GET CONNECTED.
DON'T BE SUCH A BABY.
OKAY, TRY MOVING IT.

PINAKO ROCKBELL

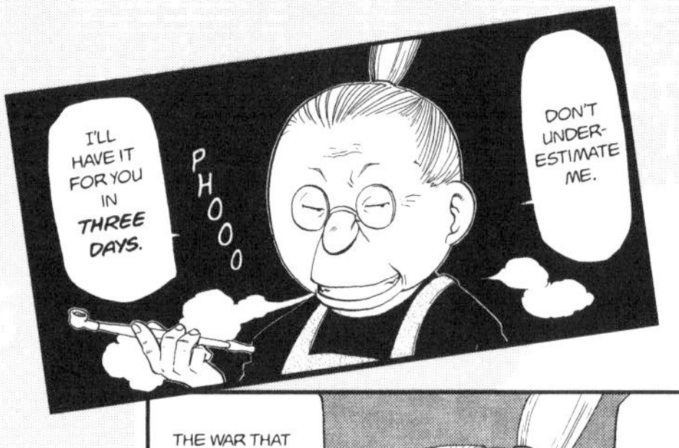
I'LL HAVE IT FOR YOU IN *THREE DAYS.*
PHOOOO
DON'T UNDER-ESTIMATE ME.

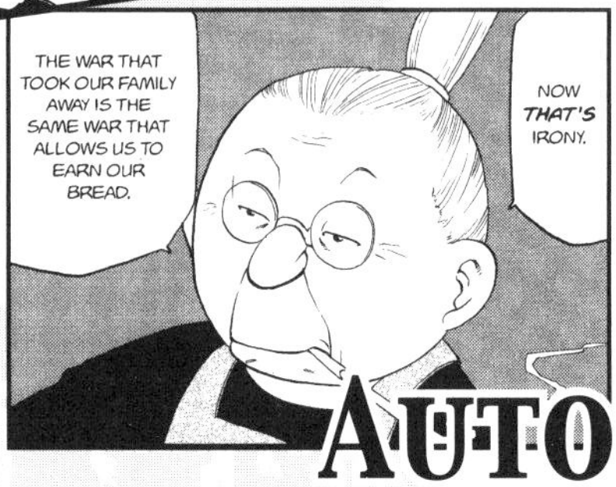
THE WAR THAT TOOK OUR FAMILY AWAY IS THE SAME WAR THAT ALLOWS US TO EARN OUR BREAD.
NOW *THAT'S* IRONY.

Wise Woman

Winry's grandmother taught her everything she knows about auto-mail. No slouch herself, she's also a skilled engineer. But right now, she's more involved in taking care of Winry and the boys than messing about in the shop. Her trademark is her pipe and her funky hairdo that defies all sense of gravity!

AUTO-MAIL ENGINEER

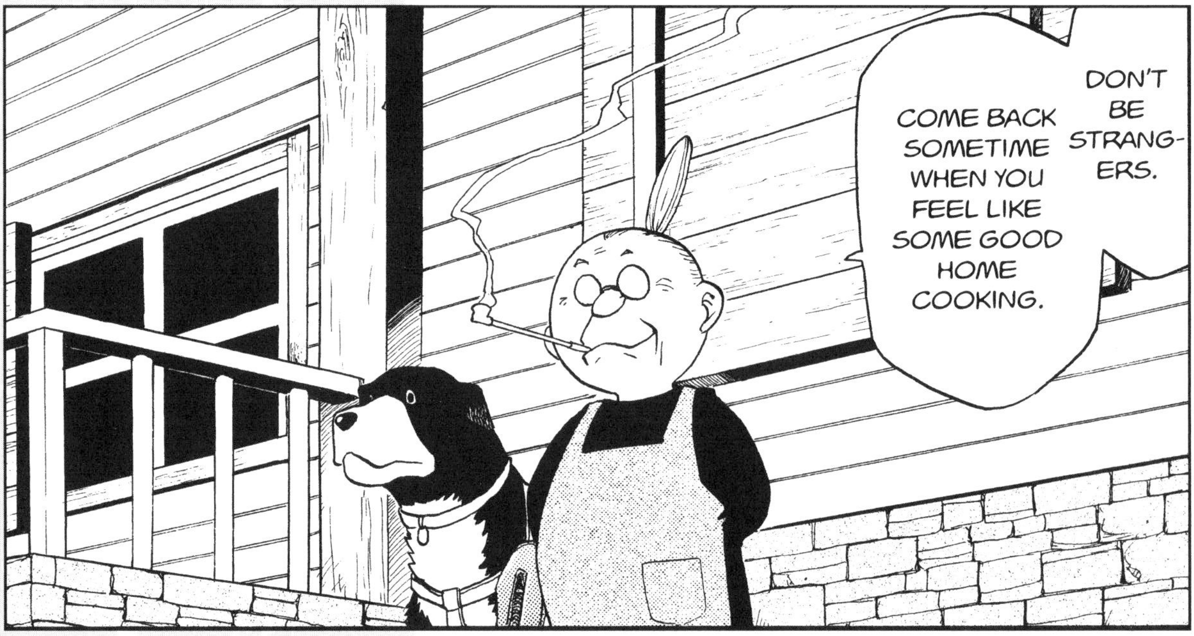
COME BACK SOMETIME WHEN YOU FEEL LIKE SOME GOOD HOME COOKING.
DON'T BE STRANG-ERS.

LOYAL PROTECTOR

DEN

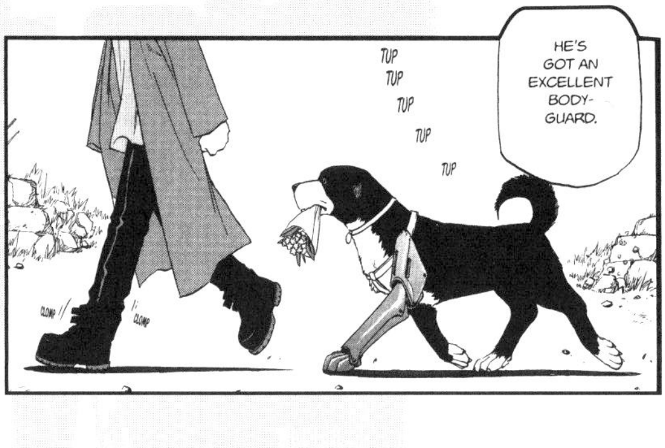
TUP TUP TUP TUP TUP
HE'S GOT AN EXCELLENT BODY-GUARD.

Faithful Companion

Den doesn't need human words to express his feelings. He grew up with Winry and the Brothers Elric and is just as much one of the family as any of his human friends.

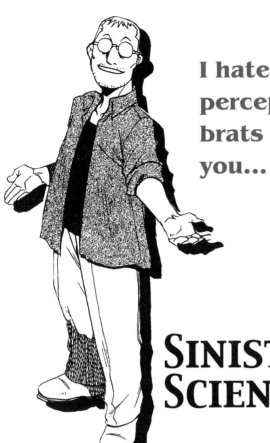

I hate perceptive brats like you...

SINISTER SCIENTIST

SHOU TUCKER

Flawed Father

An alchemist who specializes in combining life forms, he used his own wife and child as raw material in order to create chimeras that can speak human words.

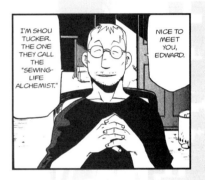

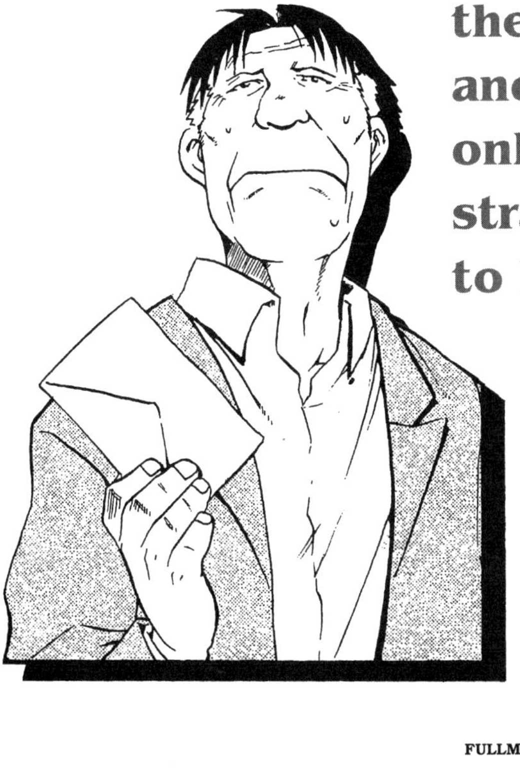

NICE TO MEET YOU, EDWARD.
I'M SHOU TUCKER. THE ONE THEY CALL THE "SEWING-LIFE ALCHEMIST."

It's the work of the devil... and it can only lead straight to hell.

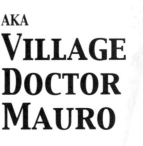

AKA

VILLAGE DOCTOR MAURO

TIM MARCOH

Paying for Past Mistakes

Tim Marcoh is an alchemist who once worked in Central City researching the Philosopher's Stone. Unable to endure the fact that the Philosopher's Stone was being used as a weapon of mass destruction, he fled Central and took his data with him. He now works as a doctor in a small country town, using the Stone's power to help the townspeople.

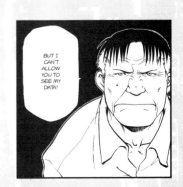

BUT I CAN'T ALLOW YOU TO SEE MY DATA!

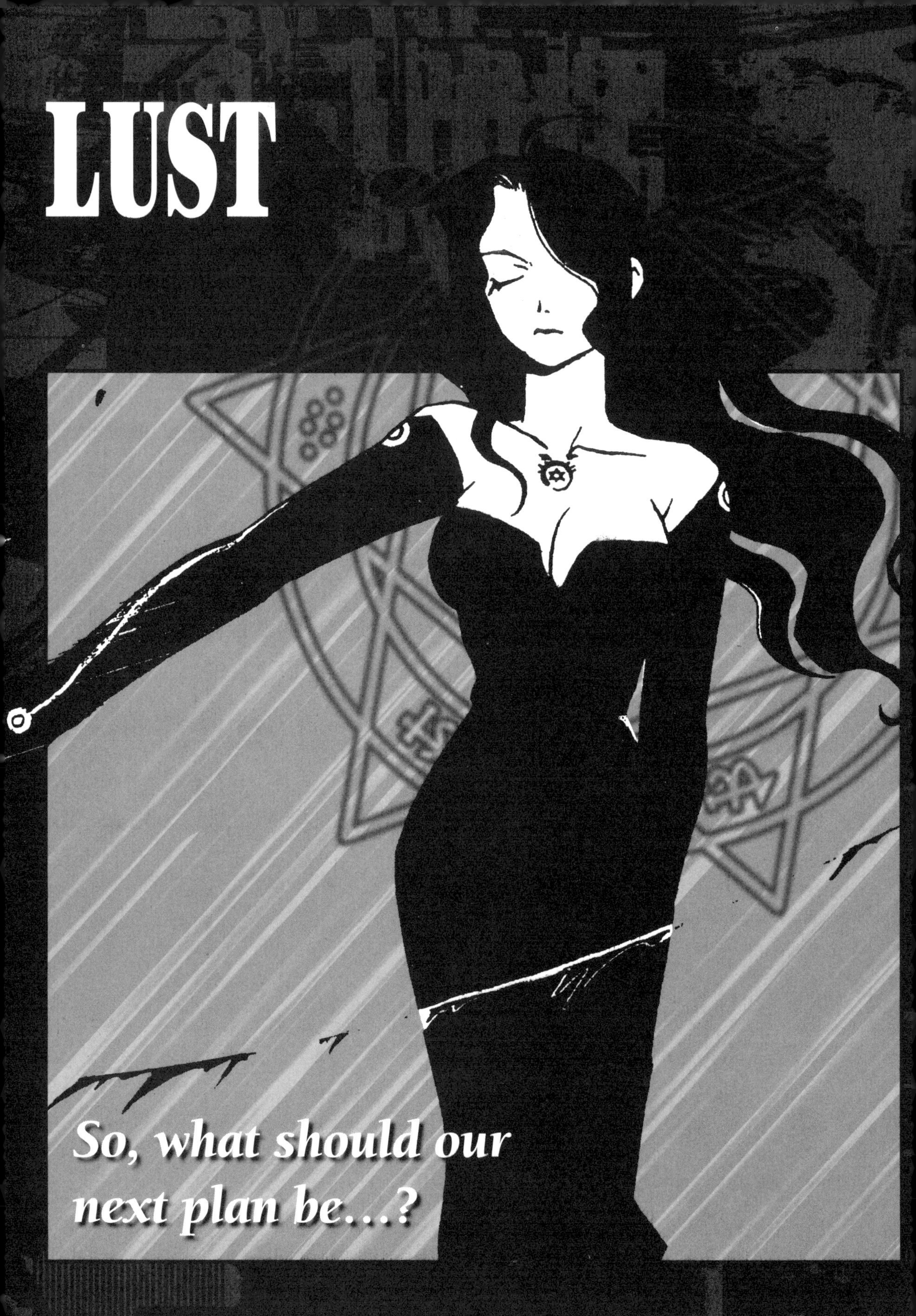
LUST
So, what should our next plan be...?

Empty Inside

The members of the mysterious Ouroboros organization all have the Ouroboros tattoo on their body. Lust is a member of that group. Her first priority in any situation is the swift execution of the "plan." Lust's cruel nature allows her to eliminate any obstacle in her way whether it is an object or a person. With power enough to match her cruelty, a nearly immortal physical body and nails that she can elongate at will, she is steadily carving out a legacy of darkness.

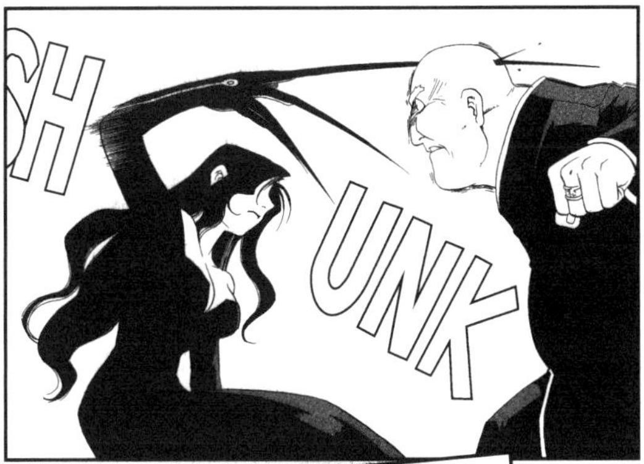
SH
UNK

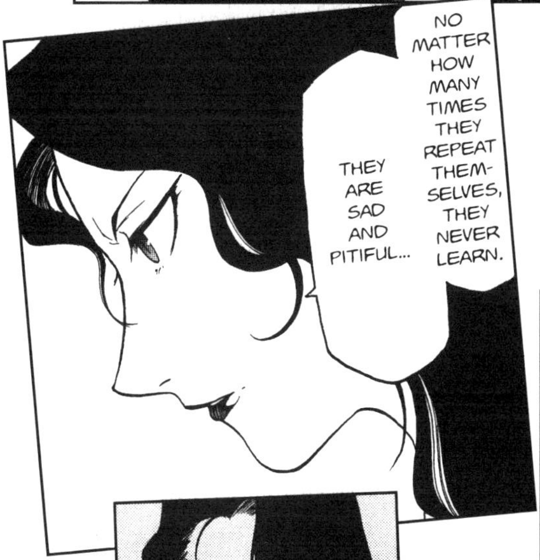
NO MATTER HOW MANY TIMES THEY REPEAT THEMSELVES, THEY NEVER LEARN.
THEY ARE SAD AND PITIFUL...

IMMORTAL

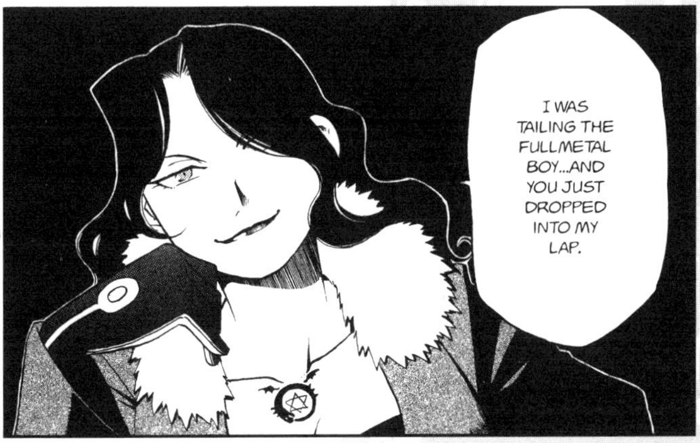
I WAS TAILING THE FULLMETAL BOY...AND YOU JUST DROPPED INTO MY LAP.

I'll erase this town from the map.

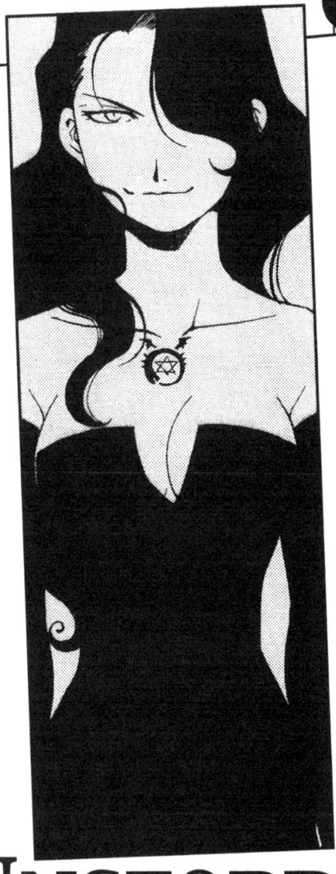

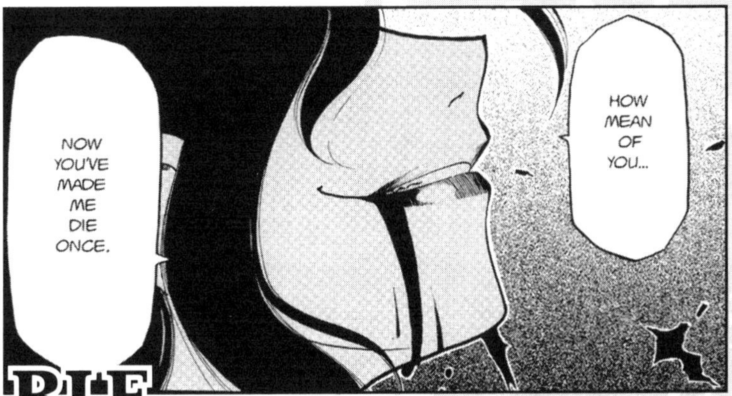
HOW MEAN OF YOU...
NOW YOU'VE MADE ME DIE ONCE.

UNSTOPPABLE

GLUTTONY

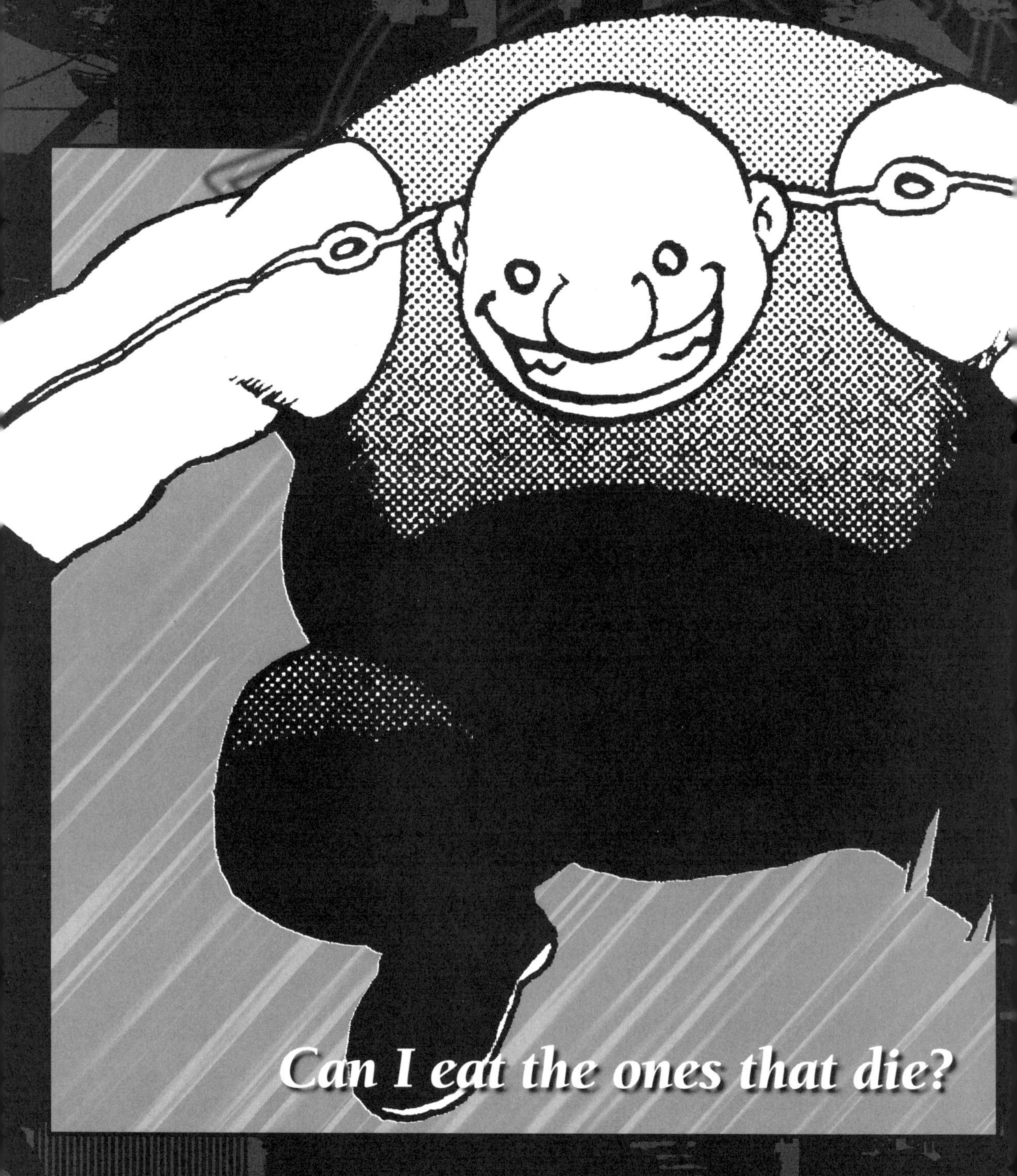
Can I eat the ones that die?

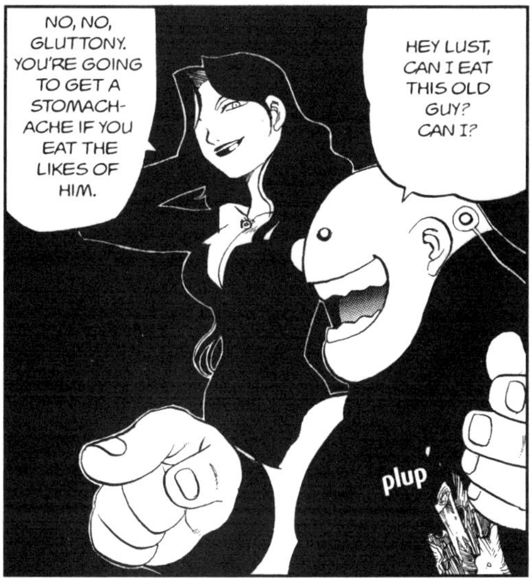
HEY LUST, CAN I EAT THIS OLD GUY? CAN I?
NO, NO, GLUTTONY. YOU'RE GOING TO GET A STOMACH-ACHE IF YOU EAT THE LIKES OF HIM.
plup

Almost an Animal

Although he also has the Ouroboros tattoo, he's completely different from Lust. To Gluttony, his appetite is everything. His every action is connected in some way to his appetite. But whether it's a human being or a chimera, everything that Gluttony eats is a living creature. But perhaps for that reason, his power is unmatched, and even though he lacks technique, he has more than enough strength to beat down the enemy.

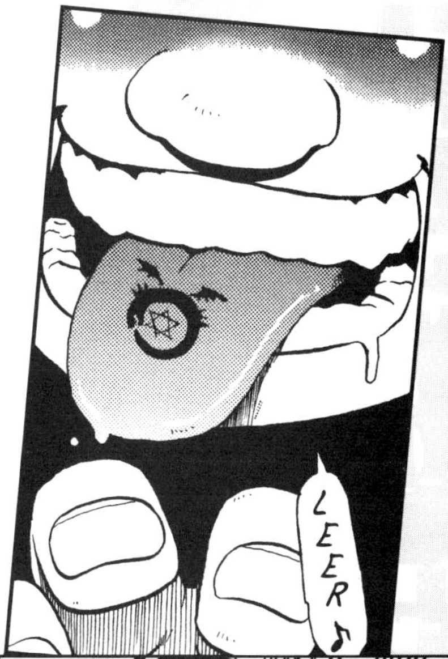
LEER♪

Lust! That was tasty!

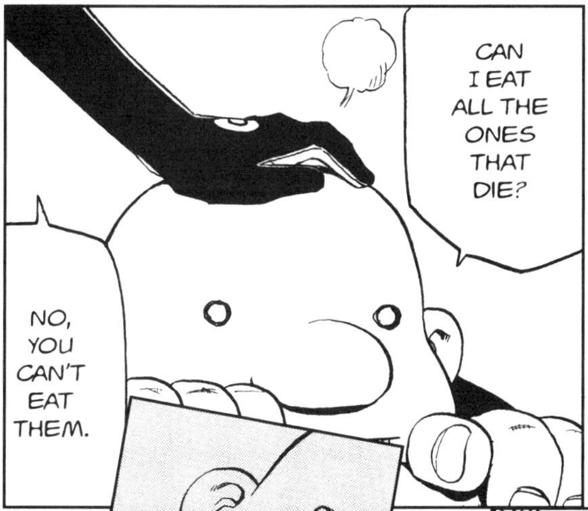
CAN I EAT ALL THE ONES THAT DIE?
NO, YOU CAN'T EAT THEM.

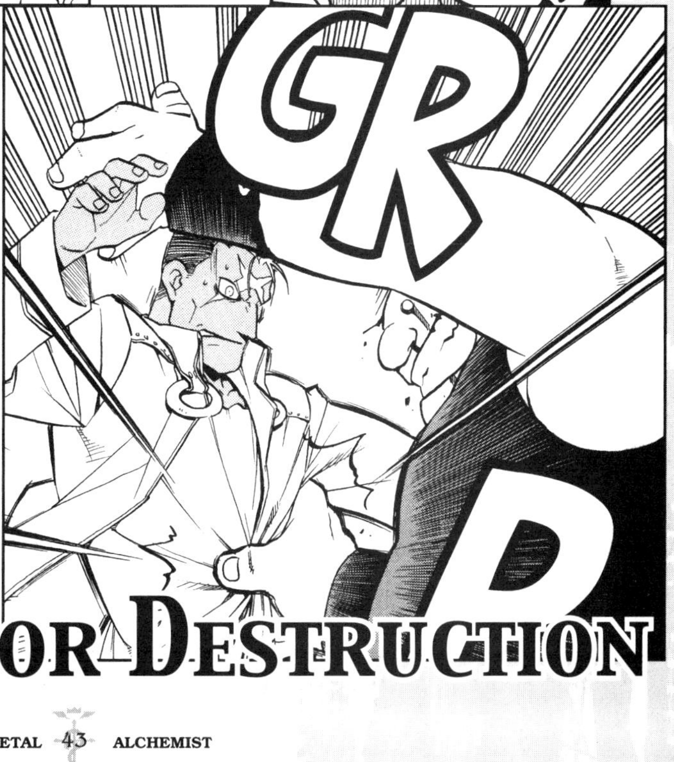
GRD

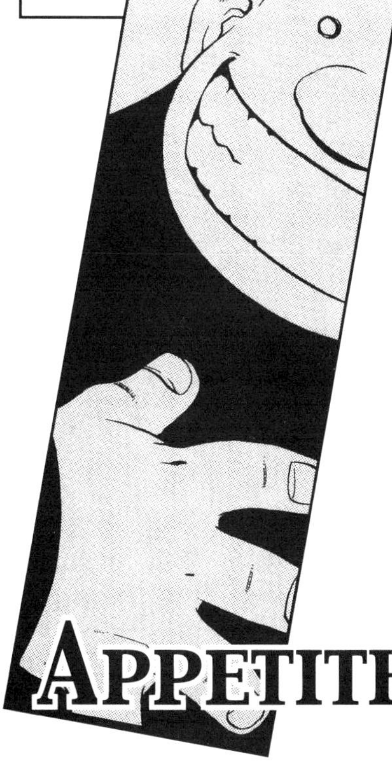

Appetite for Destruction

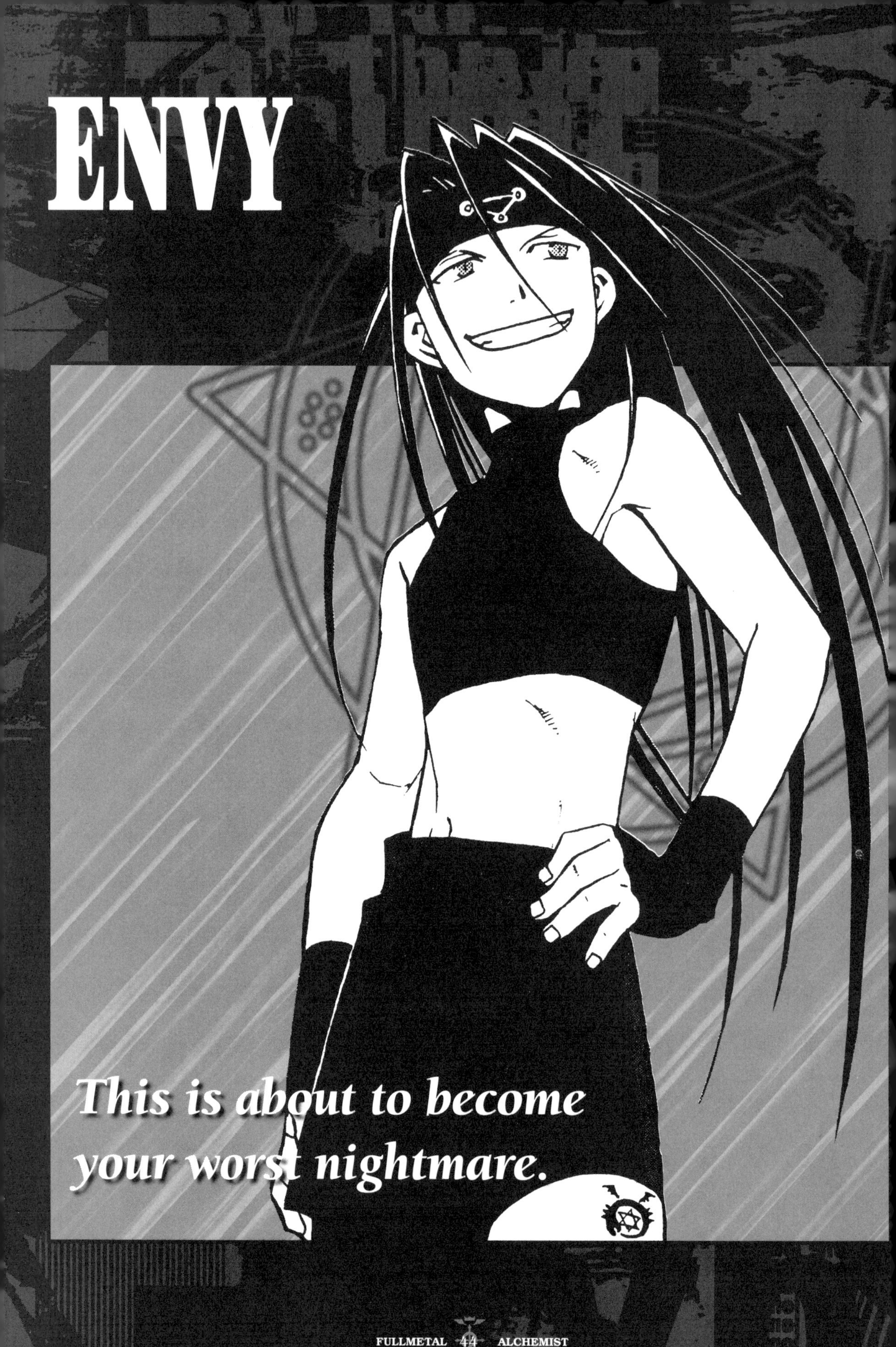
ENVY
This is about to become your worst nightmare.

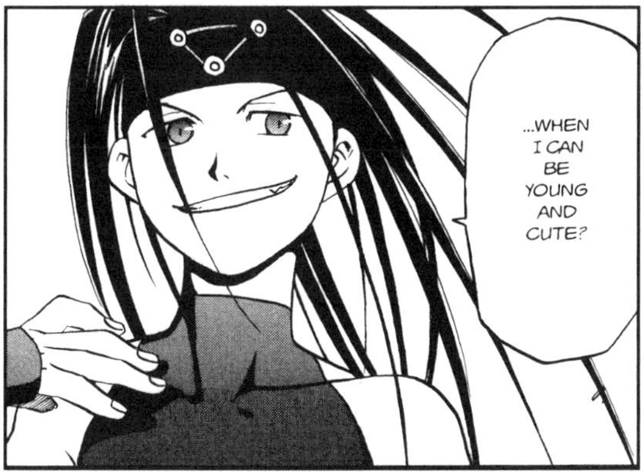
...WHEN I CAN BE YOUNG AND CUTE?

Chameleon

Of uncertain gender, Envy has the ability to transform its appearance at will. Envy can change itself into any person that it has seen at least once. No one knows Envy's true form. And even the other members of the group agree that Envy is their most depraved member. Once angered, Envy displays a terrifying cruelty and becomes uncontrollable.

Just shut the hell up before you say something else you'll regret.

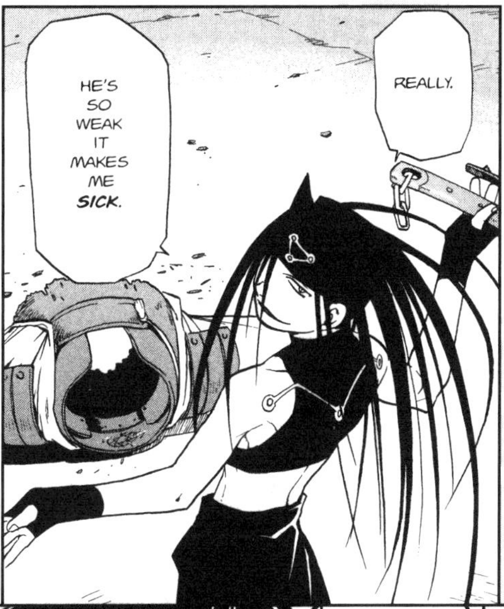
REALLY.
HE'S SO WEAK IT MAKES ME *SICK*.

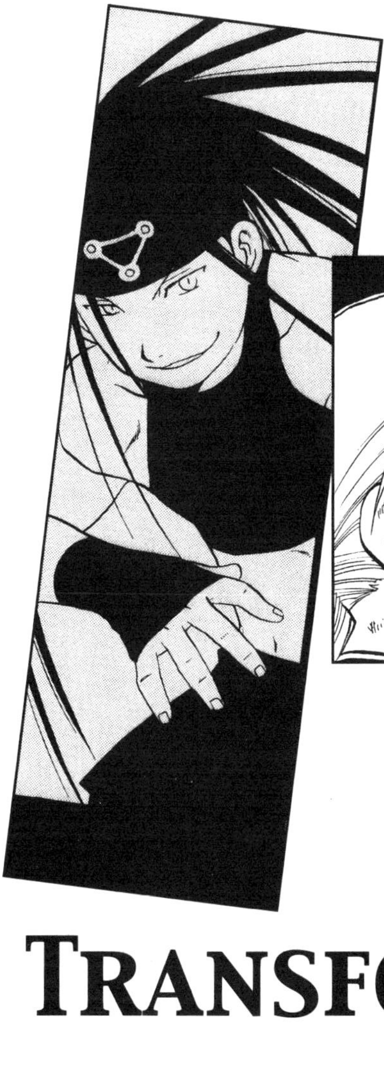

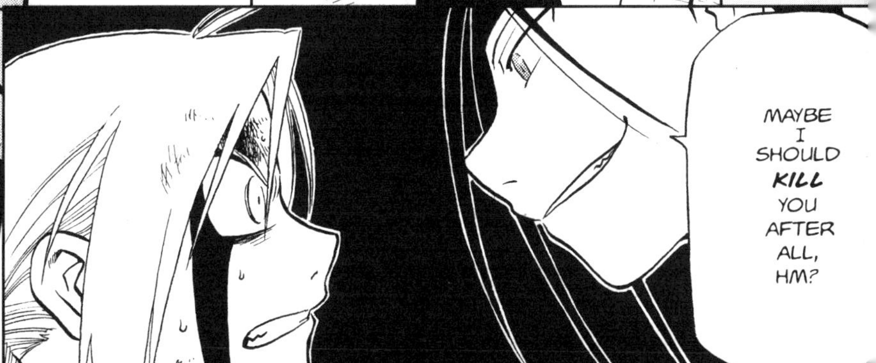
MAYBE I SHOULD *KILL* YOU AFTER ALL, HM?

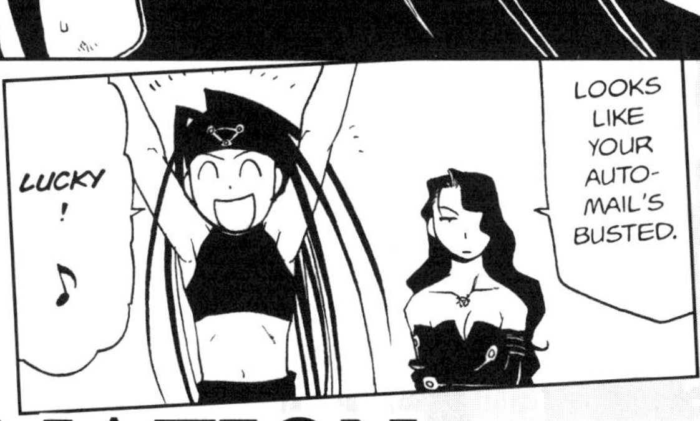
LOOKS LIKE YOUR AUTO-MAIL'S BUSTED.
LUCKY!
♪

TRANSFORMATION

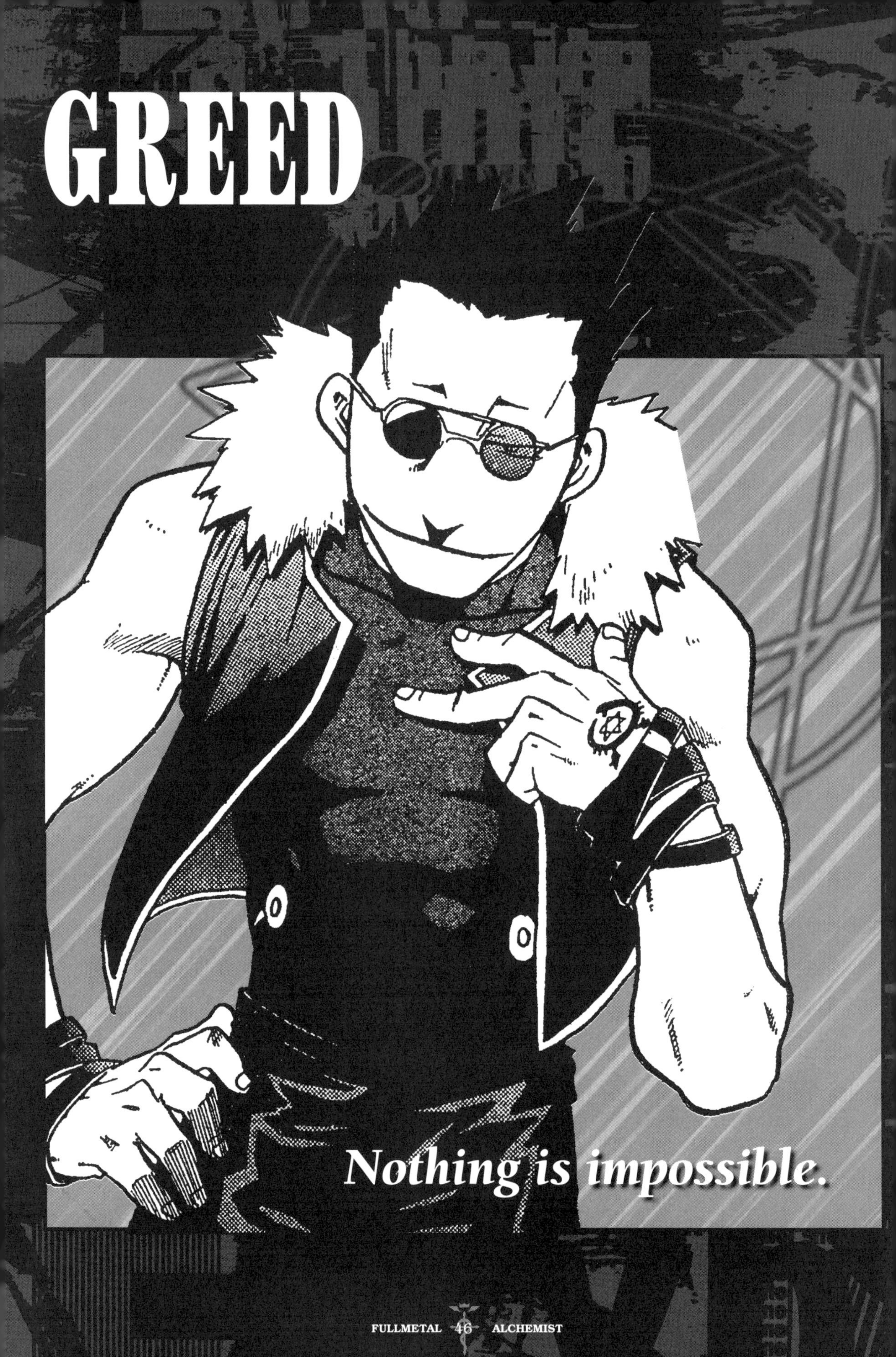
GREED
Nothing is impossible.

Almost Human

Greed has the Ouroboros tattoo on the back of his hand. His goal is to fulfill all of his desires in life, which, of course, include money, women, power, fame, and most of all immortality. Greed possesses a body that's even harder than metal, but unlike the other Ouroboros, he uses his power purely for himself. He has also been gathering chimeras that have escaped from the laboratory as his subordinates.

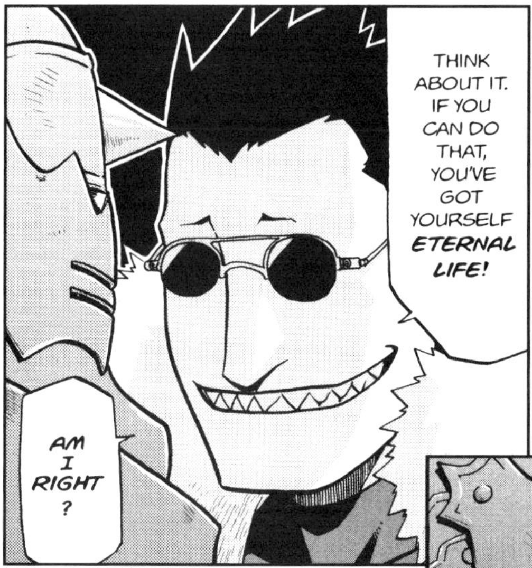
THINK ABOUT IT. IF YOU CAN DO THAT, YOU'VE GOT YOURSELF ETERNAL LIFE!
AM I RIGHT ?

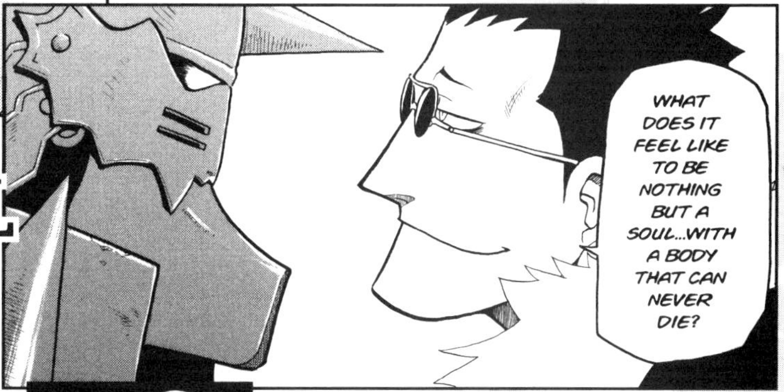
WHAT DOES IT FEEL LIKE TO BE NOTHING BUT A SOUL...WITH A BODY THAT CAN NEVER DIE?

ARTIFICIAL AVARICE

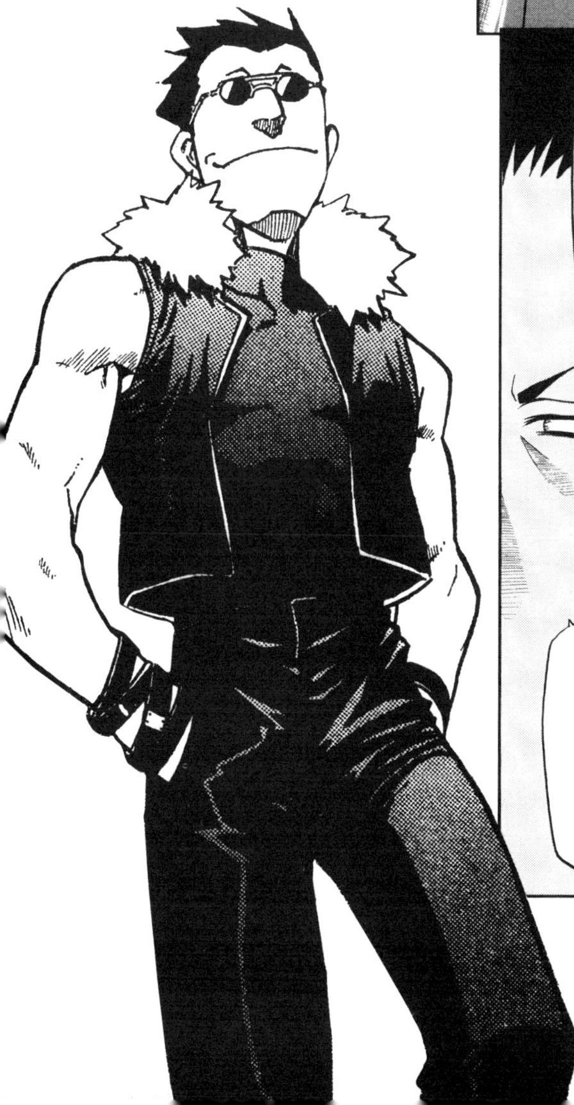

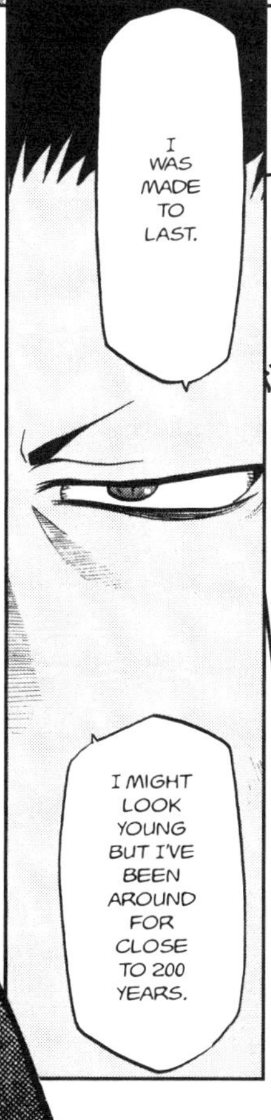
I WAS MADE TO LAST.
I MIGHT LOOK YOUNG BUT I'VE BEEN AROUND FOR CLOSE TO 200 YEARS.

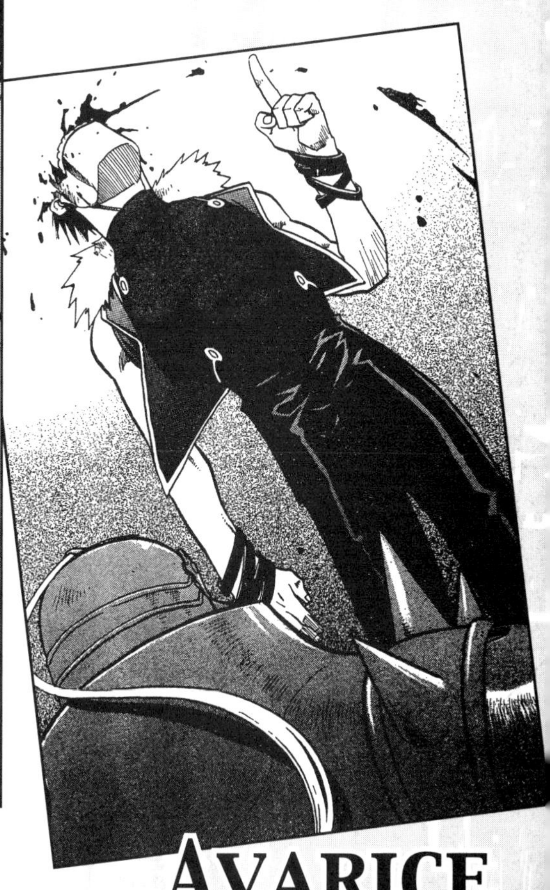

Chimeras

THEN YOU'RE GOING DOWN.
COME WITH US...
...AND YOU MIGHT FIND OUT ABOUT WHAT YOU WANT TO KNOW.

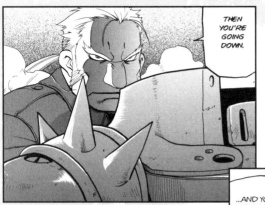

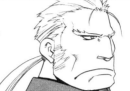

LOA

Greed's right-hand man, the chimera Loa has tremendous physical power and can easily take on Al in battle.

THAT LITTLE BRAT!
DOR-CHET!
GNG GNG GNG GNG GNG
D-D-M

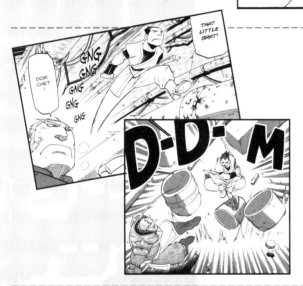

DORCHET

Another of Greed's subordinates, Dorchet was created by combining a human and a dog. Dorchet's greatest asset is his speed, and the sword is his weapon of choice. His skills, including his keen sense of smell, are, of course, more doglike than other chimeras.

SORRY TO DROP IN.
SSS
SSS
HEH HEH. THIS ISN'T A CONTEST OF STRENGTH.
KRK

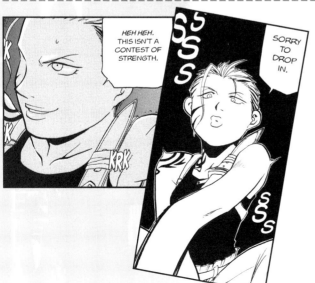

MARTEL

Severely injured in the southern border wars, soldier Martel was combined with a snake against her will. She escaped the lab only to become yet another of Greed's minions.

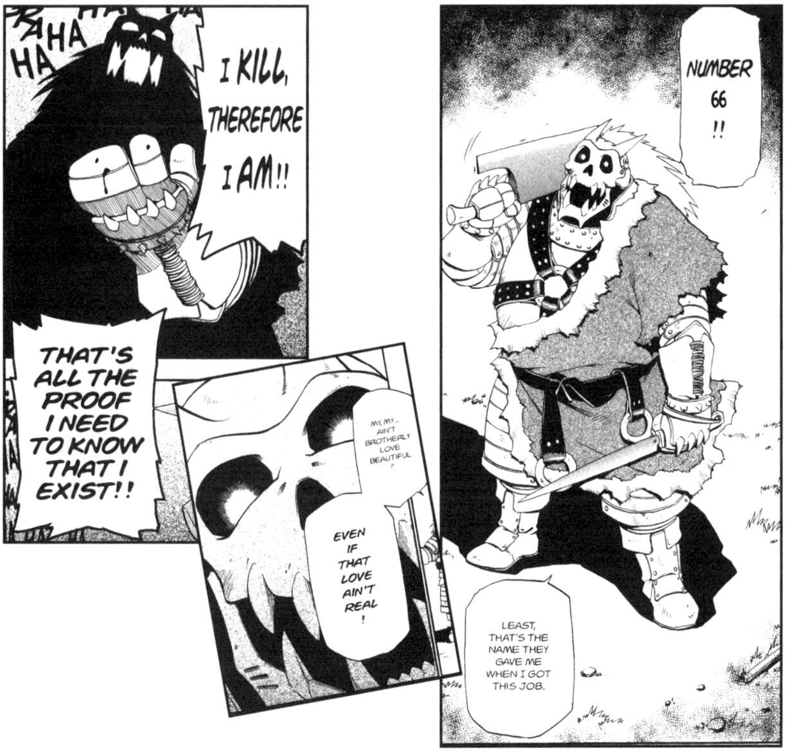
NUMBER 66 !!
LEAST, THAT'S THE NAME THEY GAVE ME WHEN I GOT THIS JOB.
HA HA HA
I KILL, THEREFORE I AM!!
THAT'S ALL THE PROOF I NEED TO KNOW THAT I EXIST!!
MY, MY... AIN'T BROTHERLY LOVE BEAUTIFUL?
EVEN IF THAT LOVE AIN'T REAL!

NUMBER 66

Mass Murderer Reborn

Barry the Chopper had his soul bound into a suit of armor by the Ouroboros. He now enjoys a new lease on life – which he uses to continue his crimes. It was reported to the public that he was executed.

GUARDIAN

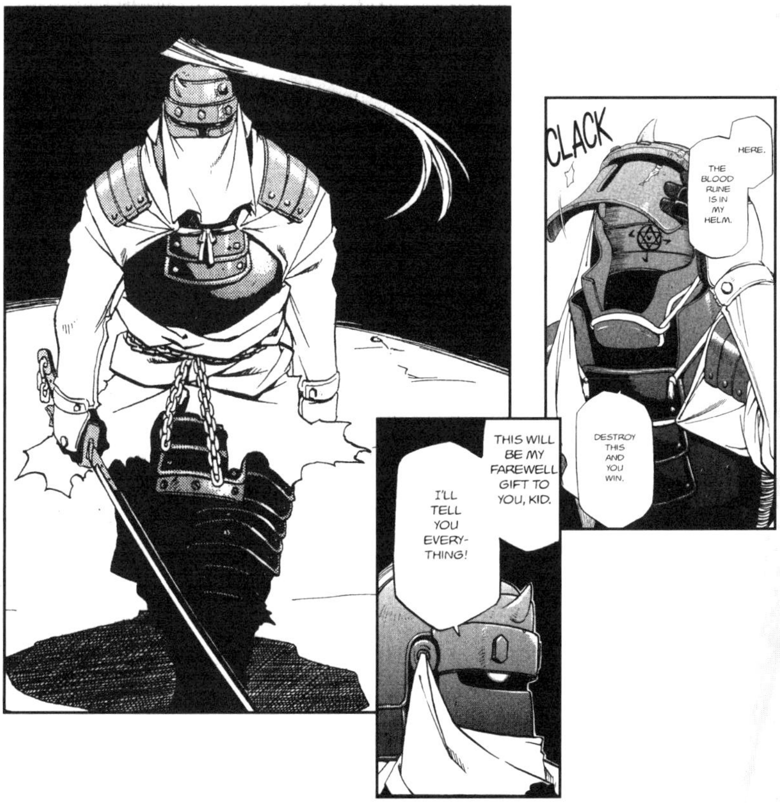
CLACK
HERE.
THE BLOOD RUNE IS IN MY HELM.
DESTROY THIS AND YOU WIN.
THIS WILL BE MY FAREWELL GIFT TO YOU, KID.
I'LL TELL YOU EVERY-THING!

NUMBER 48

Brothers Bound

The souls of two brothers who in life committed crimes as the serial killer called Slicer have been bound together into this single suit of armor.

SCAR

(The man with a scar)

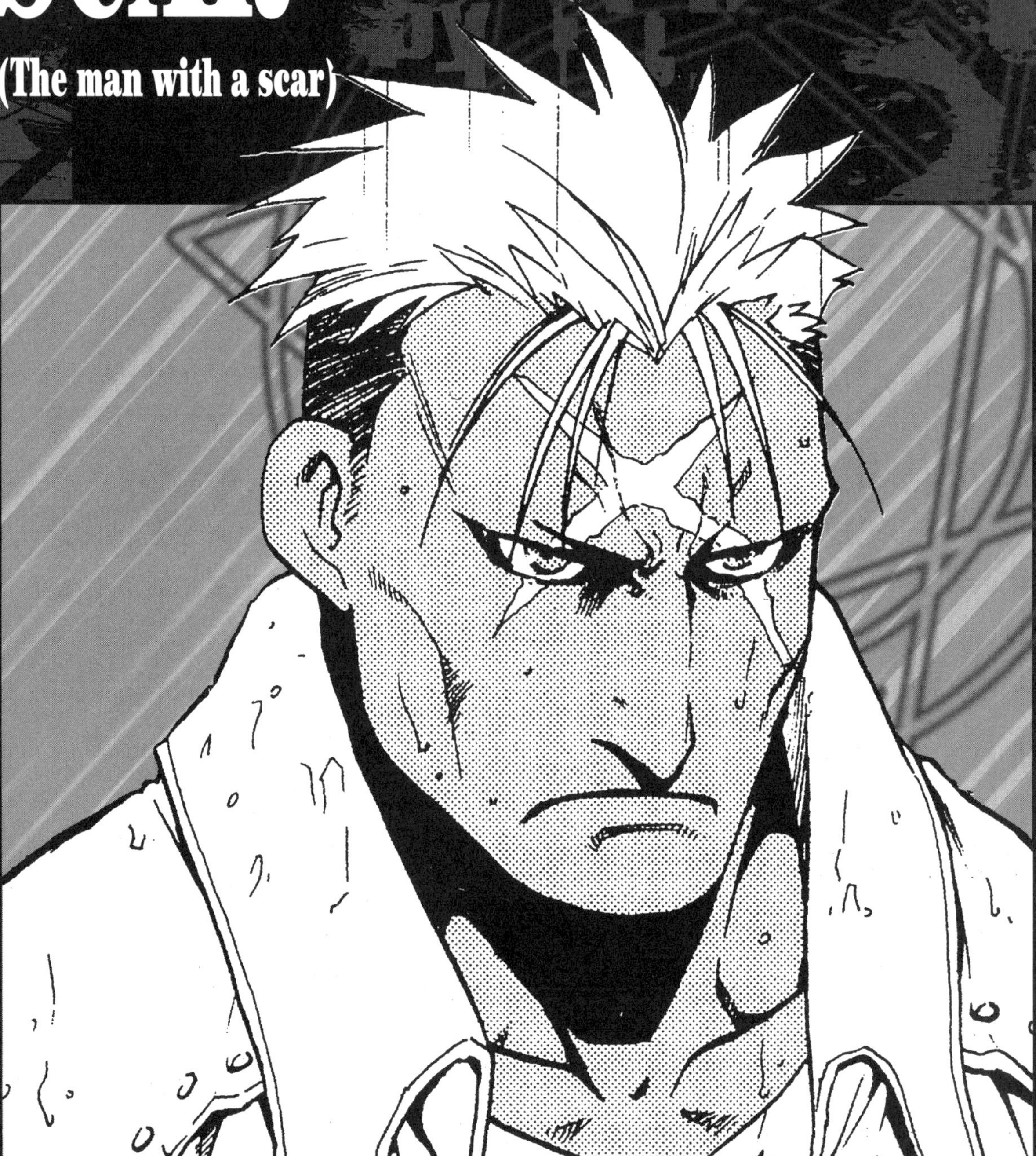
I'll give you a moment to pray.

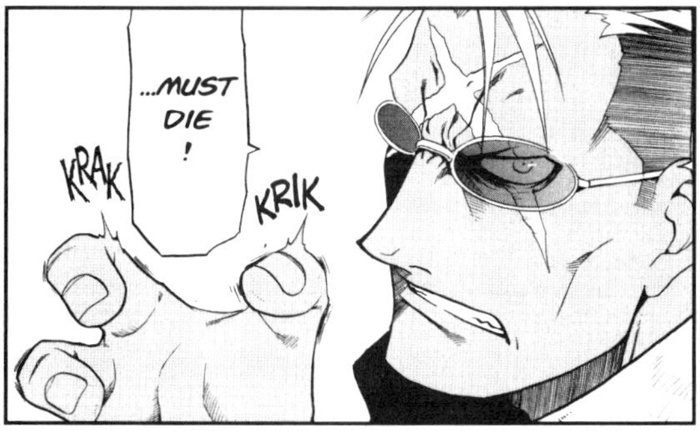
...MUST DIE!
KRIK
KRAK

After destroying the state alchemist Shou Tucker, he prays to the god Ishbala for the souls of Tucker's victims.

Killer of his own Kind

Scar is one of the last remaining members of the northern Ishbal people. After seeing his kin slaughtered in front of his very eyes by state alchemists, Scar went on a rampage of vengeance and hunted down every state alchemist he could find. His main weapon is his right arm, which has the ability to destroy anything it touches. The secret of Scar's power lies in the tattoos that cover his arms. Although he knows that vengeance only gives rise to more vengeance, he still remains true to the path he has chosen for himself.

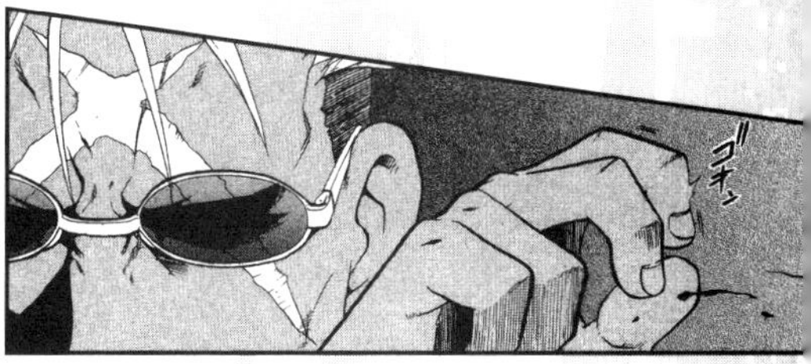

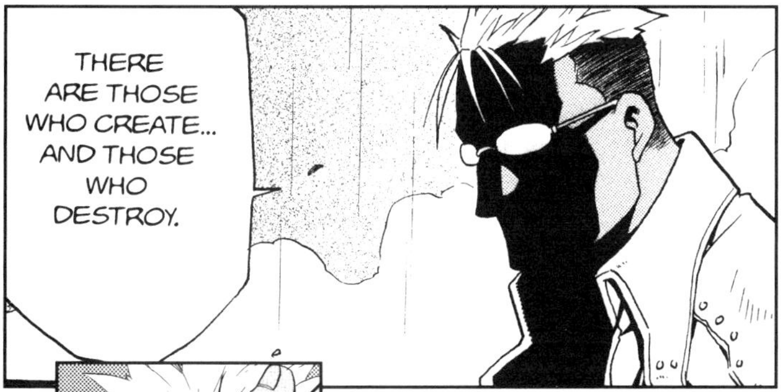
THERE ARE THOSE WHO CREATE... AND THOSE WHO DESTROY.

He calls himself the "destroyer."

THE RIGHT HAND OF DESTRUCTION

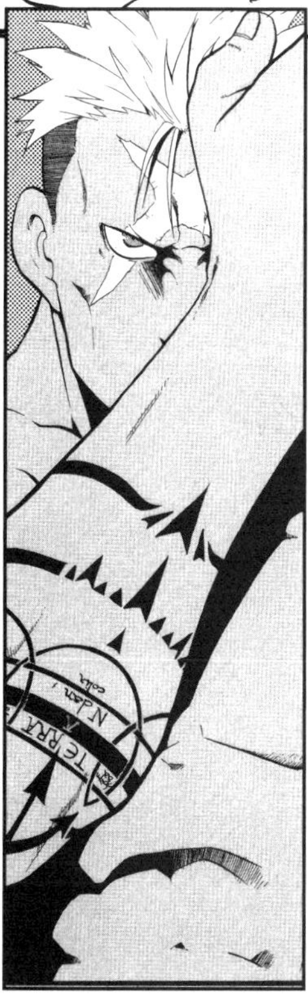

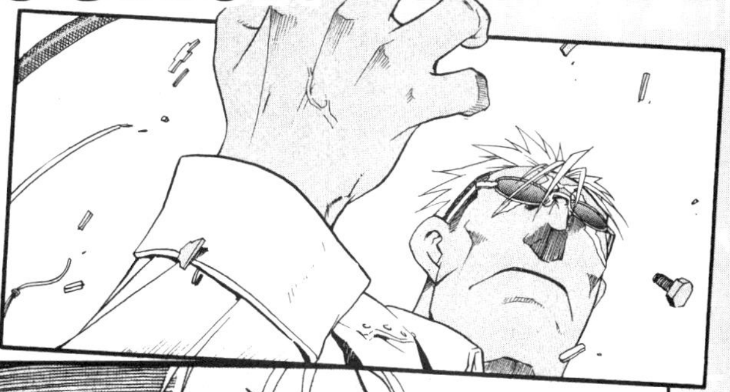

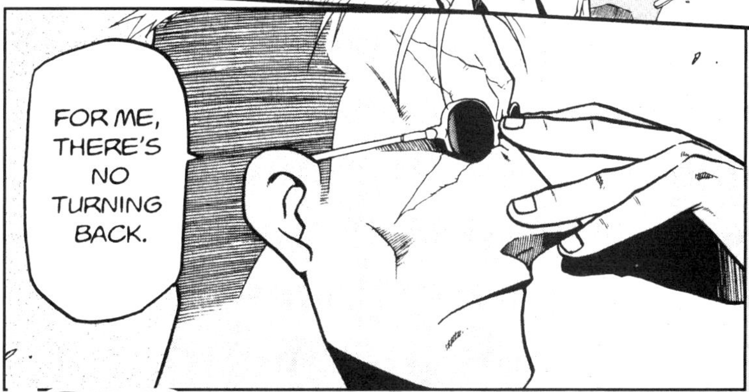
FOR ME, THERE'S NO TURNING BACK.

THE AVENGER

He calls himself the "destroyer." His own destructive technique corresponds to the first stage in alchemical transmutation, which is deconstruction.

Column Check out the mob scene!!

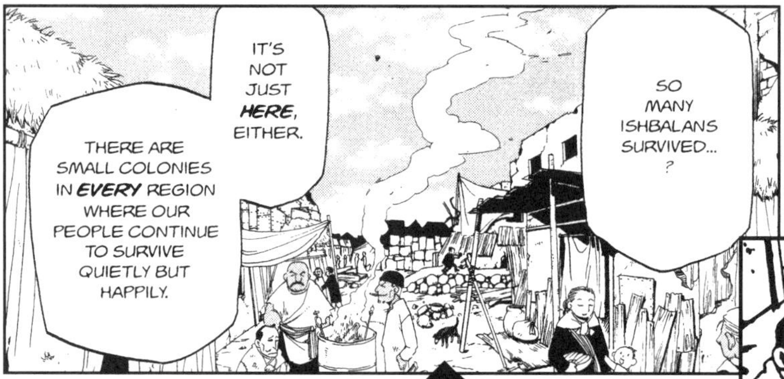
SO MANY ISHBALANS SURVIVED...?
IT'S NOT JUST **HERE**, EITHER.
THERE ARE SMALL COLONIES IN **EVERY** REGION WHERE OUR PEOPLE CONTINUE TO SURVIVE QUIETLY BUT HAPPILY.

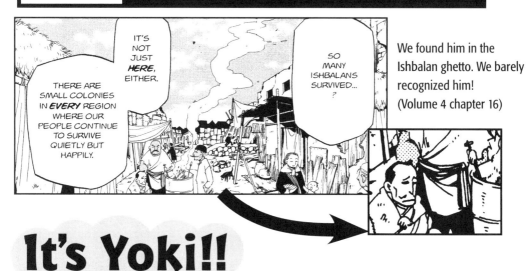

We found him in the Ishbalan ghetto. We barely recognized him! (Volume 4 chapter 16)

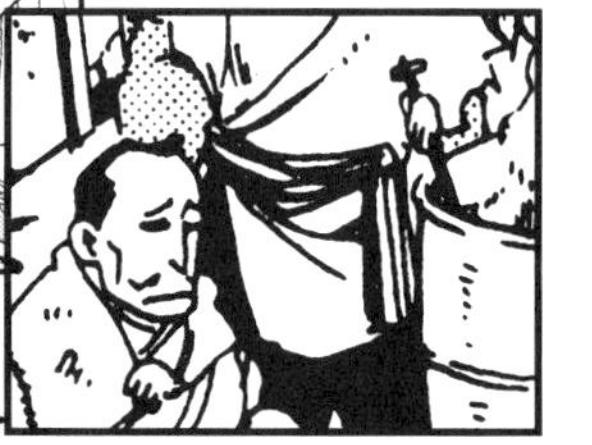

It's Yoki!!

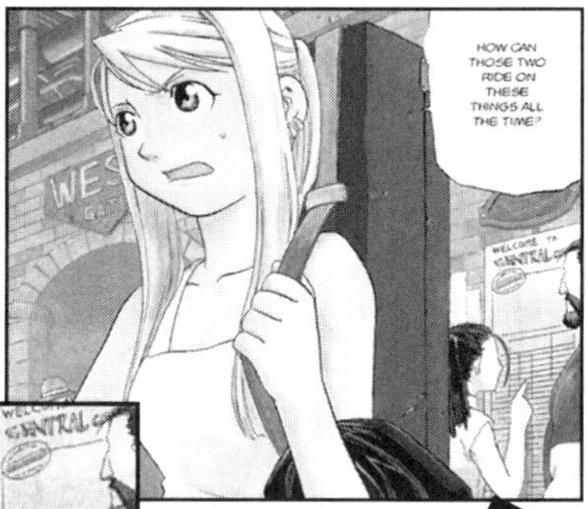
HOW CAN THOSE TWO RIDE ON THESE THINGS ALL THE TIME?

Winry came on an out-of-town assignment to repair Ed's auto-mail. Later, we discovered some unexpected people inside the train station!! (Volume 4 chapter 14)

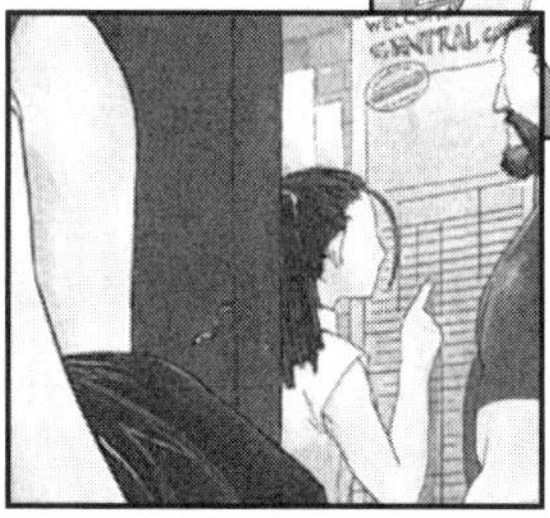

We've discovered the Curtis couple!!

Special Section

This mysterious character pops up in odd places. He's chasing someone. But who? And who is he?

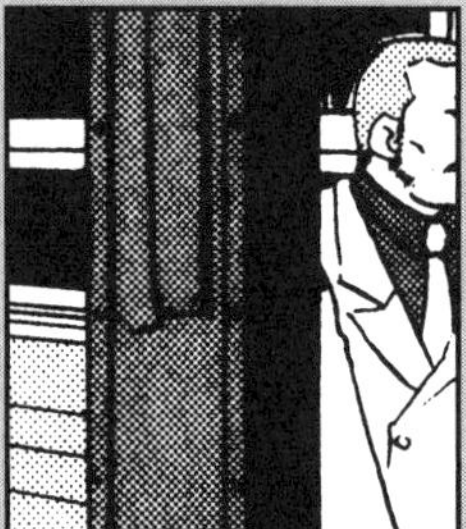

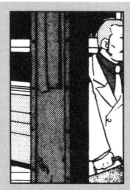

He wears a white suit and short-cropped hair. This is his first appearance. (Volume 2 chapter 8)

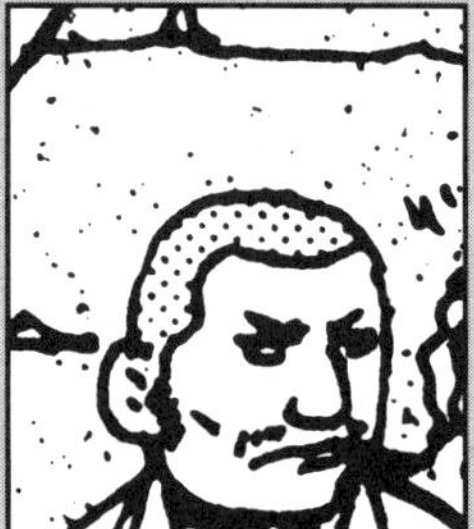

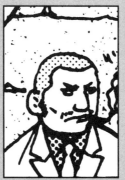

Standing on a street corner in Central City with a cigarette. (Volume 2 chapter 8)

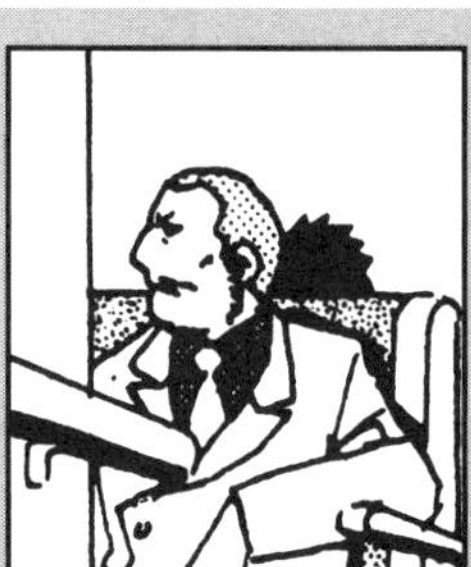

Here he is again, but this time on the train. Who's he after anyway? (Volume 4 chapter 16)

STORY DIGEST

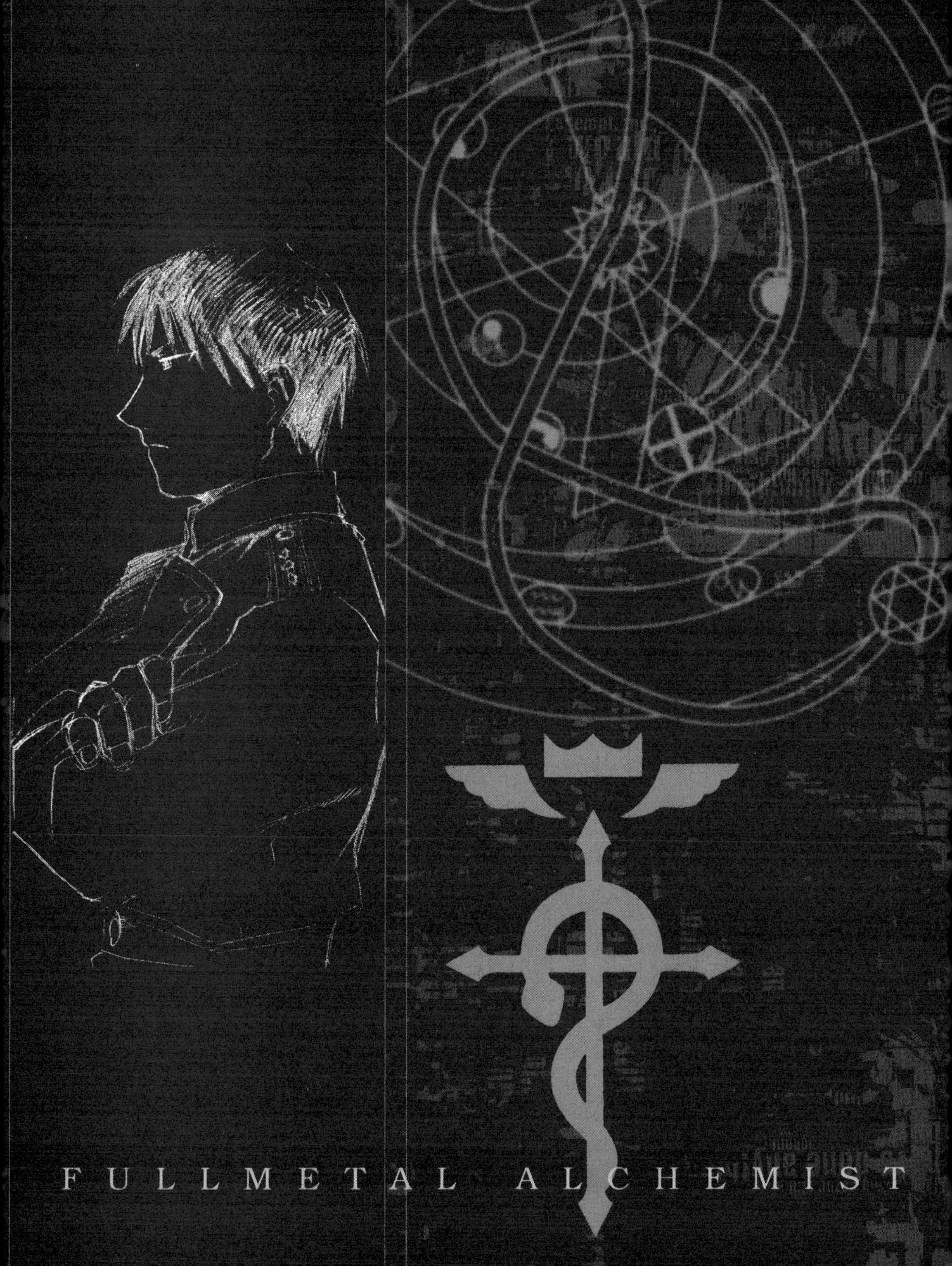

FULLMETAL ALCHEMIST

Volume 1: *The Two Alchemists*

The Chosen Path of the Elric Brothers

Due to a sin committed in their past, the Elric brothers have lost a portion of their bodies. Ed lost an arm and a leg; Alphonse lost his entire body and is now nothing but a soul in a suit of armor. Using their skills as alchemists, the two travel the world seeking a way to regain their lost bodies.

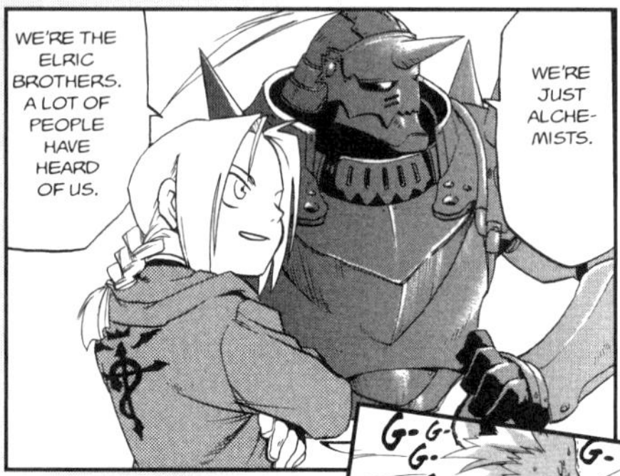
WE'RE JUST ALCHE-MISTS.
WE'RE THE ELRIC BROTHERS. A LOT OF PEOPLE HAVE HEARD OF US.

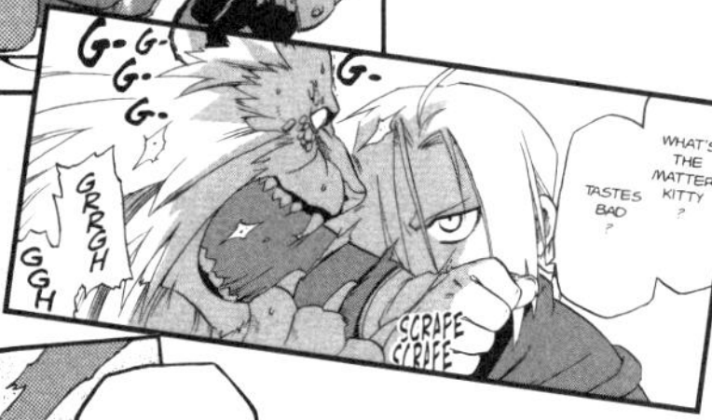
WHAT'S THE MATTER, KITTY?
TASTES BAD?
G-G-G-G-G-
GRRGH
GGH
SCRAPE SCRAPE

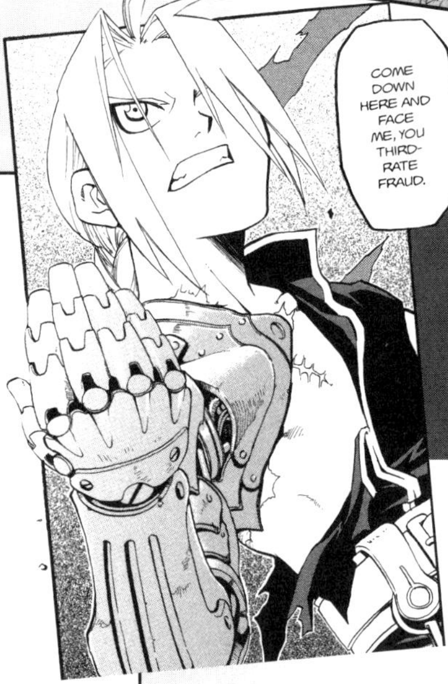
COME DOWN HERE AND FACE ME, YOU THIRD-RATE FRAUD.

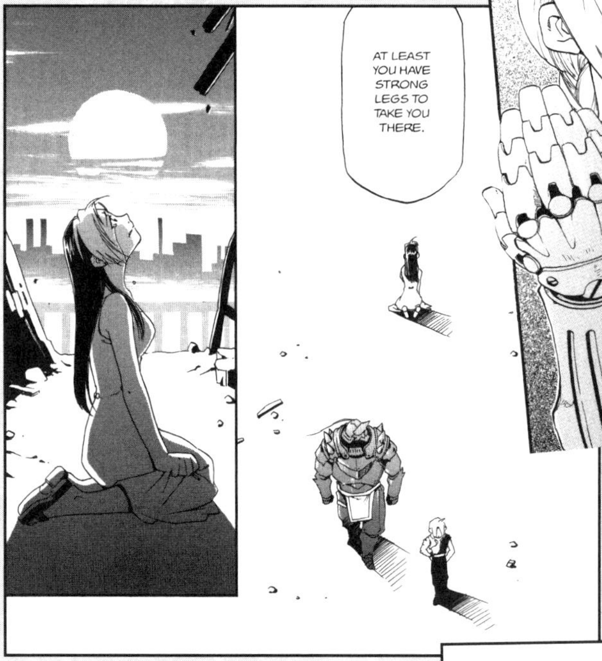
AT LEAST YOU HAVE STRONG LEGS TO TAKE YOU THERE.

I'll show you there's no comparison between us!

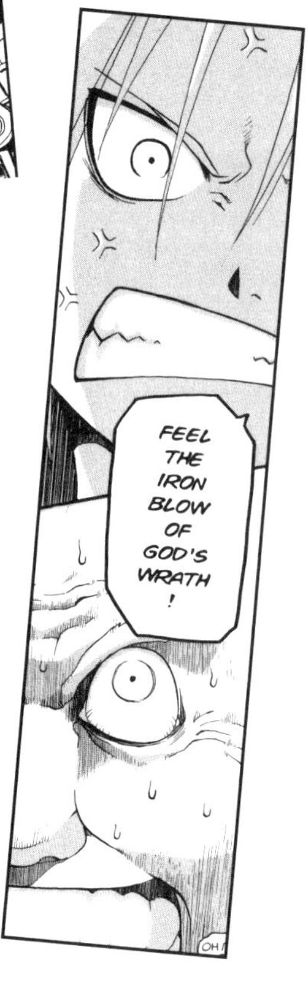
FEEL THE IRON BLOW OF GOD'S WRATH!
OH!

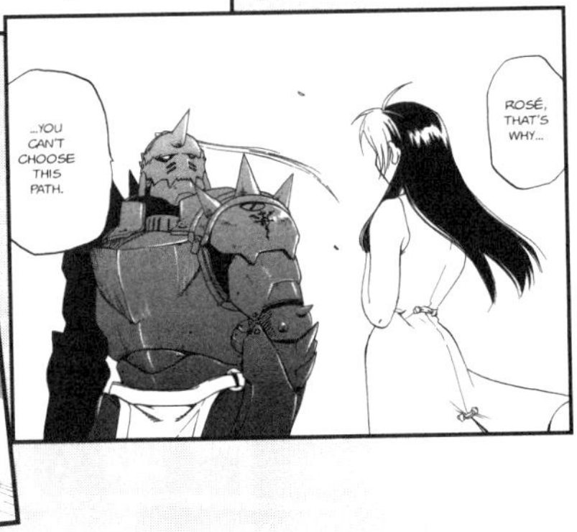
ROSÉ, THAT'S WHY...
...YOU CAN'T CHOOSE THIS PATH.

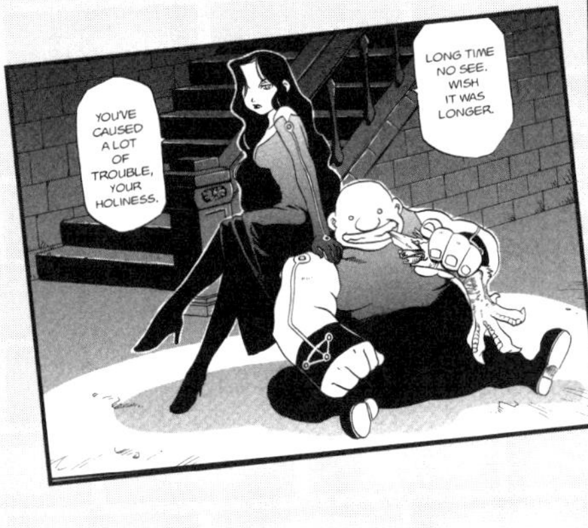
LONG TIME NO SEE. WISH IT WAS LONGER.
YOU'VE CAUSED A LOT OF TROUBLE, YOUR HOLINESS.

...THE MINES ARE OUR HOMES...
...AND OUR GRAVES.

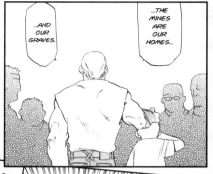

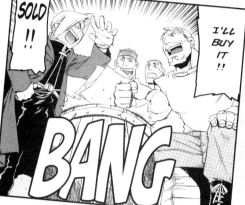

Incident in Youswell

In Youswell, a coal mining town on the outskirts of the East Area, the Elric brothers encountered and defeated the tyrannical Lt. Yoki. Leaving the liberated town by train, the boys were then attacked by terrorists during a hijacking, again using their abilities to stop the takeover and rescue the passengers.

I'LL BUY IT!!
SOLD!!
BANG

CRASH

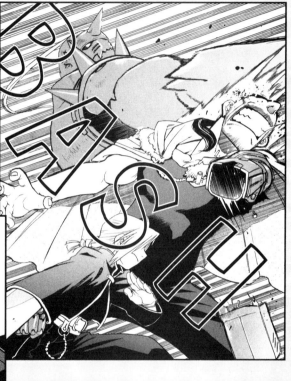

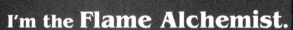

I'm the Flame Alchemist.

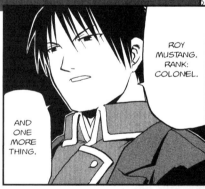

ROY MUSTANG. RANK: COLONEL.
AND ONE MORE THING.

Lighter Side

Despite his dark interior, Lt. Yoki remains the jester, carrying out his sinister plans with an air of comedic delight.

SO PLEASE LOOK FORWARD TO IT. ♡

WITH THIS MUCH GOLD I CAN SAY GOODBYE TO THIS MISERABLE POST...!
I'LL BRIBE THE HIGHER-RANKING OFFICIALS AT CENTRAL, AND THEN...
WEE HEE HEE

WELL, WELL, LIEUTENANT.
I JUST SOLD THE DEED TO THE MINE TO THE CHIEF HERE.
WHAAAT!!?

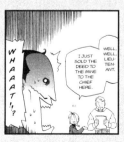

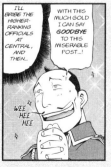

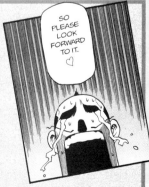

Volume 2: *Creation & Destruction*

The Many Moods of an Alchemist

While visiting a famous alchemist, the "Sewing-Life Alchemist" Shou Tucker, Ed and Al discover that the man is insane and actually used his wife and daughter for his transmutation experiments. In retribution for his crimes, Tucker is brutally murdered by the revenge-crazed Scar, who also seriously wounds Ed and Al during the fierce battle.

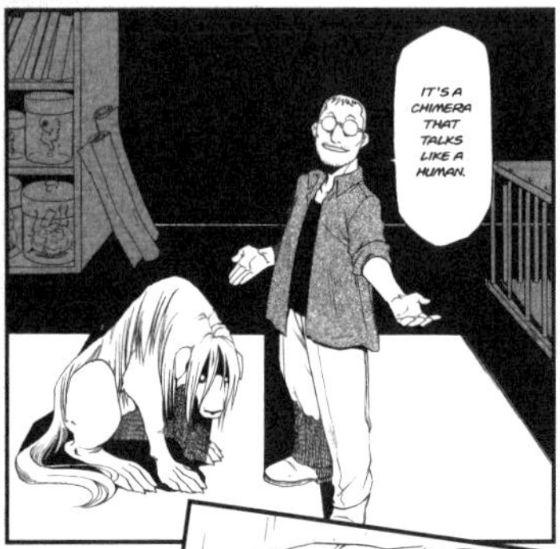
IT'S A CHIMERA THAT TALKS LIKE A HUMAN.

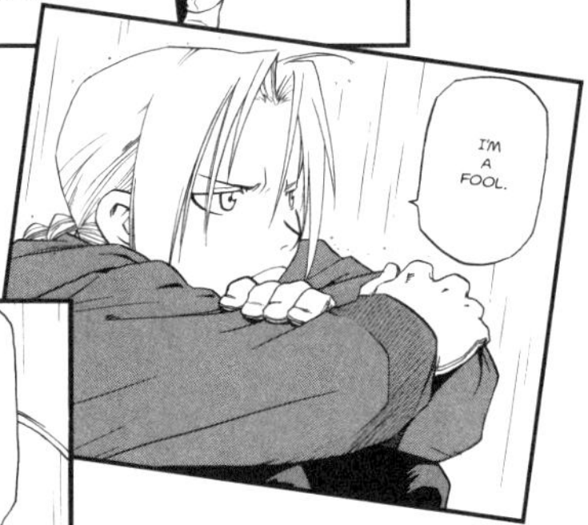
I'M A FOOL.

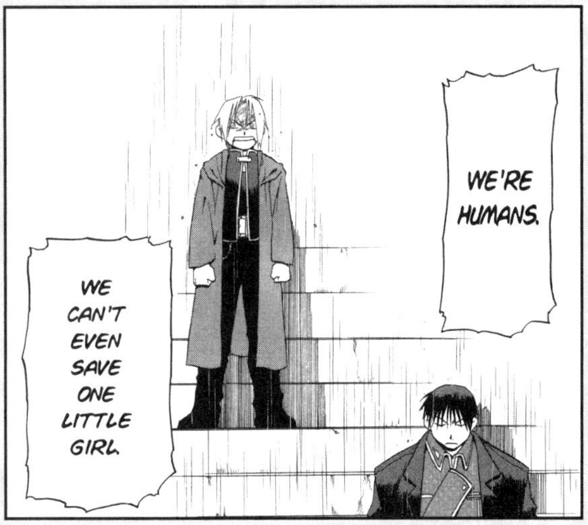
WE'RE HUMANS.
WE CAN'T EVEN SAVE ONE LITTLE GIRL.

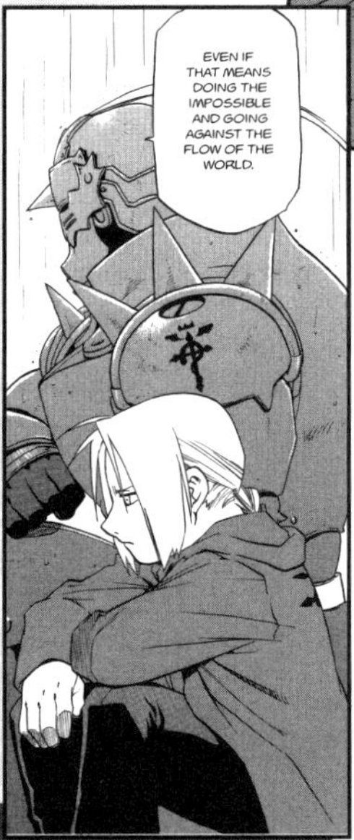
EVEN IF THAT MEANS DOING THE IMPOSSIBLE AND GOING AGAINST THE FLOW OF THE WORLD.

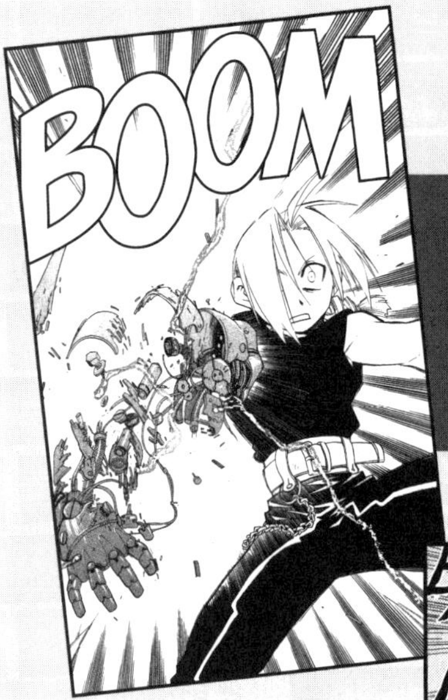
BOOM

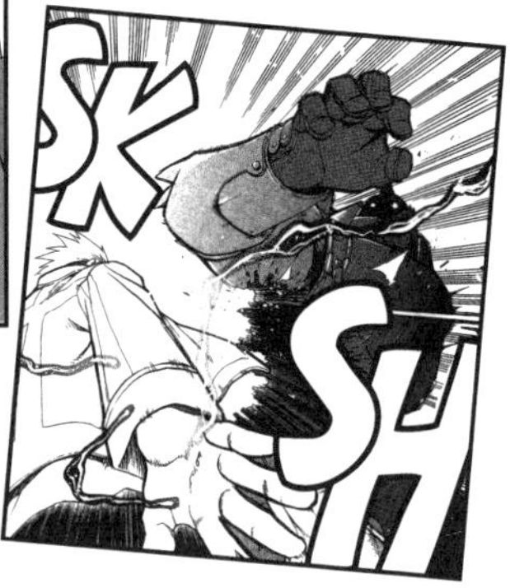
SKSH

There are those who create...and those who destroy.

Ed is defeated?!

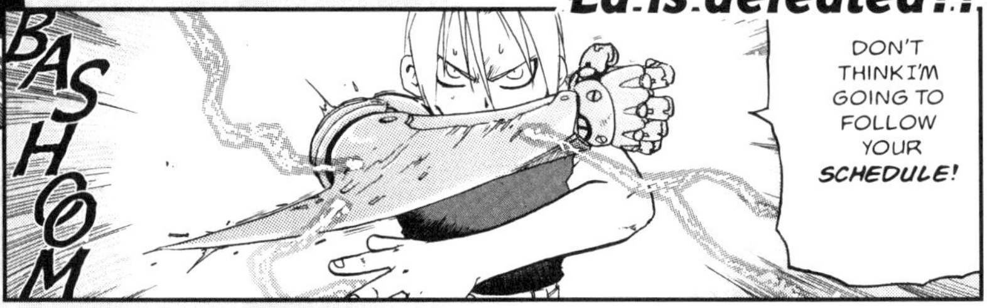
BASHOOM
DON'T THINK I'M GOING TO FOLLOW YOUR *SCHEDULE*!

Mistakes of the Past & Hope for the Future

Rescued from Scar by the military, Ed and Al are escorted by Major Armstrong to their hometown of Resembool for repairs. During the journey, they encounter Dr. Marcoh, who once researched the Philosopher's Stone. Marcoh reveals to Ed where he has hidden all of his work on the Stone.

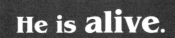

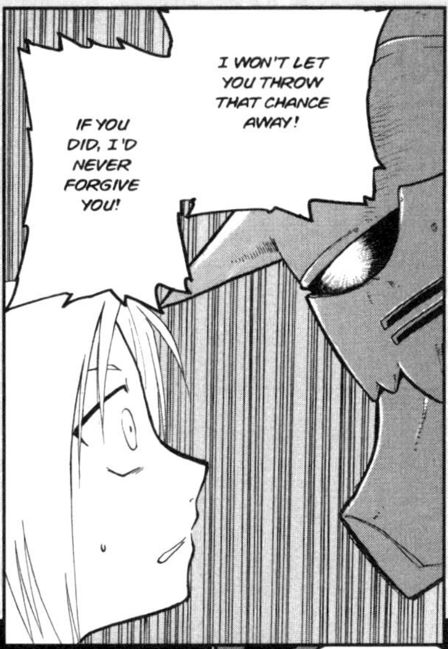
I WON'T LET YOU THROW THAT CHANCE AWAY!
IF YOU DID, I'D NEVER FORGIVE YOU!

He is alive.

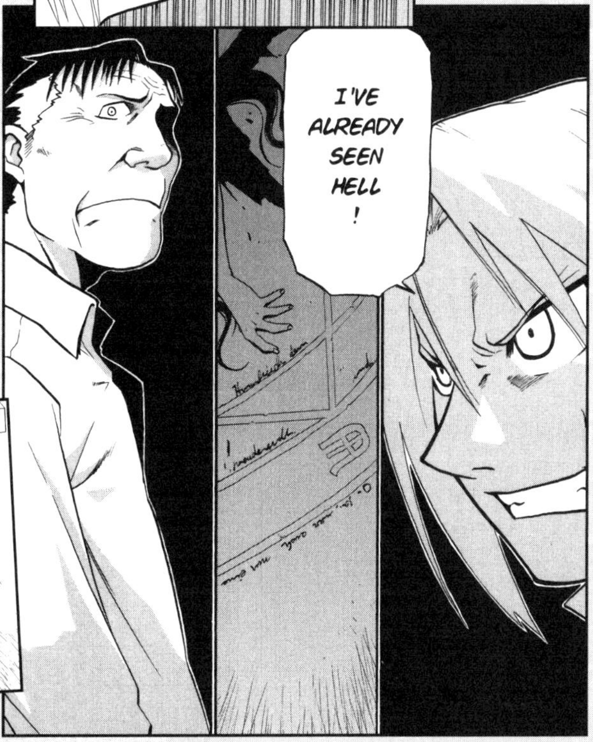
I'VE ALREADY SEEN HELL!

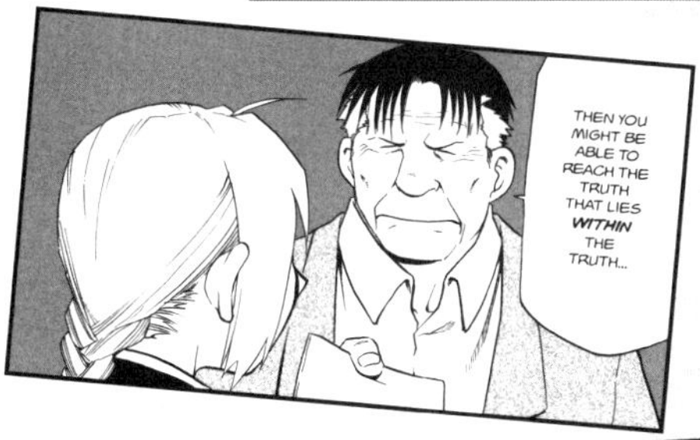
THEN YOU MIGHT BE ABLE TO REACH THE TRUTH THAT LIES WITHIN THE TRUTH...

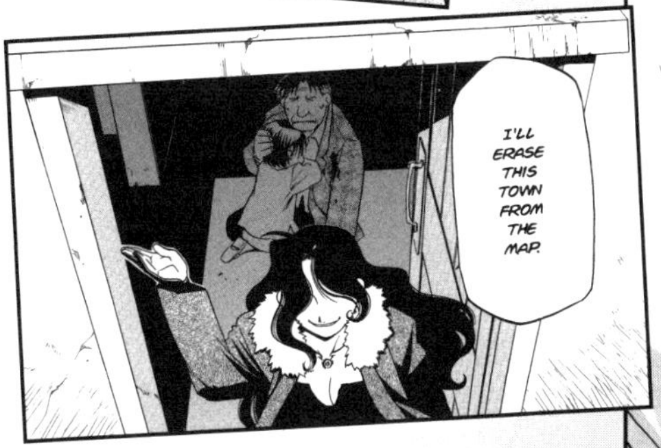
I'LL ERASE THIS TOWN FROM THE MAP.

Lighter Side

It's hard to create a spark when the air's damp. Hawkeye tells Col. Mustang he's useless on rainy days.

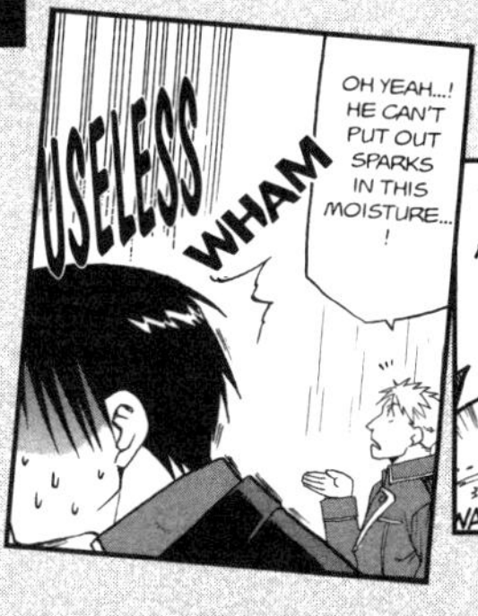
OH YEAH...! HE CAN'T PUT OUT SPARKS IN THIS MOISTURE...!
USELESS
WHAM

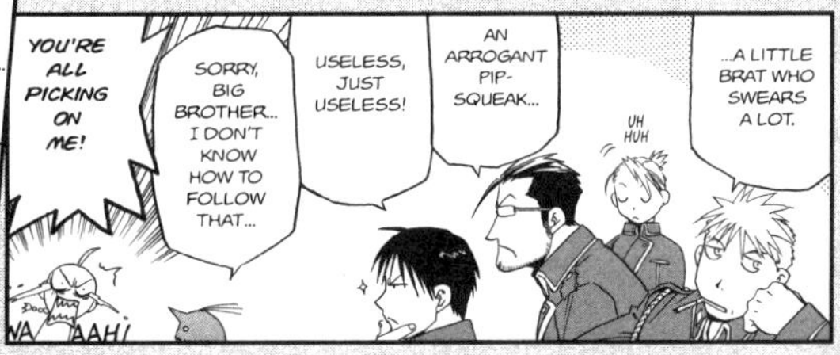
...A LITTLE BRAT WHO SWEARS A LOT.
UH HUH
AN ARROGANT PIP-SQUEAK...
USELESS, JUST USELESS!
SORRY, BIG BROTHER... I DON'T KNOW HOW TO FOLLOW THAT...
YOU'RE ALL PICKING ON ME!

Volume 3: *Past, Present & Future*

The Secret of the Philosopher's Stone

After having their auto-mail repaired by Winry and Pinako, the brothers leave Resembool and head to the Central City library, where Marcoh hid his research on the Philosopher's Stone. The truth about the Stone is more shocking than they could have imagined.

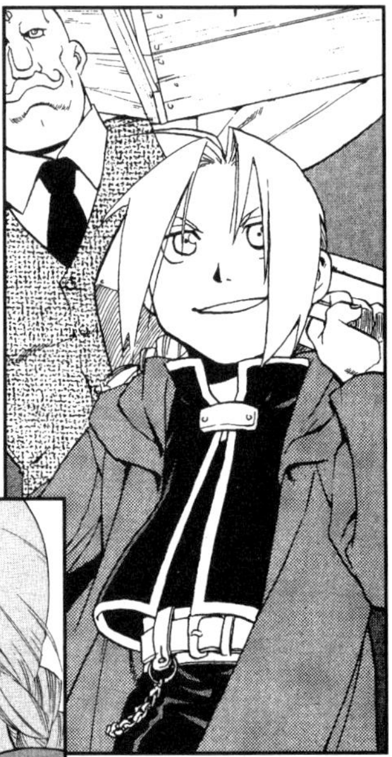

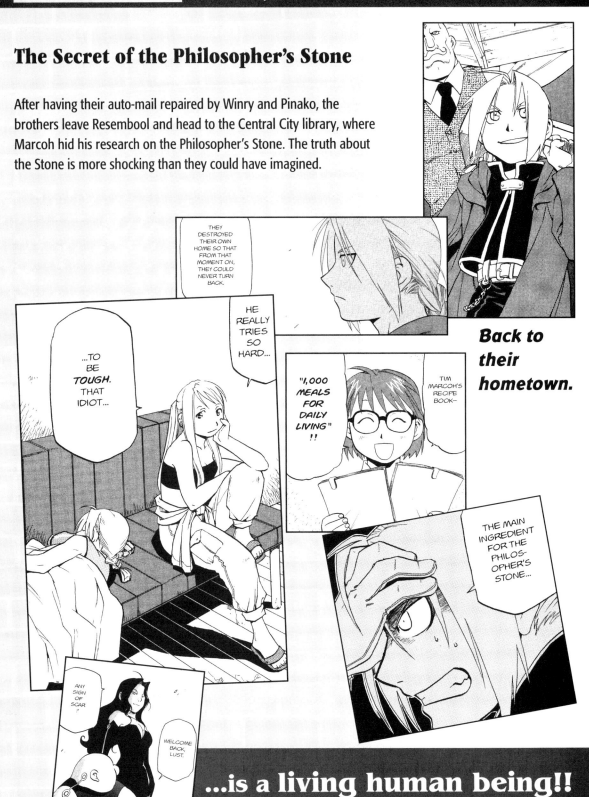

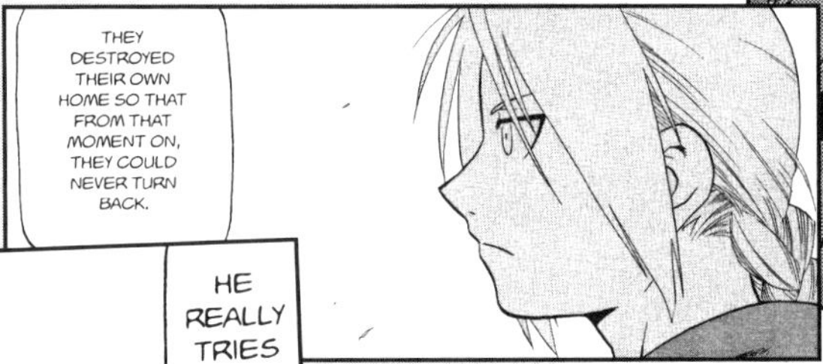
THEY DESTROYED THEIR OWN HOME SO THAT FROM THAT MOMENT ON, THEY COULD NEVER TURN BACK.

Back to their hometown.

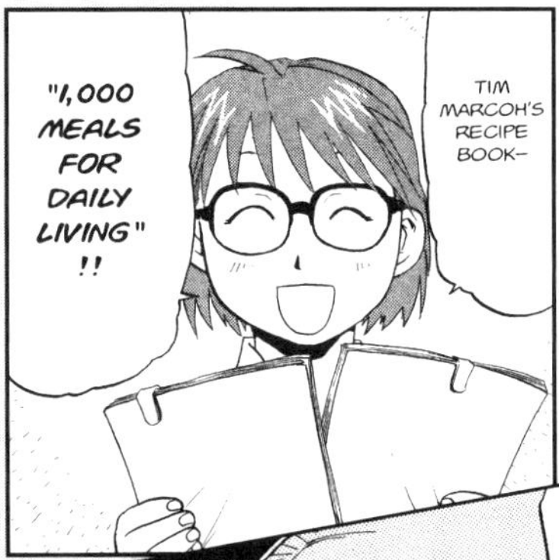
TIM MARCOH'S RECIPE BOOK—
"1,000 MEALS FOR DAILY LIVING"!!

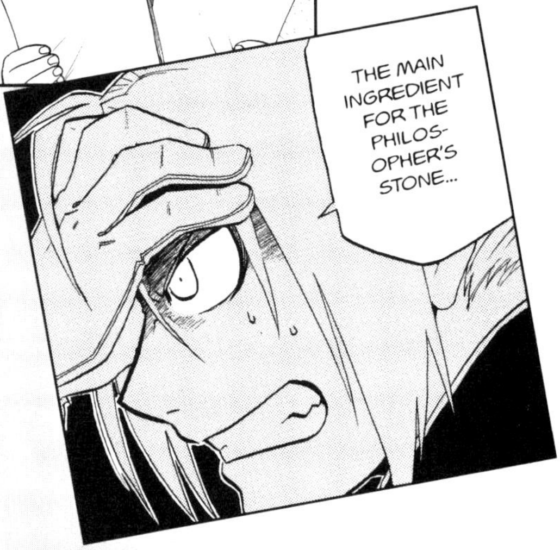
THE MAIN INGREDIENT FOR THE PHILOS-OPHER'S STONE...

...is a living human being!!

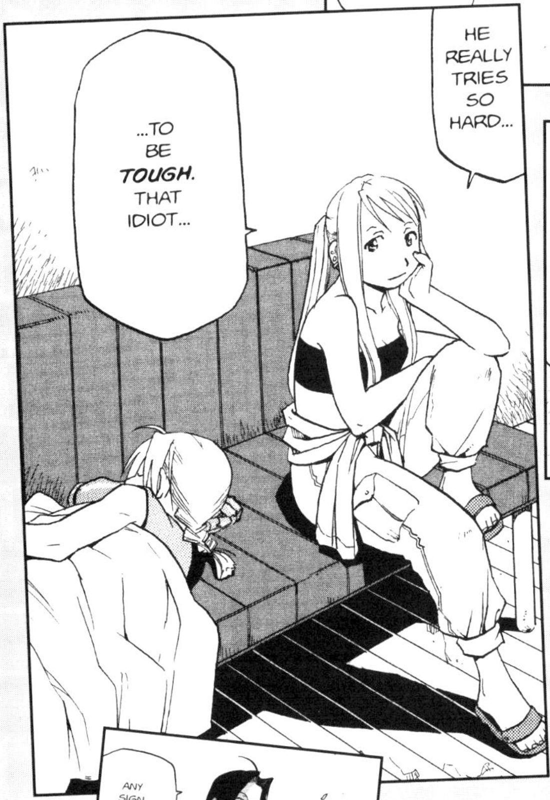
HE REALLY TRIES SO HARD...
...TO BE TOUGH. THAT IDIOT...

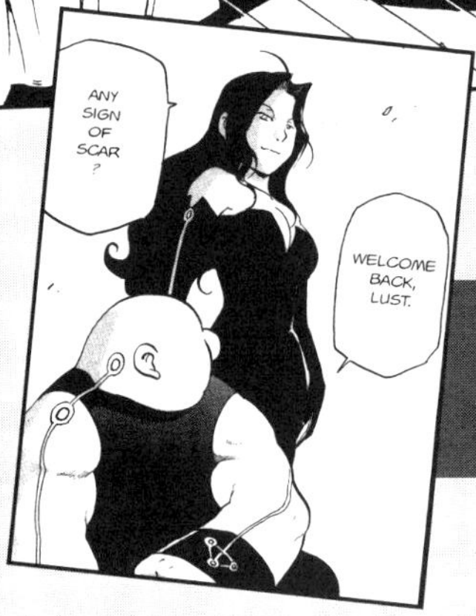
ANY SIGN OF SCAR?
WELCOME BACK, LUST.

Varying Levels of Life

Although the two brothers are shocked to find out that the main ingredient for creating a Philosopher's Stone is a live human being, they continue to look for the truth within the truth. At Marcoh's abandoned lab, they are ambushed by a suit of armor housing the souls of two mass murderers known as Slicer. During the attack, Ed and Al learn that Lust and the Ouroboros organization not only control the killers, but were also in charge of the original research on the Philosopher's Stone.

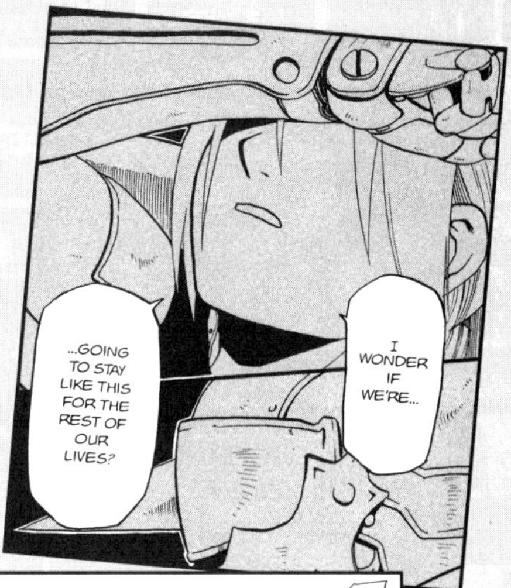
I WONDER IF WE'RE...
...GOING TO STAY LIKE THIS FOR THE REST OF OUR LIVES?

The truth within the truth

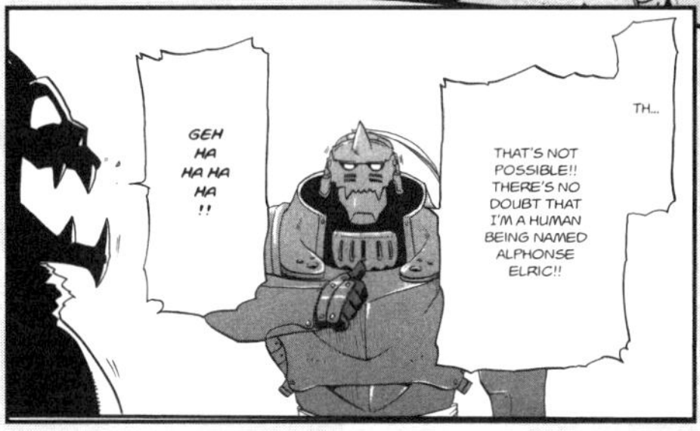
TH...
THAT'S NOT POSSIBLE!! THERE'S NO DOUBT THAT I'M A HUMAN BEING NAMED ALPHONSE ELRIC!!
GEH HA HA HA !!

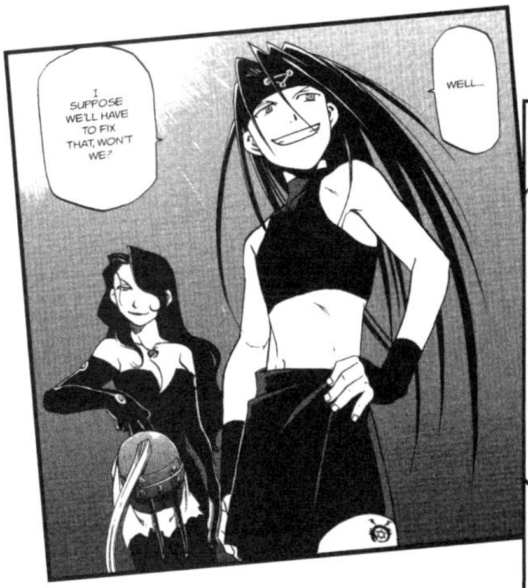
WELL...
I SUPPOSE WE'LL HAVE TO FIX THAT, WON'T WE?

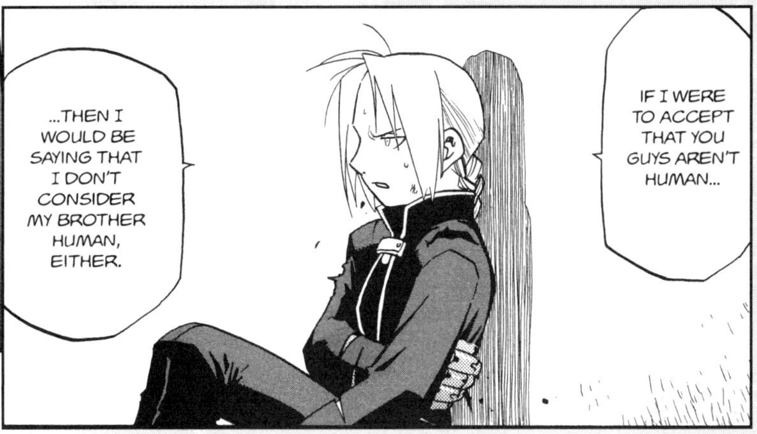
IF I WERE TO ACCEPT THAT YOU GUYS AREN'T HUMAN...
...THEN I WOULD BE SAYING THAT I DON'T CONSIDER MY BROTHER HUMAN, EITHER.

Lighter Side

Major Armstrong's muscle interrogation. No one has a chance against the sheer oppressiveness of his pose... Left: Al and 66's spontaneous comedy routine. Maybe the reason they worked so well together is because they are both souls housed in armor?

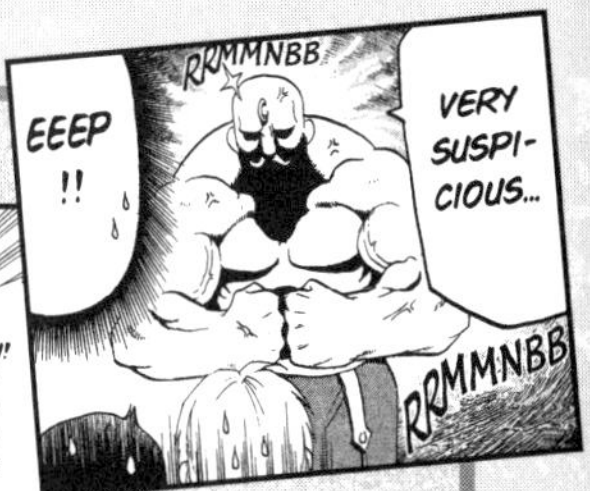
RRMMNBB
VERY SUSPI-CIOUS...
EEEP !!
RRMMNBB

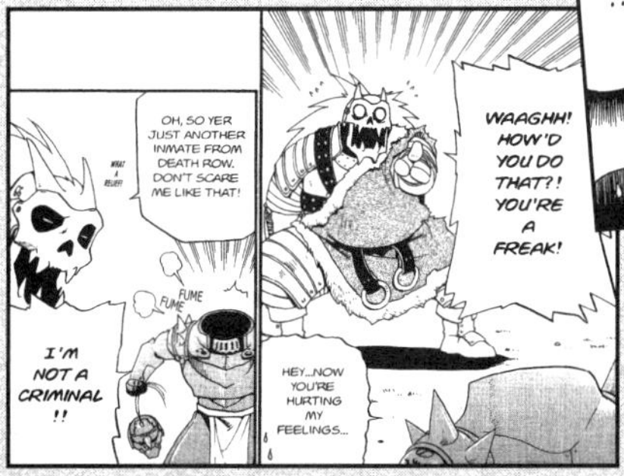
WAAGHH! HOW'D YOU DO THAT?! YOU'RE A FREAK!
HEY...NOW YOU'RE HURTING MY FEELINGS...
OH, SO YER JUST ANOTHER INMATE FROM DEATH ROW. DON'T SCARE ME LIKE THAT!
FUME
FUME
I'M NOT A CRIMINAL !!

Volume 4: *Indecision*

Unending Doubt

During the battle with the armored guardians of the lab, 66 plants a seed of doubt in Al, prompting him to believe that his memories of being human were artificially created by Ed to more easily control him as a metal pawn. At first, Al suffers in silence, but he cannot keep his worries to himself for long and finally admits his fears to his big brother.

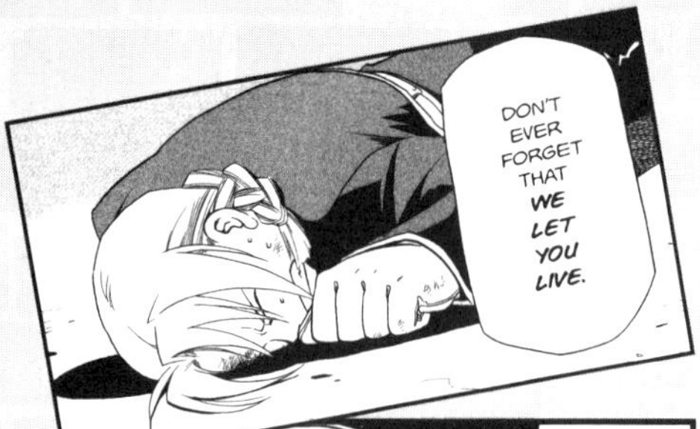
DON'T EVER FORGET THAT WE LET YOU LIVE.

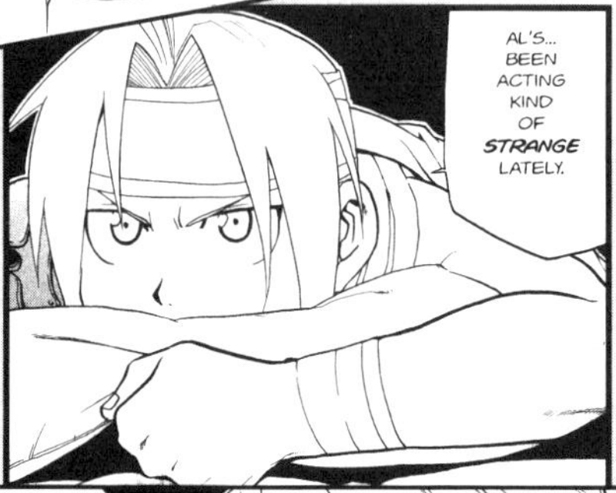
AL'S... BEEN ACTING KIND OF STRANGE LATELY.

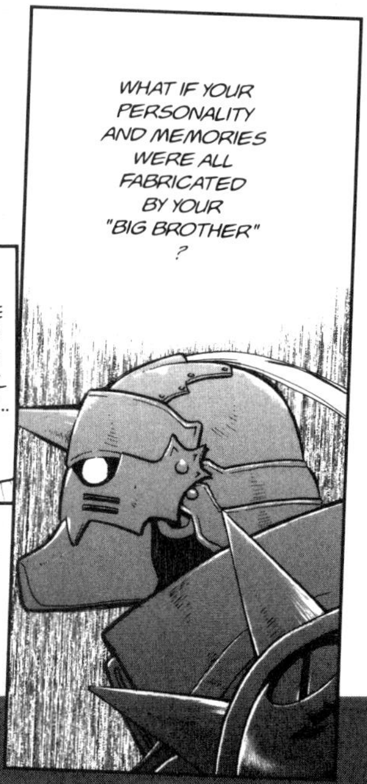
WHAT IF YOUR PERSONALITY AND MEMORIES WERE ALL FABRICATED BY YOUR "BIG BROTHER" ?

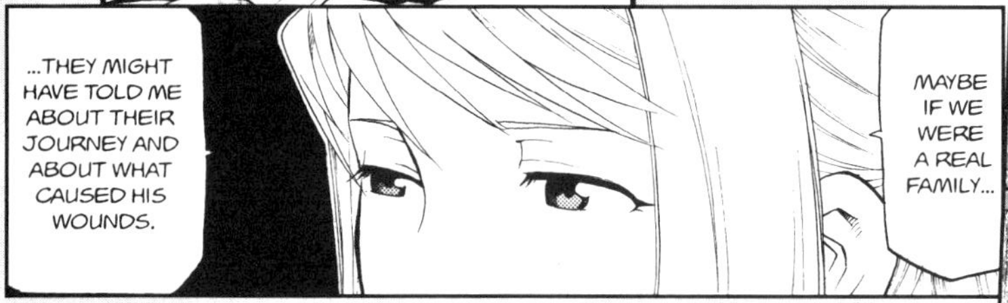
MAYBE IF WE WERE A REAL FAMILY...
...THEY MIGHT HAVE TOLD ME ABOUT THEIR JOURNEY AND ABOUT WHAT CAUSED HIS WOUNDS.

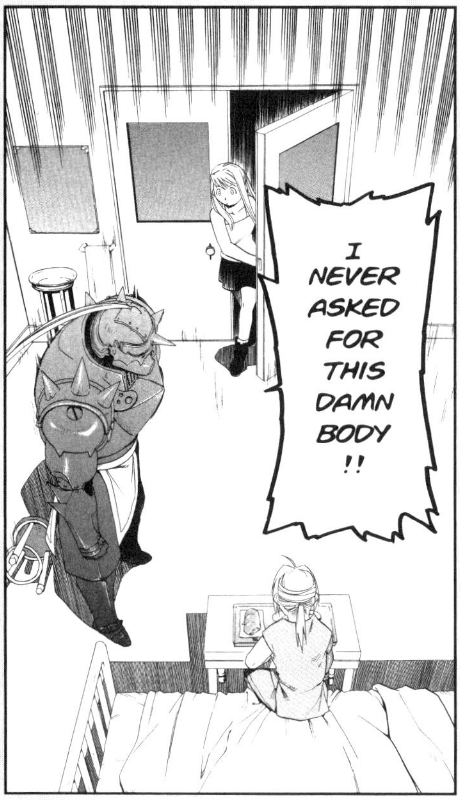
I NEVER ASKED FOR THIS DAMN BODY !!

They would rather shoulder their pain themselves than cause their loved ones to worry. That's why they won't say anything about it.

Faith Moves Them Forward

A conversation with Winry finally stops Al from doubting his own existence. Winry reminds Al of how responsible Ed feels for Al's current lack of a body and that Ed would stop at nothing to heal him and return him to a human form. Only by strengthening the bond of brotherhood can the two boys repair themselves. Doubt will only weaken and destroy them.

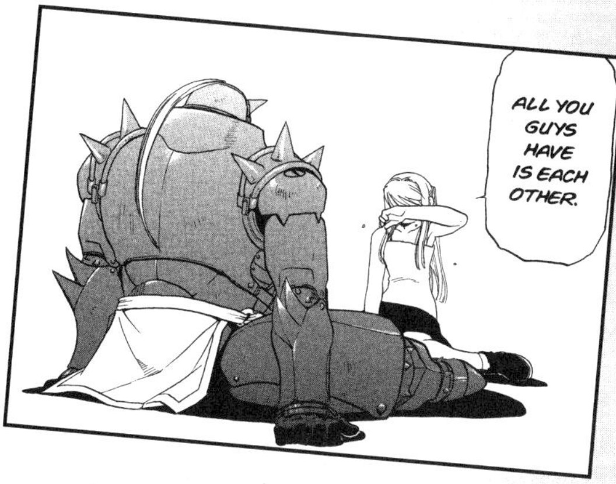
ALL YOU GUYS HAVE IS EACH OTHER.

I guess there are some things that you have to **say out loud** to understand.

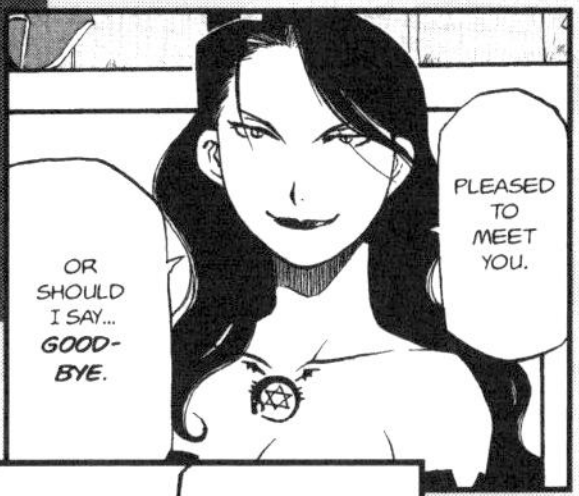
PLEASED TO MEET YOU.
OR SHOULD I SAY... GOOD-BYE.

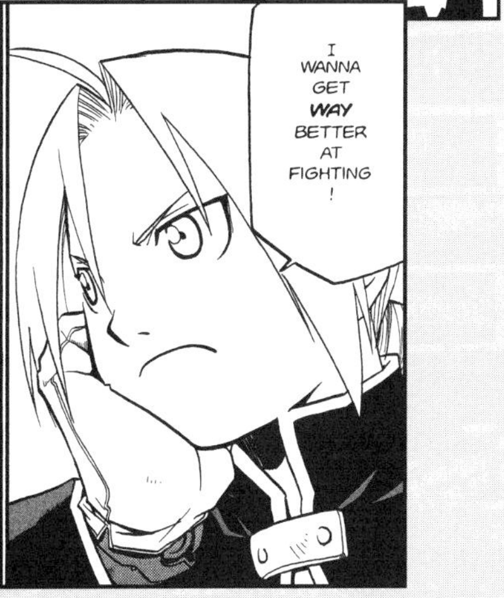
I WANNA GET WAY BETTER AT FIGHTING!

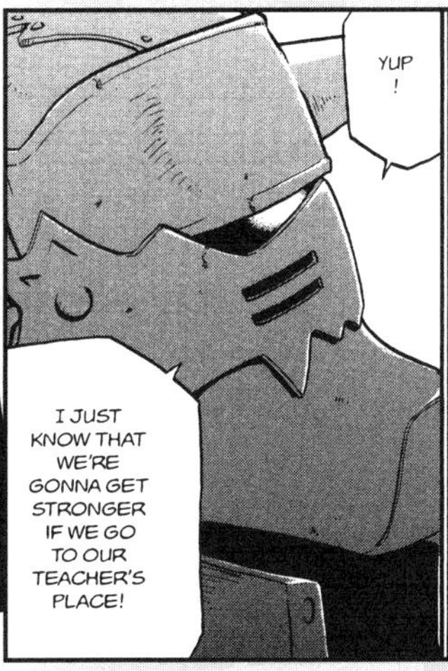
YUP!
I JUST KNOW THAT WE'RE GONNA GET STRONGER IF WE GO TO OUR TEACHER'S PLACE!

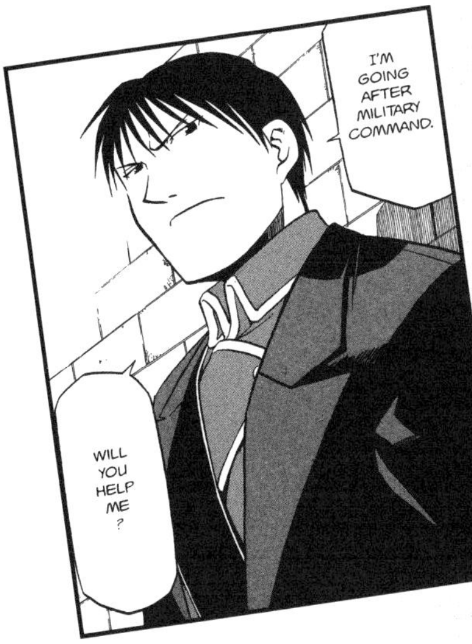
I'M GOING AFTER MILITARY COMMAND.
WILL YOU HELP ME?

Lighter Side

Ed hemorrhages when Sgt. Brosh asks if Winry is his girlfriend.
Left: Still a kid after all, Ed has a fit when he's asked to drink milk.

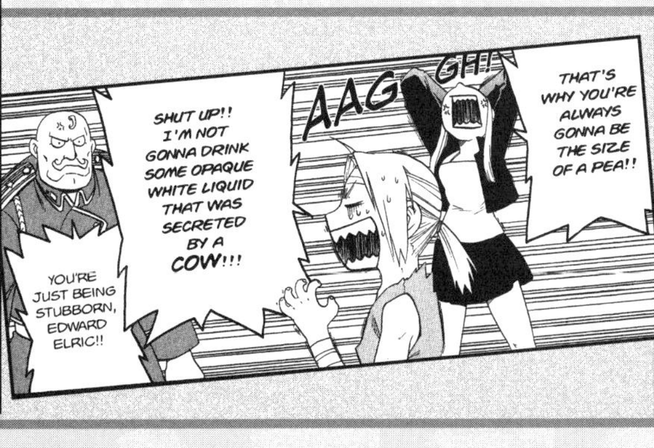
THAT'S WHY YOU'RE ALWAYS GONNA BE THE SIZE OF A PEA!!
AAGGH!!
SHUT UP!! I'M NOT GONNA DRINK SOME OPAQUE WHITE LIQUID THAT WAS SECRETED BY A COW!!!
YOU'RE JUST BEING STUBBORN, EDWARD ELRIC!!

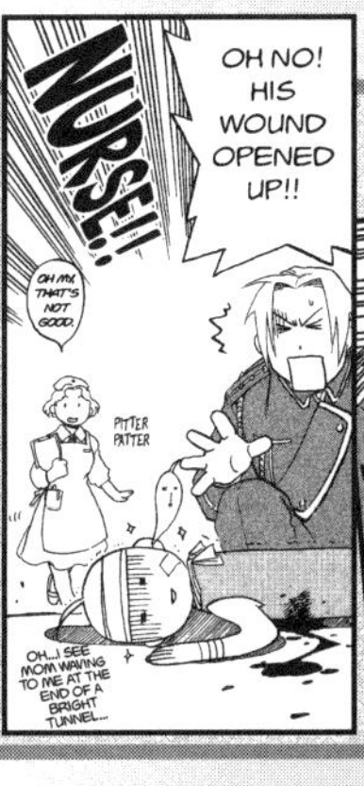
OH NO! HIS WOUND OPENED UP!!
NURSE!!
OH MY, THAT'S NOT GOOD.
PITTER PATTER
OH...I SEE MOM WAVING TO ME AT THE END OF A BRIGHT TUNNEL...

Volume 5: *About Life*

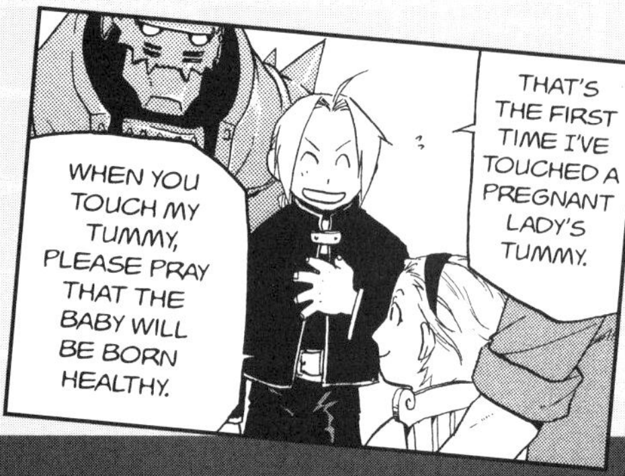
THAT'S THE FIRST TIME I'VE TOUCHED A PREGNANT LADY'S TUMMY.
WHEN YOU TOUCH MY TUMMY, PLEASE PRAY THAT THE BABY WILL BE BORN HEALTHY.

Can I feel your tummy?!

The Beauty of Life

After adding Winry to their group, Ed and his friends travel to Dublith. There, they meet the Lecourts and help with the birth of a baby. Even alchemists cannot create new life, and the experience changes the brothers' perspective forever. Witnessing new life is the greatest magic of all.

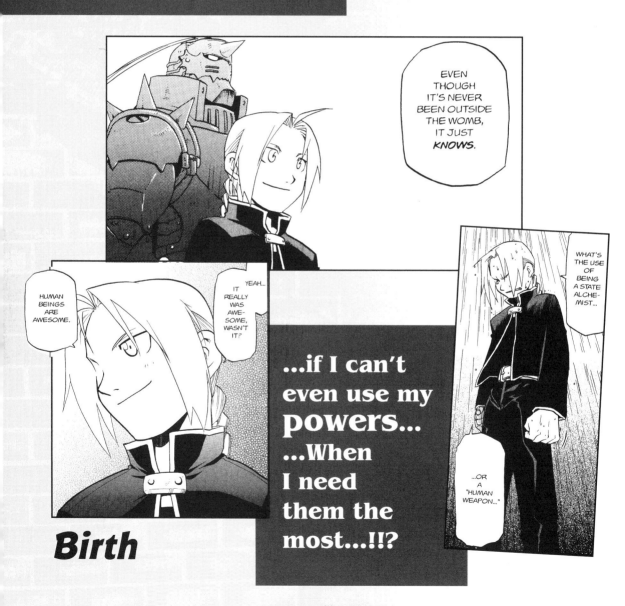

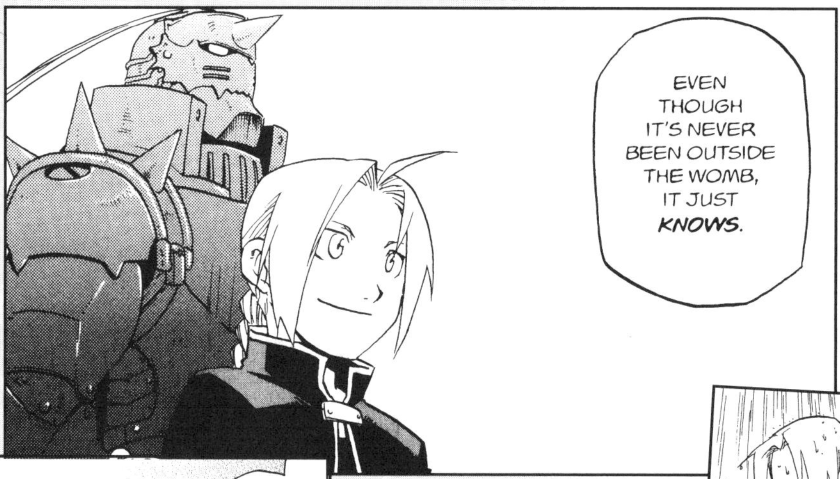
EVEN THOUGH IT'S NEVER BEEN OUTSIDE THE WOMB, IT JUST *KNOWS*.

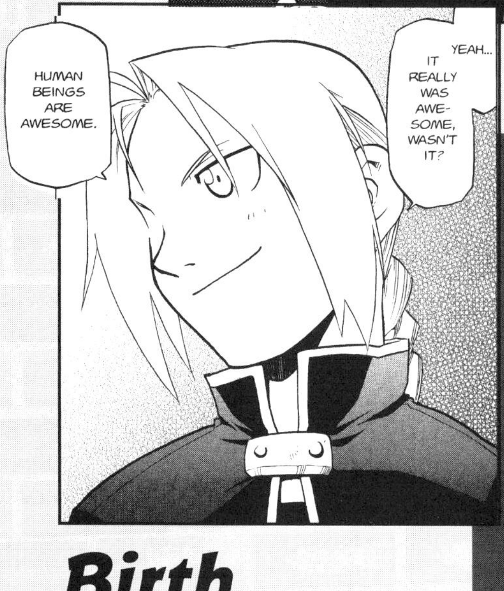
YEAH... IT REALLY WAS AWE-SOME, WASN'T IT?
HUMAN BEINGS ARE AWESOME.

Birth

...if I can't even use my powers... ...When I need them the most...!!?

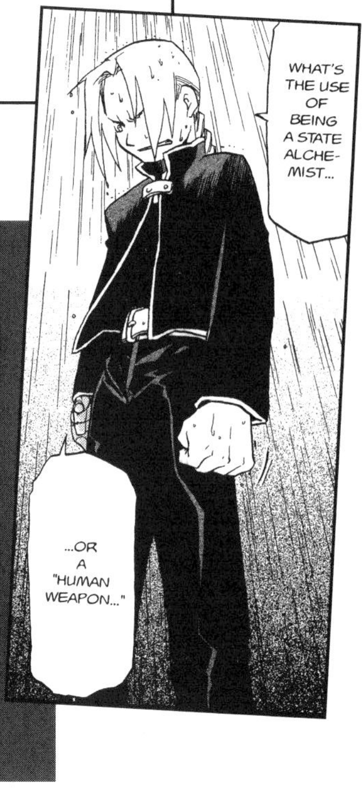
WHAT'S THE USE OF BEING A STATE ALCHE-MIST...
...OR A "HUMAN WEAPON..."

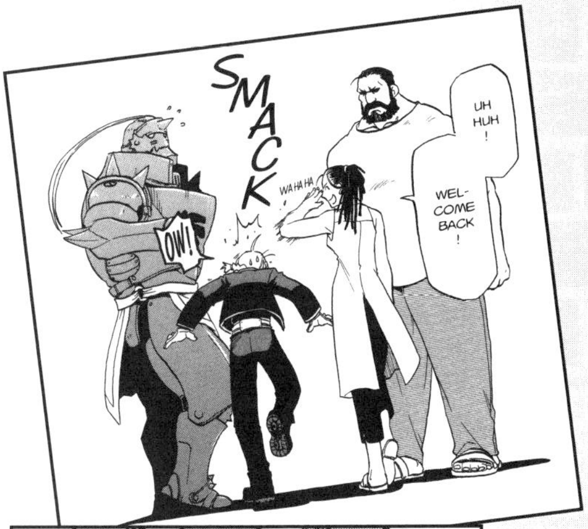
UH HUH!
WEL-COME BACK!
WAHAHA
SMACK
OW!

Reuniting with the Past

In Dublith, the boys reconnect with their alchemy teacher, Izumi Curtis, who questions them about the sins of their past. When she learns of the passing of their mother, and that they lost their bodies in a futile attempt to bring her back to life, she vows to help put them back on the straight and narrow of proper alchemy.

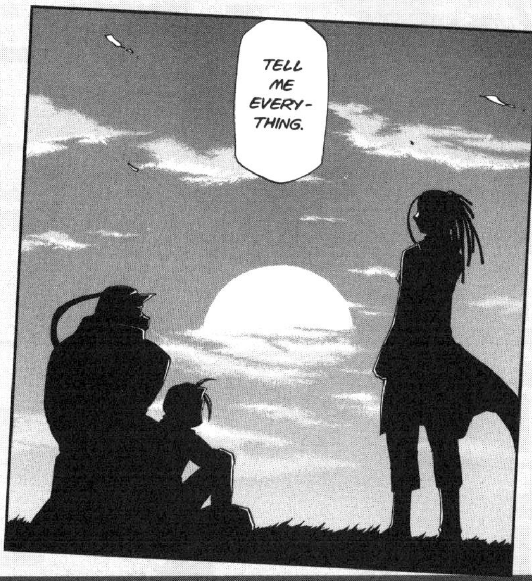
TELL ME EVERY-THING.

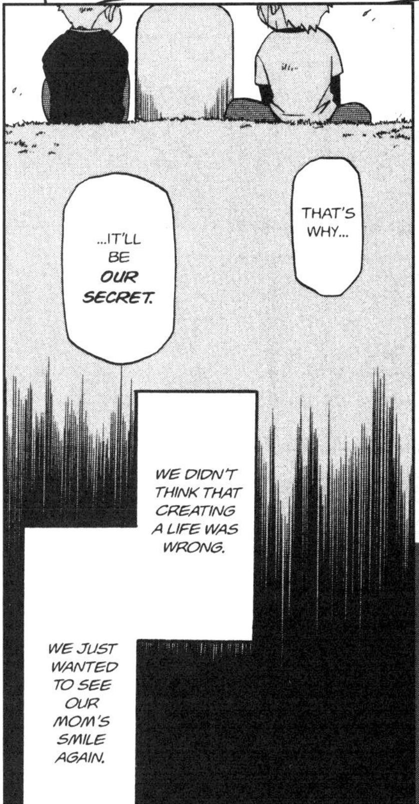
THAT'S WHY...
...IT'LL BE OUR SECRET.
WE DIDN'T THINK THAT CREATING A LIFE WAS WRONG.
WE JUST WANTED TO SEE OUR MOM'S SMILE AGAIN.

If they're trying to take the wrong path, isn't it my job as their "teacher" to put them on the correct one?

Lighter Side

Ed tries to make himself taller but it ends in failure. Even as a kid, the brothers were tough.

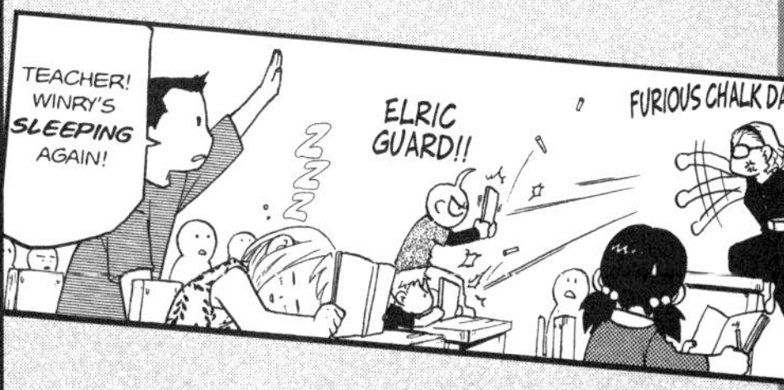
FURIOUS CHALK DANCE!!
ELRIC GUARD!!
ZZZ
TEACHER! WINRY'S SLEEPING AGAIN!

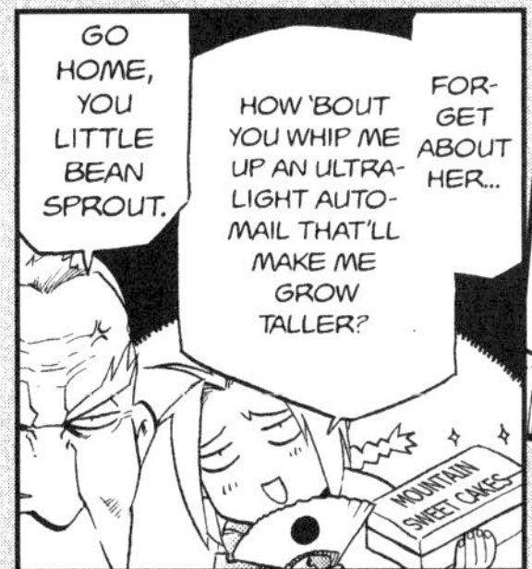
FOR-GET ABOUT HER...
HOW 'BOUT YOU WHIP ME UP AN ULTRA-LIGHT AUTO-MAIL THAT'LL MAKE ME GROW TALLER?
GO HOME, YOU LITTLE BEAN SPROUT.
MOUNTAIN SWEET CAKES

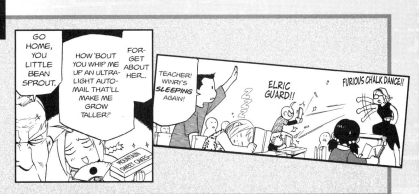

Volume 6: *The Path to Truth*

I got it!

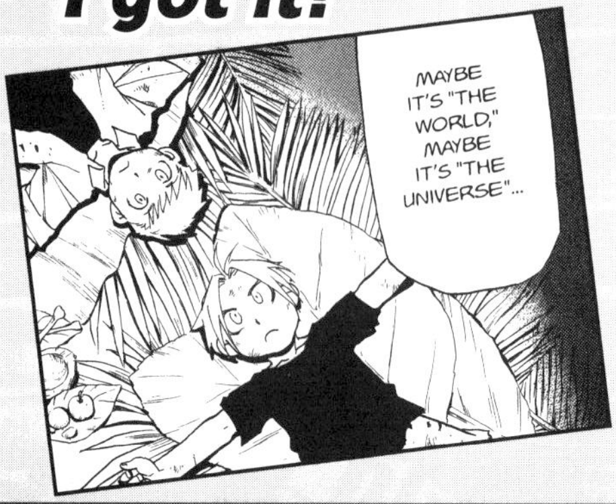
MAYBE IT'S "THE WORLD," MAYBE IT'S "THE UNIVERSE"...

Sin & Punishment

Four years ago the two brothers learned the fundamentals of alchemy from Izumi. They used that knowledge to break the greatest taboo of alchemy…attempting to resurrect their beloved mother with the forbidden art of human transmutation. But that attempt only ended in another tragedy. Their mother's transmutation failed, Ed lost an arm and a leg, and Al lost his entire body.

Life is a complex cycle, so vast we can't see it with our own eyes.

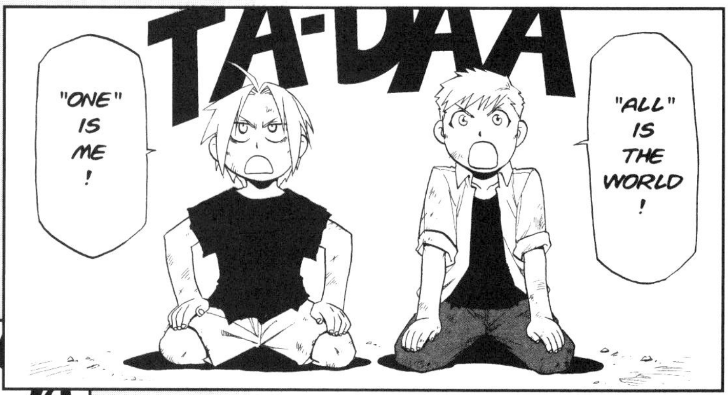
TA-DAA
"ALL" IS THE WORLD!
"ONE" IS ME!

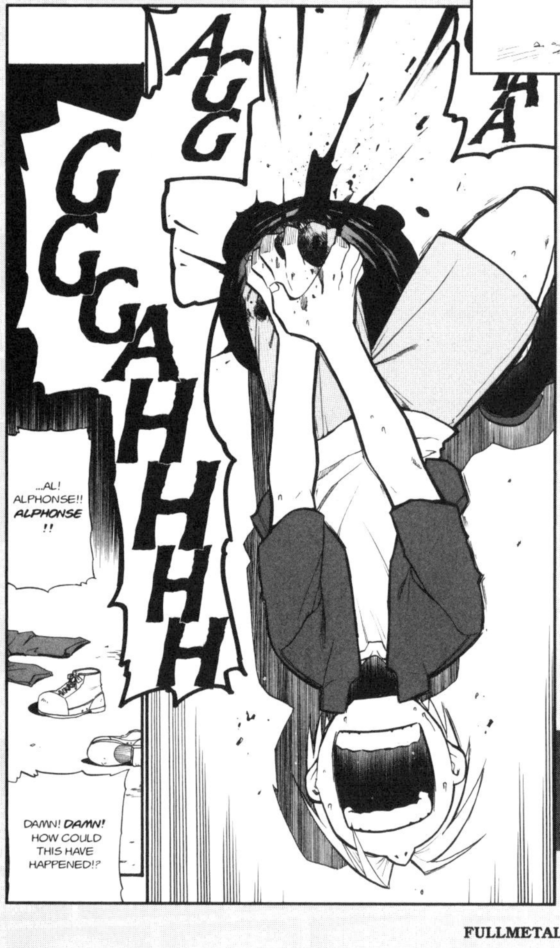
...AL! ALPHONSE!! ALPHONSE!!
DAMN! DAMN! HOW COULD THIS HAVE HAPPENED!?

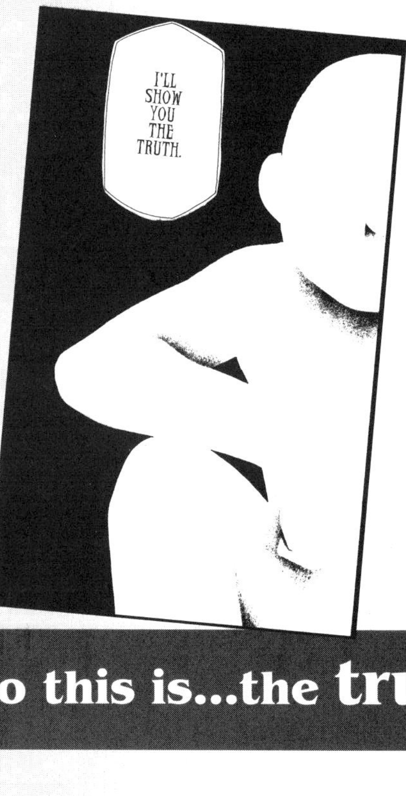
I'LL SHOW YOU THE TRUTH.

So this is...the truth!

A New Enemy...

After Ed bound his brother's soul to a suit of armor and had his own missing limbs replaced with auto-mail, the two brothers' long journey to regain their original bodies began. Izumi gently embraced the two when they told her all about their painful past. Believing that the answer to the brothers' problems may lie in Al's missing memories of his transmutation, Izumi attempts to find a way to bring Al's memories back. Meanwhile, a mysterious man with an Ouroboros tattoo begins to hatch his own plot...to kidnap Al!

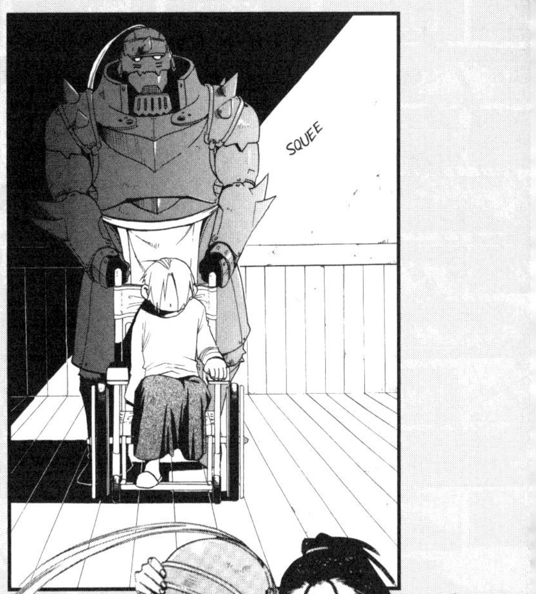
SQUEE

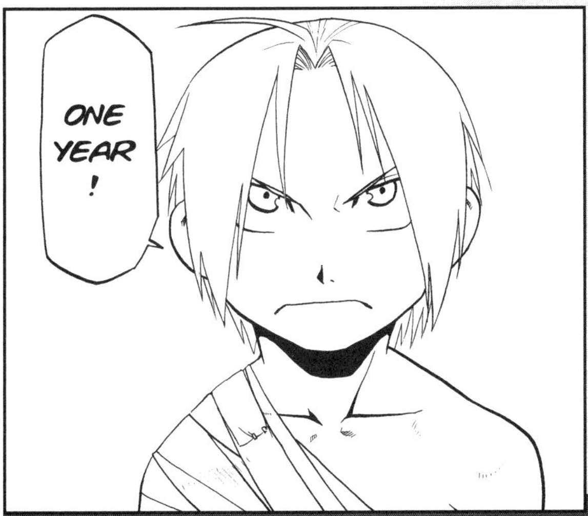
ONE YEAR!

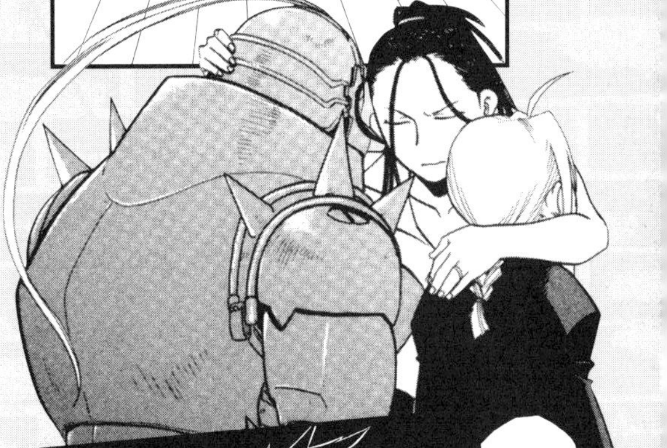

All right.
I will try and find a way to retrieve your memory.

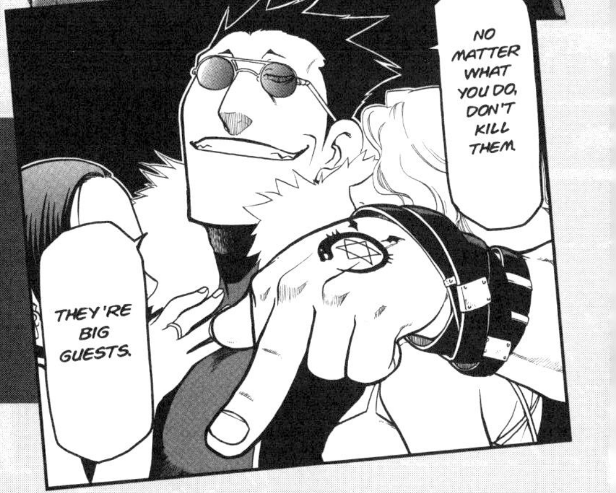
NO MATTER WHAT YOU DO, DON'T KILL THEM.
THEY'RE BIG GUESTS.

Lighter Side

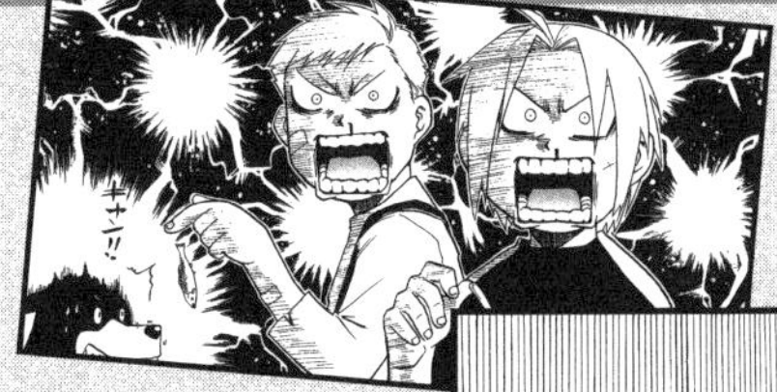

What kind of training?

The two brothers become frozen in fear even thinking about the days they spent training in Dublith. Was Izumi's training that traumatic? Right: Victims of the colonel's transfer to Central.

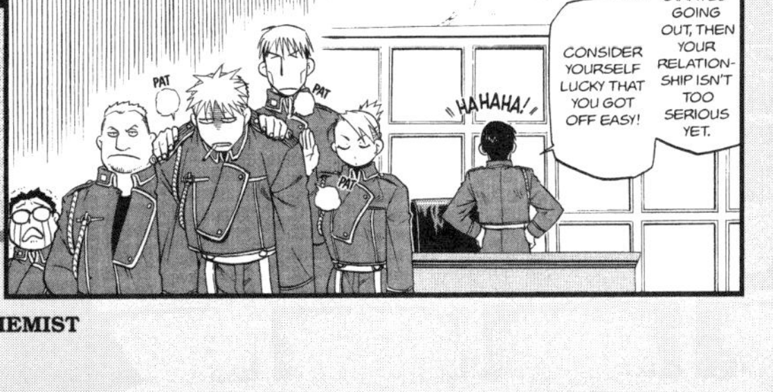
IF YOU JUST STARTED GOING OUT, THEN YOUR RELATION-SHIP ISN'T TOO SERIOUS YET.
CONSIDER YOURSELF LUCKY THAT YOU GOT OFF EASY!
HAHAHA!
PAT
PAT

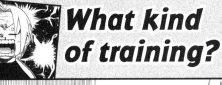

Chapter 26, Chapter 27, Chapter 28:

Lost Memories

Filling in the Gaps

Al is taken hostage by the subordinates of Greed, a man with an Ouroboros tattoo. Izumi attempts to rescue him, but Al begs her to leave him there, in case his kidnappers can somehow unlock his repressed memories. Wounded in the rescue attempt, Izumi finally tells Ed about the kidnapping, and an enraged Ed engages in a deadly battle with Greed.

YOU'RE COMING WITH US...
...TO MEET OUR MASTER.

FOR ME, THERE'S NO TURNING BACK.

KA-BOOM
SORRY TO BARGE IN.

ASSESS-MENT COM-PLETE!
EDWARD ELRIC! HOW FORTUNATE YOU ARE!
TH... THAT CAN'T BE RIGHT...
HERE.

THE NAME'S GREED.
LET'S BE FRIENDS.

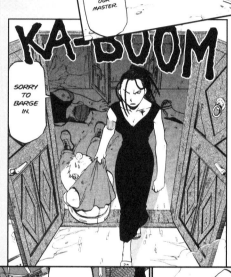

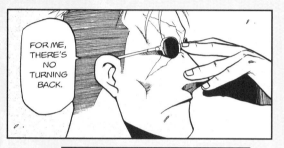

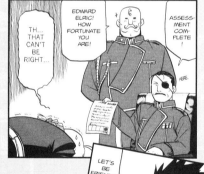

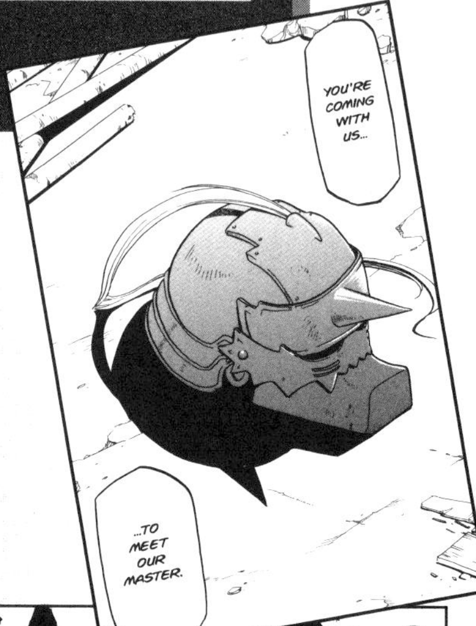

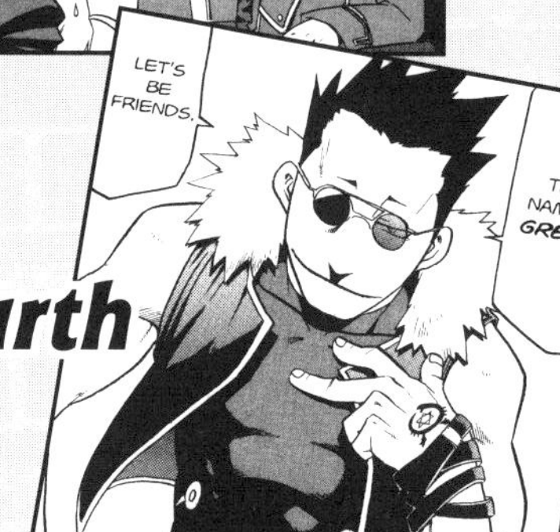

The Fourth Enemy

AND THE REST?
ELIMINATE THEM.
DEVIL'S NEST

ATTACK!!

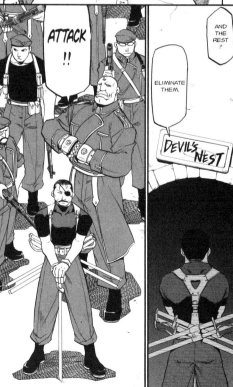

And speaking of that thing...here it comes.

The Art of Fullmetal Alchemist

THE ART OF
FULLMETAL
ALCHEMIST
Original illustrations by
Hiromu Arakawa

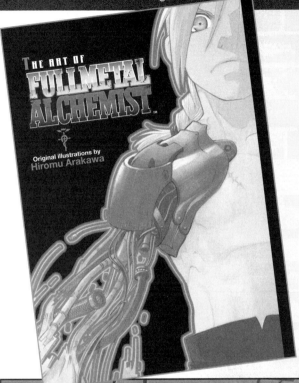

Original Illustrations by Hiromu Arakawa

The look and feel of the world of *Fullmetal Alchemist* is just as important as the story. In this large-sized art book, Hiromu Arakawa showcases her incredible vision with character sketches, backgrounds and detailed notes. Featuring full-color artwork on every page, *The Art of Fullmetal Alchemist* is a must-have for fans of the Elric Brothers and shines a bright light on the unique imagination that brings them to life in every volume.

Fullcolor Fullmetal. Paintings like this help illuminate the look and feel of the Elric Brothers and the world they live in.

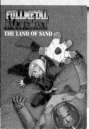

Novels

FULLMETAL ALCHEMIST
THE LAND OF SAND
MAKOTO INOUE
HIROMU ARAKAWA
VOL. 1

Fullmetal Alchemist vol.1: The Land of Sand

Original concept by: **Hiromu Arakawa**
Written by: **Makoto Inoue**

The Land of Sand

Ed and Al's search for the Philosopher's Stone brings them to the desolate gold mining town of Xenotime where they encounter two strangely familiar characters. Apparently two brothers named Elric are already in the town and searching for the Stone! Who are they? And which ones are the real Elric Brothers?!

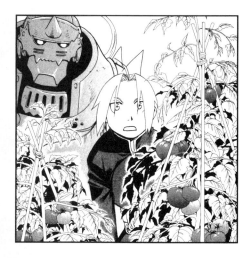

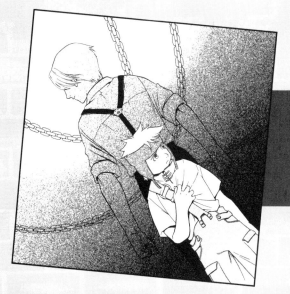

Do you really think that what you're doing is right?

The Phantom of Warehouse 13

After hearing rumors of a mysterious haunted warehouse at Eastern Command, a reluctant Roy heads out to investigate. Do ghosts really exist…and is Colonel Roy Mustang, the Flame Alchemist, a match for them?

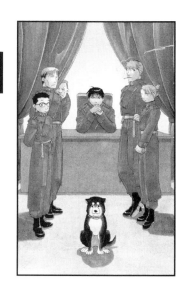

Novels

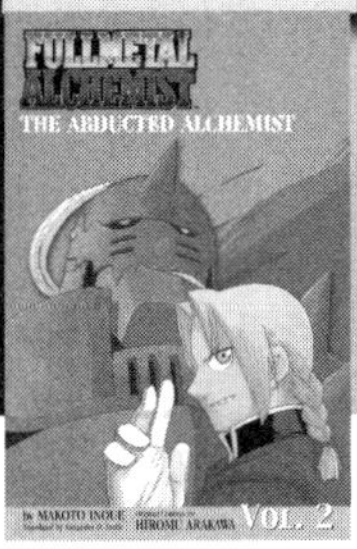
FULLMETAL ALCHEMIST
THE ABDUCTED ALCHEMIST
VOL. 2

Fullmetal Alchemist vol. 2: The Abducted Alchemist

Original concept by: **Hiromu Arakawa**
Written by: **Makoto Inoue**

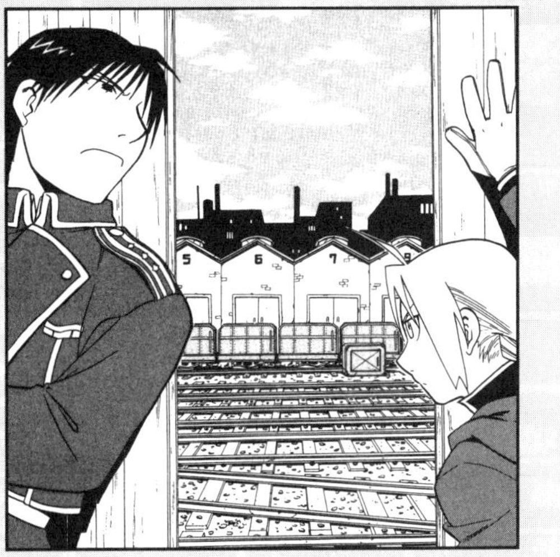

The Abducted Alchemist

Colonel Mustang and the Elric Brothers encounter criticism when a series of terrorist bombings plague the East Area. To clear their reputation, the brothers must find out who's behind the attacks and use all their combined powers to stop the path of destruction.

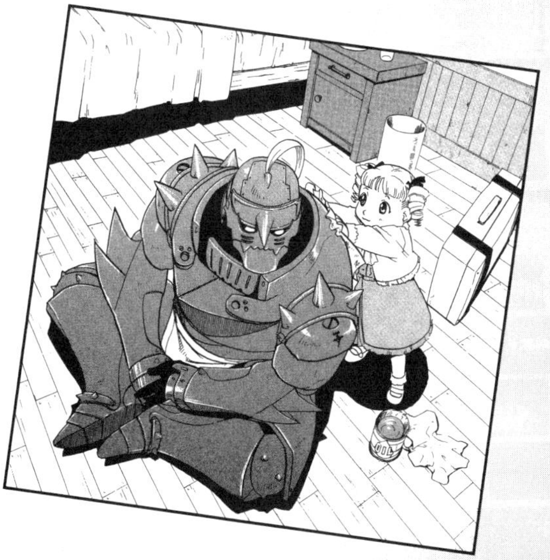

During the investigation, Roy stumbles upon a string of bizarre child abductions. Is there a connection between the kidnappings and the bombings? And can Roy find out what the connection is before Ed becomes the terrorists' next victim?

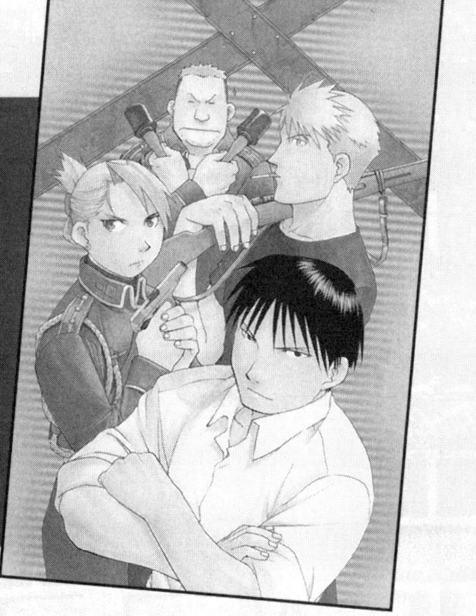

No matter what kind of path it is, if it's a path that you've chosen for yourself then you should be able to follow it through to the end.

Novels

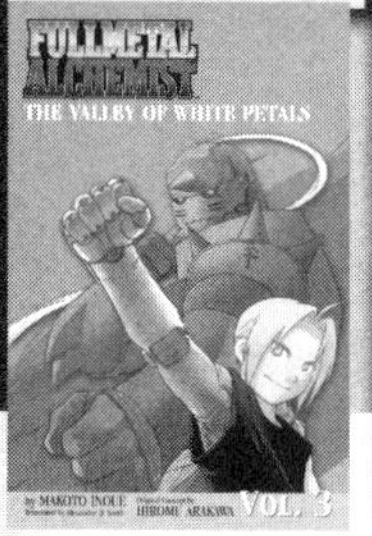
FULLMETAL ALCHEMIST
THE VALLEY OF WHITE PETALS
VOL. 3

Fullmetal Alchemist vol. 3: The Valley of White Petals

Original concept by: **Hiromu Arakawa**
Written by: **Makoto Inoue**

The Valley of White Petals

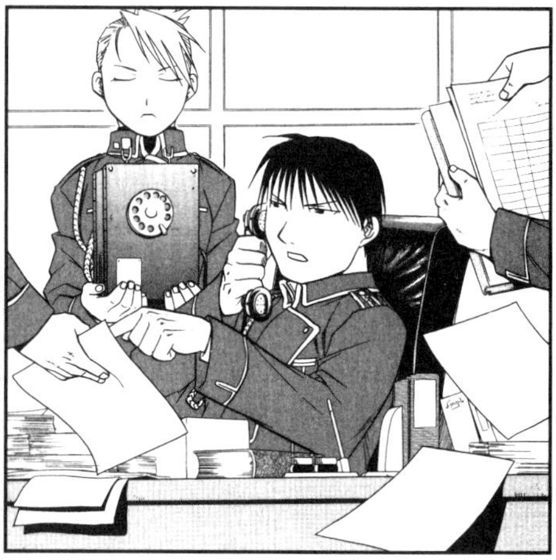

Under direct orders from their commanding officer, Edward and Alphonse journey to a Utopian society deep in the wasteland borders of Eastern Command. There, they discover that the city is ruled not by the military but by something else with which they are already all too familiar.

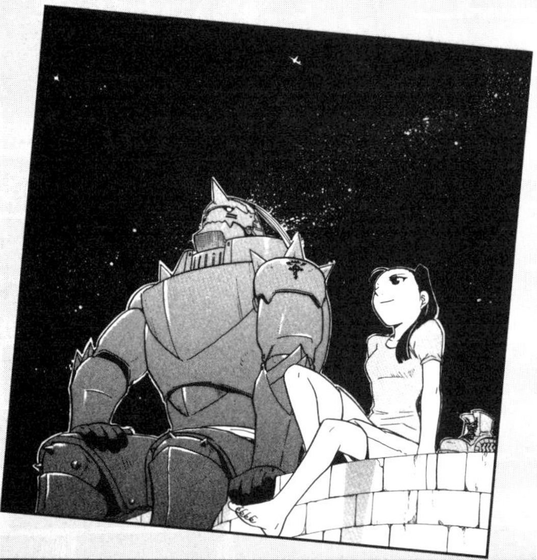

A town ruled by the laws of alchemy? Once inside the mysterious city of Wisteria, Ed and Al must make the biggest decision of their lives: Should they expose the secrets of Wisteria? Or is this alchemical paradise exactly the home they've been looking for all their lives?

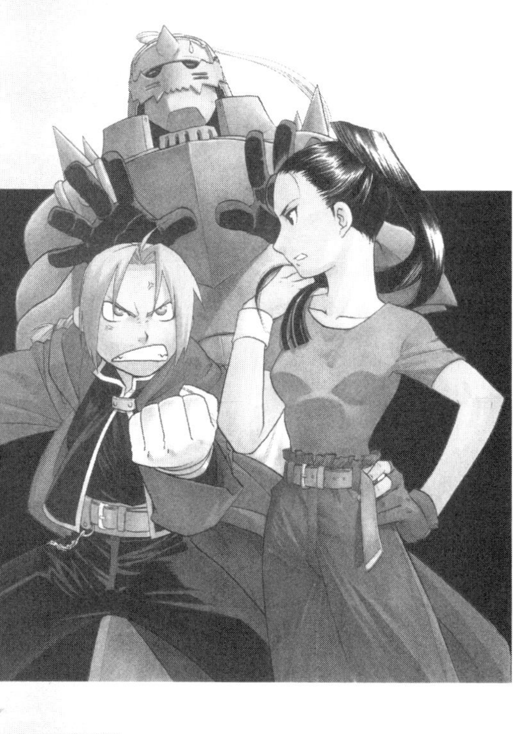

"Al," Edward began hesitantly, "do you... do you want to stay in Wisteria?"

It wasn't an entirely unreasonable question. Alphonse had seen the bad that came from Raygen's equivalent exchange, but he had also seen the good.

A STATE
ALCHEMIST'S
GROWTH RECORD

FULLMETAL ALCHEMIST

Diagram

Fullmetal Alchemist Character Connections

The Elric Brothers are not alone in their journey. Their quest has touched the lives of many.

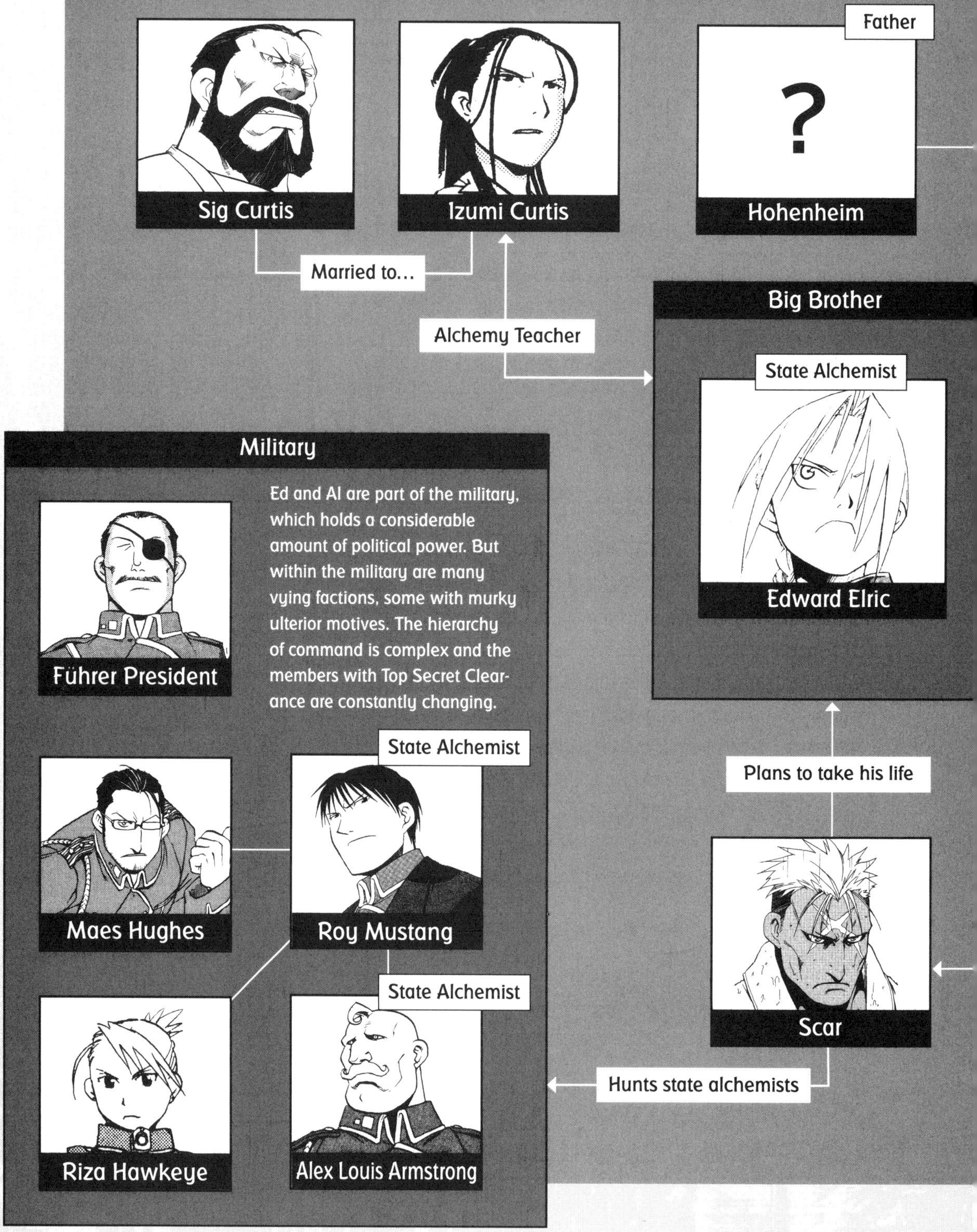

Sig Curtis
Izumi Curtis
Father
?
Hohenheim
Married to...
Alchemy Teacher
Big Brother
State Alchemist
Edward Elric
Military
Ed and Al are part of the military, which holds a considerable amount of political power. But within the military are many vying factions, some with murky ulterior motives. The hierarchy of command is complex and the members with Top Secret Clearance are constantly changing.
Führer President
State Alchemist
Maes Hughes
Roy Mustang
State Alchemist
Riza Hawkeye
Alex Louis Armstrong
Plans to take his life
Scar
Hunts state alchemists

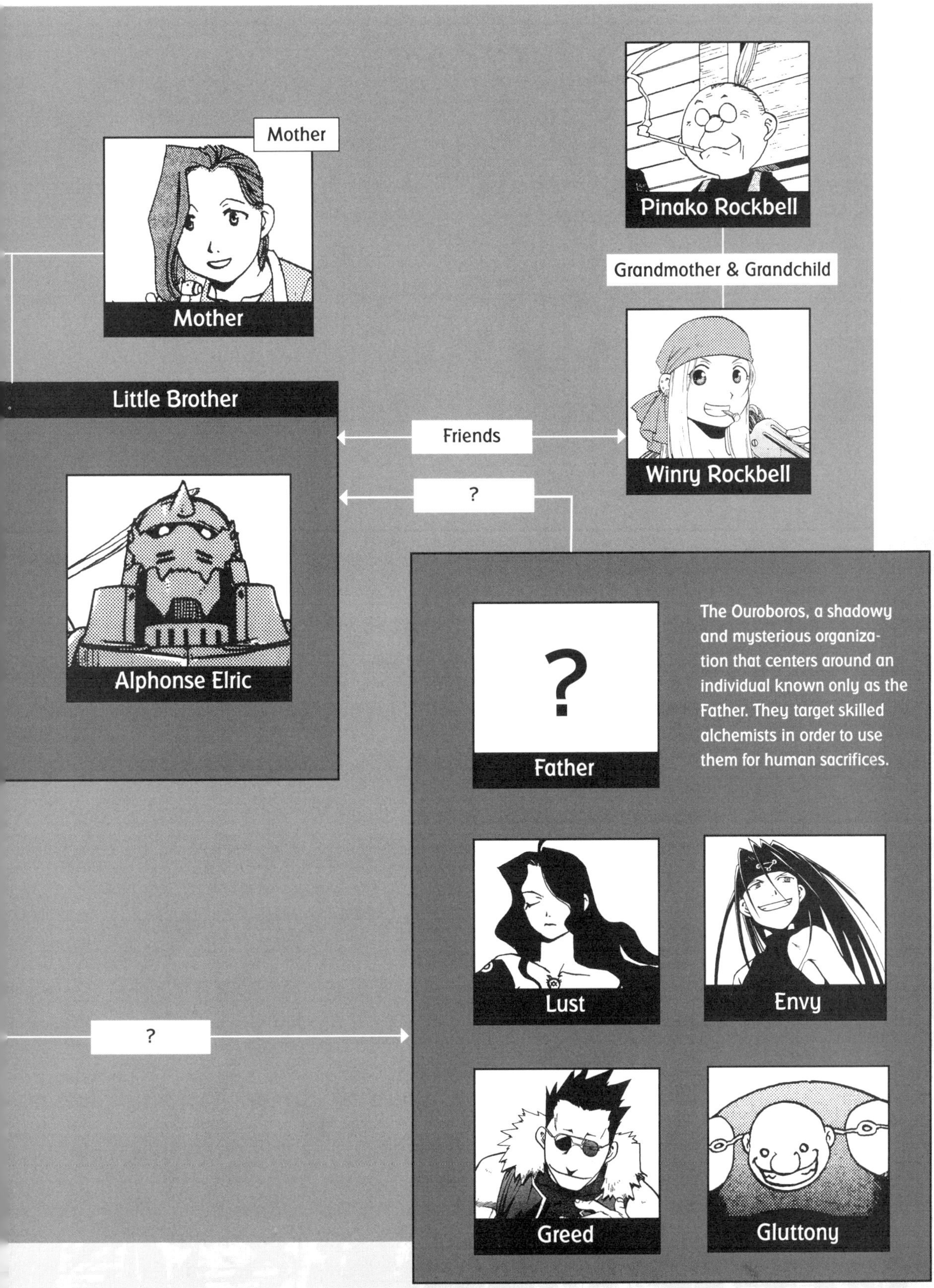
Mother
Mother
Pinako Rockbell
Grandmother & Grandchild
Winry Rockbell
Little Brother
Friends
?
Alphonse Elric
Father
The Ouroboros, a shadowy and mysterious organization that centers around an individual known only as the Father. They target skilled alchemists in order to use them for human sacrifices.
Lust
Envy
?
Greed
Gluttony

Data

The Search for the Philosopher's Stone

The Elric brothers' journey has been long and complicated. Let's follow their footprints in order to find the various places that they've visited.

Ⓐ Reole

The leader of a new religion is gathering followers in this town. Ed and Al recognize his miracles as the power of the Philosopher's Stone and expose him as a fraud.

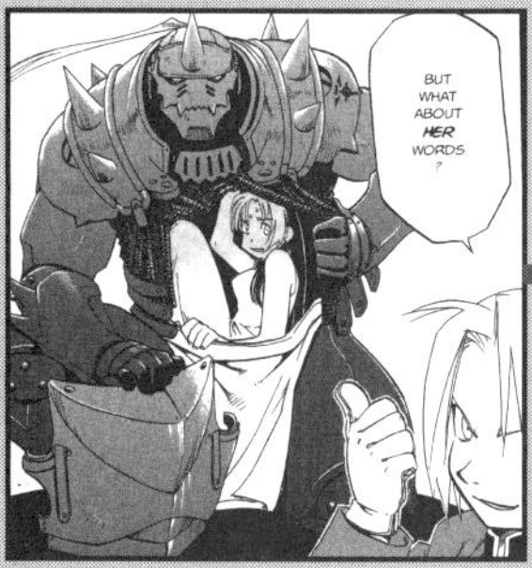
BUT WHAT ABOUT HER WORDS?

Ⓑ Youswell

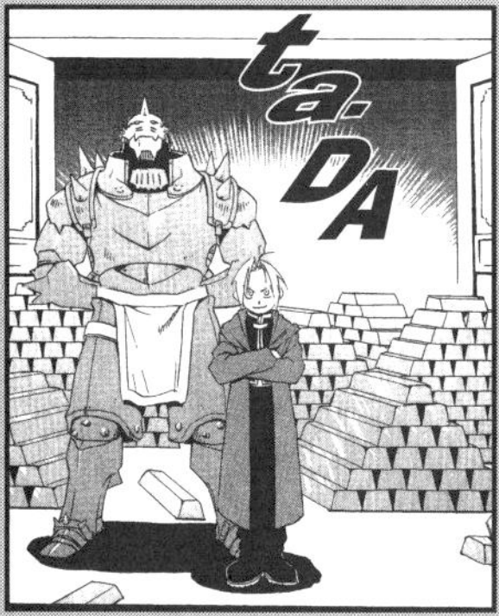
ta-DA

A mining town on the outskirts of the eastern region. The townspeople were oppressed by the tyranny of the comically villainous Lt. Yoki. Ed conducts the forbidden act of gold transmutation in order to help the townspeople.

Ⓒ The Train Hijacking

During a train heist, Ed is infuriated when the hijackers call him a runt. They learn not to mess with the Fullmetal Alchemist after the runt conquers them and puts a stop to their plans.

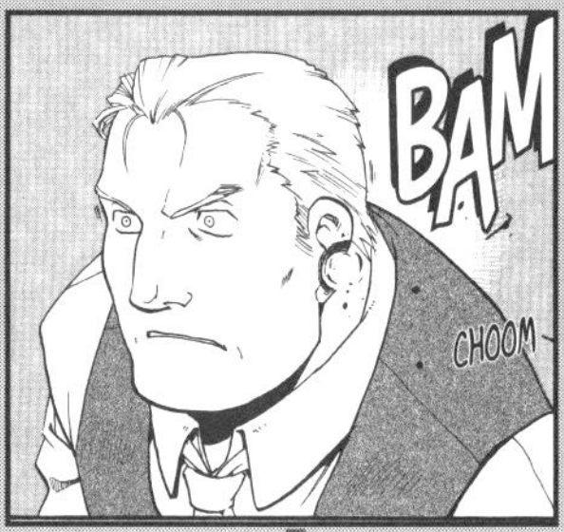
BAM
CHOOM

Ⓓ East City

The brothers expose Shou Tucker, the insane so-called "Sewing-Life Alchemist." Scar, a mysterious killer with a grudge against state alchemists, murders Tucker and gravely wounds Ed and Al.

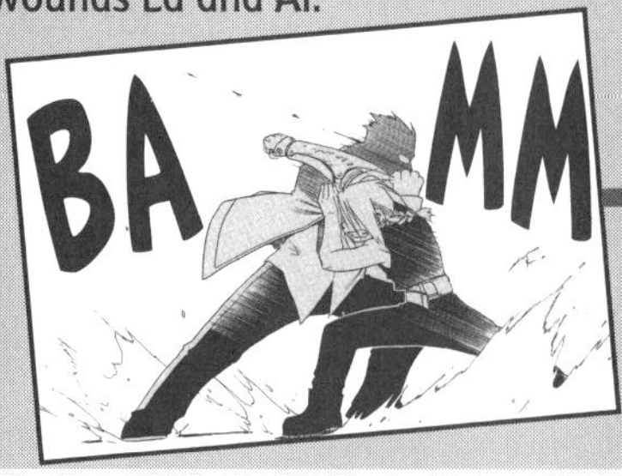
BAMM

The Elric Brothers' Travelogue

- ◆In Reole, the Elrics expose the leader of the Leto religion as a fraud. Ⓐ
- ◆In Youswell, they save the townspeople from Lt. Yoki's oppression. Ⓑ
- ◆On the way to East City they apprehend the Blue Squad who hijacks the train they are traveling on. Ⓒ
- ◆In East City, Shou Tucker creates a chimera out of his own daughter. Ⓓ
- ◆They battle Scar in East City. Ed's auto-mail and Al's armor is severely damaged. Ⓓ
- ◆The alchemist Marcoh reveals the location of the research data for the Philosopher's Stone. Ⓔ
- ◆Ed has his auto-mail repaired in Resembool. Ⓕ
- ◆The boys first encounter the Ouroboros Organization while gathering more information about the Philosopher's Stone. Ⓖ

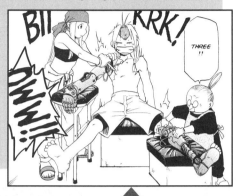

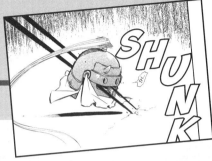

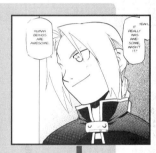

E After East City

Ed meets Dr. Marcoh, the man who originally researched the Philosopher's Stone. Marcoh tells the brothers where the notes from his secret research are hidden.

AREN'T YOU DR. MARCOH !?

F Resembool

A childhood friend, auto-mail engineer Winry, and her grandmother Pinako, welcome Ed and Al back to their hometown. Ed and Al were raised in Resembool, but burned their own house down to keep from ever having any desire to return.

THREE !!
BII KRK!
OWW!!!

G Central City

Ed and Al discover the secret ingredient for the Philosopher's Stone...people. They go to the ruins of the former laboratory and find danger waiting for them in the form of the killers called numbers 48 and 66.

SHUNK
TH...

H Rush Valley

Winry joins the brothers as they head toward a town with the nickname "the auto-mail engineer's Mecca" where yet more unexpected events wait.

YEAH... IT REALLY WAS AWE-SOME, WASN'T IT?
HUMAN BEINGS ARE AWESOME.

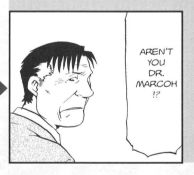

I Dublith

Ed and his friends arrive at the home of Izumi Curtis, their alchemy teacher, to discover another missing piece of their puzzle.

WHAT HAP-PENED TO YOU?
TELL ME EVERY-THING.

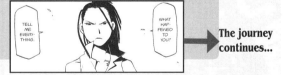

The journey continues...

The Journey So Far...

- ◆They participate in the delivery of an infant in Rush Valley. H
- ◆In Dublith, they reveal to their teacher Izumi that they attempted the sinful transmutation of their deceased mother. I
- ◆In Dublith they encounter Greed, a member of the Ouroboros. I

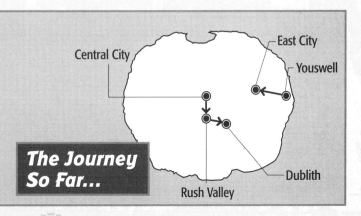

Central City
East City
Youswell
Dublith
Rush Valley

Point one

Alchemy

Let's concentrate for a minute on alchemy, really the central theme of the entire tale. We'll begin by pounding into you the Foundations of Alchemy.

The Foundations of Alchemy

◆The basic alchemic concept is equivalent exchange.

Alchemy isn't some sort of convenient magic that can create something out of nothing. It is based on the concept of "equivalent exchange," which follows the scientific principle of the conservation of matter and the laws of nature. In order to create one type of matter it is necessary to supply an equal amount of the same type of matter. For example, you can't transmute a stone statue out of water. Get it?

BUT THAT OLD GUY IS MAKING TOO MUCH OUT OF TOO LITTLE... ALCHEMY-WISE, THAT'S BREAKING THE LAW.
SEE? SO WHY DON'T YOU TWO JUST HAVE FAITH THAT IT'S A MIRACLE ALREADY ?!
BIG BROTH-ER... DO YOU THINK...?
YEAH, I DO.
THAT MEANS THAT TO OBTAIN SOMETHING, SOMETHING OF EQUAL VALUE MUST BE LOST.
IN OTHER WORDS, THE BASICS OF ALCHEMY IS THE "EQUIVALENT EXCHANGE"!

Equivalent exchange follows the logical rules of the scientific universe. With power comes responsibility.

Memo

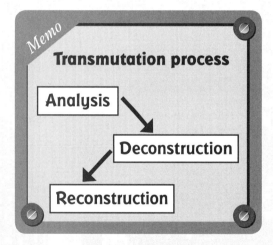

Transmutation process

Analysis → Deconstruction → Reconstruction

◆The Three Steps to Transmutation

The transmutation process can be divided into three steps: analysis, deconstruction, and reconstruction. Understanding the natural laws that exist within a substance, deconstructing it, and then reconstructing it is what alchemy is all about. All life and death follows the same law: the "flow" of energy throughout the universe. The study of alchemy is the study of how to control that flow and direct it into a new form of your choosing.

Lecturer Edward Elric

This is where I'm going to teach you what alchemy is all about. You'll want to pay close attention. If you don't understand my lecture, you won't understand the real truth of alchemy.

FSSSHH
HOW'S THAT?

Even a broken radio can be repaired by alchemy. But if a part is missing altogether, you won't be able to fix it. You have to have all the pieces to make alchemy work. You can't create something from nothing.

◆The Transmutation Circle

A transmutation circle sets in motion the alchemical energy. The circle represents the circular flow of power from one form to another. Most alchemists must use a circle to perform alchemy. However, all circles are not created equal, and each alchemist puts his own stamp on the way he or she uses one. Different runes inside the circle can mean very different things and are usually the personal imprint of the alchemist in question.

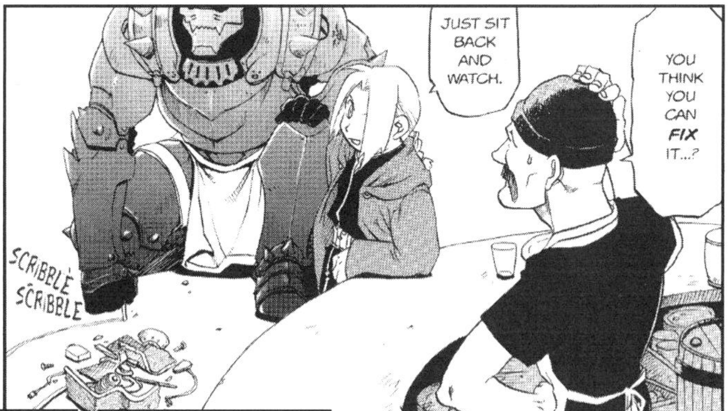
JUST SIT BACK AND WATCH.
YOU THINK YOU CAN FIX IT...?
SCRIBBLE SCRIBBLE

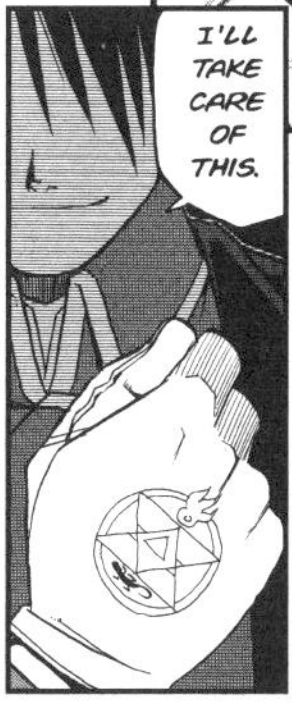
I'LL TAKE CARE OF THIS.

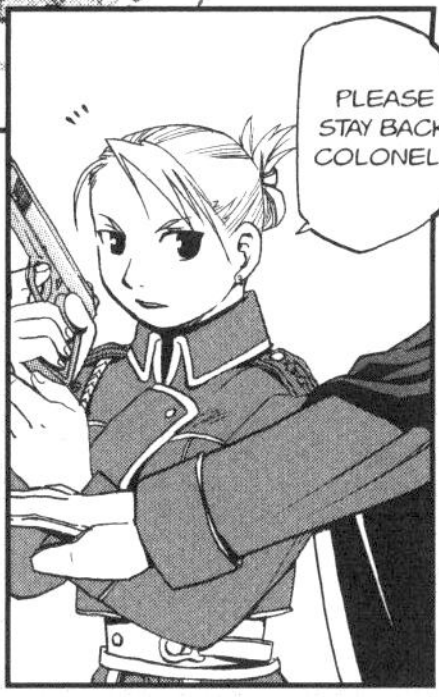
PLEASE STAY BACK, COLONEL...

Each alchemist has his own method for using the circle. Al draws a transmutation circle every time. For speed's sake, the colonel has a circle already inscribed on his glove ready to use whenever he needs.

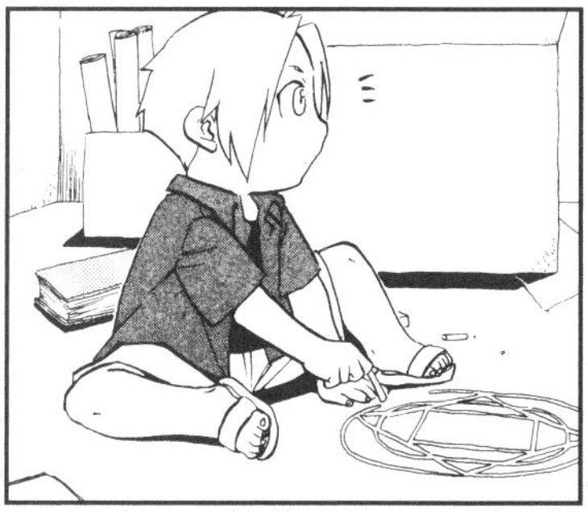

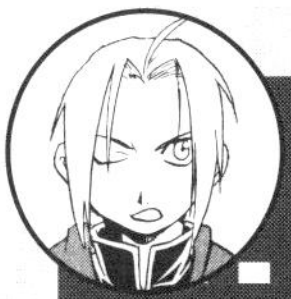

A little secret about Ed and circles

Why he doesn't use a transmutation circle...

The simple answer is that I myself am the transmutation circle, complete with runes, all ready to go. All I have to do to practice alchemy is make the sign of a circle with my hands and the circle is complete. How is this possible? That's a little more complicated. I'll let Al explain it to you.

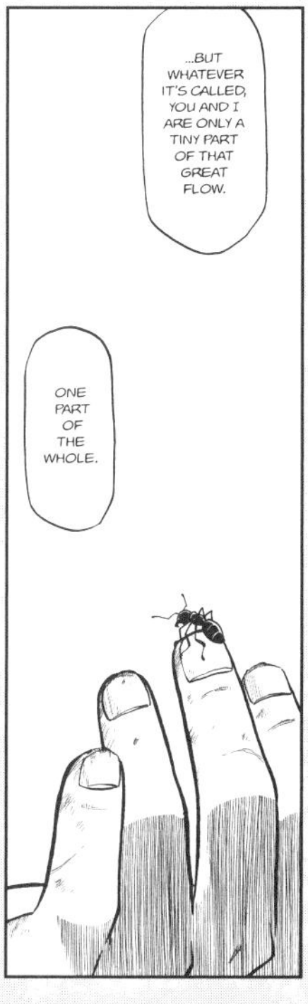
...BUT WHATEVER IT'S CALLED, YOU AND I ARE ONLY A TINY PART OF THAT GREAT FLOW.
ONE PART OF THE WHOLE.

◆The Truth of Alchemy

Back when we were apprentices, our teacher Izumi made my brother and me fend for ourselves on a deserted island. There, we learned the secret that "one is all, all is one." We are all "ones" that are part of the "all" and when we come together, we create the flow of life or energy. I know, I know, it sounds like Zen, but it's actually the fundamental truth of alchemy.

"All" is the world! "One" is me! (Ed)

Different Styles of Alchemy

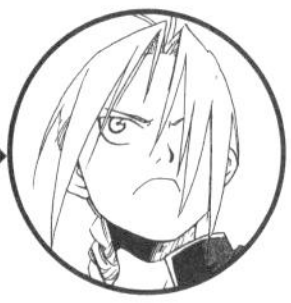

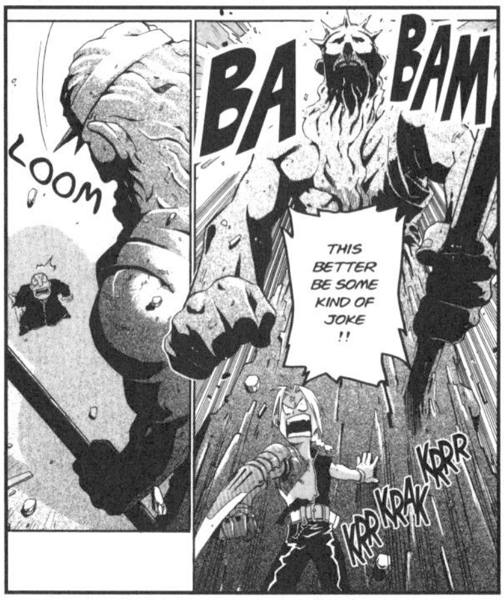
BA
BAM
LOOM
THIS BETTER BE SOME KIND OF JOKE!!
KRR KRAK KRRR

As long as I have enough for an equivalent exchange I can basically transmute anything, big or small.

◆Ed's Method

I'll go first, of course. My alchemy is totally unique. In one second, I can transmute any metal, my specialty. Spears are my favorite weapons. And I can also transmute the auto-mail of my right hand into anything I want. Though I try not to do it in front of Winry. She gets a little offended when I mess with her hard work.

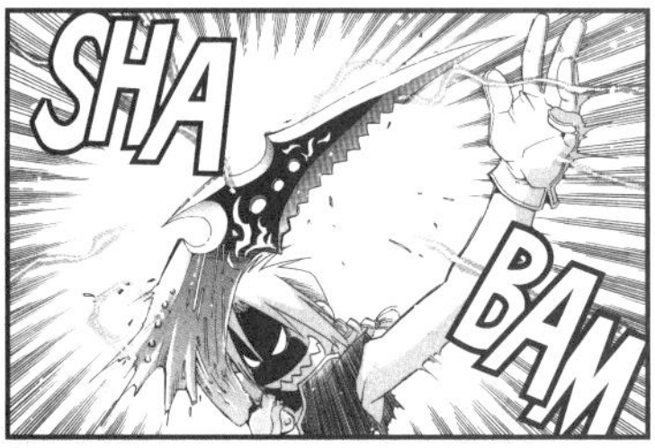
SHA
BAM

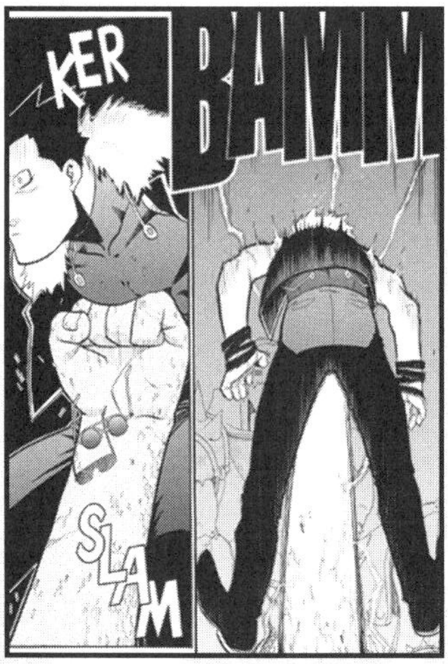
KER
BAMM
SLAM

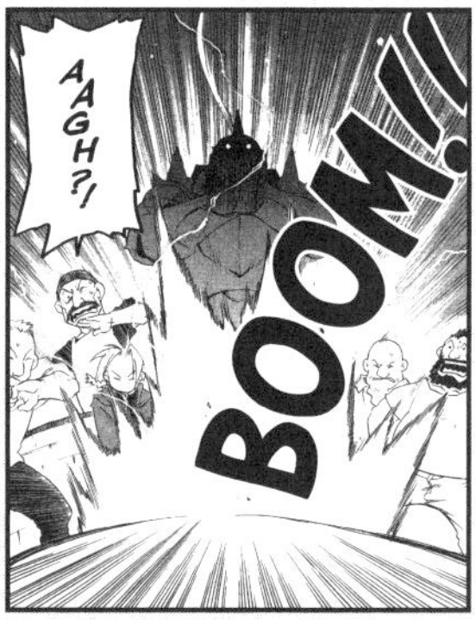
AAGH?!
BOOM!!

He's got a lot of skill but his transmutations are a little plain.

◆Al's Method

Al's not as skilled as me, but he's still pretty good. In fact, the Elric brothers are famous not just because of me, but because of Al's quick wit and strong abilities too. Al draws transmutation circles fast and I have to admit, his attention to detail is usually even better than mine.

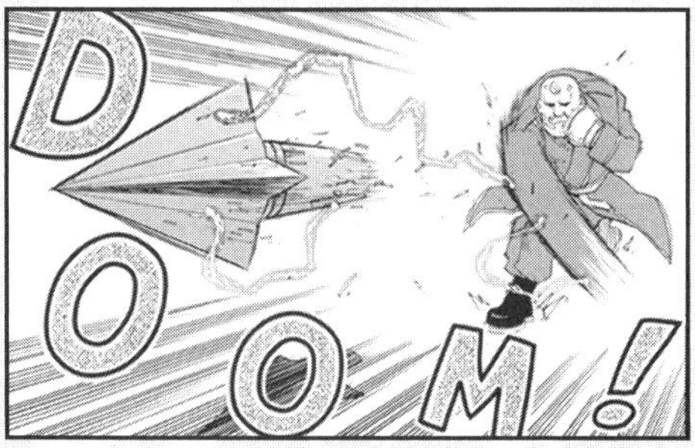
DOOOM!

His gauntlets have transmutation circles already drawn on them. It's useful for speed, but it also means he has to punch to use his alchemy, which can be a drawback if he can't use his hands.

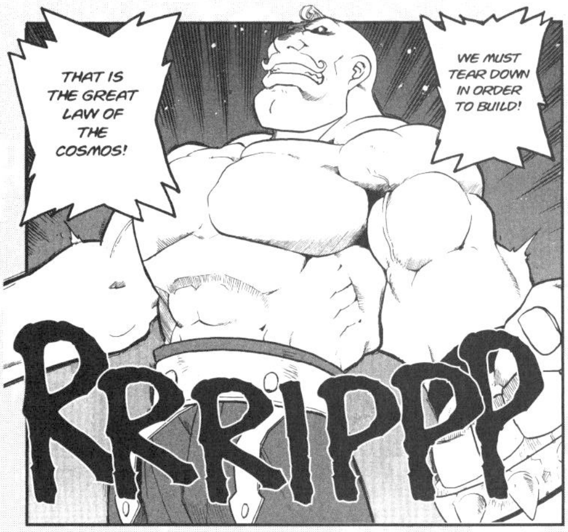
WE MUST TEAR DOWN IN ORDER TO BUILD!
THAT IS THE GREAT LAW OF THE COSMOS!
RRRIPPP

◆Major Armstrong's Method

The major's alchemy goes like this: destruction, destruction, alchemy, and more destruction. Combining his huge size with martial arts and his powerful punch, he can transmute anything in his path, provided he can hit it first!

◆Colonel Mustang's Method

In the military, there's a lot of debate over who's tougher: the colonel or me. While I could beat him super easily, it's true that he's an alchemical powerhouse. His trick: a glove made of special flammable cloth inscribed with a transmutation circle. When the cloth hits friction, it sparks. After that all he has to do is adjust the oxygen concentration level around him and stuff starts to blow up!

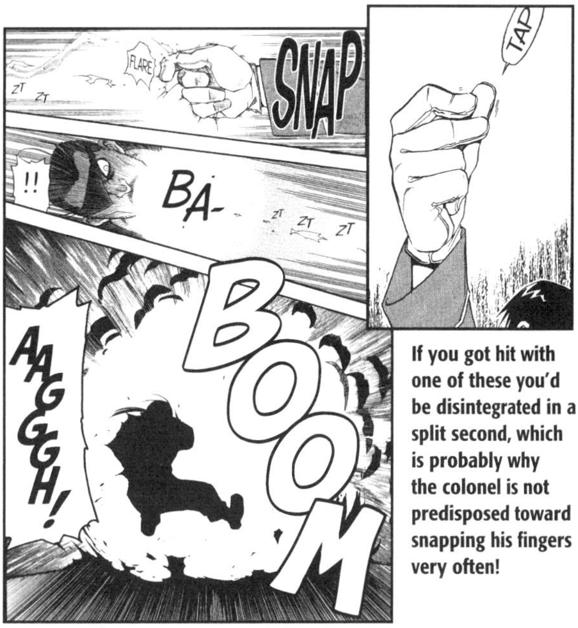
TAP
SNAP
FLARE
ZT ZT
!!
BA-
ZT ZT ZT
AAGGGH!
BOOM

If you got hit with one of these you'd be disintegrated in a split second, which is probably why the colonel is not predisposed toward snapping his fingers very often!

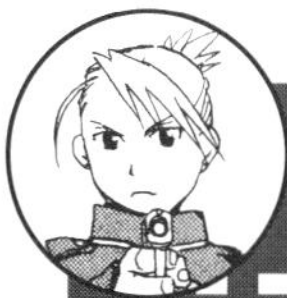

Things that give the lieutenant a headache

The Flame Alchemist's weakness

Besides being a total procrastinator and not ever finishing his work till the very last minute, the colonel also can't transmute when it's raining outside. Why? Where are you going to get sparks on a wet day? Sometimes his big ego causes him to forget this, resulting in some embarrassing, and potentially dangerous, moments. And of course, I never cease to remind the guy that he's completely useless on a rainy day.

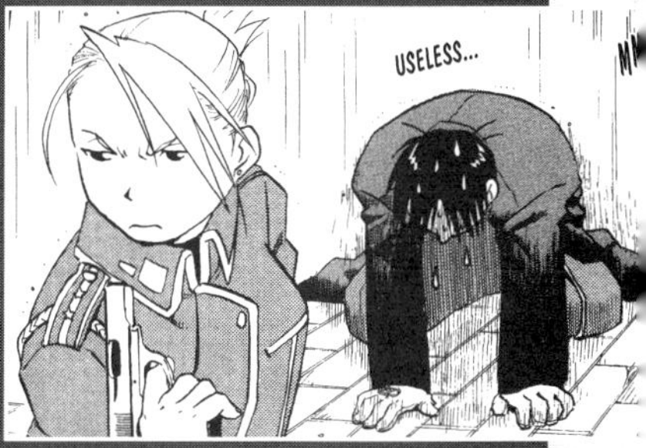
USELESS...

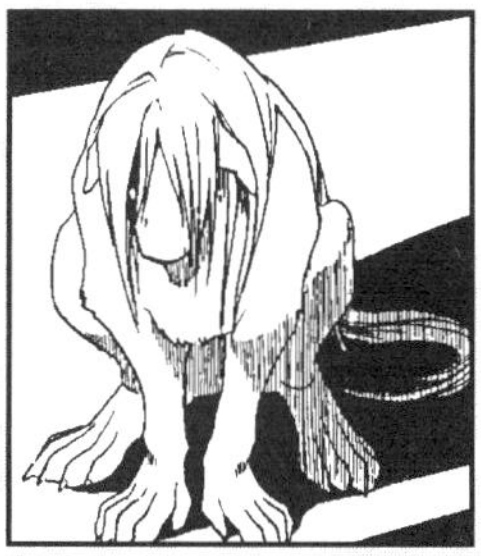

◆Tucker's Method

His specialty is combining two genetically different organisms together to create new life forms–AKA "chimeras." But there's a dark secret as to why his chimeras are capable of human speech and others are not.

◆Scar's Method

By stopping his transmutation circles in the deconstruction stage, Scar uses alchemy only to destroy rather than recreate, making him a very dangerous foe to all alchemists.

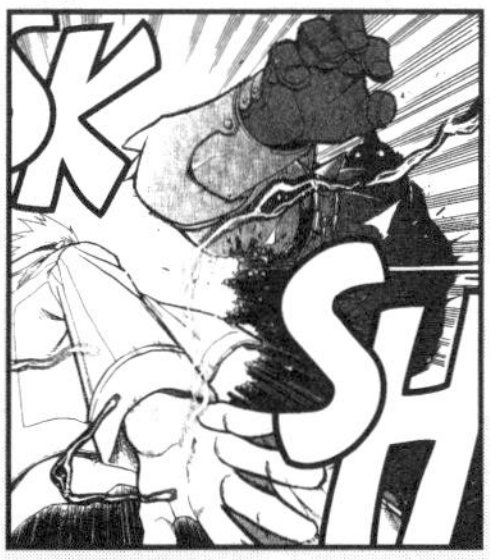

Alchemy is "a circus act for weirdoes."
(Hughes)

The Philosopher's Stone & Human Transmutation

To alchemists, the Philosopher's Stone is a sacred treasure. Why? Well, I'll tell ya. And then I'll explain why it's tied to the forbidden act of human transmutation.

The Truth About the Stone

The Power of the Philosopher's Stone

Legend has it that a stone with the power to ignore the fundamental law of alchemy, equivalent exchange, exists in a secret location somewhere in the world. We believe that harnessing its power could restore my arm and leg, and put Al back into a human body. Why? The stone is supposed to be able to allow transmutation without a circle and with only a limited amount of source material. Some don't even believe that the stone exists. But we saw a replica at Reole and it was so powerful that if the real thing is out there, it will definitely work for us. If it exists, we will find it.

It's impossible to turn a small flower into a large sunflower with the power of regular alchemy. Why is that?

Memo

A Stone by any other name:

- Sage's Stone
- Stone of Heaven
- Great Elixir
- Red Tincture
- Fifth Element

Five Names

The Philosopher's Stone that Mr. Marcoh showed us was made up of a strange-looking liquid, which made us realize that "stone" is not necessarily a literal term. The Philosopher's Stone could look like anything. As we investigated further, we found even more names by which seekers call the stone.

WOBBLE

Lecturer Alphonse Elric

My brother and I are looking for the Philosopher's Stone to repair the damage we did when we attempted a forbidden human transmutation.

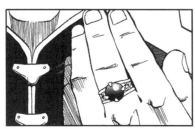

The Philosopher's Stone is very powerful and therefore incredibly dangerous. Many of those rumored to have used the Stone have had a tragic fate.

THIS REALLY IS "THE WORK OF THE DEVIL..."
DAMMIT, MARCOH... WHAT THE HELL WERE YOU DOING?!
WHAT'S WRONG?
THE MAIN INGREDIENT FOR THE PHILOS-OPHER'S STONE...

The research materials were written in code and took long hours to decipher. What we found out makes me sick to this day.

◆The Forbidden Ingredient

The true irony of the Stone is that it is apparently made up of living human tissue. Many people lost their lives to create the only thing in the world that can bring the dead to life.

"THE TRUTH THAT LIES WITHIN THE TRUTH."

It's the devil's research. That knowledge will only lead you to hell! **(Marcoh)**

◆Research for the Philosopher's Stone

It's now an indisputable fact that not only does the Stone exist, but the military was heavily involved in developing it. Marcoh told us that the Stone was even a key power in the Eastern civil war. Laboratory Number Five, now in ruins, was the center of the study of the Stone and was strategically located near a prison so that a steady flow of human captives was available to power the Stone. We now also know that the Ouroboros was controlling the experiments from the shadows. I still don't know whether they're a secret branch of the military or whether the military is working with them for some other reason.

GRANTED, WE DIDN'T EXPECT HIM TO FIND THIS PLACE, BUT JUST KNOWING ABOUT THE PROCESS OF MAKING THE STONES WON'T GET HIM ANYWHERE.
AFTER ALL, OUR PLAN IS ALREADY IN ITS FINAL STAGE.

Research for the Philosopher's Stone is most likely still being conducted somewhere, but to our knowledge, no one's successfully transmuted a perfect Philosopher's Stone yet.

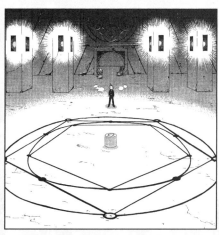

The Forbidden Act of Human Transmutation

◆The History of Human Transmutation

As a child I read in a book once that human beings are made out of the soul, the mind and the physical body. Now I know that human bodies are composed of 35 liters of water, 20 kg of carbon, 4 liters of ammonia, 1.5 kg of lime, etc. etc…I've never heard of anyone successfully conducting human transmutation and anyone who tries meets a bad end. Once an entire country was destroyed because someone tried to create the perfect human being. Human transmutation is better left alone.

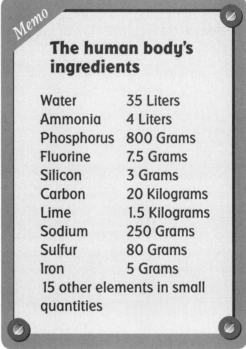

Memo

The human body's ingredients

Water	35 Liters
Ammonia	4 Liters
Phosphorus	800 Grams
Fluorine	7.5 Grams
Silicon	3 Grams
Carbon	20 Kilograms
Lime	1.5 Kilograms
Sodium	250 Grams
Sulfur	80 Grams
Iron	5 Grams

15 other elements in small quantities

I BET THE ADULTS MADE IT FORBIDDEN JUST TO COVER UP THE FACT THAT THEY DON'T KNOW HOW TO DO IT.
THINK ABOUT HOW HAPPY EVERYONE WOULD BE IF A DEAD PERSON CAME BACK TO LIFE.

...YOU COULDN'T PUT ME BACK TOGETHER TOO.

◆The Tragedy

Four years ago when my big brother was 11 years old and I was 10, we committed the ultimate sin. We just wanted to see our mom smile again… That's why we didn't have any reservations about bringing her back to life after she died. We took what we learned from our teacher Izumi and tried our best, but the "mom" that appeared in the transmutation circle couldn't be called a human being. And we were badly injured. That's what you get for trespassing in God's realm.

LET'S DO IT, AL.
OKAY!

IT...IT WASN'T SUP-POSED TO BE LIKE THIS...
DRAG
OH NO... HE'S GONE!

SOME-BODY...
HELP ME...
MOM!!

My big brother risked his life to transmute my soul and encase it in this suit of armor. Our mission now is to regain our former bodies.

◆The Price of Sin

Because we attempted a human transmutation, I lost my entire body. My big brother lost his left leg, and in order to transmute my soul into the armor, he gave up his right arm too. I don't remember much but I think my big brother does. He says he saw a doorway and the outline of someone standing in it. His left leg was taken in exchange for being allowed to go to that hidden place. But I still don't know what I got in return for my entire body being taken.

IT'S A REBOUND !!
ED, HELP ME! ED! PLEASE!
KRK
SKK
KRK
SKK
GWOO
AL---!!!
KRAK!

I should have died, but here I am thanks to my big brother. He saved me and I can't thank him enough.

YOU REMEMBER THE LAW OF EQUIVALENT EXCHANGE....

The thing in Edward's vision referred to himself as "the world," "the universe" and "one."

Izumi's soliloquy

Rebounds

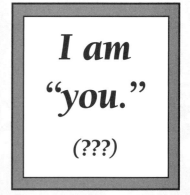

Why did Ed and Al lose parts of their bodies when they attempted a human transmutation? That's what's known as a rebound. When an alchemist attempts a transmutation beyond his skill level, the amount of material that's lacking from the equivalent exchange is taken from the alchemist's body. The same thing happened to the false prophet of the Church of Leto. I guess it just means "know your place."

I am "you."

(???)

◆The Truth

My older brother saw something when he had his limbs taken. He saw what our teacher calls "the truth." I guess it could also be called the "law of this world" or the "absolute truth of existence"… Because my big brother saw a portion of this truth he is now able to transmute without using a transmutation circle. But to get close to the truth, he lost his left leg. When our teacher got close to the truth, she lost some of her internal organs. I lost my whole body. I think that means I got closer to the truth than anybody else, but unlike Ed or our teacher, I don't remember anything that happened.

Point Three

The Ouroboros

This secret organization conducts their affairs from the shadows. This is pretty much all we know about them.

Those Who Wear the Crest

◆Why hunt alchemists?

Our goal? I guess I can tell you a little bit about it. For the past 200 years we homunculi have been working toward a single purpose, our Father's goal. But I can't tell you what that is. Though you've already gathered from Greed's hints that our master plan is already in the final stages.

◆Who is Father?

He's our "Father," plain and simple. He gave us life. And if you remember that so far we've lived more than 200 years, I think you'll get some idea of how powerful Father actually is.

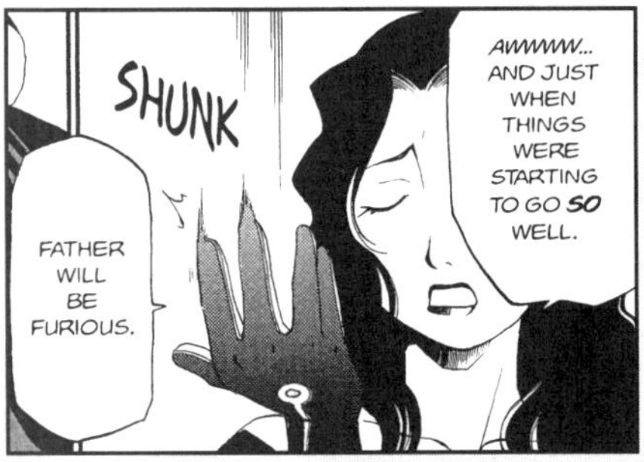
AWWWW... AND JUST WHEN THINGS WERE STARTING TO GO SO WELL.
SHUNK
FATHER WILL BE FURIOUS.

◆What is a human sacrifice?

Powerful alchemists. Their lives are necessary for the completion of our goal. That's why we're letting them live…for now. But if they keep getting in our way some of my less patient comrades might lose their tempers and kill them. Do you understand, Fullmetal boy?

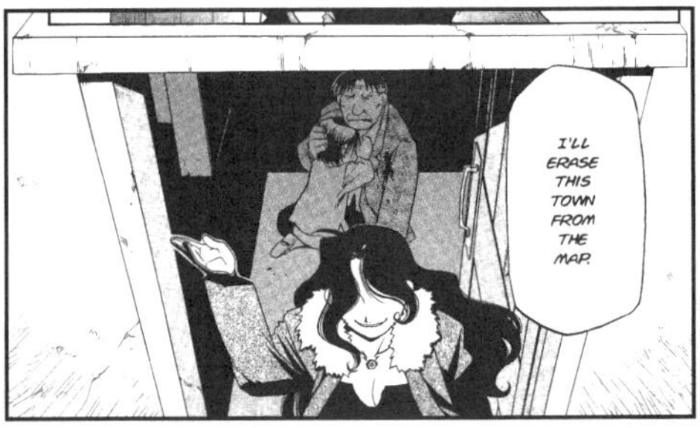
I'LL ERASE THIS TOWN FROM THE MAP.

Lecturer Lust

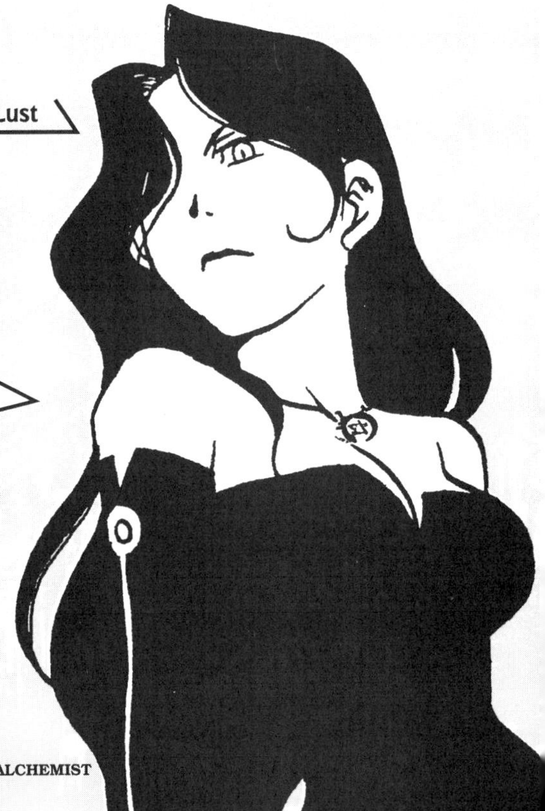

You want to know about us? I don't know who might be listening so I can't tell you everything, but I guess I can give you some hints. What's that, Gluttony? No, you can't eat them.

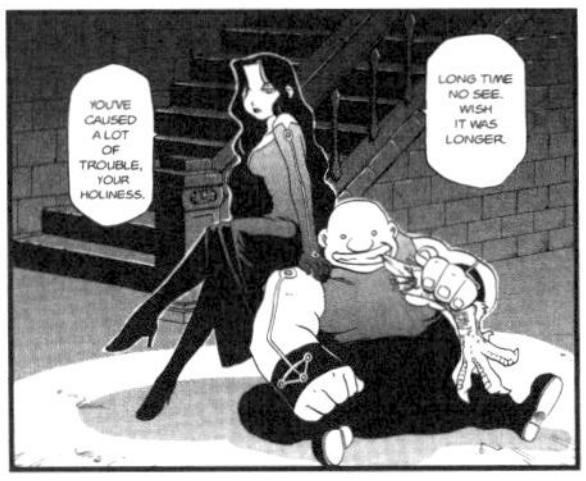
LONG TIME NO SEE. WISH IT WAS LONGER.
YOU'VE CAUSED A LOT OF TROUBLE, YOUR HOLINESS.

Our organization is large and powerful. There are many of us you haven't met.

◆The Ouroboros Crest

You can tell the Ouroboros by the tattoo of a snake biting its own tail. I'm sure you'll realize this once you think about it, but this snake symbolizes being a part of the whole, and therefore the whole as well. It also expresses the idea that the beginning and the end are the same. Understand?

YOU...
...ARE NO LONGER OF ANY USE.

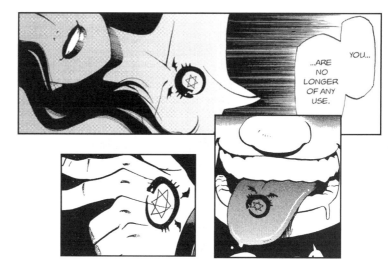

My comrades all have the tattoo. Gluttony has it on his tongue. Good place for him, right?

◆The Names of the Ouroboros

Our names come from the seven deadly sins, of course. We are Lust, Gluttony, Envy, Greed. Ah, you noticed that we are missing a few? Well, you're right to wonder about that. And I'll just let you keep on wondering.

Lust
Gluttony
Envy
Greed
?
Sloth
?
Pride
?
Wrath

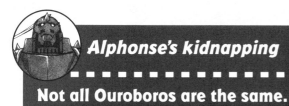

Alphonse's kidnapping

Not all Ouroboros are the same.

Hello everyone. Right now, I'm being held prisoner by an Ouroboros named Greed. He seems a little different from the other Ouroboros. He admits that he wants money, girls, power and fame as well as eternal life. I'm confused about his relationship to the rest of the group. He doesn't seem to fit at all.

MONEY!! SEX!!
POWER!!
FAME!!
I WANT EVERYTHING IN THE WORLD!

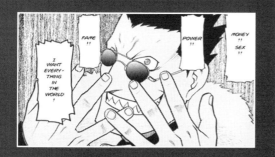

Don't forget that we're letting you live. (Lust)

Point Four

Military State

Want some real facts about our country's state of affairs? To learn that properly, we'll also need to explain some of the characters involved in the military.

National Structure

◆The military holds political power.

There's not really much more to the national structure than that. The Führer President is at the top of both the political and military chain of command. If you want to be anybody in this country, you need to join the military and be an officer like Colonel Mustang.

UNTIL THE DAY THAT I BECOME ***PRESIDENT*** AND GAIN ***COMPLETE MILITARY POWER.***

The colonel has his own goals and is steadily reaching them. I want to help him as much as possible.

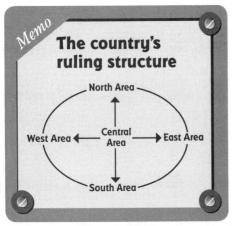

Memo
The country's ruling structure
North Area
West Area
Central Area
East Area
South Area

◆Ruling Structure

You already know that this country has a circular shape. The capital is located in the center, which makes it easy to reach the other parts of the country. Each region (north, south, east, west) has its own headquarters, which receives orders from Central. Being transferred to Central=being promoted.

Lecturer Maes Hughes

Hey, how're you doing? This time I'm going to lecture to you a little bit about this country. I'll do it for free but any presents for my beloved daughter are welcome.

"DO NOT CREATE HUMANS." "DO NOT CREATE GOLD." "SWEAR ABSOLUTE LOYALTY TO THE MILITARY."
THOSE ARE THE THREE RULES THAT A STATE ALCHEMIST MUST ***NEVER*** BREAK.

If you know that those with a state license must swear loyalty to the military, then you can begin to understand this country's state of affairs.

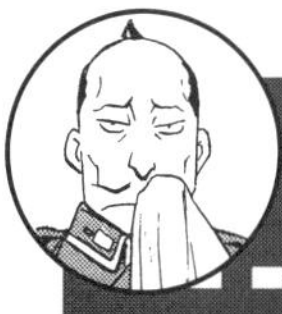

Ex-Lieutenant Yoki

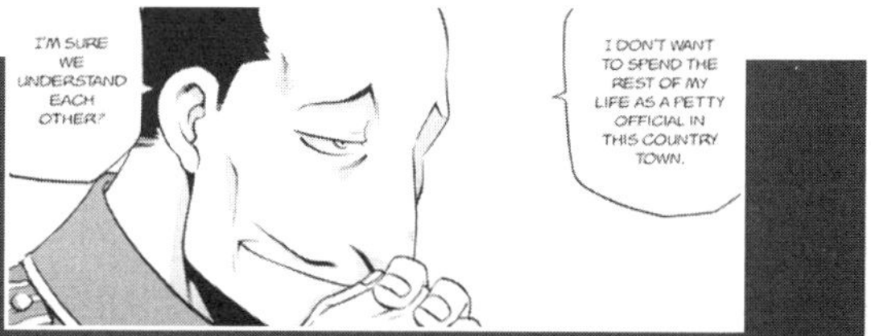
I DON'T WANT TO SPEND THE REST OF MY LIFE AS A PETTY OFFICIAL IN THIS COUNTRY TOWN.
I'M SURE WE UNDERSTAND EACH OTHER?

A loyal citizen rebuked

Hughes: It took me a long time to find you.
Yoki: That's because I was hiding in the slums of East City waiting for a chance to make my comeback…
Hughes: I heard that you used to be the owner of a coal mine?
Yoki: I knew that I was suited for a big job so I joined the military. I thought I was on the fast track to a promotion but…
Hughes: You blew it, right?
Yoki: I was deceived! By that runt of an alchemist! He's a con artist and I did nothing wrong!
Hughes: Weren't you blinded by money?
Yoki: Do you know how many bribes I sent to the high official in Central?! And those little brats, they're…so low!!
Hughes: So are you.

◆The Situation Inside and Outside the Country

This country is surrounded on all four sides by neighboring countries. Presently the border disputes in the southern and western regions are heating up. It's gotten so bad that the president went to the southern region to inspect the battle lines himself. The northern region is bordered by the treacherous Briggs Mountain and therefore is impassable. Now that I think about it the Elric brothers' teacher apparently trained on Briggs Mountain. If that's true she's really something else. To the east is nothing but a vast desert.

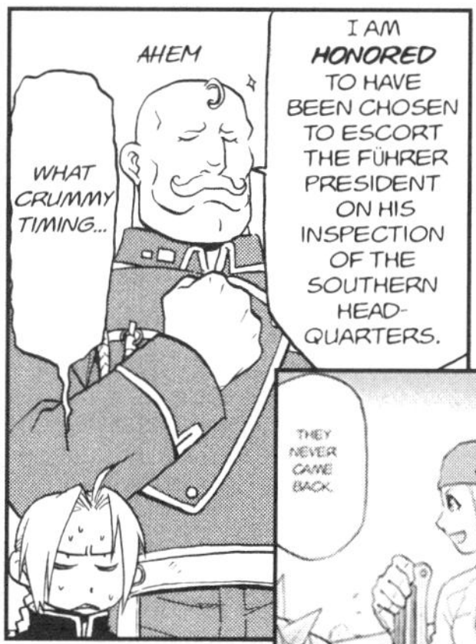
I AM HONORED TO HAVE BEEN CHOSEN TO ESCORT THE FÜHRER PRESIDENT ON HIS INSPECTION OF THE SOUTHERN HEAD-QUARTERS.
AHEM
WHAT CRUMMY TIMING...

The major's a little overbearing but I guess he's got the trust of the people around him. A state alchemist's skills are tailor made for his job as a bodyguard.

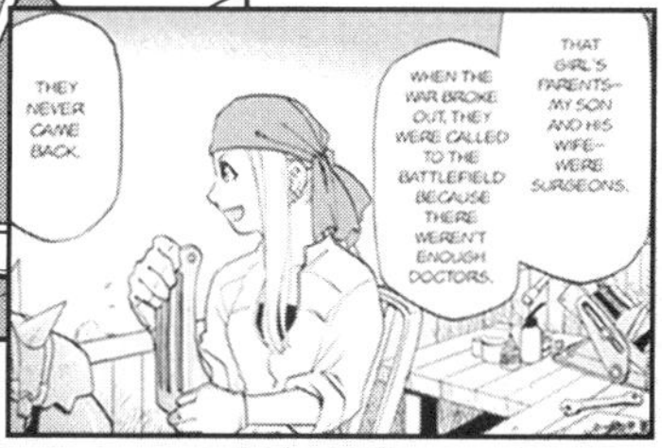
THAT GIRL'S PARENTS—MY SON AND HIS WIFE—WERE SURGEONS.
WHEN THE WAR BROKE OUT, THEY WERE CALLED TO THE BATTLEFIELD BECAUSE THERE WEREN'T ENOUGH DOCTORS.
THEY NEVER CAME BACK.

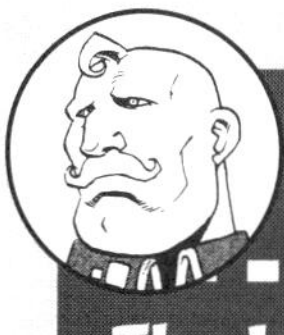

Major Armstrong speaks about his past

The Ishbalan extermination campaign

The Ishbalan extermination campaign? Even I can't bear to recollect that tragic event. After seven years of civil war, we state alchemists were called in to be used as weapons of mass destruction. Even the lives of innocent people were sacrificed indiscriminately. Although in the military we are taught to obey orders without question, it pained my soul to no end. Now that I think about it, I've heard that even the Philosopher's Stone was secretly used in the battle…

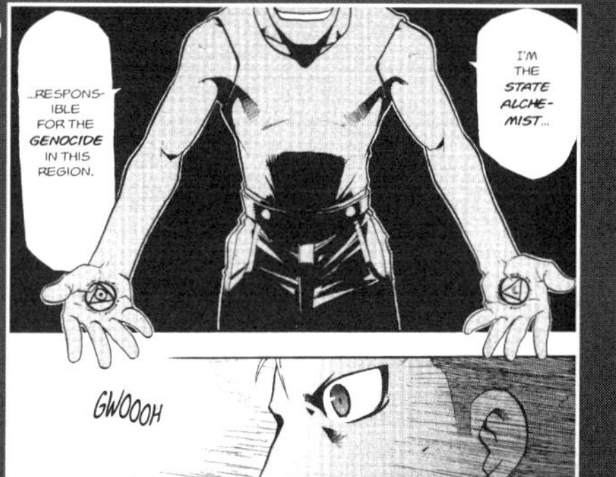
I'M THE STATE ALCHEMIST...
...RESPONSIBLE FOR THE GENOCIDE IN THIS REGION.
GWOOOH

This is the man who was in charge of the Ishbal campaign. I don't know if it's because of the atrocities which occurred during that time, but presently he is incarcerated in Central.

An Introduction to the Major Locations

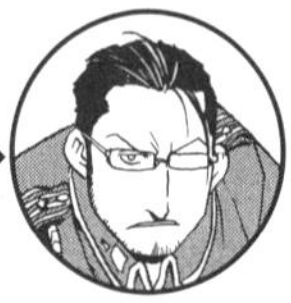

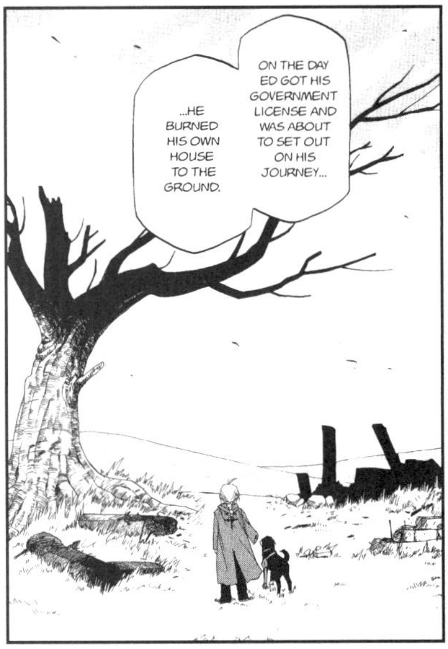
ON THE DAY ED GOT HIS GOVERNMENT LICENSE AND WAS ABOUT TO SET OUT ON HIS JOURNEY...
...HE BURNED HIS OWN HOUSE TO THE GROUND.

◆Ed's Hometown of Resembool

The East Area country village of Resembool is where the Elric brothers were born and raised. As a soldier, it makes me a little sad to think that had it not been for the Ishbalan Civil War, it might have developed into a thriving city by now. But on the other hand, it is surrounded by nature and sheep pastures, and, unlike the city, it is a nice place to relax the soul. I think it would be a good town in which to watch your grandkids grow up after retiring.

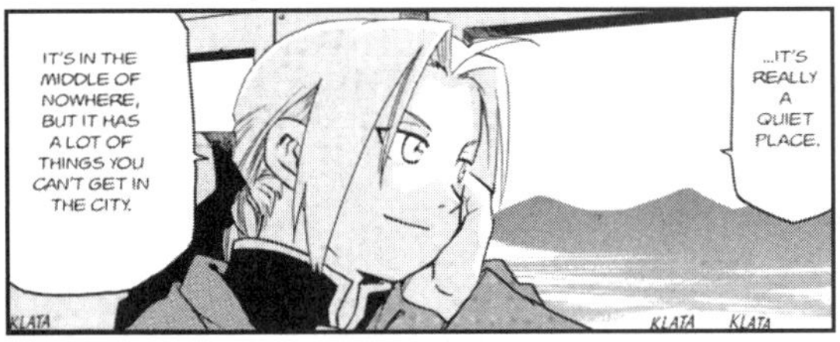
...IT'S REALLY A QUIET PLACE.
IT'S IN THE MIDDLE OF NOWHERE, BUT IT HAS A LOT OF THINGS YOU CAN'T GET IN THE CITY.
KLATA
KLATA
KLATA

The Elric brothers left their hometown with the conviction that they would never again return. It's a great feeling to know that there are people waiting for you to return and that you have a place to go home to.

◆Reole, a Town Immersed in Religion

There was nothing going on in this town until a short time ago. People began to gather there only after the new Church of Leto started to attract people to the town. Father Cornello used a fake Philosopher's Stone to create "miracles" to gather followers, erected an avenue lined with idols of Leto, and even built a large church. In the end his scam was exposed and the townspeople rioted. Now it's too depressing to even look at the place.

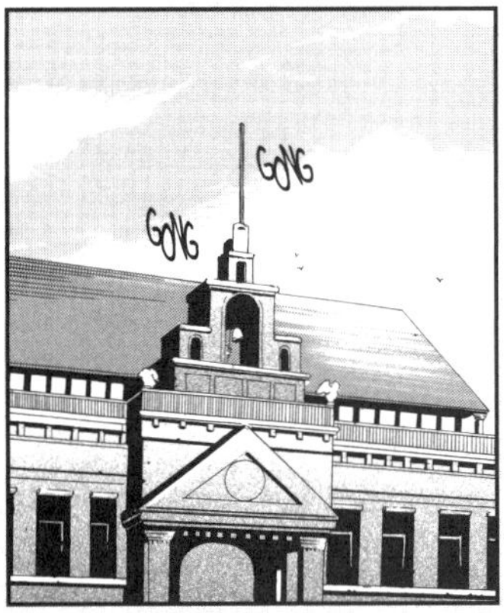
GONG
GONG

Although they were being fooled, maybe the townspeople were happier back then…

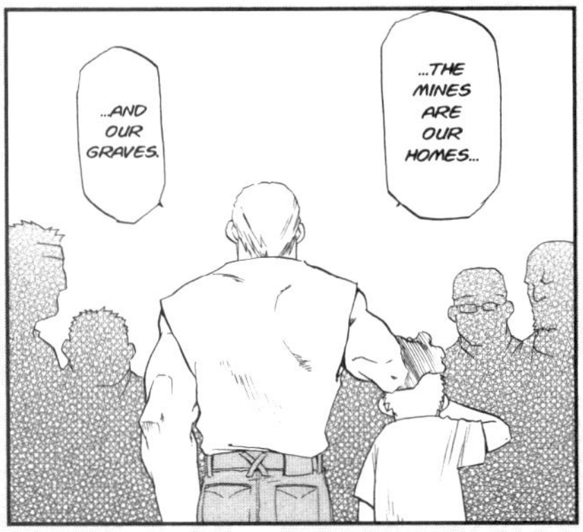
...THE MINES ARE OUR HOMES...
...AND OUR GRAVES.

No matter how much hardship a person endures they can never turn their back on their hometown.

◆Youswell, the Coal Mining Town

A coal mining town on the eastern border. The coal mine belonged to a military commander named Yoki, and because he had all the political power, the townspeople were being exploited for their labor. By the way, this town's beer is really good.

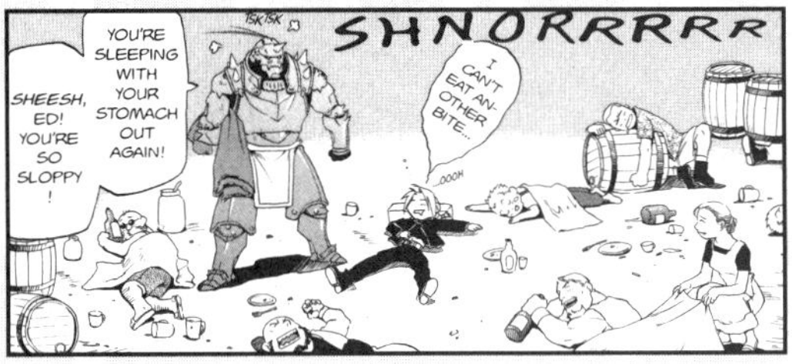
SHNORRRRRR
I CAN'T EAT AN-OTHER BITE...
YOU'RE SLEEPING WITH YOUR STOMACH OUT AGAIN!
SHEESH, ED! YOU'RE SO SLOPPY!

◆The Center of the East Area: East City

East City is the center of the East Area where Resembool and Reole are located. The East Area headquarters are also located in this town. Because of the Ishbalan Civil war and the riots in Reole, Colonel Mustang sometimes complained about how the headquarters building was falling apart. There's supposedly even an Ishbalan slum on the outskirts.

It's nothing compared to Central City, but it's a pretty hip-looking city, right?

From Central station you can go on a train journey to any station in the country.

◆The Center of the Country

Central City controls the entire country. The presidential estate, the state alchemists' office, and the National Library are all here. Even the Investigation Division where I work is here. In the largest city in the country there's nothing you can't find.

◆Rush Valley, the Auto-mail Engineer's Mecca

If you travel south by train from Central to the center of the South Area you'll arrive in Rush Valley. This hot and dry mountain town first boomed when they started developing auto-mail technology during the Ishbalan Civil War. The streets are crowded with auto-mail engineers, immersed in their research. Even the auto-mail that was used by the Blue Squad, who attempted the train hijacking, was made in Rush Valley.

IT'S ALSO CALLED "THE AUTO-MAIL ENGINEER'S MECCA."
I CAN SEE WHY.
I'VE NEVER SEEN THIS MUCH AUTO-MAIL IN ONE PLACE.
JUNK

◆Dublith, Town of the South Area

This town is slightly south of Rush Valley. It's fairly hot there because it's located in the South Area. At Kauroy Lake, which is a popular tourist spot to cool off, you'll often see couples enjoying a boat ride. There's even a deserted island in the middle of the lake, but it's a pretty big lake, so I'm sure not too many people go there.

GLARE
OH MAN...
THE SOUTH AREA SURE IS HOT, HUH, ED...?
DUBLITH

Point Five

The Military

As we've mentioned before, the military holds a considerable amount of power.

Military Structure

◆The Purpose of the Military

Our purpose is obviously to ensure the peace and well-being of this country. This country is in conflict both outside and inside its borders. Our duties also include maintaining military outposts in preparation for another war, and gathering information from the provinces. So as you can see we have many things we have to do.

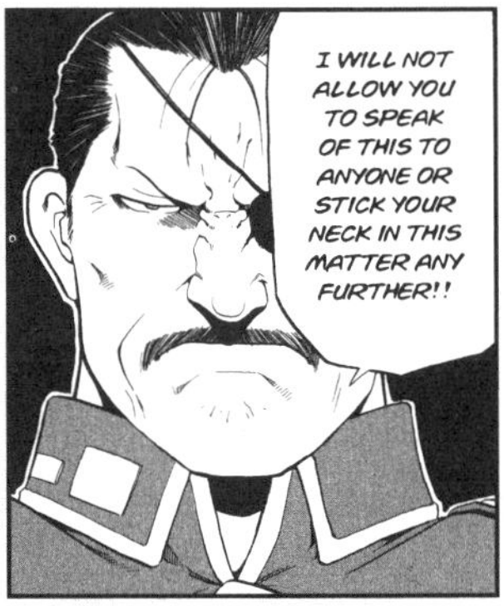
I WILL NOT ALLOW YOU TO SPEAK OF THIS TO ANYONE OR STICK YOUR NECK IN THIS MATTER ANY FURTHER!!

The president is also the commander-in-chief of the military. It's his position that I want.

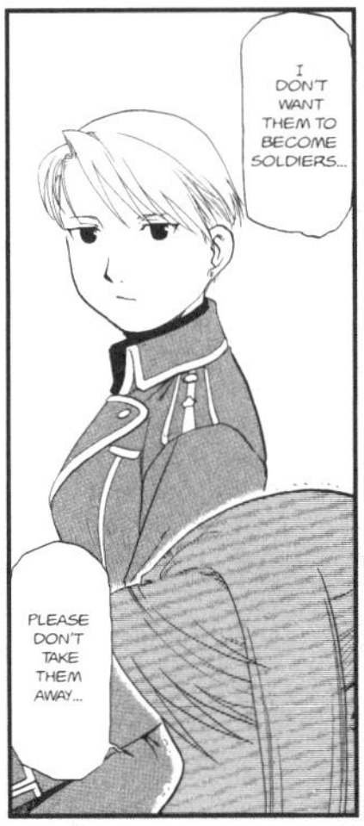
I DON'T WANT THEM TO BECOME SOLDIERS...
PLEASE DON'T TAKE THEM AWAY...

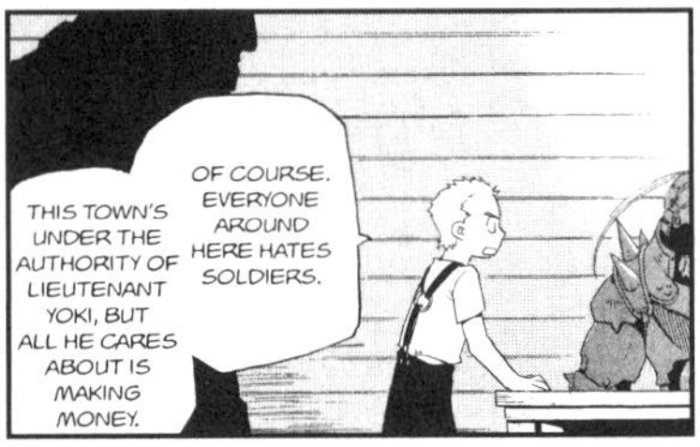
OF COURSE. EVERYONE AROUND HERE HATES SOLDIERS.
THIS TOWN'S UNDER THE AUTHORITY OF LIEUTENANT YOKI, BUT ALL HE CARES ABOUT IS MAKING MONEY.

People who can only measure the success of their lives through money are pathetic.

◆Everyone hates the military.

The citizens have a hard time understanding what the military does. Most of us military personnel work to better the country, but some of us abuse the power that is given to us. I also often hear about people who borrow money in order to offer bribes so that they can be promoted. That's the present situation.

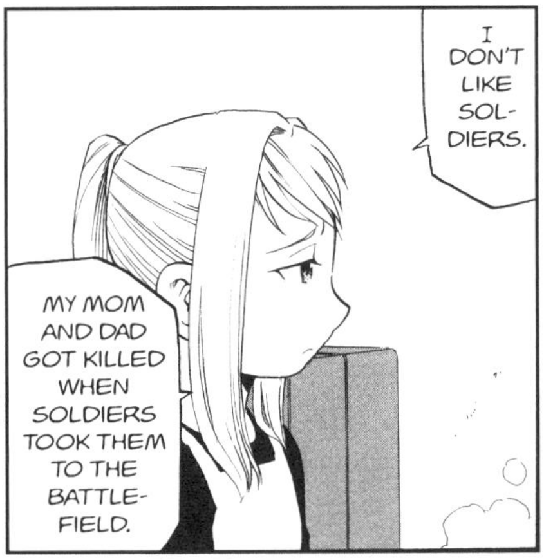
I DON'T LIKE SOLDIERS.
MY MOM AND DAD GOT KILLED WHEN SOLDIERS TOOK THEM TO THE BATTLEFIELD.

Lecturer Roy Mustang

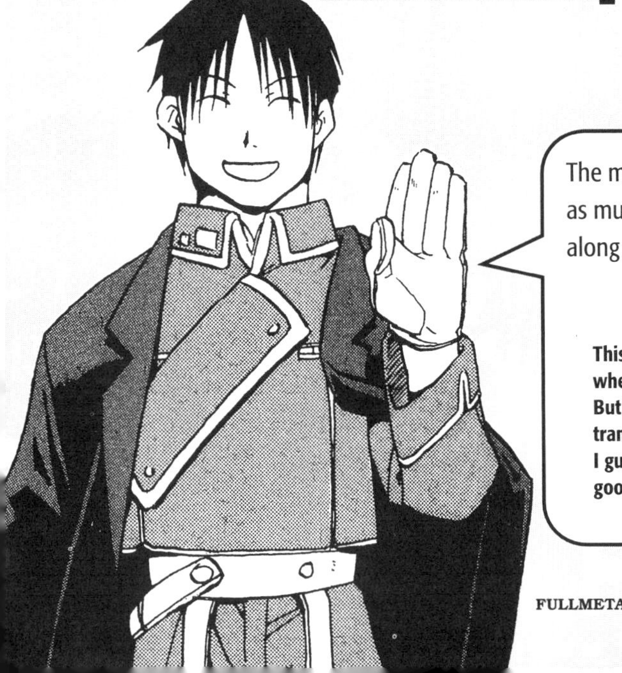

The military is the pillar that supports this nation. I'll explain as much as I can without being late for my next date. Follow along as best you can.

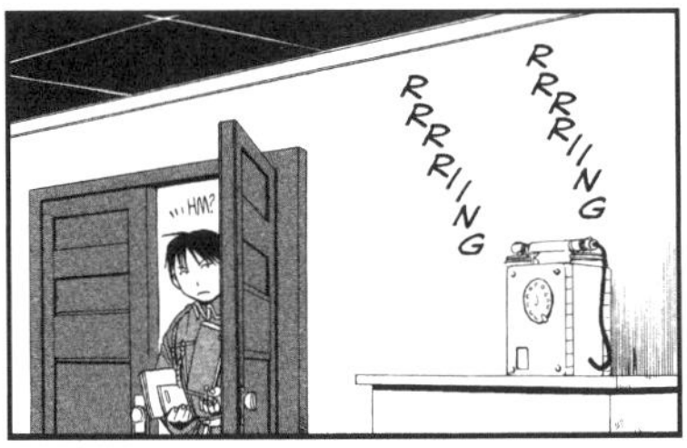
RRRRING
RRRING
HM?

This is the East H.Q., where I used to work. But since I'm being transferred to Central I guess I have to say goodbye to this place.

Chart Of Military Ranks

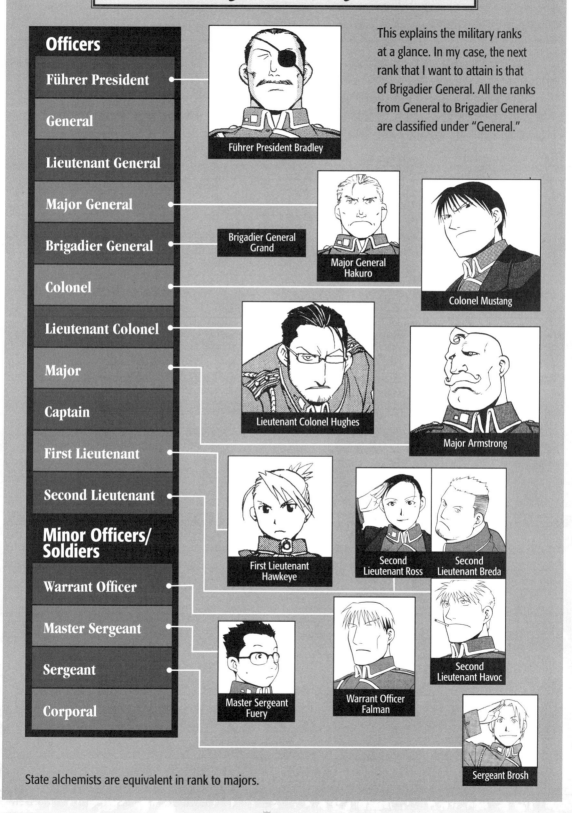

This explains the military ranks at a glance. In my case, the next rank that I want to attain is that of Brigadier General. All the ranks from General to Brigadier General are classified under "General."

Officers

Führer President

General

Lieutenant General

Major General

Brigadier General

Colonel

Lieutenant Colonel

Major

Captain

First Lieutenant

Second Lieutenant

Minor Officers/ Soldiers

Warrant Officer

Master Sergeant

Sergeant

Corporal

Führer President Bradley

Brigadier General Grand

Major General Hakuro

Colonel Mustang

Lieutenant Colonel Hughes

Major Armstrong

First Lieutenant Hawkeye

Second Lieutenant Ross

Second Lieutenant Breda

Second Lieutenant Havoc

Master Sergeant Fuery

Warrant Officer Falman

Sergeant Brosh

State alchemists are equivalent in rank to majors.

State Alchemists

◆Position and Privilege

The role of state alchemist puts the scientist's intellectual pursuits to practical use. As state alchemists they have access to various privileges and are able to conduct high-level research that would be impossible for civilians. By the way, up to now, only about 200 people have successfully passed the test and acquired the state alchemist license. But I hear that many people fail the assessments or quit of their own accord.

Memo

Notable privileges

- **Abundant research funds**
- **Access to special research materials**
- **Access to various government organizations**
- **Rank equivalent to major**

WHY ARE YOU GUYS SO POLITE TO ME?
ALTHOUGH YOU'RE NOT A STANDARD SOLDIER, YOUR RANK IS EQUIVALENT TO *MAJOR*.
ONE WORD FROM YOU AND WE COULD BE DISCHARGED.

A state alchemist has a high position within the military. In other words the military relies on them quite a bit.

...
MAYBE I SHOULD GET CERTIFIED AS A STATE ALCHEMIST TOO.

Al's gentle nature would never allow Ed to walk this dangerous path alone. The two brothers share a strong bond.

◆Dogs of the Military

"Alchemists work for the people." That's the alchemists' credo. Although alchemy is based on equivalent exchange, to most people it must seem like we're performing miracles. Because state alchemists have sold our souls to the military in exchange for power and privilege, people call us "dogs of the military."

GO TO THE STATE ALCHEMISTS' OFFICE IN THE PRESIDENTIAL PREFECTURE, WITHDRAW THE AMOUNT I WROTE DOWN ON THERE FROM MY RESEARCH GRANT FOR THE YEAR AND GIVE IT TO SHESKA.
EH? WHAT'S THIS?

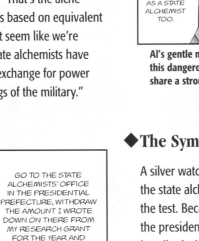

A state alchemist is given tens of thousands of *sens* a year to fund their research.

◆The Symbolic Silver Watch

A silver watch is given to those who possess the state alchemist's license as proof of passing the test. Because the state alchemist is under the president's direct control, the silver watch is inscribed with the presidential seal, which is the six pointed star. This also acts as an ID, and is necessary for withdrawing research funds and for utilizing various organizations. In Edward Elric's case, I've heard he's scratched some words on the other side of the watch lid. Usually defacing the watch is not allowed, but it probably won't be discovered if it's under the lid.

◆The Test and the Assessment

In order to become a state alchemist, a person must pass a written test, a practical skill test, a psychiatric test and finally an interview. After that they can't just sit back and enjoy the privileges without doing anything. Once a year it is also necessary to pass an assessment based on practical achievement. If high marks aren't earned on this assessment then it is possible to get your license revoked. Most alchemists, including myself, write their research notes in code.

Memo

Alchemical notes written in code

- **Marcoh's research: cooking recipe**
- **Mustang's research: women's names**
- **Ed's research: travelogue**

SHNK
BAM

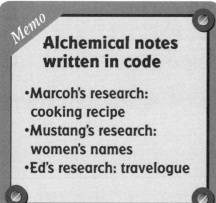

This was the first time that anyone had ever pointed a spear at the president during a test and gotten out alive. But I wonder just how skilled at combat the president really is?

WELL, SWEETIE... WHEN YOU BECOME A STATE ALCHEMIST YOU HAVE TO SHOW THE RESULTS OF YOUR RESEARCH ONCE A YEAR.
AND IF THEY DON'T LIKE HOW YOU'RE DOING, THEY TAKE AWAY YOUR LICENSE.

BETTER TO CHAIN HIM TO THE MILITARY NOW BEFORE HE GETS INVOLVED WITH ANOTHER ORGAN-IZATION.
VERY WELL. IF THAT IS WHAT YOU WISH.
HAVE YOU DECIDED ON HIS SECOND NAME?
YES.
IT MAY SOUND A LITTLE IMPOSING FOR A 12-YEAR-OLD, BUT HE'LL GROW INTO IT WITH TIME.

◆A Second Name

All state alchemists are given a second name by the president. This name takes into account their skills and specializations. Now I have an interesting story to tell. Apparently someone overheard the president deferring to another individual on whether or not to accept someone as a state alchemist and choosing their second name. Who is this other person? If I could find that out then I might have something that I could use against the president. I'm going to investigate it.

Memo

Presently known state alchemists

Fullmetal Alchemist	Edward Elric
Flame Alchemist	Roy Mustang
Strong Arm Alchemist	Alex Louis Armstrong
Sewing-Life Alchemist	Shou Tucker
Iron Blooded Alchemist	Basque Grand

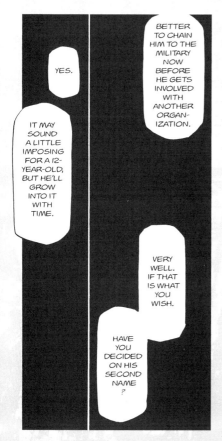

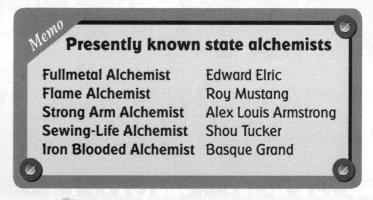

Point Six

Civilization and Culture

This last lecture will focus on the world that Ed and his friends live in, from a cultural perspective.

The Lifestyle of the People

◆Food and Common Items

You want to know about what kind of things we eat? The same as everyone else really. Meat, fish, fruits, vegetables, and bread. We eat as much bread as we want from the pile of bread that is placed in the middle of the table. Rice? That's the staple food from the island country in the east right? We don't really eat that. Now that I think about it, even though Ed hates milk, he loves stew, which has milk in it. What a weirdo huh?

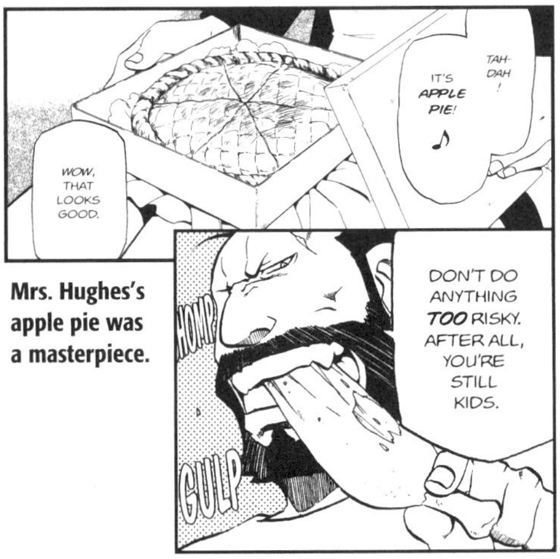
TAH-DAH!
IT'S APPLE PIE! ♪
WOW, THAT LOOKS GOOD.
DON'T DO ANYTHING TOO RISKY. AFTER ALL, YOU'RE STILL KIDS.
CHOMP
GULP

Mrs. Hughes's apple pie was a masterpiece.

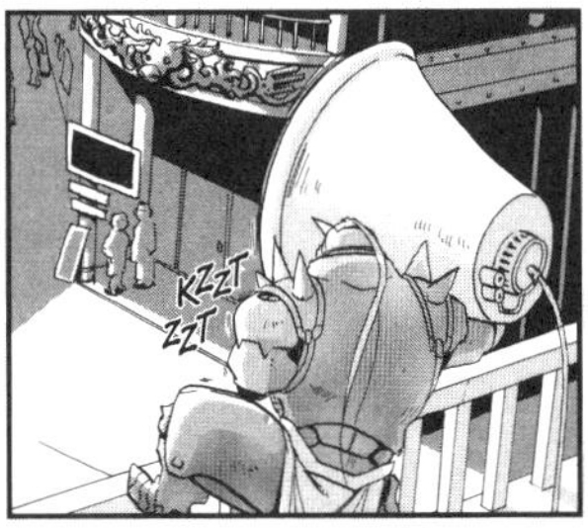
KZZT
ZZT

Speaker

This is a speaker. You can amplify your own voice through a microphone. It seems like a lot of fun. I bet it would feel great to use it to sing a song.

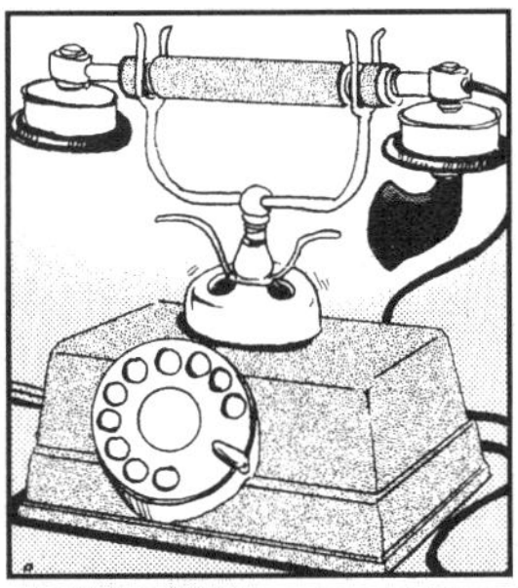

Phone

This is our house phone. Isn't it nice? Rotary phones are standard. In the city they even have payphones.

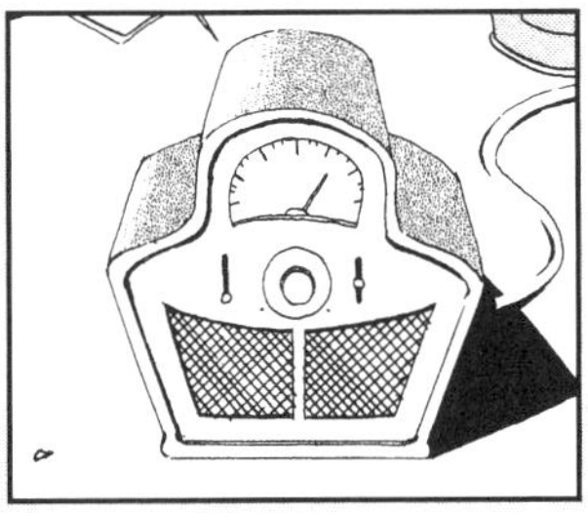

Radio

The radio is one form of entertainment. But there still aren't very many stations yet. It's used mainly for listening to special announcements.

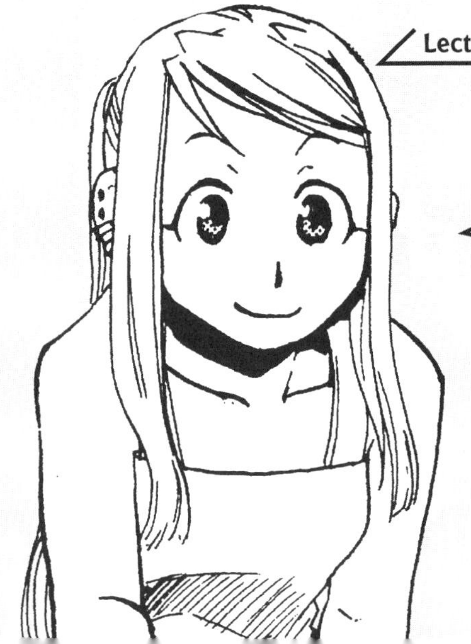

Lecturer Winry Rockbell

Why do I have to talk about our daily lives? Wait, I can talk about auto-mail too? Then leave it to me!

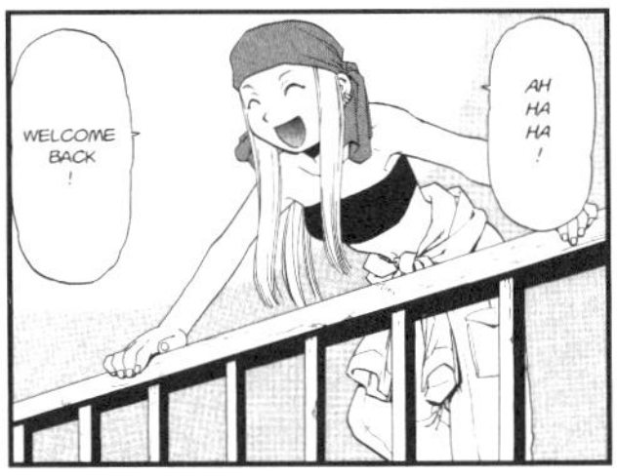
AH HA HA!
WELCOME BACK!

I welcome them back with a smile. But Ed only comes back when he needs to get his auto-mail repaired.

200 THOU-SAND !
SLAM

◆Currency=Sens

The currency that we use is called *sens*. At Izumi's shop, it's 128 *sens* for 100 grams of pork loin and 200 *sens* for 100 grams of beef shoulder. It's probably roughly equivalent to the value of yen in your world. Auto-mail costs anywhere from 100 thousand *sens* to a few million *sens*.

The rate for two people to spend one night at this inn is 200,000 *sens*? That's beyond ridiculous!

◆Means of Transportation

The main modes of transportation in this country are trains, cars and horse drawn carriages. Trains are basically for long distance trips. I've ridden on one a few times myself, but it's not a very comfortable way to travel. It made my butt hurt so much that I could hardly stand it. Cars are used mainly for getting around in the city, and in the countryside carriages are the most common. By the way, vehicles for air travel haven't been invented yet. But I think they're conducting tests of the technology.

HE GOT HIS STATE ALCHEMIST'S CERTIFICATION TWO YEARS AGO WHEN HE CREATED A CHIMERA THAT COULD SPEAK.

Not very many people own automobiles yet. You hardly ever see any in the countryside. It's too bad, because they look so cool.

13.
12.

I don't see how Ed can always travel around on such uncomfortable things. In a way I sort of admire him. But on the other hand, maybe he's just not that delicate...

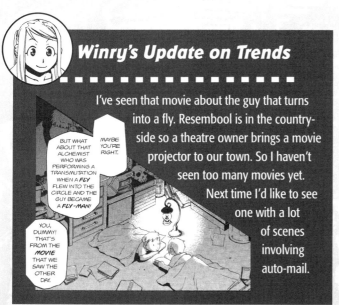

Winry's Update on Trends

I've seen that movie about the guy that turns into a fly. Resembool is in the country-side so a theatre owner brings a movie projector to our town. So I haven't seen too many movies yet. Next time I'd like to see one with a lot of scenes involving auto-mail.

MAYBE YOU'RE RIGHT.
BUT WHAT ABOUT THAT ALCHEMIST WHO WAS PERFORMING A TRANSMUTATION WHEN A *FLY* FLEW INTO THE CIRCLE AND THE GUY BECAME A *FLY-MAN!*
YOU, DUMMY! THAT'S FROM THE *MOVIE* THAT WE SAW THE OTHER DAY.

Whoever invented stew was brilliant! It has milk in it and it still tastes that good! (Ed)

Who hates milk.

Artificial Limbs (Auto-mail)

◆Auto-mail: Recent Development

Auto-mail is the result of recent developments in engineering. Think of it as electrically powered artificial limbs. (They utilize the electricity created by the movement of muscles.) Thirteen years ago when the Ishbalan Civil War began, many people were severely injured, and as a result, auto-mail technology began to develop rapidly. Auto-mail as we know it today was developed during that time. I lost both my parents during that civil war, but at the same time it increased the demand for auto-mail, so my feelings are kind of divided about it.

THE SMELL OF OIL, THE CREAKING OF ARTIFICIAL MUSCLES, THE WHIRRING OF BEARINGS...
...AND THE BEAUTIFUL FORM BASED ON THE PRINCIPLES OF BIOPHYSICAL RESEARCH!
OH MY... HOW WONDERFUL AUTO-MAIL PROSTHETICS ARE!!

I can't express the allure of auto-mail in words. Oh gosh, just thinking about it makes me…

KREEK

Ed's right arm (front view)

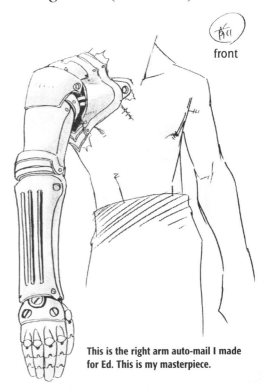

front

This is the right arm auto-mail I made for Ed. This is my masterpiece.

Ed's right arm (rear view)

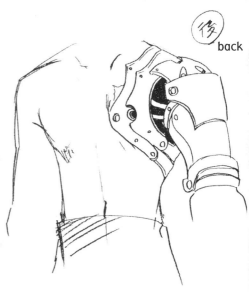

back

At Rush Valley they told me this was a rare style of auto-mail. The style of auto-mail varies quite a bit from region to region.

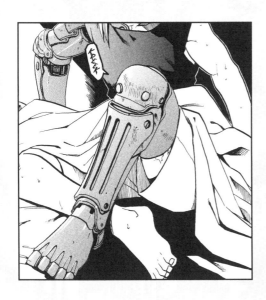

Ed's right arm (movable parts)

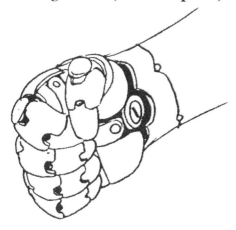

The great thing about auto-mail is that unlike regular artificial limbs, you can move it by your own will. Not only that, but it can perform movements that aren't possible with the normal human body. Isn't it wonderful?

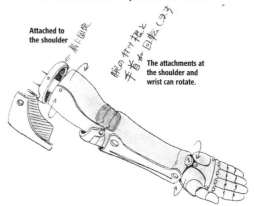

Attached to the shoulder

The attachments at the shoulder and wrist can rotate.

◆The Engineer's Job

An auto-mail engineer needs more than just knowledge of auto-mail. After all, auto-mail is a part of someone's body, right? That's why it's necessary to have some medical knowledge too. Usually it's enough to perform periodic maintenance adjustments, but in Ed's case, he always manages to go somewhere and come back with his auto-mail all broken down. Geez.

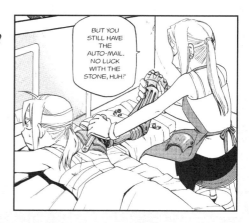

BUT YOU STILL HAVE THE AUTO-MAIL. NO LUCK WITH THE STONE, HUH?

ARE YOU SURE YOU'RE NOT GOING TO REGRET THIS?

YES. I'VE MADE UP MY MIND.

When Ed made the decision to get the auto-mail surgery, I'd swore I'd always be there to help him. I feel the same way now, and I'll always feel that way.

◆A Bit More About Auto-mail

I think that what I just explained to you should help you understand about auto-mail for the most part. If I were to add one more thing, it would be about the relationship between auto-mail and water. Auto-mail is very heavy, so it's impossible to swim when you're wearing it. That's why you have to be careful when around a large body of water. But they are waterproof, so showers and baths are no problem. However, maintenance is very important.

Dominic's Opinion?

Auto-mail and height

The reason Ed is still small might be because his auto-mail is too heavy for his size. It's not good to put a burden on the auto-mail wearer. A craftsman needs to follow that one rule. Maybe if you improve your skill, little girl, and build him lighter auto-mail, he might grow a little taller.

IT'S POSSIBLE.

◆The Auto-mail Engineers of the World

Now that auto-mail has become so widespread, of course there're going to be some engineers that are better than others. There are a few engineers that I really respect. First of all there's Granny Pinako. I might be biased because we're family, but I think she's got a lot of skill. Also Dominic Lecourt from Rush Valley, and Mr. Garfiel to whom I'm apprenticed. They are my idols.

I'LL HAVE IT FOR YOU IN THREE DAYS.
PHOOO

HELLO? ROCKBELL AUTO-MAIL SHOP.
HEY, WINRY? IT'S ME.

Granny Pinako was my first teacher. She taught me a lot of things at home.

IT'S THE 11TH GENERATION MODEL FROM GODS STUDIO!!
I NEVER THOUGHT THERE'D COME THE DAY WHEN I'D SEE IT WITH MY OWN EYES!! ♡

I love the auto-mail from Gods Studio. One day I'd like to build an auto-mail that could compete with theirs.

INTERNAL AUTO-MAIL CARBINES...
...ARE THE CULMINATION OF MY LIFE-LONG DREAM.

Ed's left leg (connection)

①
②
ちょい押し下げでジョイント

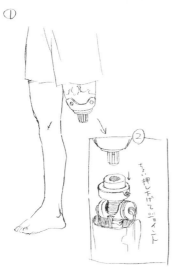

Presses down a bit to connect

Ed's left leg (main)

This is what the inside of the auto-mail looks like. It looks a little shabby with the wires in plain view.

← 緩衝

Shock absorber

...!!

This one was made by Dominic. Not only is it light and agile, but it also has a weapon hidden in it. I was really surprised.

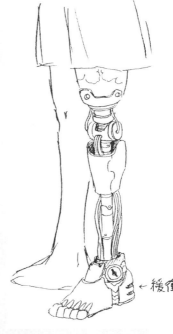

◆Rehabilitation

Auto-mail is much more durable and useful than the artificial limbs that were available before. But the surgery and the rehabilitation process of learning to use auto-mail are very difficult. The pain is so great that it's enough to make a grown man cry. It's amazing that Ed was able to go through such pain while he was still a child.

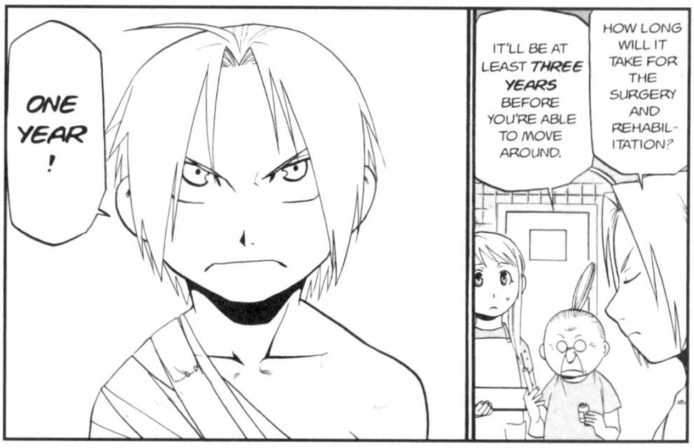

HOW LONG WILL IT TAKE FOR THE SURGERY AND REHABIL-ITATION?
IT'LL BE AT LEAST THREE YEARS BEFORE YOU'RE ABLE TO MOVE AROUND.
ONE YEAR!

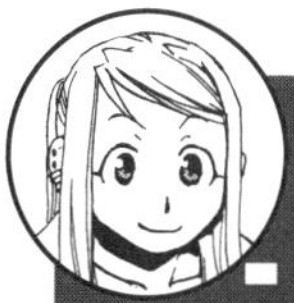

It's news to Winry too.

Pinako's glamorous past

Granny Pinako used to be called the "Pantheress of Resembool" when she was younger. Pantheress. Can you believe it? Not only that but I also heard that she used to pick on Mr. Lecourt who always puts up such a tough front… I know she's kind of strict in some ways, but I have a hard time imagining that. I'm gonna ask her about it when I get home.

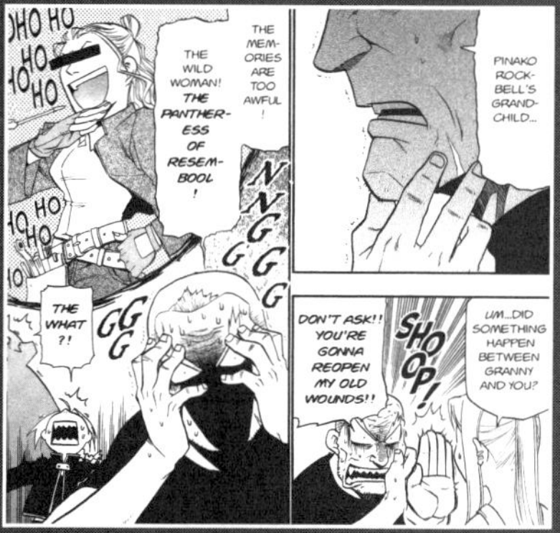

PINAKO ROCK-BELL'S GRAND-CHILD...
UM...DID SOMETHING HAPPEN BETWEEN GRANNY AND YOU?
SHOOP!
DON'T ASK!! YOU'RE GONNA REOPEN MY OLD WOUNDS!!
THE MEM-ORIES ARE TOO AWFUL!
THE WILD WOMAN! THE PANTHER-ESS OF RESEM-BOOL!
HO HO HO HO
NNGGGG
GGG
HO HO HO HO
THE WHAT?!

Ed's left leg (bottom of foot)

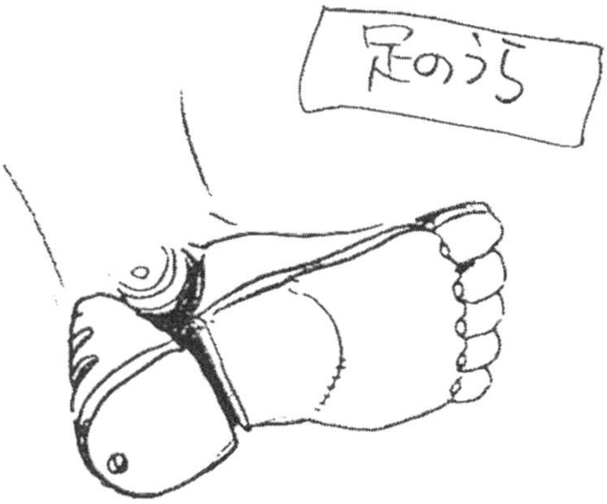

足のうら

The bottom of the foot looks very similar to that of a human foot. The shape of the foot is ideal for absorbing shock.

I've decided to keep helping you until you get your former body back! (Winry)

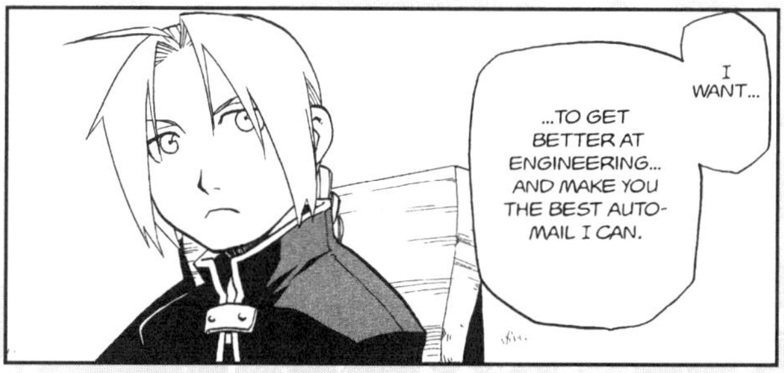

I WANT...
...TO GET BETTER AT ENGINEERING... AND MAKE YOU THE BEST AUTO-MAIL I CAN.

One on One

Exclusive Interview With Hiromu Arakawa

Arakawa-sensei leads a busy life but was kind enough to sit down with us to answer a few questions about her work and her life.

How did you come to be a manga artist?

Arakawa: When I was a kid I doodled on everything near me...advertisements, my textbooks. I kept that up till the artist thing just happened.

Like drawing a moustache on self-portraits in history textbooks? *(chuckle)* Did you do any other job before becoming a comics professional?

Arakawa: My family runs a dairy farm in Hokkaido so I used to work for them. For seven years I took care of cows and cultivated the fields.

Is that why your self-portrait is a cow?

Arakawa: Yes, and because I think I look a little like a cartoon cow, so it fits.

In other words you were born with your destiny tied to cows. So, of course you must love cows?

Arakawa: Of course. I love to take care of them and also eat them.

Which do you prefer, Japanese food or Western food? Which dish is your favorite?

Arakawa: Japanese! And my favorite food is ramen![1] Hokkaido's ramen is really good.

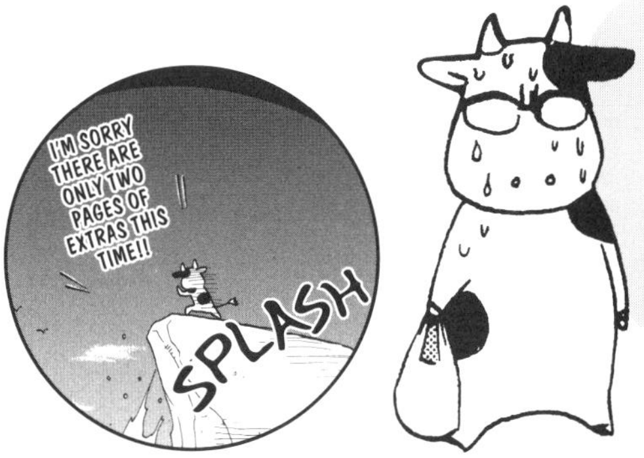
I'M SORRY THERE ARE ONLY TWO PAGES OF EXTRAS THIS TIME!!
SPLASH

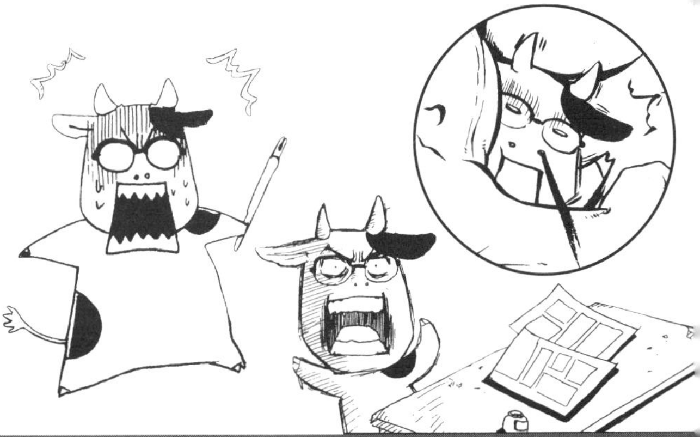

1:
Ramen: She especially likes miso ramen, as you'll see later on.

2:
***Star Wars*: The famous six part space opera that depicts a war between an evil empire and the rebel army.**

The ramen from Sapporo and Asahikawa is quite famous, isn't it? Do you have other hobbies or interests?

Arakawa: I like to watch movies. Also I like to go to antique flea markets and buy all kinds of strange things.

Which movies?

Arakawa: I like the *Star Wars*② series and the *Indiana Jones series*. Darth Vader is the greatest villain of all time and Sean Connery③ is the greatest old man.

Would you say any other manga artists have influenced you?

Arakawa: The manga artist that I look up to the most is Suiho Tagawa, the author of *Norakuro*.④ He is the root of my style as an artist. I also love Rumiko Takahashi⑤ and *Kinnikuman* or *Ultimate Muscle*⑥ by Yudetamago. As far as composition and how to draw, I learned that when I was apprenticed to Hiroyuki Eto, the author of *Mahoujin Guru Guru*⑦ for *Shonen Gangan*.

An unusual combination. So you combined *Norakuro* and *Mahoujin Guru Guru* to get the inspiration for the world of *Fullmetal Alchemist*?

Arakawa: Well, first I came up with the Philosopher's Stone. I don't remember how I got the ideas for the plot, but it came to me while I was working on something else. Then I did some research on the Philosopher's Stone and ended up reading about alchemy. I was fascinated, and that, in turn, became the framework for the whole manga.

So was it easy researching something as obscure as alchemy?

Arakawa: No! It was difficult because the descriptions and interpretations differed from author to author. I wish they could just unify their findings. *(sob)*

Too bad there's no book entitled *Everything You Ever Wanted to Know About Alchemy!* But the research is over. Now you create. What's your most and least favorite part about creating Fullmetal Alchemist?

3:
In *Indiana Jones and the Last Crusade,* the third in the trilogy, Sean Connery plays the role of Indiana Jones's father in an inspired performance.

4:
Black Stray Dog: A classic children's manga from the 1930s. A military story starring anthropomorphic animals.

5:
Rumiko Takahashi: The extremely successful female manga artist who authored such hits as *Lum*Urusei Yatsura, Ranma 1/2* and *Inuyasha.*

6:
Kinnikuman/ Ultimate Muscle: A classic comedy-action shonen manga. *Ultimate Muscle* is the sequel to the original 1970s series.

7:
Magic Circle Spin-Spin: A comedy manga parodying fantasy role-playing games.

Arakawa: My favorite task is inking[8] the characters. It's fun to see the characters taking shape. On the other hand, my least favorite task is the storyboard stage,[9] drawing out the panels and writing the dialogue.

What time period is your work based on?
Arakawa: I based it on the industrial sectors of England during the industrial revolution.[10] It's a city with rows of factories wrapped in smoke, smog and steam. But I've given it my own original flavor and made it into a fantasy world.

Your train stations definitely have a feeling of old-time Europe to them. Okay, moving on to the next question. Who's your favorite character?
Arakawa: Favorite character?! I really can't decide. If I had to force myself to pick they would be Ed, Al, Winry and Lt. Hawkeye. But the characters that are easiest to draw are Major Armstrong, animals and the mobs.[11] *(chuckle)*

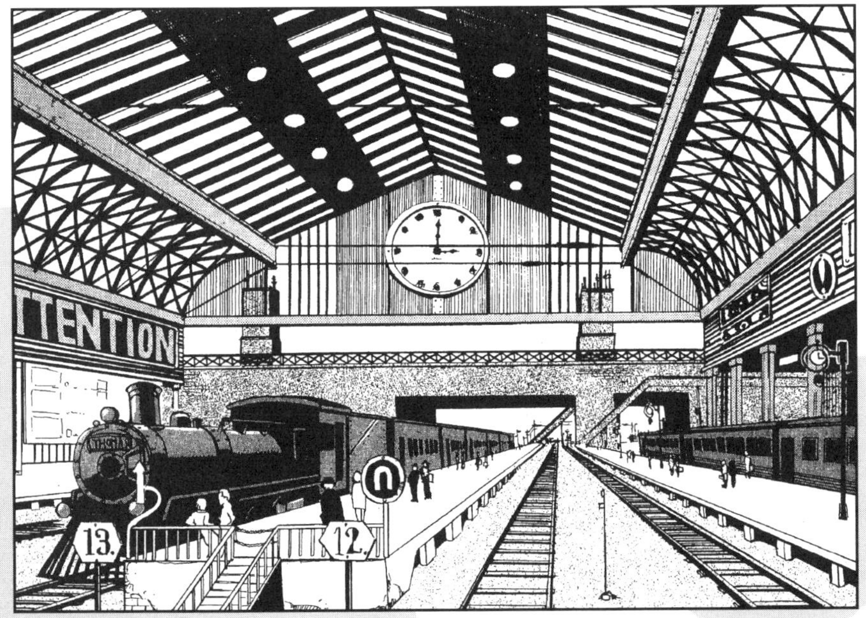
TTENTION
13.
12.

8:
Inking: The process in which the lines of the underlying sketch are drawn over with ink in order to create the final drawing. To learn more about the process of drawing comics refer to pg. 111.

9:
Storyboard stage: A stage of the comic book creation process in which the panel layout is sketched out and the dialogue is written. Known in Japan as the Name Stage.

10:
Industrial revolution: The transformation from tools to machines that occurred in the second half of 18th century England. This caused various changes in the country's economy, industry and society.

11:
Mobs: When there are many people gathered in one spot. The crosswalk at Tokyo's Shibuya Station is always like that.

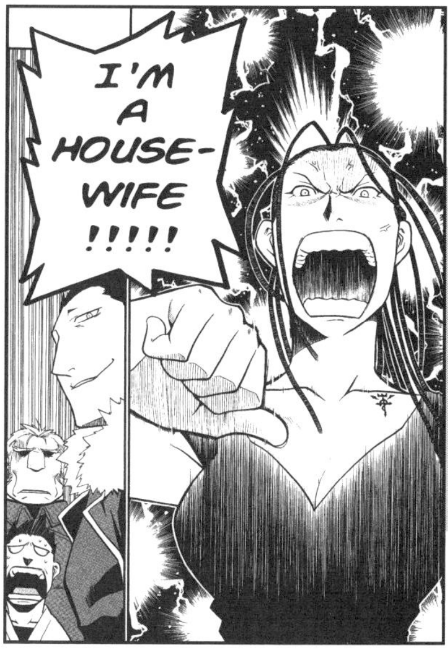
I'M A HOUSE-WIFE !!!!!

Armstrong must be fun to draw. So you draw animals quite a bit. Do you like any other animals besides cows?
Arakawa: I like dogs. I guess that's why there are quite a few in the story: Den, Alexander and Black Hayate.

If you had to choose a favorite episode, which one would it be?
Arakawa: It would be the side story "Dog of the Military."[12] It was really easy to draw. From a recent episode, I would have to say volume 7, the end of chapter 27.[13] The interaction of "Who the hell are you!?" "I'm a housewife!!!!!" That's a scene that I wanted to do for a long time.

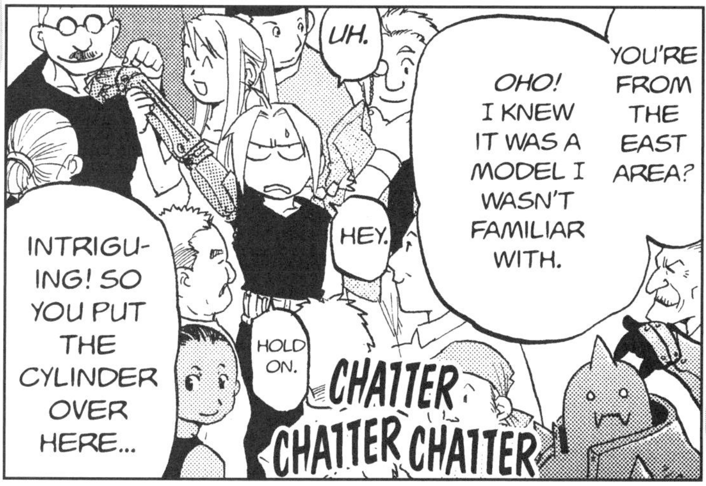
YOU'RE FROM THE EAST AREA?
OHO! I KNEW IT WAS A MODEL I WASN'T FAMILIAR WITH.
UH.
HEY.
HOLD ON.
INTRIGU-ING! SO YOU PUT THE CYLINDER OVER HERE...
CHATTER CHATTER CHATTER

I liked that a lot. That's the scene that makes you say, "That's Izumi!" Speaking of compelling scenes, I'm sure there was quite a strong reaction from everyone when Lt. Col. Hughes died. What do you remember from working on that episode?
Arakawa: Every month, before we start work on the comic, I have the assistants read the dialogue in the

12:
"Dog of the Military": An extra story included in the last part of volume 4. The story depicts the experiences of a stray puppy at East H.Q.

13:
The end of chapter 27: The encounter between Greed and Izumi.

rough draft so that they can get an idea of how the story is going to flow. This was the one where everyone who read it cried, "Ohhhhh!!!" I had to apologize profusely.

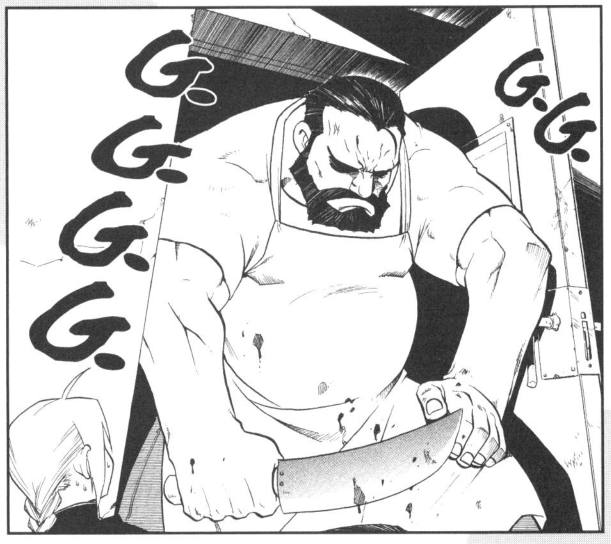
G.G.G.
G. G. G. G.

We've assembled a special collection of your illustrations in this book.[14] You seem to put a lot of effort into even the illustration on the back of the cover and the bonus manga at the end of the volume. Where do you get your ideas?

Arakawa: They come out of nowhere, really. Sometimes I just think of new things while working on the original book, and then reading all of it over again, I noticed that a lot of it is about Colonel Mustang. Maybe he's a character that's easy to mess with?

Out of all the characters, who is modeled after you the most?

Arakawa: Well, since all of the characters came from me, there must be a part of each of them that resembles me in some way...For instance, my assistant Yuzuka tells me that I resemble Ed. And my other assistant Takaeda tells me that I resemble Izumi. But I'm not that hot-headed!!! *(flustered)*

So between those two, if you lived in your own manga world, what would you be like?

Arakawa: I'd follow three simple rules:
-Never go within 2KM of circus freaks.[15]
-Never go near the butcher shop in Dublith.
-Always spend under 300 sens on snacks.[16]
That ought to keep me alive! *(chuckle)*

14:
Arakawa-sensei wishes that all 180 pages of this book could be new comics!

15:
Circus freaks: A less formal name for alchemists. Lieutenant Colonel Hughes holds the honor of coining the phrase.

16:
***Always spend under 300 sens on snacks, Bananas aren't snacks,* and countless other wise sayings were invented as rules for elementary school field trips.**

Well then, for good or for ill, if you could become a circus freak, or alchemist, what sort of powers would you have?

Arakawa: I would use ink and paper to transmute manga pages. There might be problems with some of the details though. (heh)

Your code name might be "The G Pen Alchemist"?[17] So with those alchemy skills, what other manga genres would you like to do?

Arakawa: High school martial arts romantic comedy!

That's quite a genre *(chuckle).* That would be interesting to see and maybe a bit scary too… Now I'd like to start wrapping things up. Could you give a little hint as to what we can expect in the upcoming episodes?

Arakawa: When the Elric brothers' father, Hohenheim, finally makes an appearance, things are going to start happening very quickly… I think everyone is going to be very surprised when they find out who he really is.

I'll be looking forward to that. So is there any specific message you're trying to get through to fans with *Fullmetal Alchemist*?

Arakawa: Nothing in particular. If 100 people read it there are going to be 100 different interpretations, so I think whatever each person gets out of reading the comic is the message. The Elric brothers grit their teeth every day trying to get back their original bodies but I hope the readers don't dwell too much on the painful things and just enjoy the story. If people think it's cool, that's enough for me!

Okay, what would you like to say to your fans today?

Arakawa: Love!!

17:
G Pen: A popular type of Japanese pen that allows the manga artist to change line width by varying the pressure on the pen.

Trivia Info You Can't Live Without!

❶ Whose mythical fate does Ed compare his punishment to?

The Greek mythological character Icarus, who made wings out of wax but flew too close to the sun, melting his wings and sending him plummeting back to earth. Ed feels like he too was burned by flying too close to the sun.

WELL... IT'S LIKE THAT MYTH ABOUT THE HERO...
HE MADE WINGS OUT OF WAX SO HE COULD FLY... BUT WHEN HE GOT TOO CLOSE TO THE SUN... TO GOD... THE WAX MELTED AND HE CRASHED TO THE GROUND...

❷ Is Den stronger than Ed?

URR

Who knows… but her left leg is auto-mail. And she is an excellent body-guard for the family.

HE'S GOT AN EXCELLENT BODY-GUARD.
TUP TUP TUP TUP TUP

MAY I HAVE THE CODE, PLEASE ?
@#$%! ARE YOU SERIOUS !!?
UNCLE-SUGAR-OLIVER-EIGHT-ZERO-ZERO!

❸ What's the secret in the secret phone code?

Hughes uses a secret code when he calls Eastern H.Q. from an outside line. When the first letter of each word on the right is lined up it spells USO800! That means uso happyaku, or "lie" in Japanese.

❹ Izumi loves ramen?

When Ed forgets about his assessment date, Izumi grabs the phone in an attempt to make Ed finally quit being the military's dog. But she accidentally calls the Ramen House. She must love ramen if the first number she dials without thinking is for a take-out joint!

I'VE BEEN MEANING TO GO TO HEAD-QUARTERS, ANYWAY.
RAMEN HOUSE, HELLO?

Enlarged diagram.

BEHIND THE SCENES

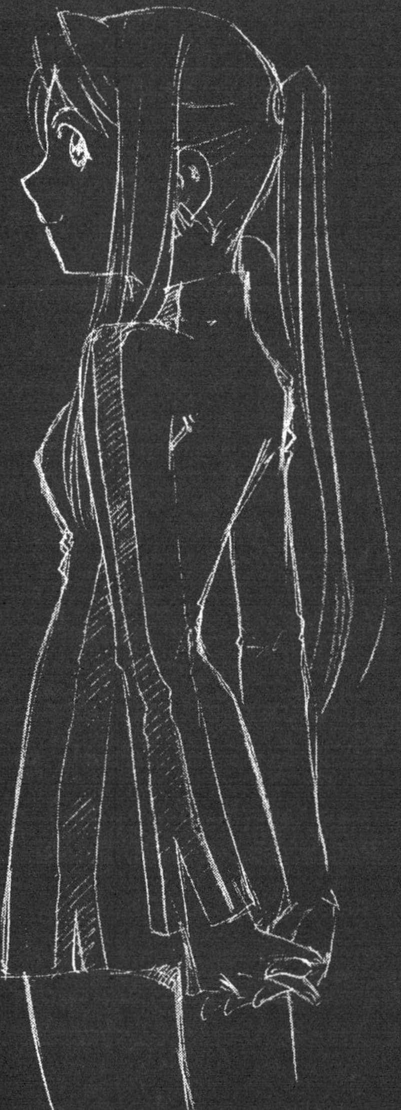

FULLMETAL ALCHEMIST

A VISIT TO THE COWSHED

Inside the Studio

A sneak peek at Arakawa-sensei's workplace, where *Fullmetal Alchemist* comes to life!

Workroom

This is truly where *Fullmetal Alchemist* is born. Besides Arakawa-sensei and the assistants' desks, this is the room that contains the vast reference library. When things get really busy, it's pretty crazy in here.

Is that Arakawa-sensei at her desk working? Why, Arakawa-sensei looks exactly like her self-portrait!

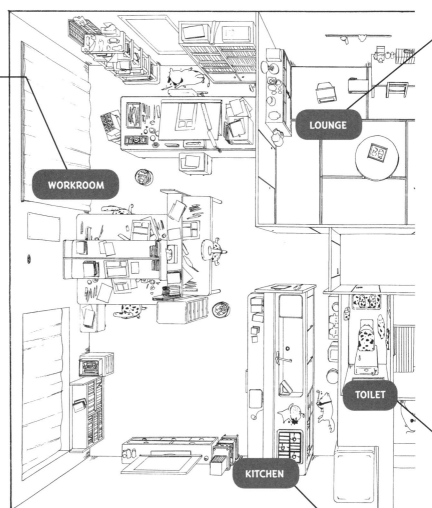

LOUNGE

WORKROOM

TOILET

KITCHEN

Mysterious Bodies

Why are all the animals, really self-portraits of all the artists, throwing up? Maybe because deadlines are coming up?

Kitchen

A clean and spacious kitchen. Everyone takes turns cooking. It's the source of power for *Fullmetal Alchemist*.

Diagram of the Cowshed

Lounge

Tatami, small table, and green tea are all ready to go in this Japanese-style room ideal for thinking and creating new stories.

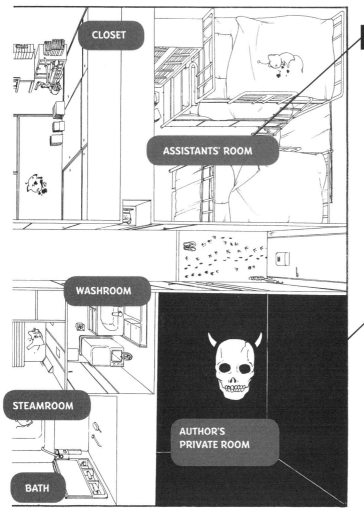

CLOSET

ASSISTANTS' ROOM

WASHROOM

STEAMROOM

BATH

AUTHOR'S PRIVATE ROOM

Assistants' Room

A manga artist's work is very hard. Sometimes they end up sleeping over to give me extra help.

The Author's Private Room

Arakawa-sensei's private room. Sometimes cries of "moo moo moo" can be heard, or could that be just a rumor?

Toilet

It's decorated in a way that's fit for the name "cowshed." This is where all the four-panel manga are born...

THINGS WE FOUND AT THE COWSHED

A few items really caught our eye at Arakawa-Sensei's house. They represented the cowshed theme so well that we just had to take a photo so you could see what we mean!

The rumors are true

Not only the toilet seat but everything in the bathroom is cowhide patterned! Arakawa-sensei loves cows.

We discovered the rough sketch for a relay manga, where one artist starts a few panels and then another picks up where they left off, then another artist keeps going and so on, and so on.

They're just for... reference...right?

These weapons are for reference. Is the one on the right Lieutenant Hawkeye's favorite gun?

Ed captured!

The iron array!!

Arakawa-sensei works out with these. They weigh 8kg (about 17 1/2 lbs) each!

ガンコな肉屋の主よ!!
見よ!! 国家錬金術師のすばらしさ!!
その瞳にとくと刻むがよい!!!

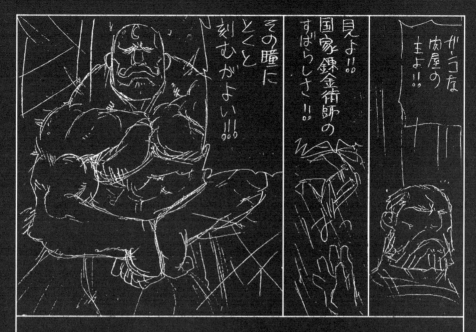

Creating
FULLMETAL ALCHEMIST
Learn step-by-step how comics come to life

等価交換で。
そう!
おまえらも人造人間に興味があるって言うじゃねえか
いい取引きだろうて。

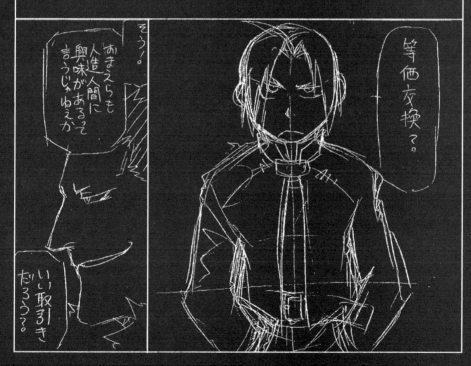

~ Storyboards ~

Page 1

This is where the real work begins. In the storyboard, or Japanese "name" stage, the basic drawings and the characters' dialogue are put in. There's still a long ways to go before it's finished!

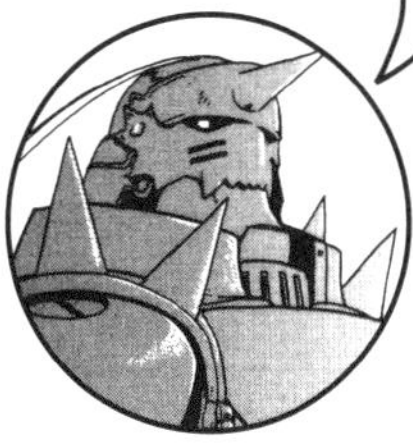

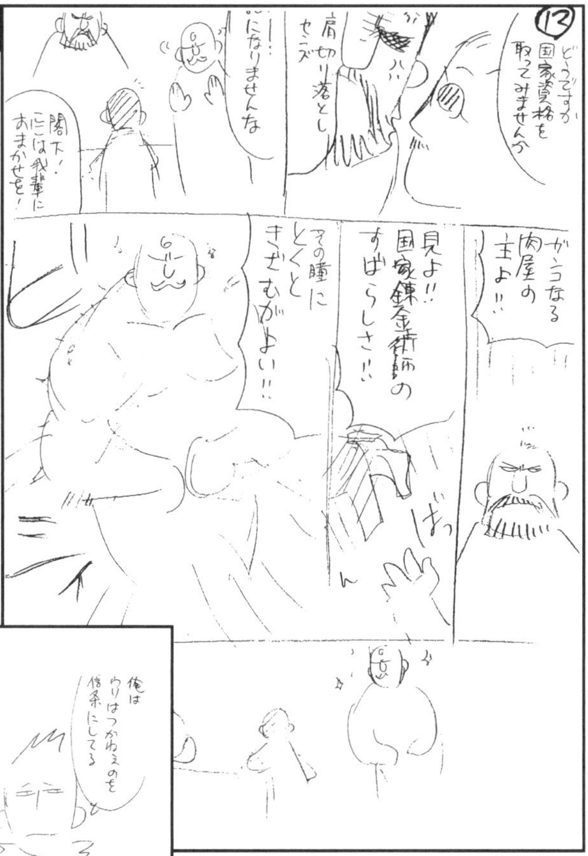

どうですか 国家資格を取ってみませんか
閣下！ここは我輩におまかせを！
ガラなる肉屋の主よ!!
見よ!! 国家錬金術師のすばらしさ!!
その瞳にとくときざむがよい!!
ばっ

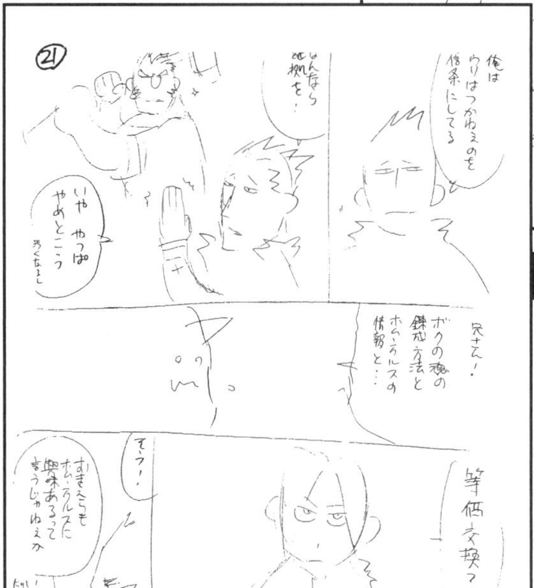

俺はウソはつかねえのを信条にしてる
いや やっぱ やめとこう
兄さん！ ボクの魂の錬成方法とホムンクルスの情報と…
等価交換？
そう！
おまえらもホムンクルスに興味あるって言うじゃねえか
いい取引きだろう？

Page 2

The above panels show Major Armstrong and the president when they arrived at Dublith with Ed. It also shows the muscle contest between Sig and the Major. Pretty crazy, eh?

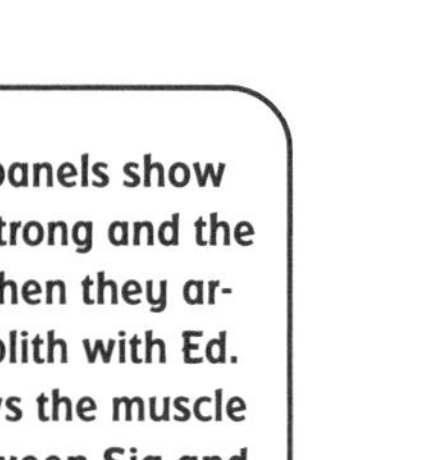

~ Pencils ~

Page 1

どうですか 国家資格を 取ってみませんか
牛豚合びき 98センズ!!
ふー… 話になりませんな
閣下! ここは我輩に おまかせを!
ガンコな肉屋の主よ!!
見よ!! 国家錬金術師のすばらしさ!!
その瞳にとくと刻むがよい!!!

Even at this early stage, you can start to see background details take shape. Character detail is tightened up. And the size of the word font inside the balloons is finalized. We're almost done!

Page 2

俺はウソはつかねえのを信条にしてる
なんなら証拠を…
いや やっぱやめとこう
兄さん
ボクの魂の錬成方法と人造人間の情報と…
等価交換?
そう! おまえらも人造人間に興味があるって言うじゃねえか
いい取引きだろう?

This is where Ed comes to rescue Al and ends up face-to-face with Greed. Do you remember Ed's response to Greed's villainous proposition?

~ Inks ~

Page 1

どうですか 国家資格を 取って みませんか
牛豚合びき 98センズ!!
ふー… 話になりませんな
閣下! ここは我輩に おまかせを!
ガンコな 肉屋の 主よ!!
見よ!! 国家錬金術師の すばらしさ!!
その瞳に とくと 刻むがよい!!!
ばっ
……

This is what it looks like after inking. The characters' expressions are clearer now. And the word balloons are finished. Darling, you look really handsome!

俺はウソを つかねぇのを 信条にしてる
なんなら 証拠を…
いや やっぱ やめとこう
兄さん
ボクの魂の 錬成方法と 人造人間の 情報と…
等価交換?
そう! おまえらも 人造人間に 興味があるって 言うじゃねえか
いい取り引き だろう?

Page 2

I have to say, on page 1, I was quite taken with the spectacle of two fine specimens of humanity engaged in a muscle contest. A well-toned physique will indeed save the world someday, I tell you. Of course, on page 2, I suppose wits are somewhat necessary to add tension to the story...

The Assistants Present...

THE COWSHED DIARIES

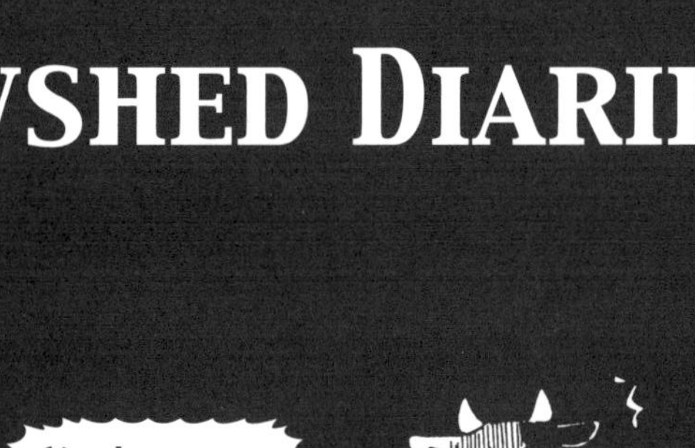

You're gonna *print this?!!*

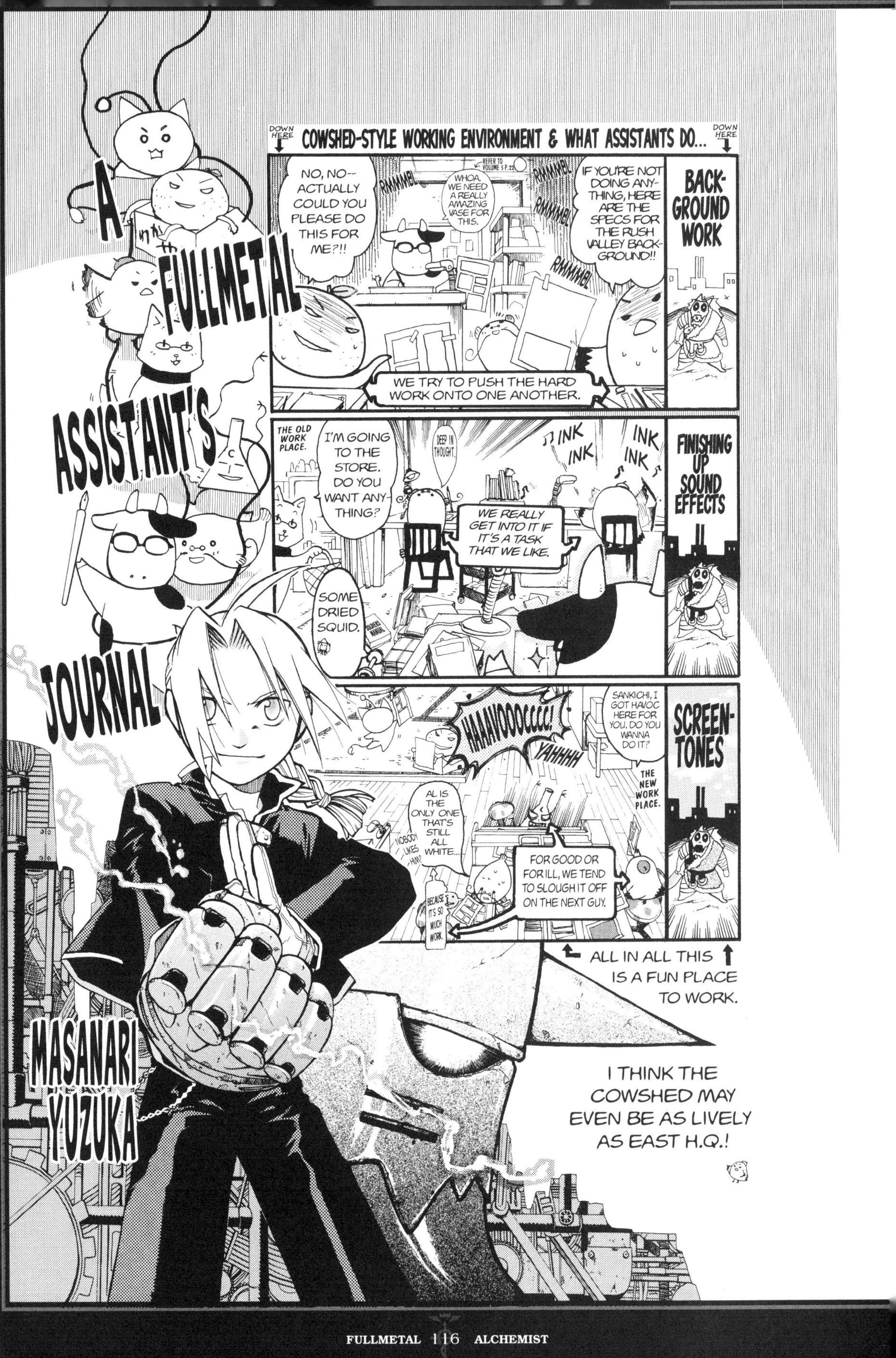
A FULLMETAL ASSISTANT'S JOURNAL
MASANARI YUZUKA
DOWN HERE
COWSHED-STYLE WORKING ENVIRONMENT & WHAT ASSISTANTS DO...
DOWN HERE
BACK-GROUND WORK
IF YOU'RE NOT DOING ANY-THING, HERE ARE THE SPECS FOR THE RUSH VALLEY BACK-GROUND!!
RMMMBL
RMMMBL
RMMMBL
RMMMBL
REFER TO VOLUME 5 P.22
WHOA, WE NEED A REALLY AMAZING VASE FOR THIS.
NO, NO-- ACTUALLY COULD YOU PLEASE DO THIS FOR ME?!!
WE TRY TO PUSH THE HARD WORK ONTO ONE ANOTHER.
FINISHING UP SOUND EFFECTS
INK INK
INK INK
DEEP IN THOUGHT.
I'M GOING TO THE STORE. DO YOU WANT ANY-THING?
THE OLD WORK PLACE.
WE REALLY GET INTO IT IF IT'S A TASK THAT WE LIKE.
SOME DRIED SQUID.
SCREEN-TONES
SANKICHI, I GOT HAVOC HERE FOR YOU. DO YOU WANNA DO IT?
THE NEW WORK PLACE.
HAAAVOOOCCCCC!
YAHHHH
AL IS THE ONLY ONE THAT'S STILL ALL WHITE...
NOBODY LIKES HIM?
FOR GOOD OR FOR ILL, WE TEND TO SLOUGH IT OFF ON THE NEXT GUY.
BECAUSE IT'S SO MUCH WORK.
ALL IN ALL THIS IS A FUN PLACE TO WORK.
I THINK THE COWSHED MAY EVEN BE AS LIVELY AS EAST H.Q.!

Keisui Takaeda's

COWSHED DIARIES

CONGRATULATIONS ON THE *FULLMETAL ALCHEMIST* ANIME!

THE COWSHED IS AN ENJOYABLE WORKPLACE. WHEN A DEADLINE LOOMS, ARAKAWA-SENSEI AND THE ASSISTANTS SECRETE SOME SORT OF STRANGE FLUID FROM THEIR BRAINS, MAKING FOR SOME VERY INTERESTING TALKS. **WE CALL IT THE MANGA BRAIN STATE.**

IF ARAKAWA-SENSEI IS THE PARENT OF THE MANGA, THEN THE ASSISTANTS ARE THE NANNIES.
...LITTLE MASTER HAS GOTTEN SO BIG...!! SOB...
SQUISH
TAKAEDA!! I CAN'T SEE THE TV!!
GRRR
DUM-DA-DUM-DUM
GEEZ, WHAT AN ANNOYING CATFISH!!
TATERS
8kg

THE 0.1 SECOND OFFENSIVE AND DEFENSIVE BATTLE

THERE'S ONE WORD THAT'S FEARED AT A MANGA ARTIST'S WORK-PLACE... THIS IS...!!
WHEN THE BOSS SAYS
OH.
...JUST THAT SIN-GLE WORD!!!
DRAW DRAW DRAW DRAW
NORTH SEA POTATOES
GAAASSSP
WHAT'S WRONG ARAKAWA-SENSEI?!!!
DO WE HAVE TO RE-DO IT?!
WE DON'T HAVE ENOUGH PAGES?!
HOW MANY HOURS TILL THE DEAD-LINE?!
WHAT HAPPENED?!!!
oh NOOOOOO
...I DREW...
EYE-LASHES ON THE COL-ONEL...
PRETTY
WHAAT?!!! SHOW IT TO ME!!!
WOW!
WHAAA
ERASE
NO!! STAY BACK!!!
THE ASSISTANTS ARE QUICK.
BUT ARAKAWA-SENSEI IS EVEN FASTER.

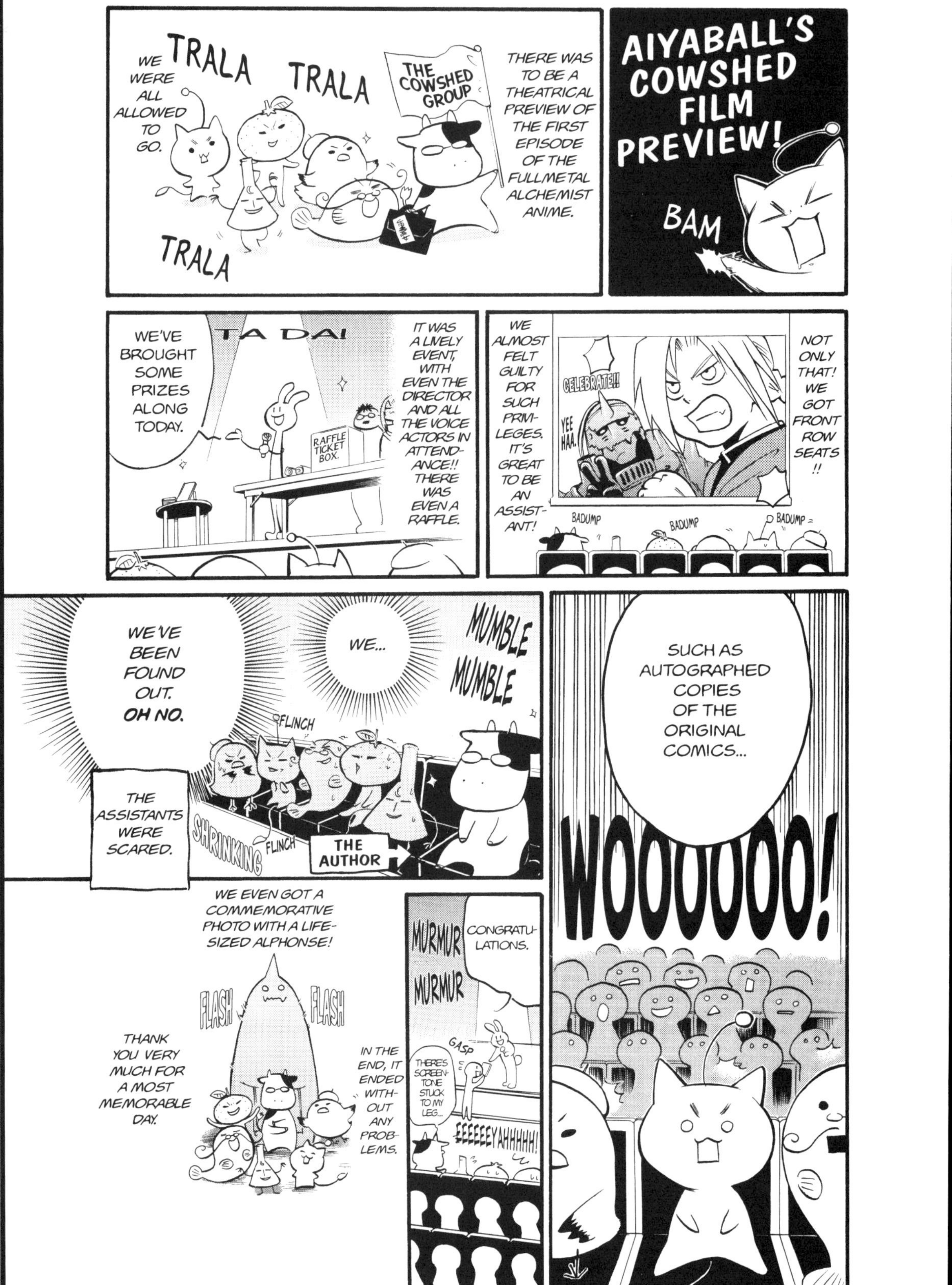
AIYABALL'S COWSHED FILM PREVIEW!
BAM
THERE WAS TO BE A THEATRICAL PREVIEW OF THE FIRST EPISODE OF THE FULLMETAL ALCHEMIST ANIME.
THE COWSHED GROUP
TRALA TRALA
WE WERE ALL ALLOWED TO GO.
TRALA
NOT ONLY THAT! WE GOT FRONT ROW SEATS!!
CELEBRATE!!
YEE HAA.
WE ALMOST FELT GUILTY FOR SUCH PRIVILEGES. IT'S GREAT TO BE AN ASSISTANT!
BADUMP BADUMP BADUMP
IT WAS A LIVELY EVENT, WITH EVEN THE DIRECTOR AND ALL THE VOICE ACTORS IN ATTENDANCE!! THERE WAS EVEN A RAFFLE.
TA DA!
WE'VE BROUGHT SOME PRIZES ALONG TODAY.
RAFFLE TICKET BOX.
SUCH AS AUTOGRAPHED COPIES OF THE ORIGINAL COMICS...
WOOOOOO!
MUMBLE MUMBLE
WE...
WE'VE BEEN FOUND OUT. OH NO.
FLINCH
THE ASSISTANTS WERE SCARED.
SHRINKING
FLINCH
THE AUTHOR
CONGRATULATIONS.
MURMUR MURMUR
GASP
THERE'S SCREENTONE STUCK TO MY LEG...
EEEEEEYAHHHHH!!
WE EVEN GOT A COMMEMORATIVE PHOTO WITH A LIFE-SIZED ALPHONSE!
FLASH FLASH
IN THE END, IT ENDED WITHOUT ANY PROBLEMS.
THANK YOU VERY MUCH FOR A MOST MEMORABLE DAY.

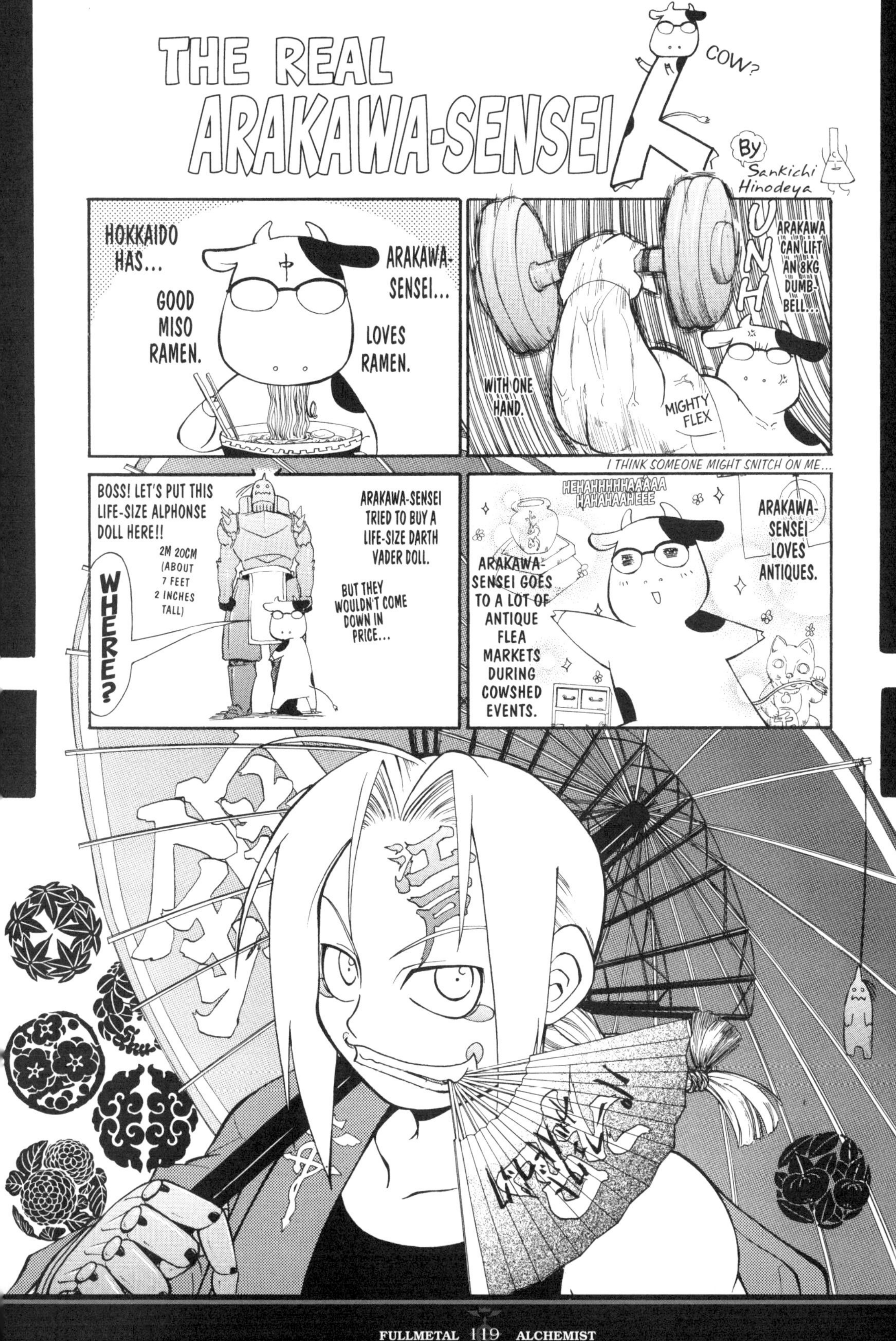
THE REAL ARAKAWA-SENSEI
COW?
By Sankichi Hinodeya
ARAKAWA CAN LIFT AN 8KG DUMBBELL...
UNH
WITH ONE HAND.
MIGHTY FLEX
ARAKAWA-SENSEI...
HOKKAIDO HAS...
LOVES RAMEN.
GOOD MISO RAMEN.
I THINK SOMEONE MIGHT SNITCH ON ME...
ARAKAWA-SENSEI LOVES ANTIQUES.
HEHAHHHHHAAAAA HAHAHAAHEEE
ARAKAWA-SENSEI GOES TO A LOT OF ANTIQUE FLEA MARKETS DURING COWSHED EVENTS.
ARAKAWA-SENSEI TRIED TO BUY A LIFE-SIZE DARTH VADER DOLL.
BOSS! LET'S PUT THIS LIFE-SIZE ALPHONSE DOLL HERE!!
BUT THEY WOULDN'T COME DOWN IN PRICE...
2M 20CM (ABOUT 7 FEET 2 INCHES TALL)
WHERE?

Fullmetal Laboratory Number One

Letters to the Team

The Fullmetal Laboratory Number One is a Q&A corner that's got almost as many fans as the manga itself! We collected some of the best notes here...

I found an ________.

This is what one reader noticed. "In volume 5 page 10 panel 1, there's a photograph stuck on the board that looks like Bald."

AS LONG AS BATTLES KEEP FLARING UP AROUND THIS COUNTRY, THERE WILL ALWAYS BE A DEMAND FOR THE GOODS AND SERVICES THIS CITY OFFERS.
AS MUCH AS I LOVE AUTO-MAIL, I PRAY FOR THE DAY WHEN THIS BUSINESS WON'T BE SO PROSPEROUS.

Hey, that's true. Now that I look closely at it, that looks like the guy who was involved in the train hijacking incident!! So, that auto-mail with the built-in knife was made in Rush Valley, huh? That makes sense.

"In volume 2 page 10, among the files that the colonel is holding, isn't there a file of a certain individual...?"

"CHIMERA: AN ARTIFICIAL FUSION CREATED BY ALCHEMICALLY 'MARRYING' TWO GENETICALLY DISSIMILAR LIFE FORMS."
IN OTHER WORDS, THERE'S A CHIMERA RESEARCHER IN THIS CITY.

That hairstyle that's a little too unique and the moustache... that's got to be Major Armstrong! You guys really have good eyes.

This one says, "On page 100 of volume 1 Mount Fuji is on the map!!"

Let me see here... Mount Fuji... Yeah I guess there is a Mount Fuji in the eastern region! There might even be other locations if you look closer.

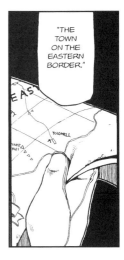

"THE TOWN ON THE EASTERN BORDER."

So Many Questions...

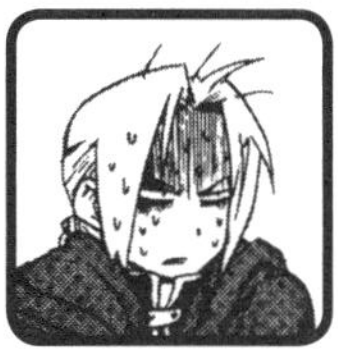

A reader wants to know, "Are there different types of military uniforms?"

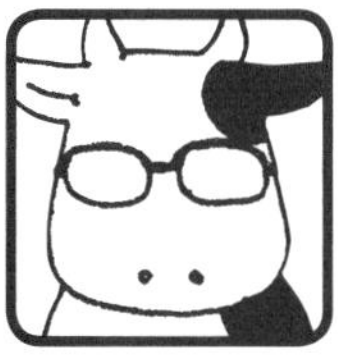

The soldiers' uniforms are blue but the military police have different types depending upon the occasion.

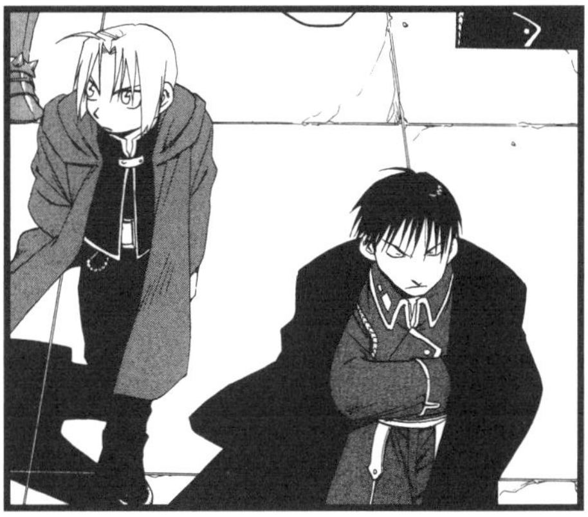

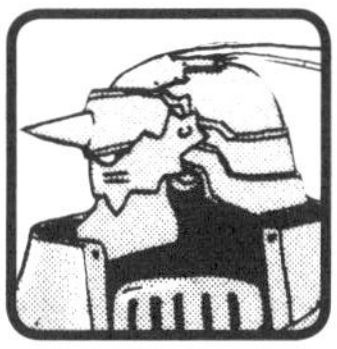

"Dr. Marcoh's research notes are disguised as cooking recipes and the colonel's are disguised as women's names. So what kind of research notes does Major Armstrong have?"

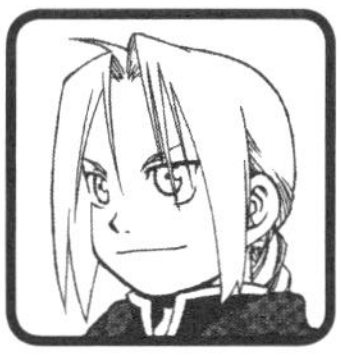

He draws very artistic portraits, so maybe he disguises his research notes as drawings. By the way, mine are written down in the form of a travelogue.

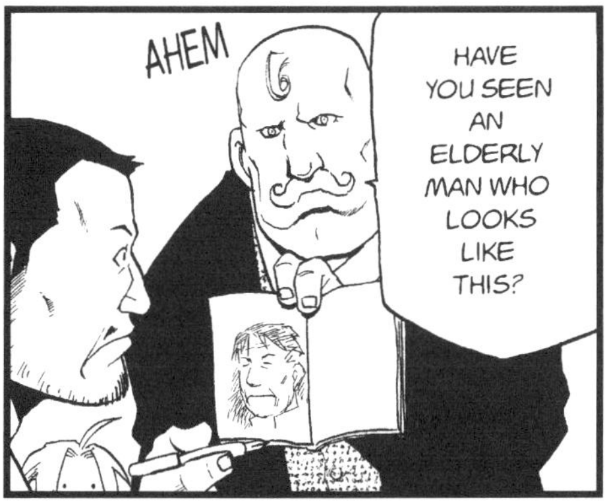
AHEM
HAVE YOU SEEN AN ELDERLY MAN WHO LOOKS LIKE THIS?

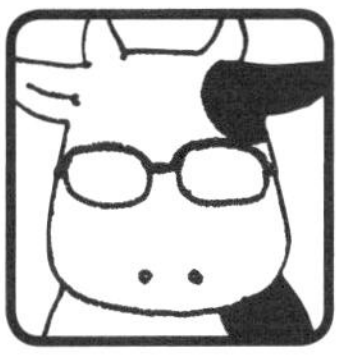

No, no, he uses the "Armstrong style muscle memory technique"!

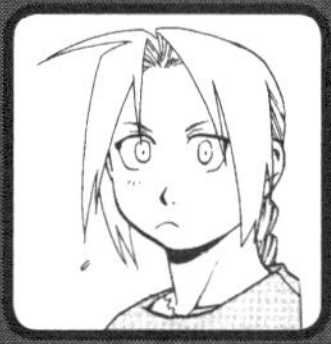

This letter asks... "Do you like dogs, Arakawa-sensei?"

You may have noticed that a lot of dogs and cats make an appearance in *Fullmetal Alchemist*. I love them. Especially shiny black ones! Strong, cool-looking black ones! A black that hides the dirt! The ex-sumo Grand Champion, Chiyonofuji's loincloth was black too. Yup, Chiyonofuji is cool. To me he's the world's ultimate hero. His overhand toss move that seems as though he's picking someone up and over is a work of art...but if I keep going on about Chiyonofuji it's going to be another 1000 pages. So I'm going to leave it at that. Huh? What was the original topic?

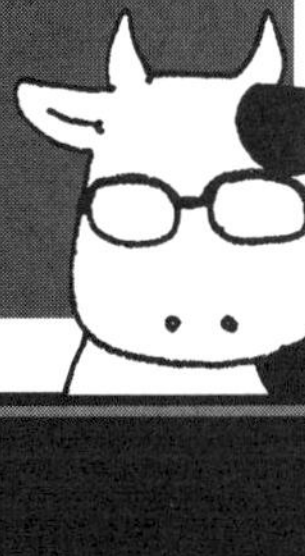

THE MAIN CHARACTER

An Investigation

Ed
Al
Winry
1
2
3

Who appears most?

We counted up all the panels our main characters have been in and came up with three winners. Ed shines brilliantly in the first place spot! The fact that he had almost twice as many appearances as Al in second place shows that it's a lot of work to be the main guy. All panel results are up to Chapter 28.

1st place	Edward Elric	2145 panels
2nd place	Alphonse Elric	1250 panels
3rd place	Winry Rockbell	353 panels
4th place	Izumi Curtis	283 panels
5th place	Roy Mustang	246 panels
6th place	Alex Louis Armstrong	229 panels
7th place	Scar	188 panels
8th place	Maes Hughes	152 panels
9th place	Number 48	115 panels
10th place	Riza Hawkeye	113 panels

A comment from the winner.

I'm number one! Viva me! The fact that I got almost twice as many appearances as Al proves how amazingly popular I am. They should have called this book the "Edward Elric Profile Book" instead.

Guess who... is in ninth place...!!

A comment from Number 48.

CLACK

Who could've guessed? Since I'm no longer in this world and will most likely be phased out soon, I am going to enjoy this reverberation of my former life. Hmm, I wonder what 66 is up to these days...

▣ Anger Management

Anger, anger, anger. Who needs calcium the most in this comic? Here's the total percentage of angry panels for our most angry characters. Of course, Number One is...

Izumi
Winry
Ed
1
2
3

Ed fails to win two consecutive victories!!

1st place	***Izumi Curtis*** 9.2% (26 panels)
2nd place	***Winry Rockbell*** 4.8% (17 panels)
3rd place	***Edward Elric*** 4.6% (98 panels)

A comment from the winner.
So that means I'm mad one out of every ten times I show up? This is all my idiot apprentices' fault!

I'M A HOUSE-WIFE !!!!!

▣ Crybaby Contest

Who's the biggest baby? Pre-count predictions were split between crybaby Winry and two more. Let's see who won.

NIFF
SNIF

1st place	***Alex Louis Armstrong*** 5.2% (12 panels)
2nd place	***Winry Rockbell*** 3.7% (13 panels)
3rd place	***Alphonse Elric*** 1.7% (21 panels)

Armstrong
Winry
Al
1
2
3

The pathetic victory!!

A comment from the winner.
I can't believe that I'm the winner! I'm so touched. I mean, it's such an honor to be recognized for something that's just been so common in my family for generations (sob)!

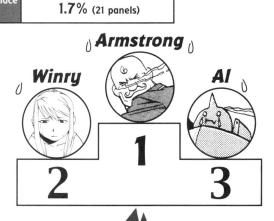

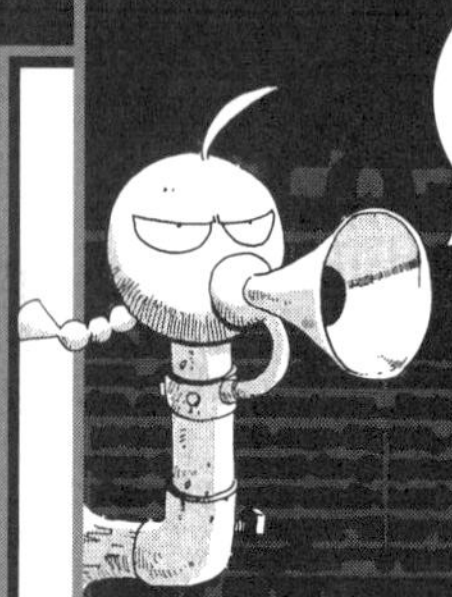
Crazy Stuff!

SHORT STUFF SELECTION

We decided to say "that word" to Ed repeatedly.

Edward Elric is a genius alchemist. But the one thing that troubles him is "that" problem of his. If you slip up and mention that taboo subject you'll really be in for it... Our condolences to anyone who suffered because of this itty bitty tiny little, er, problem...

You mean the little guy?

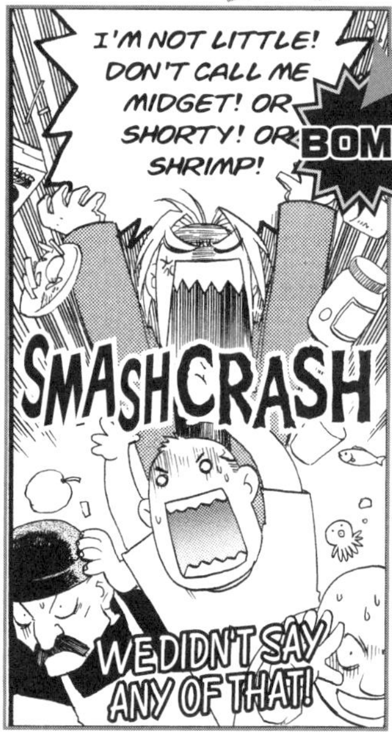
I'M NOT LITTLE! DON'T CALL ME MIDGET! OR SHORTY! OR SHRIMP!
BOMB
SMASHCRASH
WE DIDN'T SAY ANY OF THAT!

...Have you gotten a lot smaller?

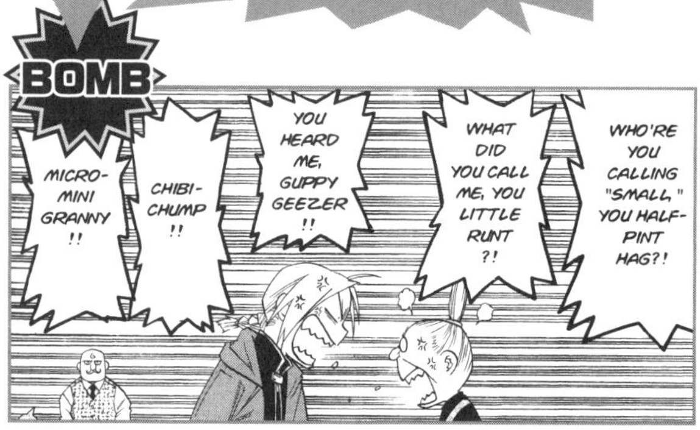
BOMB
WHO'RE YOU CALLING "SMALL," YOU HALF-PINT HAG?!
WHAT DID YOU CALL ME, YOU LITTLE RUNT?!
YOU HEARD ME, GUPPY GEEZER!!
CHIBI-CHUMP!!
MICRO-MINI GRANNY!!

I don't want to shoot a runt like you, but...

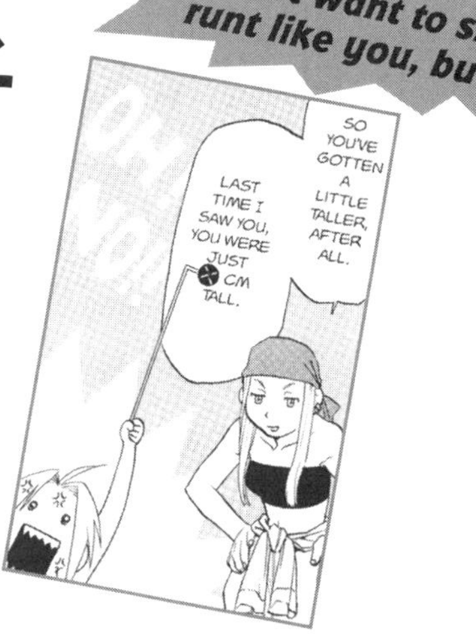
SO YOU'VE GOTTEN A LITTLE TALLER, AFTER ALL.
LAST TIME I SAW YOU, YOU WERE JUST ⊗ CM TALL.

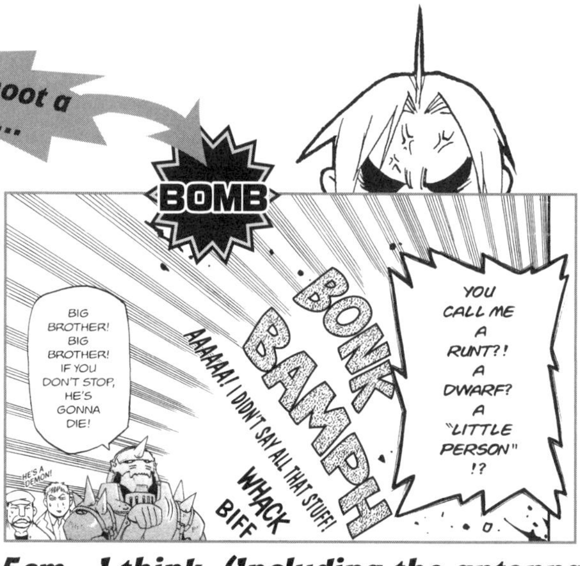
BOMB
YOU CALL ME A RUNT?! A DWARF? A "LITTLE PERSON"!?
BONK
BAMPH
AAAAAA! I DIDN'T SAY ALL THAT STUFF!
WHACK
BIFF
BIG BROTHER! BIG BROTHER! IF YOU DON'T STOP, HE'S GONNA DIE!
HE'S A DEMON!

My height is...165cm...I think. (Including the antenna and the high-heeled shoes.) (That's about 5'4".)

Fullmetal Firsts: Alphonse's Experiences

He has a big suit of armor for a body, but he still has the heart of a 14-year-old. "I want to be treated like a kid sometimes too." Now we're going to reveal some of the experiences he's had, which granted Al this wish after getting the armor body!

First time treated as a kid

NOW, YOU BOYS... PLEASE LISTEN TO YOUR ELDERS.
DON'T TREAT ME LIKE A KID!!
GRRAAA!!
OH, ED!
THIS IS THE FIRST TIME SOMEONE'S TREATED ME LIKE A KID SINCE MY BODY BECAME ARMOR!
WOWW!
IT'S NO USE...

First time as luggage

TA-DA
BAGGAGE FEES ARE CHEAPER THAN TRAVEL FEES!
THIS IS THE FIRST TIME SOMEONE'S TREATED ME LIKE LUGGAGE SINCE MY BODY BECAME ARMOR...
GLOOM GLOOM GLOOM
MY POOR BROTHER...

First pat on the head

BULGE
GLARE
I SEE...
RUB RUB
THAT'S THE FIRST TIME I'VE GOTTEN A PAT ON THE HEAD SINCE I BECAME A SUIT OF ARMOR...
YOU'VE REALLY GOTTEN BIG.

"The first time... is always the best!"

The Perfect Parent

Lieutenant Colonel Hughes best embodies one of the main themes of *Fullmetal Alchemist*. What is it? The love of one's family, of course. Family, fathers, and love...After reading this, you may be able to learn what love really is...

Doting parent file No.01

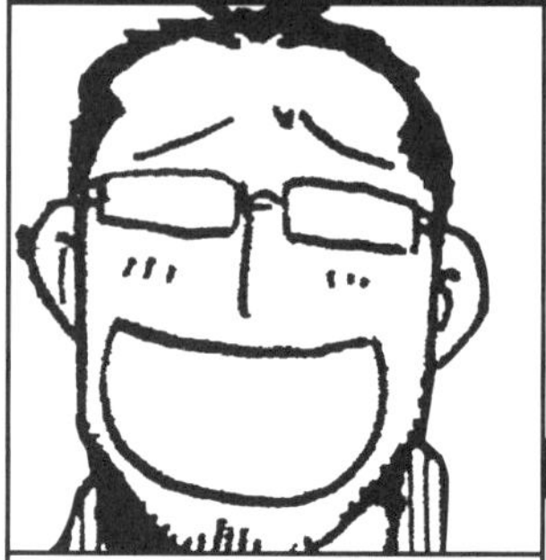

Lieutenant Colonel Hughes's attitude of placing family above work and his daughter above his subordinates might not be correct for a soldier, but it is correct for a human being.

RANK

Maes Hughes | A

Evidence number 1

With the military's private line...!

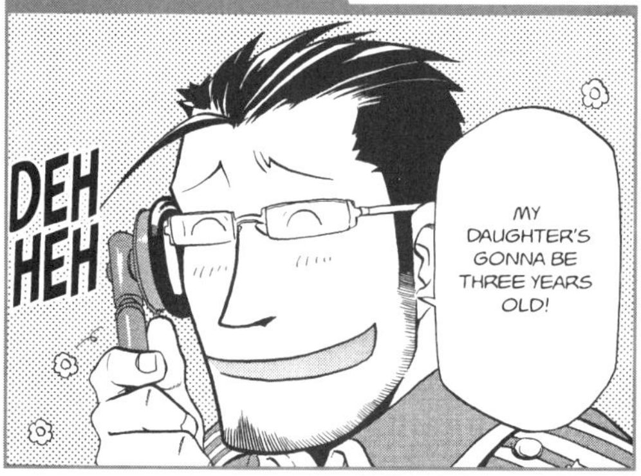
MY DAUGHTER'S GONNA BE THREE YEARS OLD!
DEH HEH

An example of Hughes using the military's private line to brag about his daughter. It's easy to believe the rumor that 70 percent of his call time is dedicated to talking about his family.

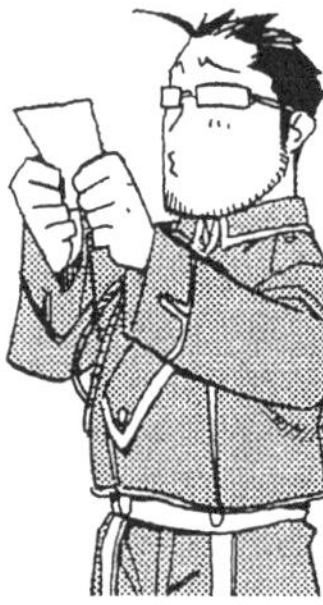

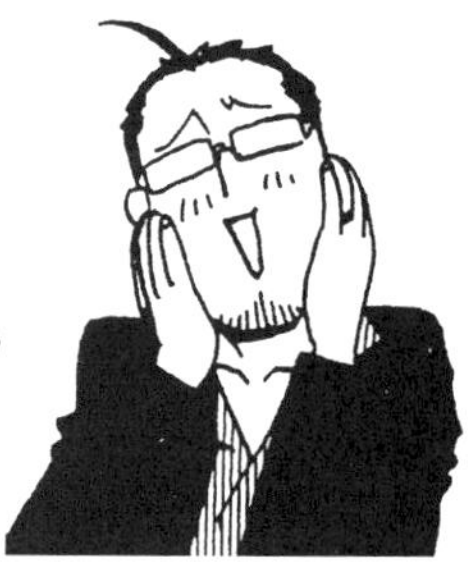

Evidence number 2

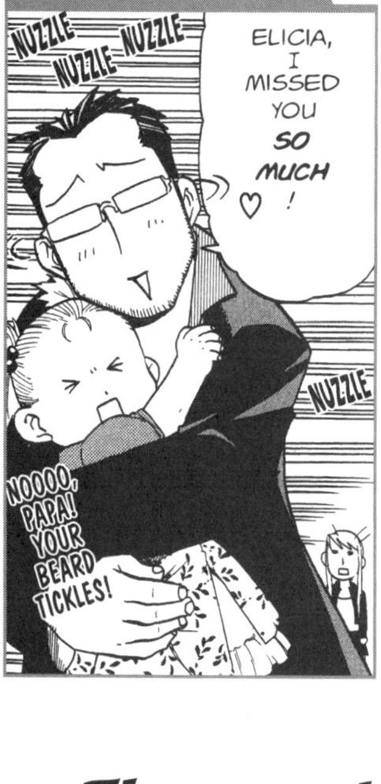
ELICIA, I MISSED YOU SO MUCH!
NUZZLE NUZZLE NUZZLE
NUZZLE
NOOOO, PAPA! YOUR BEARD TICKLES!

When he sees his daughter...!

The lieutenant colonel's shameless method of displaying his love. Winry's dazed expression in the back is nice.

Evidence number 3

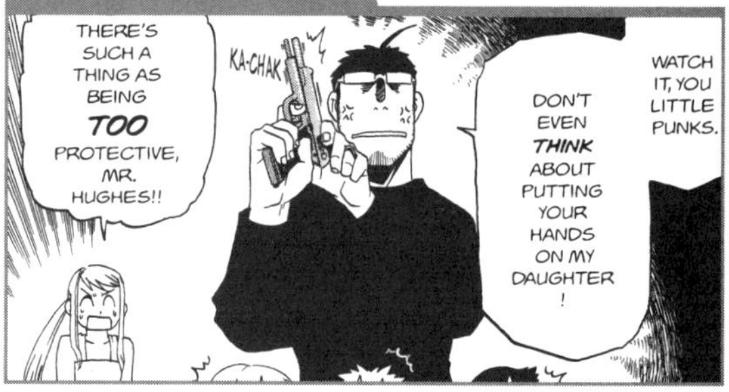
WATCH IT, YOU LITTLE PUNKS.
DON'T EVEN THINK ABOUT PUTTING YOUR HANDS ON MY DAUGHTER!
KA-CHAK
THERE'S SUCH A THING AS BEING TOO PROTECTIVE, MR. HUGHES!!

To his daughter's friends...!

An example of Hughes threatening his daughter's male friends with a gun. Actually his daughter Elicia is only 3 years old...

The wonderful life of doting parents!

The Body Perfect

Emotional and physical, Major Armstrong is one of the most unique characters on the *Fullmetal Alchemist* roster. He has a strong sense of justice. And his body is beautifully sculpted with precision and care. Gentle, strict, and oh-so-manly, there's still much more to Armstrong than meets the eye.

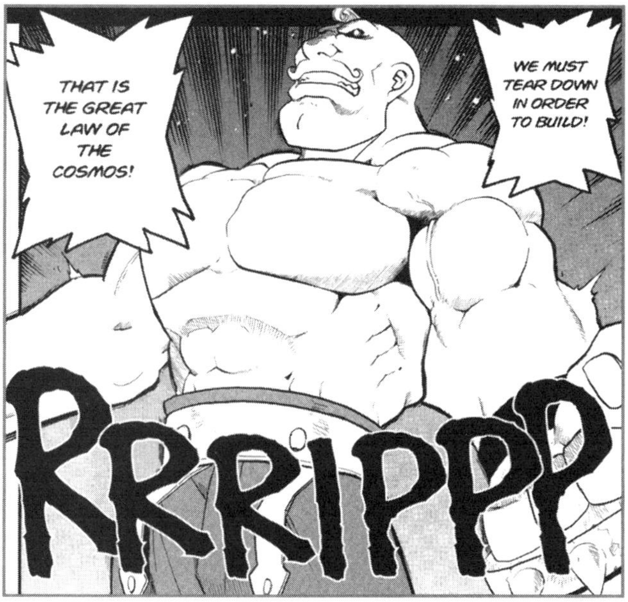
WE MUST TEAR DOWN IN ORDER TO BUILD!
THAT IS THE GREAT LAW OF THE COSMOS!
RRRIPPP

A healthy soul...

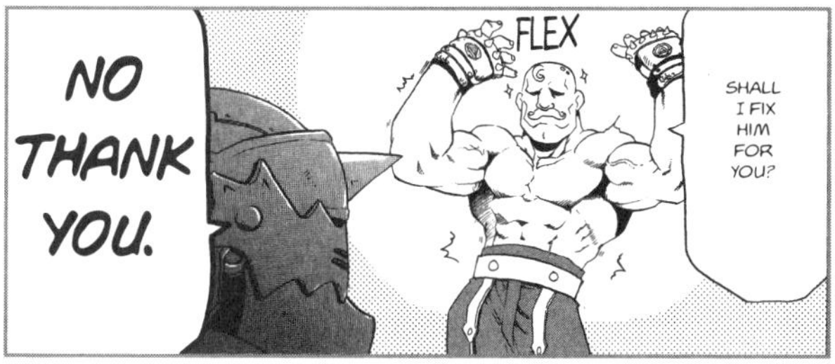
FLEX
SHALL I FIX HIM FOR YOU?
NO THANK YOU.

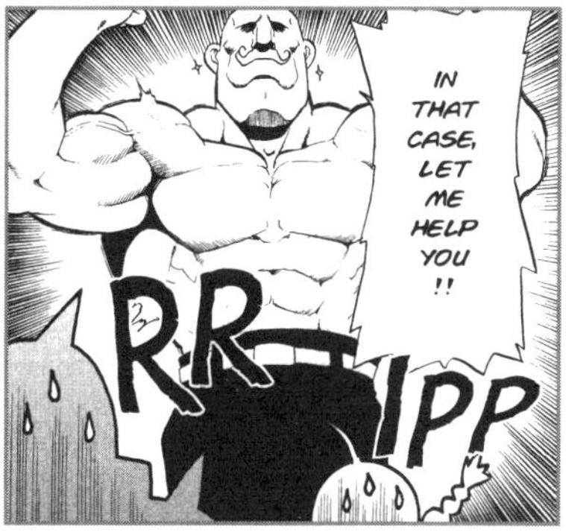
IN THAT CASE, LET ME HELP YOU !!
RR-IPP

...resides in a...

...well-trained body!!

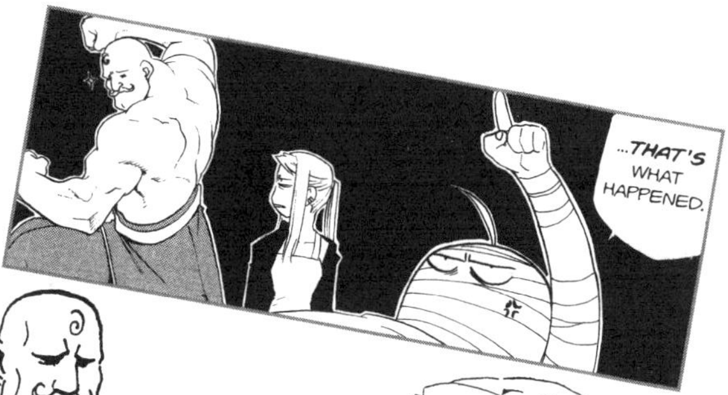
...THAT'S WHAT HAPPENED.

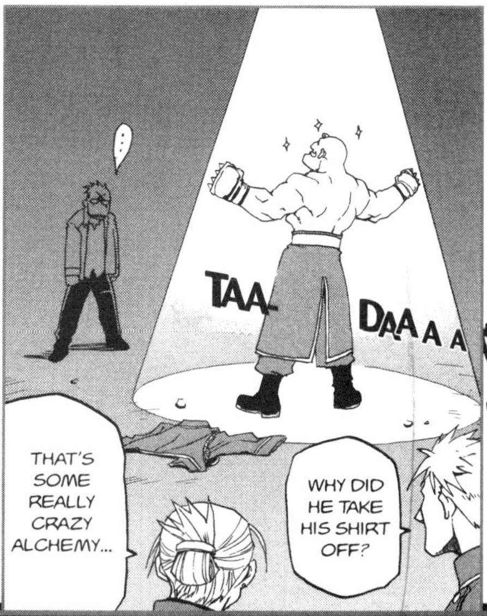
TAA-DAAAA
WHY DID HE TAKE HIS SHIRT OFF?
THAT'S SOME REALLY CRAZY ALCHEMY...

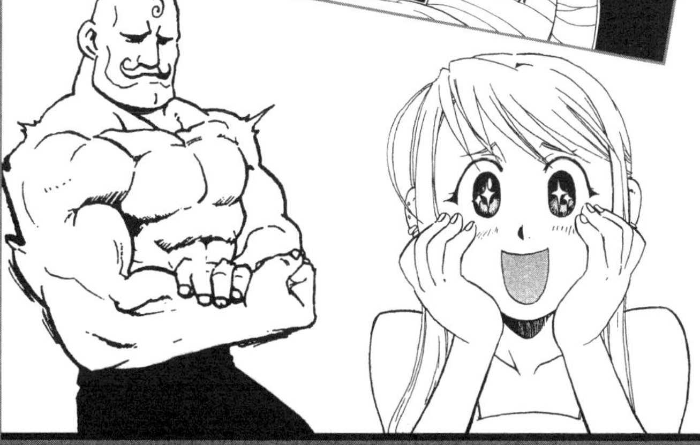

IDENTIFY YOURSELF! PERSONALITY ANALYSIS TEST
Who are you most like?
Take our test and find out!

Answer each question by choosing yes or no. We'll diagnose you and let you know which character you best match up with. Results are on the following page. Now, begin with question number 1!

FUN BOAT RIDE ?

1 You've been worried about your height before.

Y➤**2** / N➤**3**

2 You're almost invincible when it comes to sibling quarrels.

Y➤**4** / N➤**5**

3 You have a secret future ambition.

Y➤**5** / N➤**6**

4 You think that you're easily prone to tears.

Y➤**7** / N➤**8**

5 You love to play with children.

Y➤**8** / N➤**10**

6 You love fiddling with mechanical gadgets.

Y➤**9** / N➤**10**

7 You are a moody person.

Y➤**11** / N➤**12**

HMH, HMH! FOLLOWING A CHILD IS NO CHALLENGE FOR ME!

USELESS, JUST USELESS!

8 You tend to keep your troubles to yourself.

Y➤**9** / N➤**11**

9 When you were young you were called a child prodigy.

Y➤**12** / N➤**13**

10 You tend to worry a lot.

Y➤**13** / N➤**11**

11 When you are subjected to a strong shock, it takes you a long time to regain your composure.

Y➤**14** / N➤**15**

12 You can't overlook evil no matter what.

Y➤**14** / N➤**16**

13 When you teach someone something you do so with a lot of enthusiasm.

Y➤**16** / N➤**15**

14 You tend to forget things often.

Y➤**17** / N➤**18**

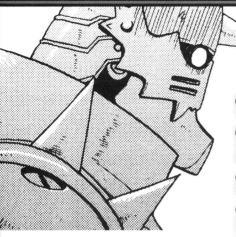

⑮ You are presently following some kind of plan. **Y➤⑲ / N➤⑰**

⑯ In a tight situation, you say "please God!" and pray without thinking. **Y➤⑳ / N➤⑱**

⑰ You have a goal that you need to see through. **Y➤㉑ / N➤㉒**

⑱ You have a sibling that is one year younger or older than you. **Y➤㉑ / N➤㉓**

⑲ You think that you will go far in life. **Y➤㉓ / N➤㉔**

⑳ You have a surprising talent. **Y➤㉒ / N➤㉔**

㉑ People say that your face looks angry even though you're smiling. **Y➤㉕ / N➤㉖**

㉒ If you were going to be reborn you'd like to come back as a woman. **Y➤㉖ / N➤㉕**

㉓ You like people that are better at something than you are. **Y➤㉚ / N➤㉑**

㉔ You'd like to join the army to train yourself to be tougher. **Y➤㉙ / N➤㉚**

㉕ You hate milk. **Y➤㉗ / N➤㉙**

㉖ You often throw things. **Y➤㉘ / N➤㉗**

㉗ Someone has said to you, "One day you're going to work for the government." **Y➤ B-type / N➤ A-type**

㉘ The person that you love is next to you right now. **Y➤ E-type / N➤ F-type**

㉙ You're given to melodramatic displays of emotion. **Y➤ D-type / N➤ C-type**

㉚ Your family and friends mean a lot to you. **Y➤ H-type / N➤ G-type**

FULLMETAL PERSONALITY TYPES

(A) Ed

Always Searching

You worry more about others than yourself. You're responsible and trustworthy and your biggest flaw is your picky eating habits.

(B) Al

Brotherly Spirit

You are compassionate and polite to a fault. Sometimes you should promote yourself a bit too, and your biggest fault is that you often seem a little too serious.

(C) Roy

Girl/Boy Crazy

The opposite sex is your weakness. You're cool but passionate. If you can successfully merge these two sides of your personality, you're sure to be very popular.

(D) Armstrong

Muscles

You have a direct and excitable personality. You are susceptible to emotions and have a tendency to be moved very easily. If you build up your body from now on it might bring you luck.

WHERE DO YOU FIT IN?

Match your results to the character who fits your test score. We think you'll be surprised at how accurately we've rated you!

E Izumi

The Teacher

You can't help but show the strict side of your personality to others. Having people understand the gentleness within you is the key to your being able to lead a happy life.

F Winry

The Fix-It Champ

You're likely to go all out for someone you care about. You don't mind spending a lot of effort in order to progress. But just be careful that you don't get so wrapped up that you lose sight of your surroundings.

G Envy

The Leader

You're not very good at controlling your feelings. If you get too carried away you might hurt someone. You might want to consider practicing Zen meditation to attain a little more level-headedness.

H Scar

Patience

Because you care so much about your friends, you tend to keep your painful thoughts to yourself, overburdening your own heart. You have a lot of drive, but remember, sometimes getting advice from others can be helpful and may open up a new path.

FULLMETAL ALCHEMIST CULT QUIZ

CULT QUIZ

This is a cult quiz of common sense questions that any *Fullmetal* fan should know the answer to, though we threw in a few that we can't imagine anyone will get at all. If you do, you definitely have earned your bragging rights. In case you're wondering, these questions were designed by Gluttony so it's going to take all your brainpower to figure out the answers!

TIM MARCOH...
LET'S SEE...

Cult Quiz Research Group President

Gluttony

The strength to make quizzes and also to solve them comes from food. If you're hungry anything is possible!

Cult Quiz Research Group

Number 66 | Lieutenant Hawkeye | Pinako

Q01

What body part other than his right arm did Ed lose when he was young?

A. left arm **B.** right leg **C.** left leg

Q02

Long hair is one of Ed's trademarks. How does he usually keep his hair back?

A. braid
B. bangs
C. topknot

TWIST TWIST
ALL RIGHT THEN... SHALL WE?

Common sense

Well, these are the most basic questions. If you miss these, you ought to be embarrassed. Right?

Beginner's level

Q03

Something important was stolen from Ed by Paninya. What was it?

A. wallet
B. height
C. silver watch

Q04

This is Hughes's beloved daughter, Elicia. How old did she become at the birthday party Winry was invited to?

A. 2 years old
B. 3 years old
C. 10 years old

Q05

There are two large scars on Scar's body. One of them is the scar on his face, and where is the other one?

A. left leg
B. right arm
C. back

Q06

Something that Ed has a habit of doing while sleeping. What is the habit that Al calls untidy?

A. He sleeps with his stomach out.
B. He sleeps with his eyes open.
C. He sticks his tongue out.

Q07

Winry and Pinako are auto-mail engineers. What was Winry's parents' profession?

A. physicians
B. dentists
C. surgeons

Heh heh heh. Some of the choices are already becoming kind of misleading. Ha ha ha.

IT'S GONE...

Q08

Scar, who hunts state alchemists, is one of the last surviving Ishbalans. What was the first thing he said during his very first appearance?

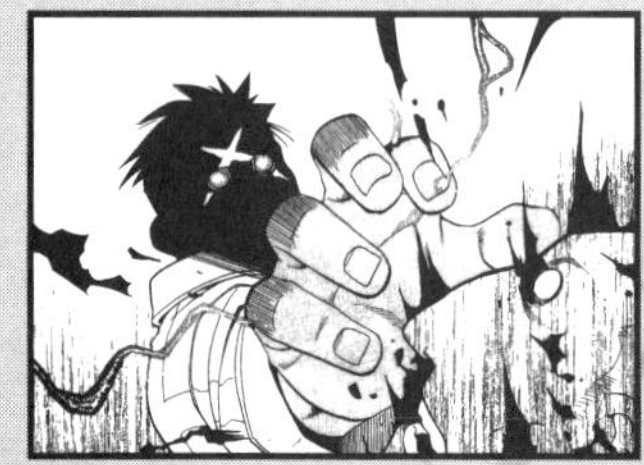

A. Destruction upon you!!
B. I'm going through.
C. ...

Q09

What branch is General Hakuro affiliated with in the eastern region?

A. New Option branch
B. New Oprain branch
C. New Optain branch

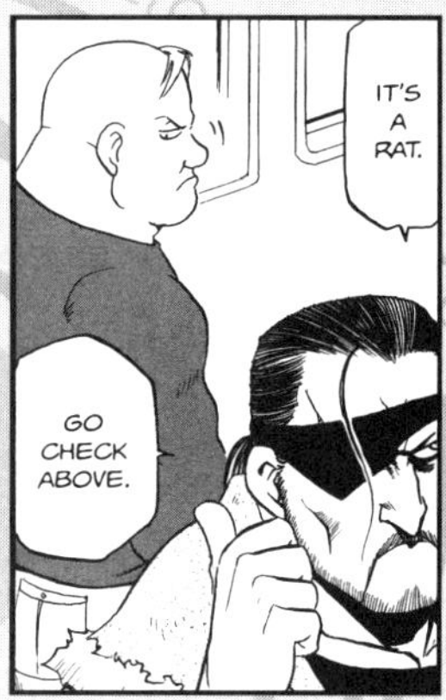
IT'S A RAT.
GO CHECK ABOVE.

Q10

Bald is the leader of the "Blue Squad," which is an extremist group from the East Area. What was the hidden weapon that was built into his auto-mail?

A. knife B. Japanese sword C. chainsaw

Intermediate level

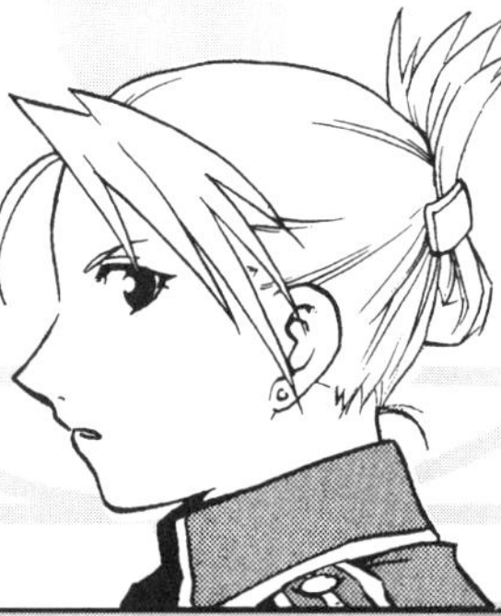

At this point, knowledge from casual reading will start to become less effective. If you can answer the questions in this section without any trouble that means you have a pretty good head on your shoulders. Would you like to do some target practice with me?

Q11

What number was on the part that Winry forgot to put on Ed's auto-mail when she was repairing it?

A. 04-B
B. A-5b
C. A-08

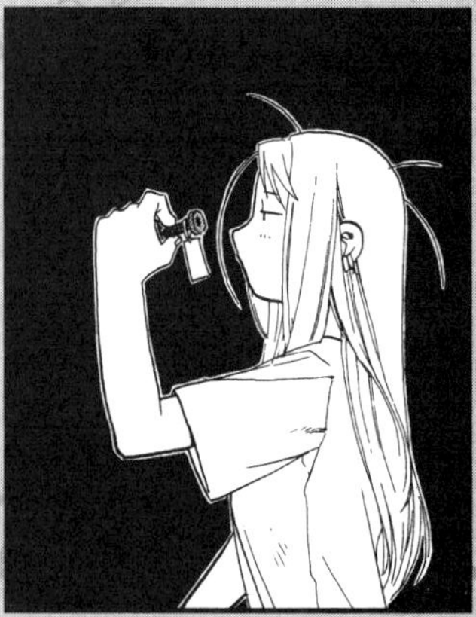

Q 12

King Bradley came to see Ed when he was hospitalized. What gift did he bring?

A. melon
B. watermelon
C. durian

Advanced level

HUH? BUT IF I DON'T KEEP UP MY BUSINESS, THEN I'LL *NEVER* BE ABLE TO PAY IT OFF...

Q 13

When Ed was small, what was the name of the attack that the teacher hit the Elric brothers with for being inattentive in class?

A. furious chalk dance
B. lunch confiscation
C. blackboard nail scrape

Q 14

There's a weapon built into Paninya's left leg. What is that weapon, which is the culmination of an auto-mail engineer's dream?

A. mega wave-motion gun
B. 1.5 inch carbine
C. Walter-P38

Q 15

What kind of shoes was Izumi wearing when she was reunited with Ed and Al?

A. toilet slippers
B. high heels
C. beach sandals

I TOLD YOU NOT TO STRAIN YOURSELF.
HERE'S YOUR PILLS, DEAR.
UGH KOFF GLUB

These next couple of questions take more than a little brains to figure out. Speaking of "little," Ed and the others have really grown up.

Q 16

There are many skills that have been passed down for generations in the Armstrong family. As of chapter 28, the skills that have been revealed are alchemy, tracking, and what other skill?

A. fake crying **B.** seduction **C.** portraiture

From this level on, the questions are going to get a lot harder. To find the answers to these questions, you're going to need to check every panel in the series.

Q 17

After finishing with repairs on the auto-mail, what train did Ed and El take to Central City?

A. 10:10
B. 12:00
C. 15:00

Q 18

Colonel Mustang was transferred to Central City. How many chess games did he win, lose, and draw against the general of the eastern headquarters?

A. 1 win 97 losses 15 draws
B. 2 wins 95 losses 13 draws
C. 1 win 96 losses 17 draws

NO TAKING BACK MOVES, GENERAL.

HEY!!

Q 19

Presently the arsonist Kimbley is incarcerated. What's his cell number?

A. 29
B. 44
C. 37

Difficult questions

...I GUESS I HAVE NO CHOICE.

WHERE IN CENTRAL?

HUH?

Q 20

Winry went to Central City to repair Ed's auto-mail. Which train station exit did she meet Major Armstrong at?

A. north exit
B. east exit
C. west exit

Q21

Major Armstrong is the military's number one gentleman. A picture of what animal is on his handkerchief?

A. panda
B. rabbit
C. dog

Q22

The "Blue Squad" is an extremist group from the eastern region. How many people total were involved in the hijacking of the train that Ed and the others were on?

A. 15 people **B.** 12 people **C.** 20 people

SO, UM... WHO ARE THESE GUYS?
SIGH
SO HE WAS JUST SUBCON-SCIOUSLY REACTING TO THE WORD "RUNT"...

Extreme cult

Q23

Izumi and Sig own a butcher shop. On the sign outside the shop what type of meat is listed other than beef, pork, and chicken?

A. mammoth
B. bear
C. lion

Q24

In Rush Valley, what was the name of the dog that bit Ed when he was trying to capture Paninya?

A. Jerry **B.** Jolly **C.** Julie

I'll give you your favorite food if you can solve these problems. Don't be shy, eat up.

Q25

Winry has pierced ears. How many earrings does she wear in her right and left ears?

A. 2 in the right, 2 in the left
B. 4 in the right, 2 in the left
C. 2 in the right, 4 in the left

Find out how you did. Answers to the Cult Quiz on page 156.

An Analysis ALCHEMY IN EUROPE

Alchemy is not some kind of fictitious magic, but a scientific field of learning studied across a significant area of the world ranging from Asia to Europe. We'll focus on the alchemy of Europe and the specific history of that region.

What is it?

Alchemy is much more than changing metal to gold. Indeed, it is possible, at least in the world of *Fullmetal Alchemist*. But that's only one use of this ancient science. In fact, the alchemists of Europe had a much more elaborate goal.

AFTER ALL, SOME PEOPLE SAY THAT ALCHEMY ORIGINATED IN THE KITCHEN.

The Birth of Alchemy

The word "alchemy" is thought by some to have originated from Arabic, though another theory states that the word came from Chinese, which was then incorporated into Arabic and then finally spread throughout Europe. The earliest known literature regarding alchemy goes back to the days of ancient Greece and Egypt. At that time, much research was being done on coloring metal and textiles. There is some confusion about the exact origin of the modern definition, but since decorating textiles was a household chore, not an industry, it was mainly performed by housewives. This idea of household magic seems to have given birth to the modern term.

All Is One

Soon, alchemy developed beyond practical household wisdom and practice and evolved into a scientific pursuit with the lofty goal of discovering the truths of the world. The oldest and most well-known literature from this period is the Emerald Tablet discovered in the fourth century and attributed to the god Hermes Trismegistus. The Emerald Tablet contains the most important concept in alchemy: the rule of "all is one."

Fundamental Material

Alchemists believe that before the world became divided into the all, it was composed of a single substance, the fundamental material called Prima Materia. The Greek philosopher Aristotle stated that out of this Prima Materia came the four basic elements of fire, air, water, and earth. At the fundamental level, everything in the world is composed of these four elements.

God & Alchemy

To put it bluntly, in the world of alchemy Prima Materia was essentially God. In Christianity, the world is thought to be created by God. If this is true then everything in the physical world that we live in used to belong the ethereal world of God.

1
Kether
(crown)
2
Chokmah
(wisdom)
3
Binah
(understanding)
4
Chesed
(mercy)
5
Geburah
(power)
6
Tiphereth
(beauty)
7
Netzach
(victory)
8
Hod
(splendor)
9
Yesod
(foundation)
10
Malkuth
(kingdom)

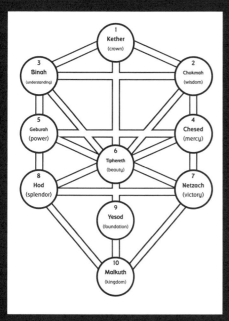

The Kabbalah and Alchemy

The Kabbalah is an esoteric teaching of Judaism, the mother religion of Christianity. The Kabbalah is said to contain the wisdom of God and to contain hidden codes so complex that it takes great study to truly understand them. To the casual reader, the writings of the Kabbalah won't mean much.

Some time in the 16th century, the Kabbalah became known throughout the whole of Europe. It seems unlikely that it has any prior connection to alchemy, which developed on its own individual course, but there is one thing that the Kabbalah shares with alchemy: both teach that the world came out of God (=one) who created it, and that the human beings (=all) who inhabit the physical world can become closer to God through study.

The Sephiroth tree diagram shows the Kabbalah's Arcana. The Sephiroth tree is comprised of ten spheres (Sephira), three pillars, and 22 paths (channels). (Each number has a very specific meaning but we will abbreviate it here.)

The tree is essentially a map that shows how the things that came from God's world, a nebulous, untouchable domain, become connected to the physical world of the four basic elements.

The Meaning of Alchemy

This is where the concept of an alchemist making gold takes on a different meaning. Turning metals of little value into pure gold means taking the impure Prima Materia that has been dispersed throughout the world and returning it once again to a state of pure Prima Materia.

Or rather, purifying a substance and returning it to its correct state is alchemy. Of course, this process is not only done to metal but also to the soul of the person conducting the alchemy. So alchemists refine their own souls through alchemy.

It's all rather grandiose, but if you think about it in terms of the Japanese concept of *do*, which means path, it's very easy to understand. For example, kado is the art of arranging flowers, but that isn't all it's about. Judo and kendo are fighting techniques on the surface, but their true goal is not about defeating the opponent. The same dual nature exists in alchemy.

The End of Alchemy

LIFE IS A COMPLEX CYCLE, SO VAST THAT WE CAN'T SEE IT WITH OUR OWN EYES.

Alchemy died out after the age of reason. The sad truth is that charting the steps to refining a soul does not have a practical place in the real world. It's easy to see how people dealing with only the reality in front of their eyes would turn their backs on something like that. But the refinement of the soul, which was the goal of alchemy, was taken up by literature and art. In some cases, the data from the alchemical experiments and their by-products became the foundation for modern science and medicine.

The Philosopher's Stone

The religious element aside, the value of alchemy has for the most part been placed on its ability to create gold. Certain aspects of the science have been based in medicine and the search for an all-cure elixir. But most historians focus only on the transformation of metals.

The common notion was that the Philosopher's Stone could convert any type of metal into gold immediately, or could be used as an all-curing elixir. According to other speculations, it could turn base metals into gold, but only when properly applied.

Without the metal being properly prepared the Stone had no effect. It's safe to say that the method for refining the Philosopher's Stone was different for almost every alchemist, but, among the very few similarities, the one most often mentioned is the change in color during the refining process.

The ingredients for the Philosopher's Stone were placed in specialized containers and then heated. The color of the stone first turned black, next white, and then in the end a beautiful red. By the way, there are hardly any examples of someone claiming that they successfully refined a Philosopher's Stone. But it is said that a certain alchemist named Paracelsus was never without one.

Paracelsus (Philippus Aureolus Theophrastus Bombastus Von Hohenheim)

When discussing the greats of alchemy, it is impossible to leave out Paracelsus, who supposedly succeeded in refining a Philosopher's Stone.

Paracelsus took Aristotle's four basic elements and condensed them into the three principles of mercury, salt, and sulfur. According to legend, this concept is the beginning of the scientific method. Not only would you end up creating new matter, you would be using yourself to do it. It sounds like wacky spiritualism, but if you look underneath the mumbo jumbo, it does make a bit of sense.

Seriously, think about how much more scientists can accomplish when they are passionate about their work. Paracelsus was not just a scientist and alchemist but a very popular professor at the University of Basel. But even that couldn't save him when he went up against the corrupt university officials who finally ran him out after only one year of teaching his beloved students. The majority of his known works are from the period following his dismissal, when he was simply a wandering alchemist.

Bibliography

Roberts, Gareth. *The Mirror of Alchemy*. Translated by Mera Kimikazu as *Renkinjutsu Daizen* [Toyoshorin, 1999].

Tanemura, Suehiro. *Kuroi Renkinjutsu* [Black Alchemy]. Hakusuisha, 1991.

Sone, Kozo. *Renkinjutsu no Fukkatsu* [The Rebirth of Alchemy]. Shokabo, 1992.

Dobbs, B.J.T. *Newton's Alchemy*. Translated by Etsuo Terashima as *Newton no Renkinjutsu* [Heibonsha, 1995].

Shinpigaku no Hon [Book of Mysticism]. Book Esoterica, issue 18 [Gakushu Kenkyusha, 1996].

COLLECTOR'S BOX

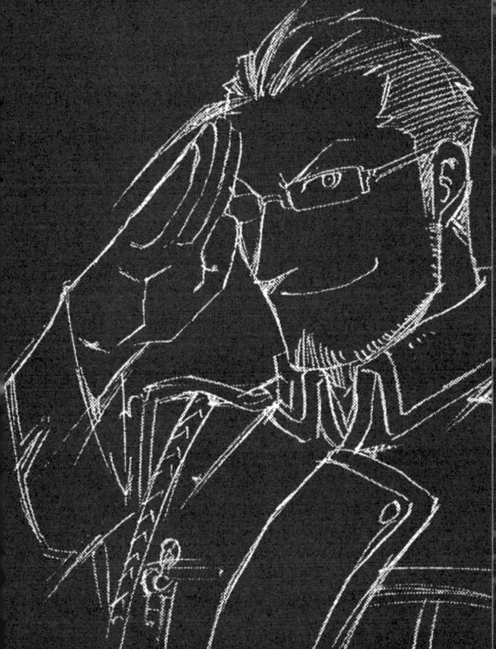

FULLMETAL ALCHEMIST

ONE-PANEL MANGA FROM VOLUMES 1-6!

In the original Japanese, these manga were hidden under the slipcovers on the covers.

VOLUME

They finally caught the elusive prey! It's not an alien but a strangely short state alchemist?!

A real live alchemist is captured.

Big brother!

A chimera of Al and a dog. This is the armor-faced dog we've been hearing so much about! Maybe it's been seen scampering along the freeway at midnight...?!

VOLUME 2

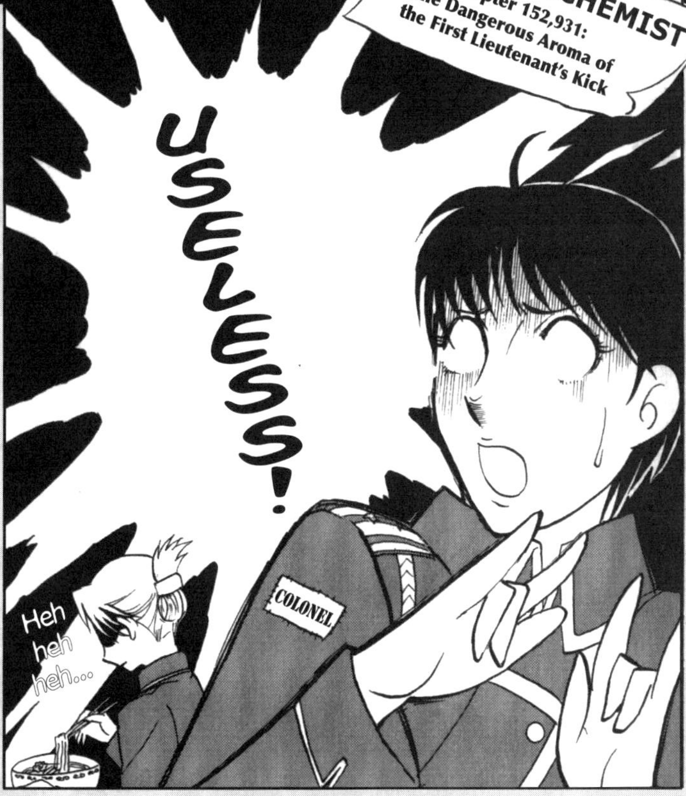
FLAME ALCHEMIST
Chapter 152,931:
The Dangerous Aroma of
the First Lieutenant's Kick
USELESS!
COLONEL
Heh heh heh...

The old Shôjo manga cliché where the sensitive heroine gets bullied. What will be the future of the colonel who's been bullied 152,931 times?

Ed opens the forbidden door. Is the major naked under the armor to keep from getting too hot? What a shock.

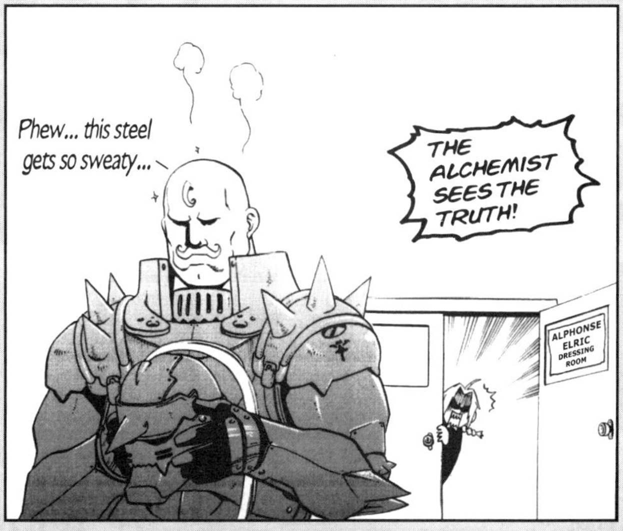
Phew... this steel gets so sweaty...
THE ALCHEMIST SEES THE TRUTH!
ALPHONSE ELRIC DRESSING ROOM

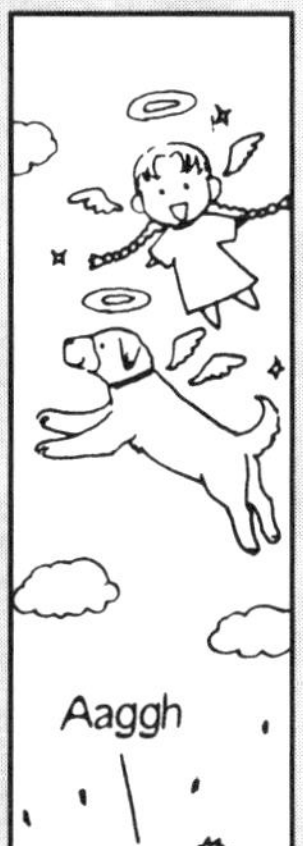
Aaggh
HELL

VOLUME 3

It's surprising how natural Lieutenant Hawkeye looks in this situation. They've been officially named the state thugs!

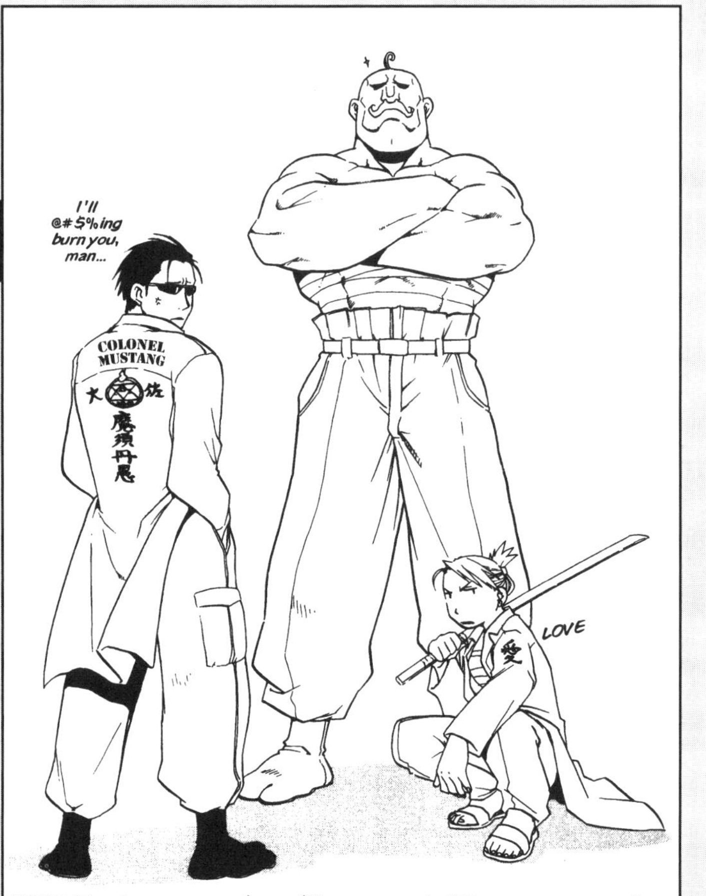
I'll @#$%ing burn you, man...
COLONEL MUSTANG
LOVE

NOTE: The characters are dressed like stereotypical Japanese gang members.

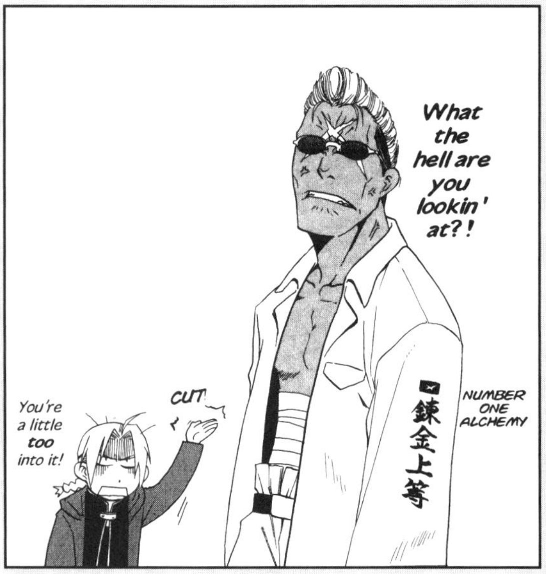
What the hell are you lookin' at?!
NUMBER ONE ALCHEMY
錬金上等
CUT
You're a little too into it!

I know a guy like this! There are multiple knife scars under the bandages...Brrr.

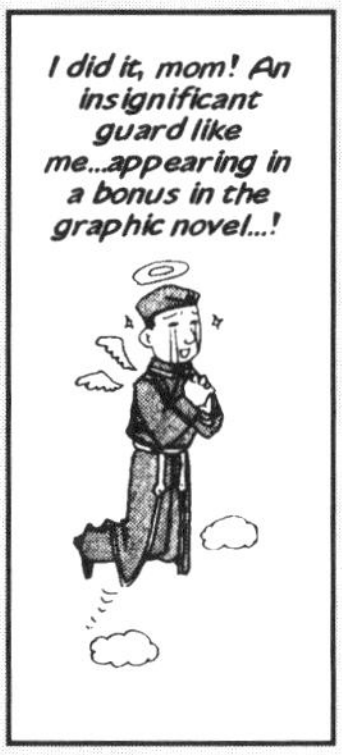
I did it, mom! An insignificant guard like me...appearing in a bonus in the graphic novel...!

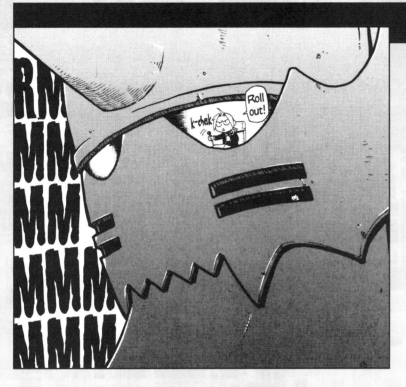

VOLUME 4

Roll out!
k-chak
RMMMMMMMMMMMMM

Allow me to name this robot Yoroiga-R! Don't overlook the cat peeking out.

Individually they aren't so strong, but when unified, they're invincible... right?

SUPER FUSION

Want to see some photos of my daughter? Look, look!
Sigh...

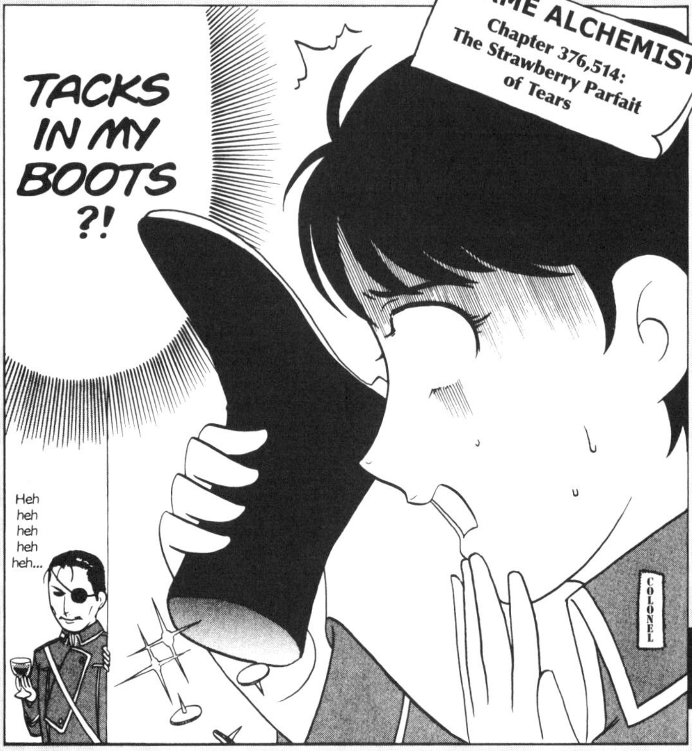
FLAME ALCHEMIST
Chapter 376,514: The Strawberry Parfait of Tears
TACKS IN MY BOOTS ?!
Heh heh heh heh heh...
COLONEL

The *Fullmetal* drama has finally reached its 376,514th episode. Even though someone put tacks in his shoes, the colonel won't be kept down!

VOLUME 5

Al, you have too many cats! Those one hundred supernatural-looking eyes have gone beyond cute and are just scary...

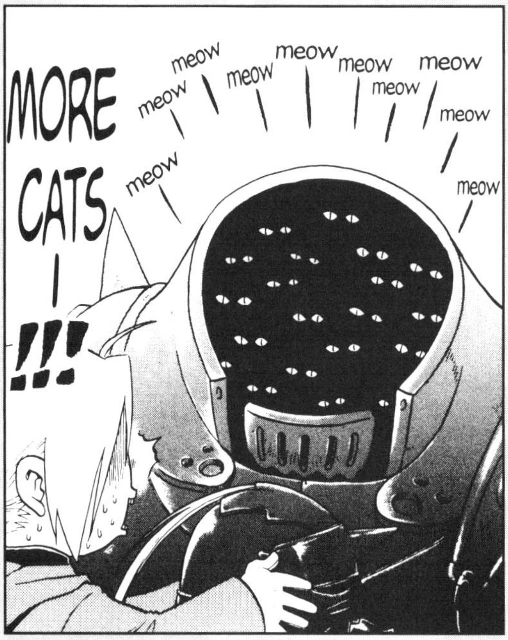
MORE CATS!!!!
meow meow meow meow meow meow meow meow meow meow

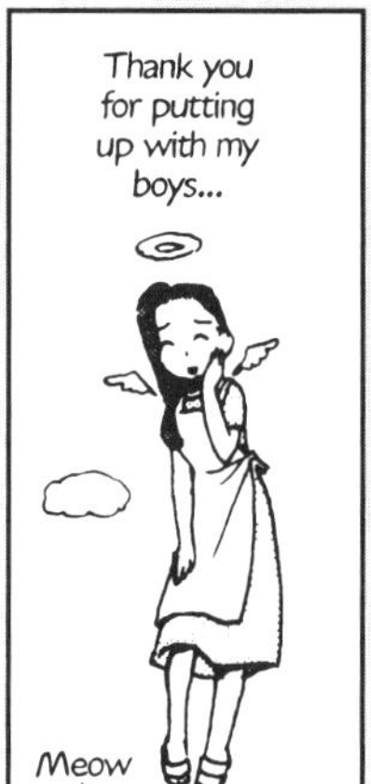
Thank you for putting up with my boys...
Meow

VOLUME 6

Mason left his boss behind and took the cover spot for himself! Where's the dull blade headed...?

What's a bit-part character like *you* doing on the cover...?
FULLMETAL ALCHEMIST
6
Forgive me!
Ulp!

Even with his 50cm elevator shoes, he's still no match for Al's height. It seems as though a battle for the heroine's love is about to begin at any minute!

FULLMETAL BANCHO*
The Boss
meow
Demon Beast
The Pawn of the Military Commanders
Heroine
Elevator Geta (sandals)

***Bancho=A stereotypical Japanese delinquent**

The Elric brothers ate us...
The fox ate me...
Guhh...

COWSHED DIARIES RELAY

(Note: Relay comics a.k.a "round-robin comics" are when each person switches off to do one panel in the comic.)

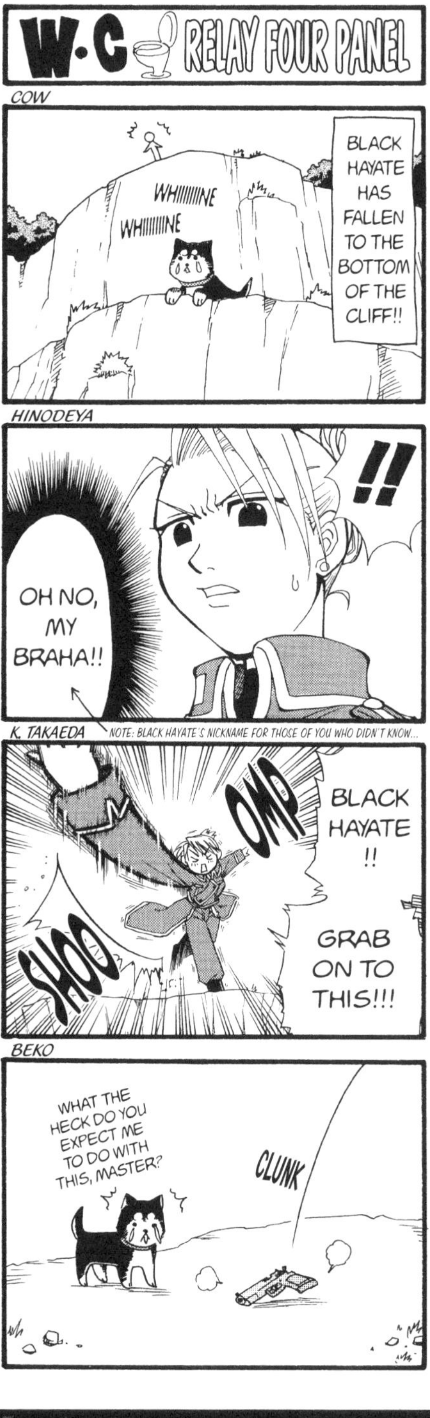

W·C RELAY FOUR PANEL
COW
BLACK HAYATE HAS FALLEN TO THE BOTTOM OF THE CLIFF!!
WHIIIIIINE
WHIIIIINE
HINODEYA
!!
OH NO, MY BRAHA!!
NOTE: BLACK HAYATE'S NICKNAME FOR THOSE OF YOU WHO DIDN'T KNOW...
K. TAKAEDA
BLACK HAYATE!!
OMP
SHOO
GRAB ON TO THIS!!!
BEKO
WHAT THE HECK DO YOU EXPECT ME TO DO WITH THIS, MASTER?
CLUNK

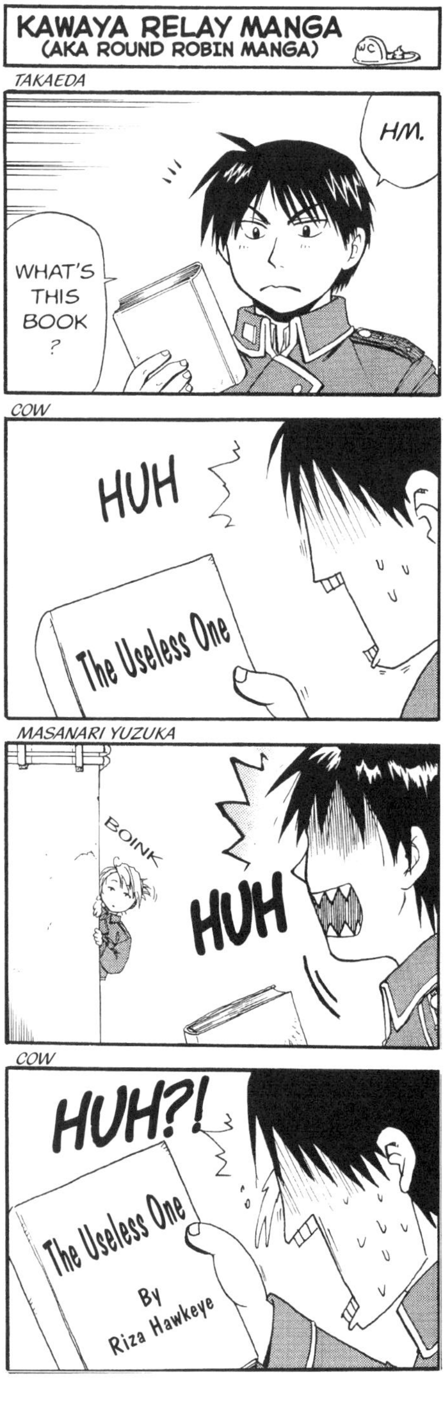

KAWAYA RELAY MANGA
(AKA ROUND ROBIN MANGA)
TAKAEDA
HM.
WHAT'S THIS BOOK?
COW
HUH
The Useless One
MASANARI YUZUKA
BOINK
HUH
COW
HUH?!
The Useless One
By Riza Hawkeye

W.C. RELAY FOUR-PANEL

Arakawa and her assistants switched off drawing one panel each in the bathroom for these four-panel manga masterpieces!

KAWAYAN MANGA!
TAKAEDA
THE DAYS WHEN SCAR STILL HAD A SCAB.
IT'S BEGINNING TO GET PUFFY.
MIRROR
HINODEYA
I WANT TO PEEL OFF MY SCAB!
OHHH MAN, I REALLY WANT TO PEEL IT OFF!!!
BABA
RRRRRIPP!
BUT IF I MESS UP IT'S REALLY GONNA HURT.
TEAR
BUT, BUT...!!!
ARAKAWA
WHAT, A SCAB?
RIP!
ARRRRGH!!!
THERE.
ELDER!!
TMP TMP
YOU MUST ENDURE IT...

BATHROOM RELAY MANGA
HINODEYA
CRUNCK
SQUISH
CRUNCH
SMACK SMISH
TAKAEDA FIRST SHOT.
YOU'RE EATING SOMETHING AGAIN, GLUTTONY?
YOU WANT SOME, LUST?
ARRRMY ARRRMM MARMMM
TAKEDA SECOND SHOT
HERE.
SWISSH
ARAKAWA
ENVY CALLED ME AN "OLD LADY" SO YOU CAN EAT EVERY LAST SCRAP!!

FOUR-PANEL EXHIBITION ROOM

SPECIAL GIFT ALCHEMIST

SHONEN GANGAN SPECIAL GIFT PLASTIC UNDERLAY FOUR-PANEL MANGA.

SAMPLE USE OF PLASTIC UNDERLAY.
NOOOOOOOO
AAAAHHHHHH
RUB RUB RUB RUB
RISE
MY NEW HEIGHT....
...170 CM !!!
I DON'T THINK SO.
SLAM

ALCHEMY IS GREAT

TV ANIME COMMEMORATIVE FOUR-PANEL MANGA.

ALCHEMY IS WONDERFUL !!
HEY.
THERE'S NO TOILET PAPER !!
EVEN IN CASES LIKE THIS!
OTOKI KOROKU
NO NEED TO WORRY !!
WAMP
TRANS-MUTING
BAM
TOILET PAPER !!!
ka
SO AS YOU CAN SEE, ALCHEMY IS A VERY USEFUL SKILL!!! FOR THE WORLD AND FOR THE PEOPLE!!
GLARE
GET OUT !!

RARE HILARITY

We've carefully selected four previously unpublished rare four-panel gag manga and collected them here. These are truly collector's items!

CHARACTER POPULARITY CONTEST COMMEMORATIVE COMIC

THE OBSCURE PERSON'S SONG

SPECIAL FULLMETAL ALCHEMIST 2ND ANNIVERSARY PROJECT, "CHARACTER POPULARITY CONTEST" FOUR-PANEL MANGA.

A CHARACTER POPULARITY CONTEST?!
IT'S OUR BIG CHANCE!!
GANGAN 5 GONBUTO VOLUME
NOW IS THE TIME TO SHOW OUR STRENGTH!!
WE'LL MAKE FATHER COME IN NUMBER ONE BY CASTING A GROUP VOTE!!
YEAAAAAAHHHH
FATHER
FATHER
DAD
ONLY THREE VOTES...

A JAPANESE PUN

TV ANIME MEMORIAL FOUR-PANEL MANGA

FULLMETAL ALCHEMIST IS BEING MADE INTO ANIME?
WHAT?! AN ANIME?!
OR IN JAPANESE, ANIME-KA!
ANIME-KA?!
ANI-MECHA?!
BEEP
SHOOOOOOOO
I DON'T CARE WHAT YOU CALL ME!!!
MECH OTAKU!

NOTE: THIS MANGA ONLY MAKES SENSE IN JAPANESE DUE TO THE PUN ON THE WORDS "ANIME" AND "KA," BUT IT'S FUNNY ANYWAY IF YOU JUST WANNA LOOK AT THE PICTURES! OR YOU CAN TRY TO MAKE SENSE OF IT. ANIME KA = BECOME AN ANIME. ANI-MECHA = BIG BROTHER. GET IT? HAHAHAHAHAHA. FUNNY, RIGHT?!

ROUGH SKETCH MUSEUM

Sketches | Behind the page

We've discovered another side to the Fullmetal Alchemist from Arakawa-sensei's rough sketches!
We've collected some of the more playful rough sketches from the back of some of the papers!

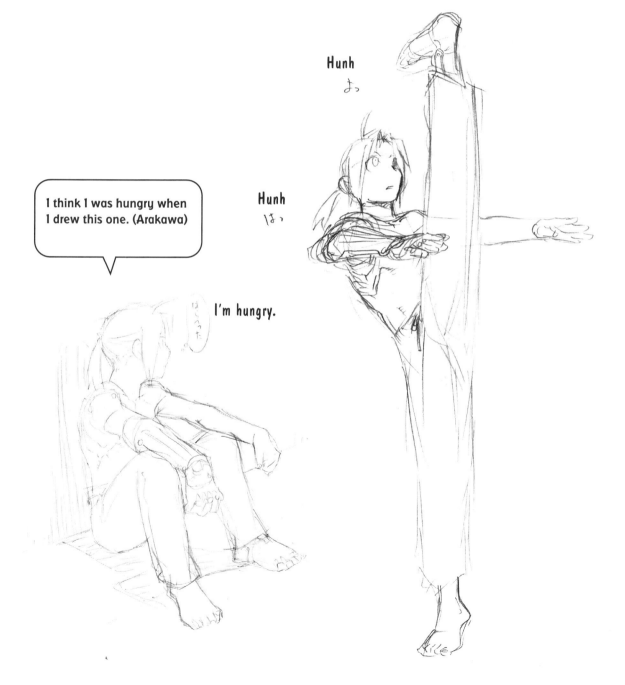

Hunh
よっ

Hunh
はっ

I think I was hungry when
I drew this one. (Arakawa)

I'm hungry.

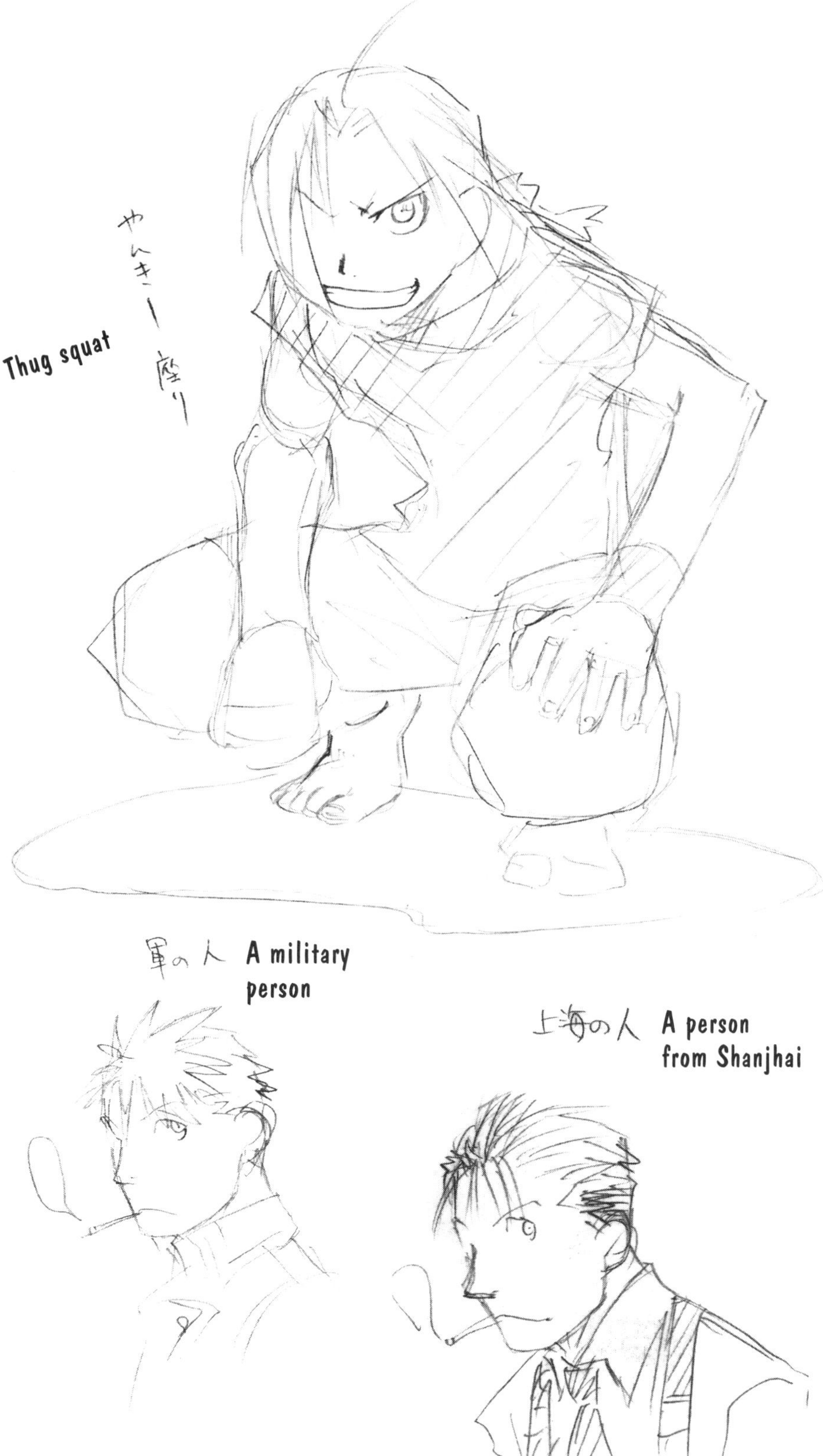
やんきー座り
Thug squat
軍の人
A military person
上海の人
A person from Shanjhai

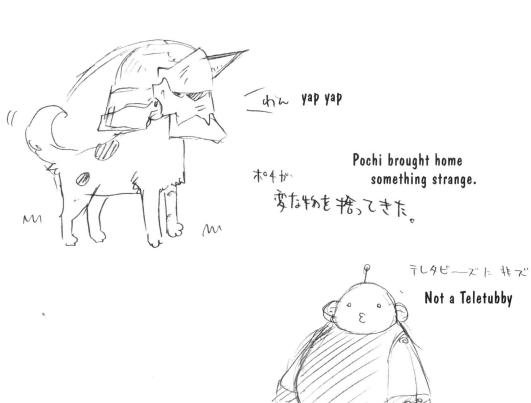

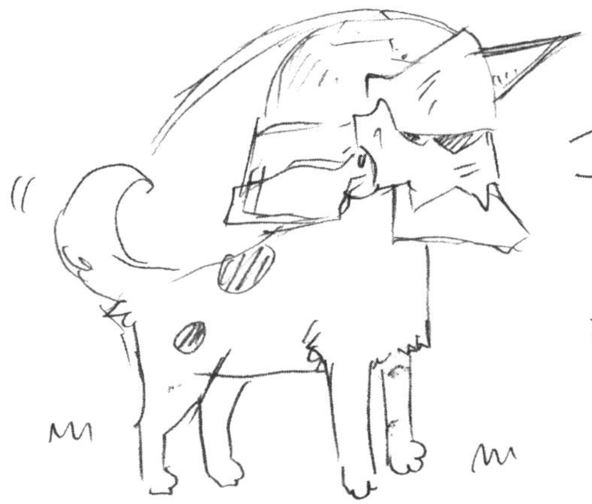
わん yap yap
ポチが
変な物を拾ってきた。
Pochi brought home something strange.

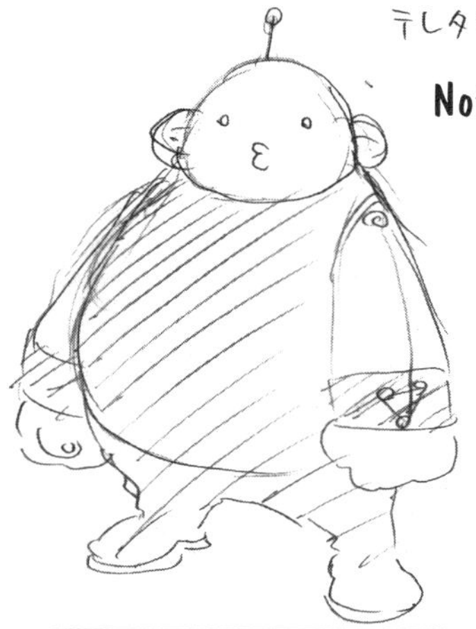
テレタビーズに非ズ
Not a Teletubby

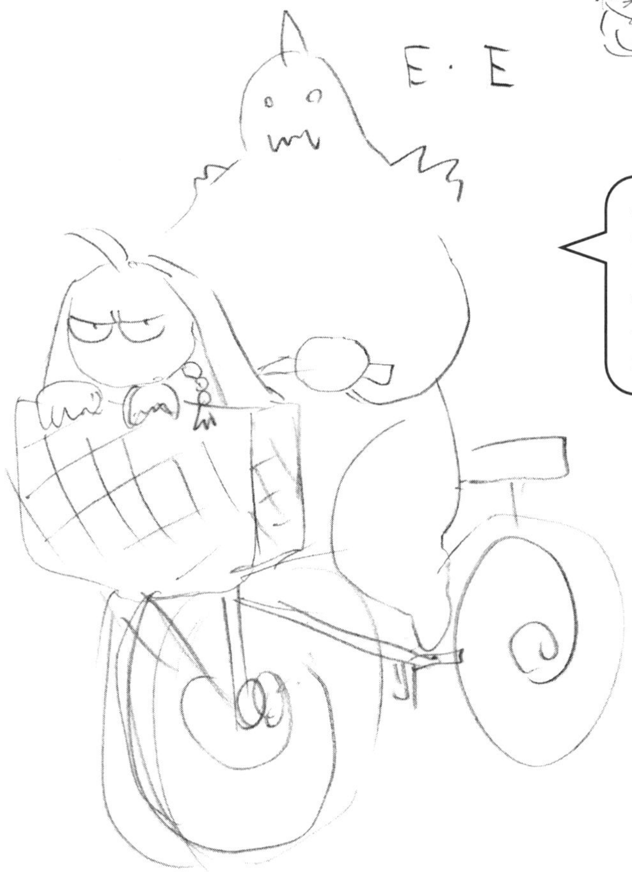
E・E
A heartwarming story about the compassionate young boy Alphonse and the small alien that came from outer space. (E.E. Edward Elric)

Rough Sketch Museum

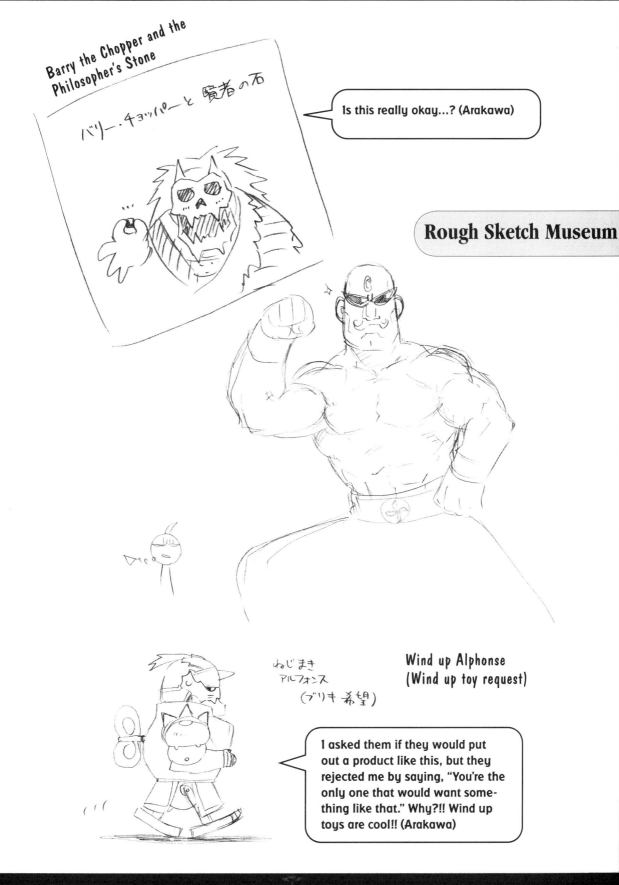

Barry the Chopper and the Philosopher's Stone

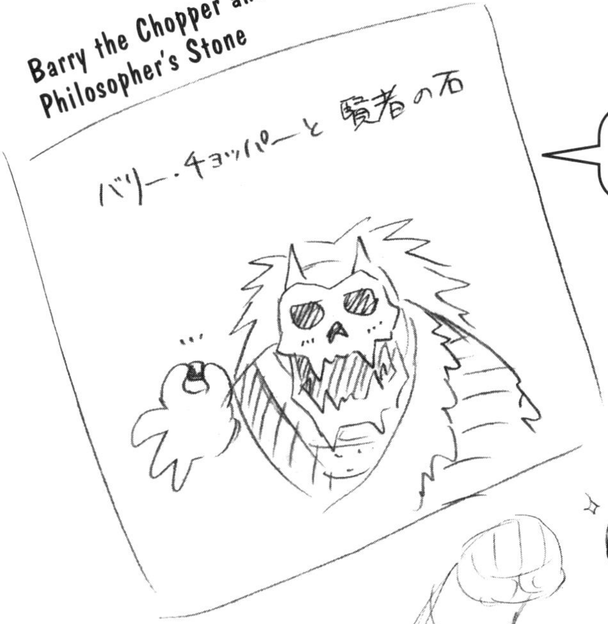
バリー・チョッパーと賢者の石

Is this really okay...? (Arakawa)

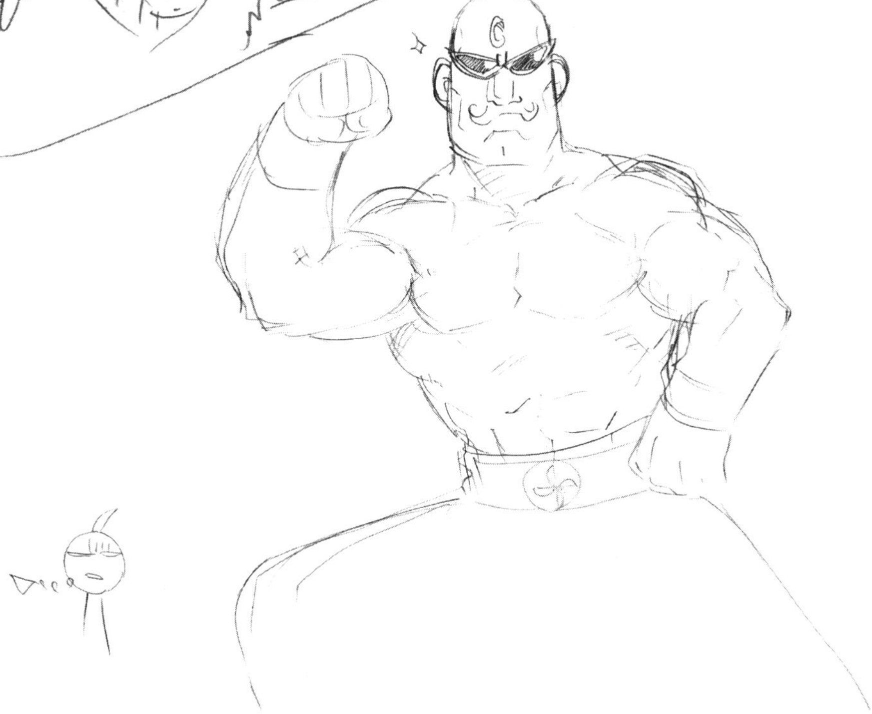

Wind up Alphonse
(Wind up toy request)

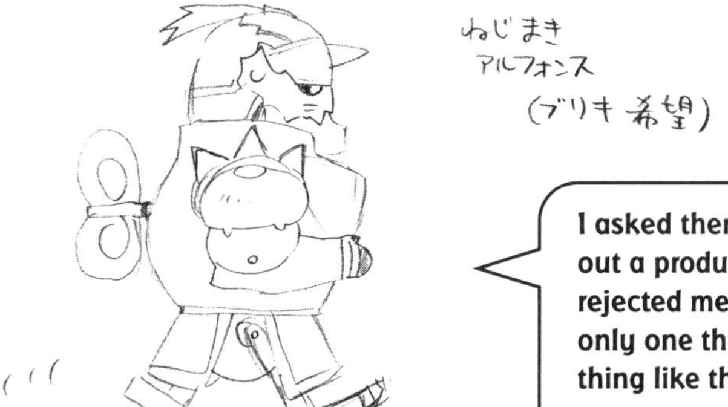
ねじまき
アルフォンス
(ブリキ希望)

I asked them if they would put out a product like this, but they rejected me by saying, "You're the only one that would want something like that." Why?!! Wind up toys are cool!! (Arakawa)

BONUS MANGA

FULLMETAL ALCHEMIST IS SHONEN MANGA, WHICH IS FOR BOYS ONLY, BUT GIRLS LOVE IT TOO!
BUT IT DOESN'T HAVE ANY OF THE THEMES OF A REGULAR BOYS' COMIC.
LIKE "EF-FORT."
NOPE, I STARTED OFF AT LEVEL 100 FROM THE BEGIN-NING.
AND "FRIENDSHIP." I GUESS WE DON'T HAVE TOO MANY FRIENDS EITHER.
DON'T SAY THAT.
AND A "COOL HERO"...
ED, YOU'RE KIND OF TINY.
WHAT ABOUT OUR TEAM?
CRUNCH CRUNCH
THEY'RE ALL OLD GEEZ-ERS.
SHUT UP!
HUMPH! EFFORT AND FRIEND-SHIP ARE TRIVIAL!
WE'RE OVERFLOWING WITH A QUALITY THAT MOST YOUNG BOYS DON'T POSSESS.
HUH?! WHAT'S THAT?!
MONEY AND POWER.
WHAT AN IMMORAL MANGA.
STATE ALCHEMIST
HE SHOULD HAVE SAID IT WAS ALL ABOUT BROTHERLY LOVE OR SOMETHING.

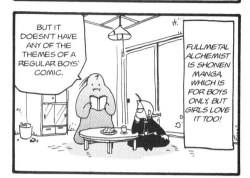

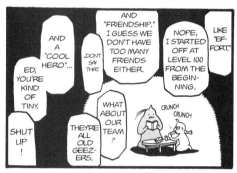

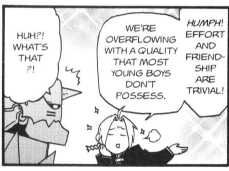

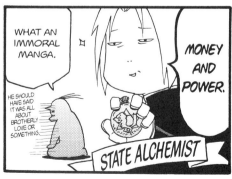

The Answers to the Cult Quiz

Answers!

P.132-133

Q01 ...C left leg
Q02...A braid
Q03...C silver watch
Q04...B 3 years old
Q05...B right arm
Q06...A He sleeps with his stomach out.
Q07...C surgeons

P.134-135

Q08...B I'm going through.
Q09...C New Optain branch
Q10...C A-08
Q12 ...A melon
Q13 ...A furious chalk dance
Q14 ...B 1.5 inch carbine
Q15 ...A toilet slippers
Q16 ...C portraiture

P.136-137

Q17 ...C 15:00
Q18...A 1 win 97 losses 15 draws
Q19 ...A 29
Q20...C west exit
Q21 ...B rabbit
Q22...B 12 people
Q23...A mammoth
Q24...C Julie
Q25...B 4 in the right, 2 in the left

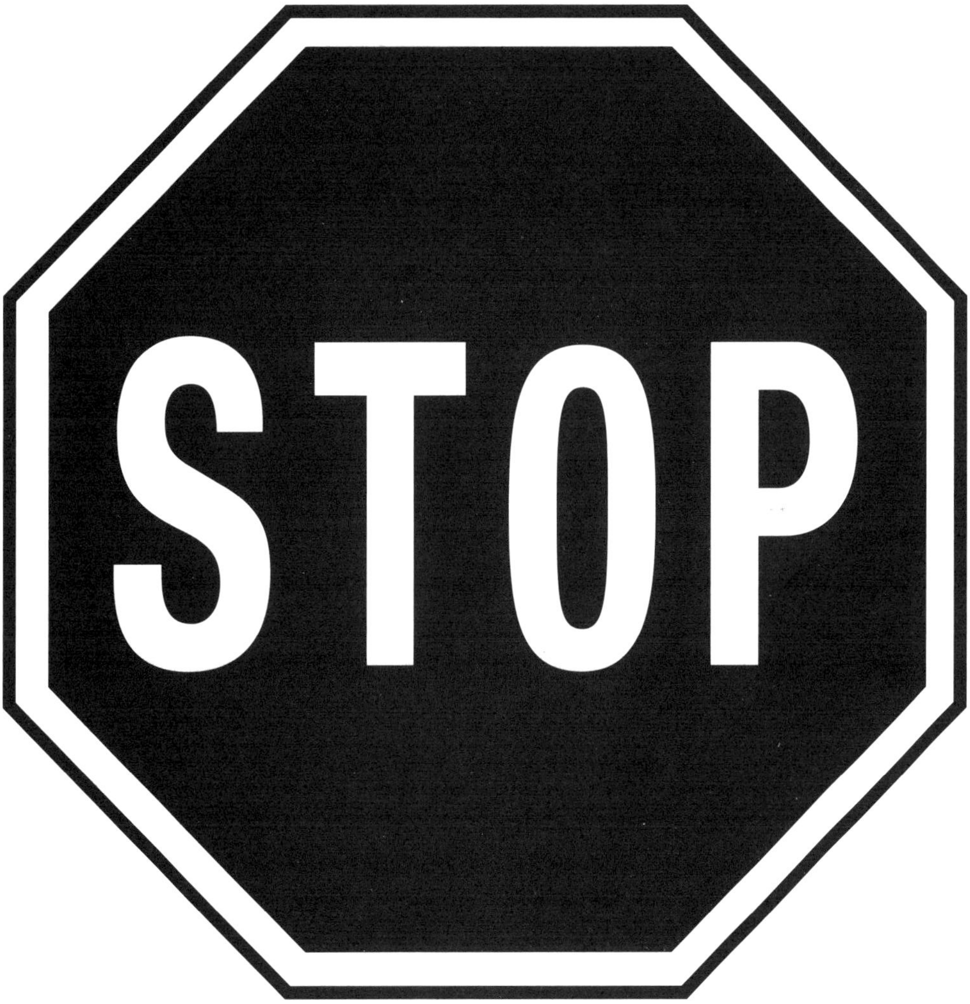
STOP

Thank you for reading *Fullmetal Alchemist Profiles.*
Now please turn to the last page
to discover a bonus manga,
"The Blind Alchemist," which begins on page 183
and reads the opposite direction from the pages
you've already been enjoying.

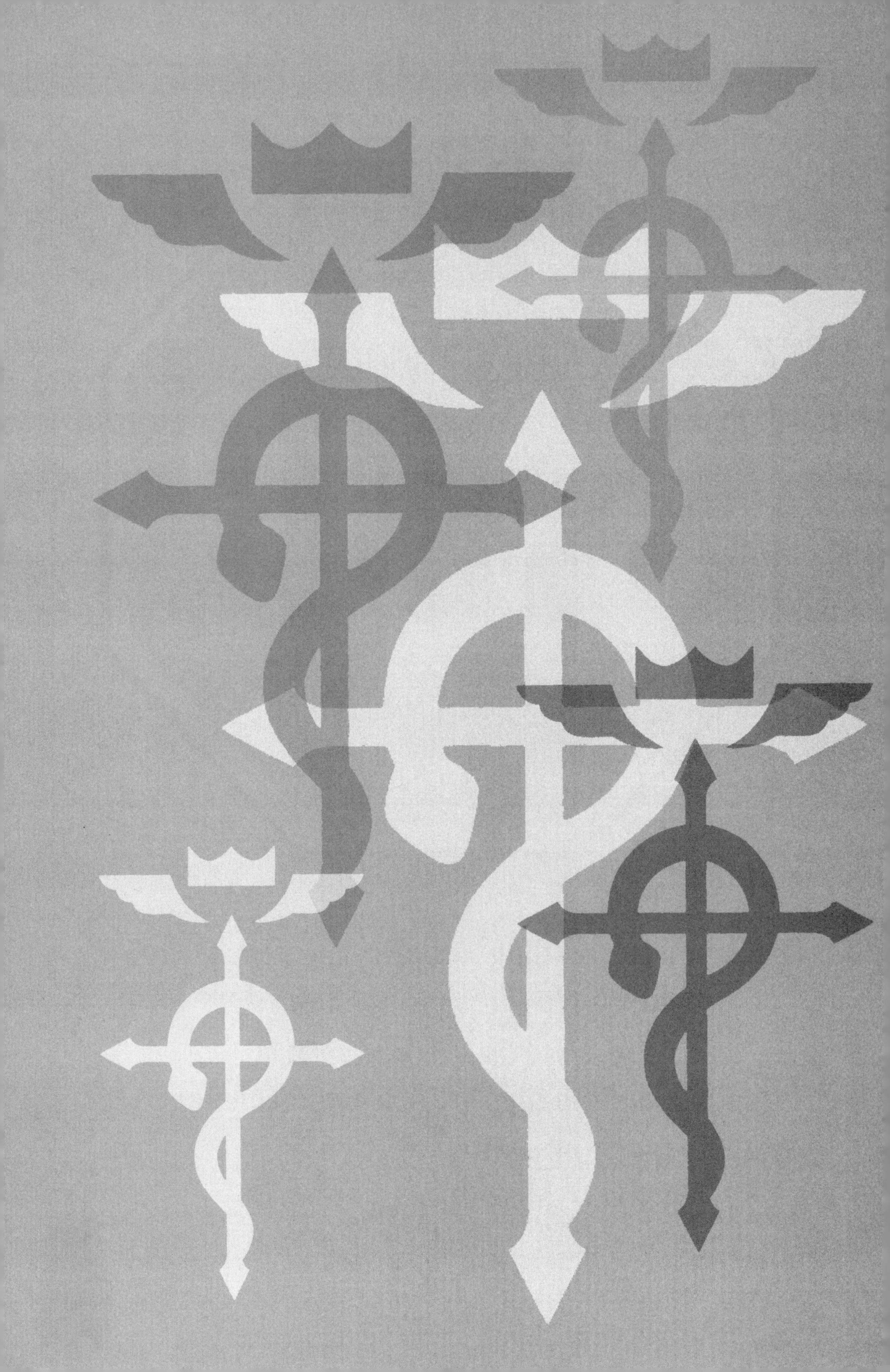

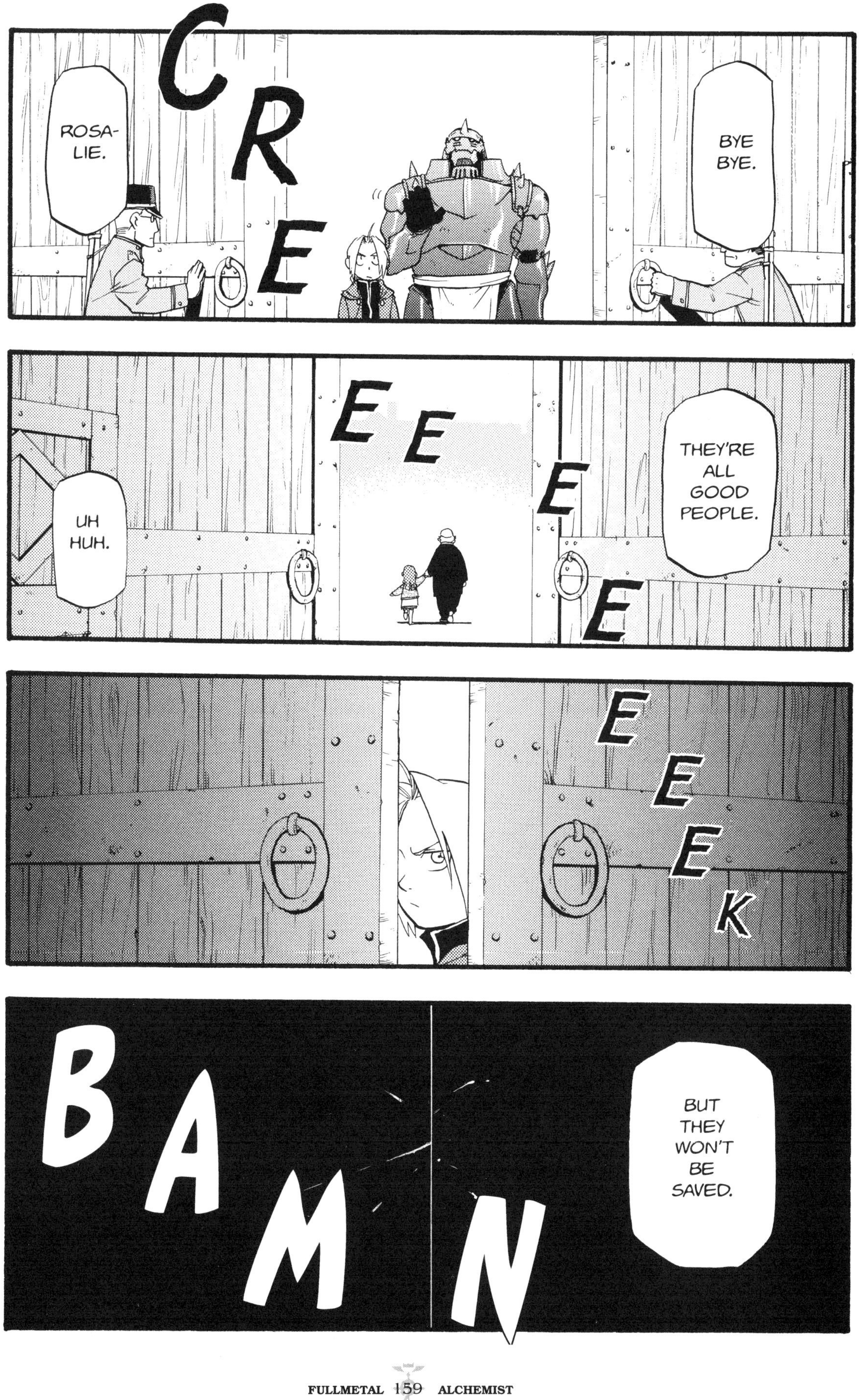

BYE BYE.
ROSA-LIE.
CRE
THEY'RE ALL GOOD PEOPLE.
UH HUH.
EEEE
EEEK
BUT THEY WON'T BE SAVED.
BAMN

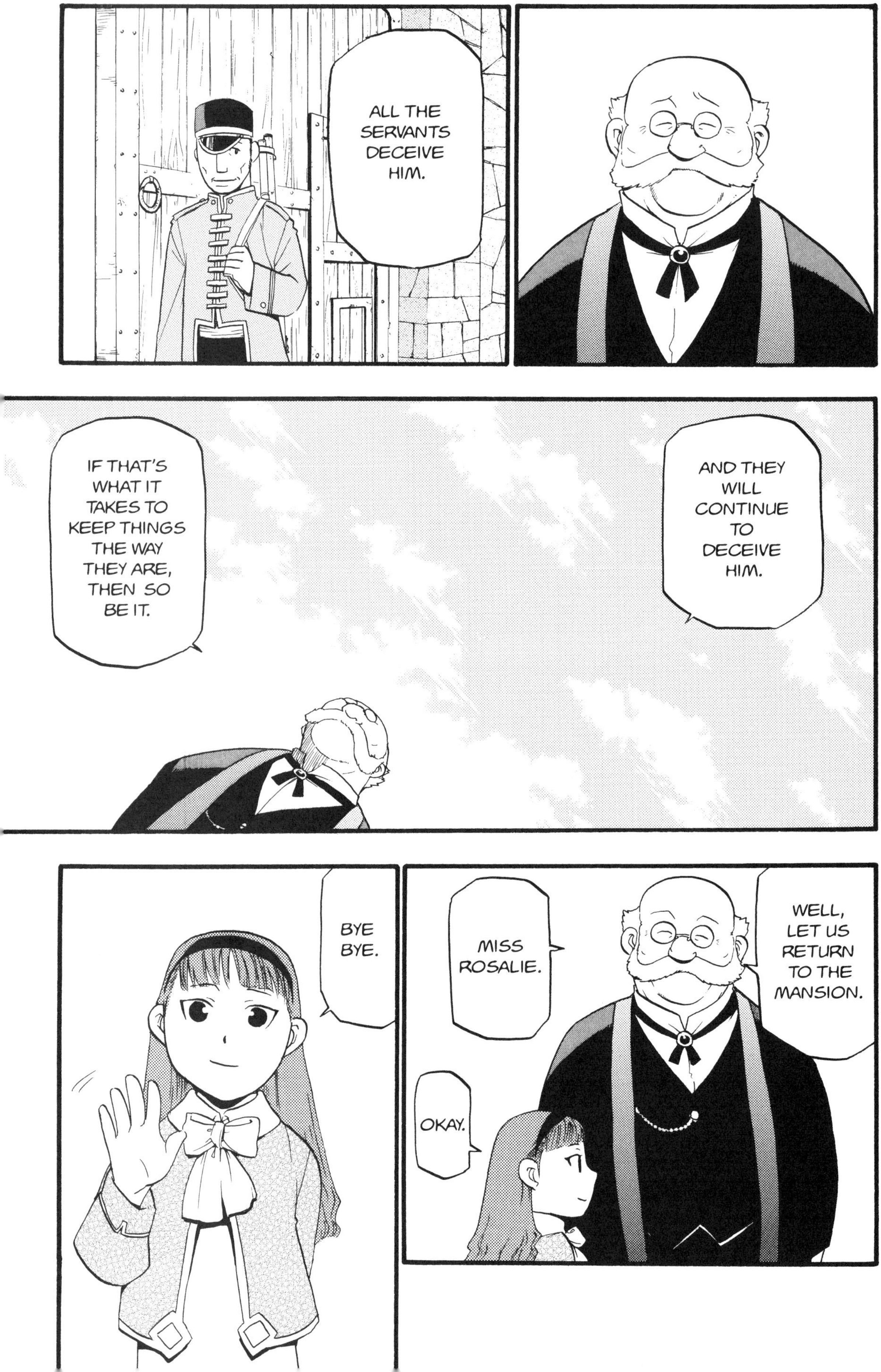
ALL THE SERVANTS DECEIVE HIM.
AND THEY WILL CONTINUE TO DECEIVE HIM.
IF THAT'S WHAT IT TAKES TO KEEP THINGS THE WAY THEY ARE, THEN SO BE IT.
WELL, LET US RETURN TO THE MANSION.
MISS ROSALIE.
OKAY.
BYE BYE.

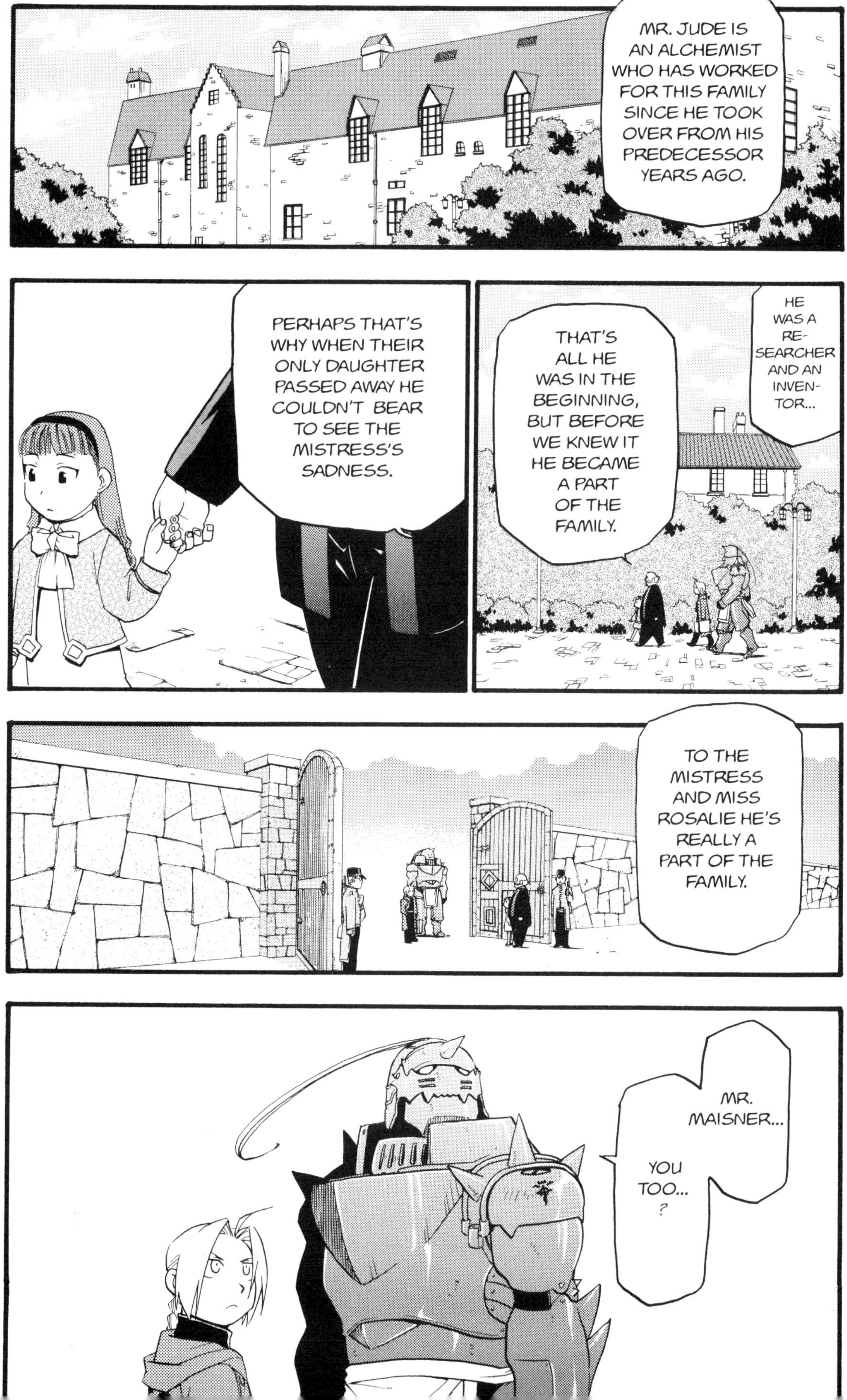
MR. JUDE IS AN ALCHEMIST WHO HAS WORKED FOR THIS FAMILY SINCE HE TOOK OVER FROM HIS PREDECESSOR YEARS AGO.
HE WAS A RE-SEARCHER AND AN INVEN-TOR...
THAT'S ALL HE WAS IN THE BEGINNING, BUT BEFORE WE KNEW IT HE BECAME A PART OF THE FAMILY.
PERHAPS THAT'S WHY WHEN THEIR ONLY DAUGHTER PASSED AWAY HE COULDN'T BEAR TO SEE THE MISTRESS'S SADNESS.
TO THE MISTRESS AND MISS ROSALIE HE'S REALLY A PART OF THE FAMILY.
MR. MAISNER...
YOU TOO... ?

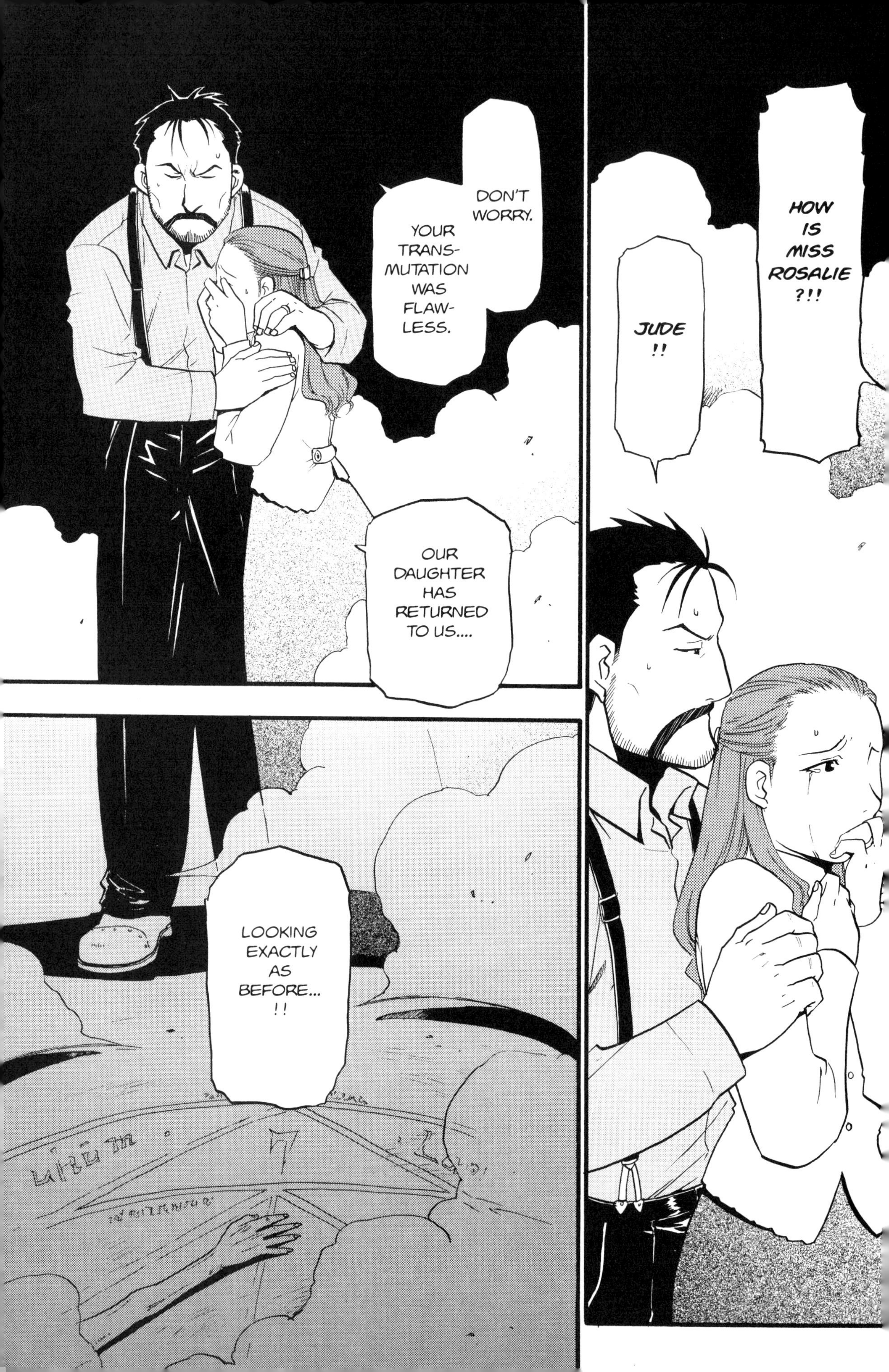
HOW IS MISS ROSALIE ?!!
JUDE !!
DON'T WORRY.
YOUR TRANS-MUTATION WAS FLAW-LESS.
OUR DAUGHTER HAS RETURNED TO US....
LOOKING EXACTLY AS BEFORE... !!

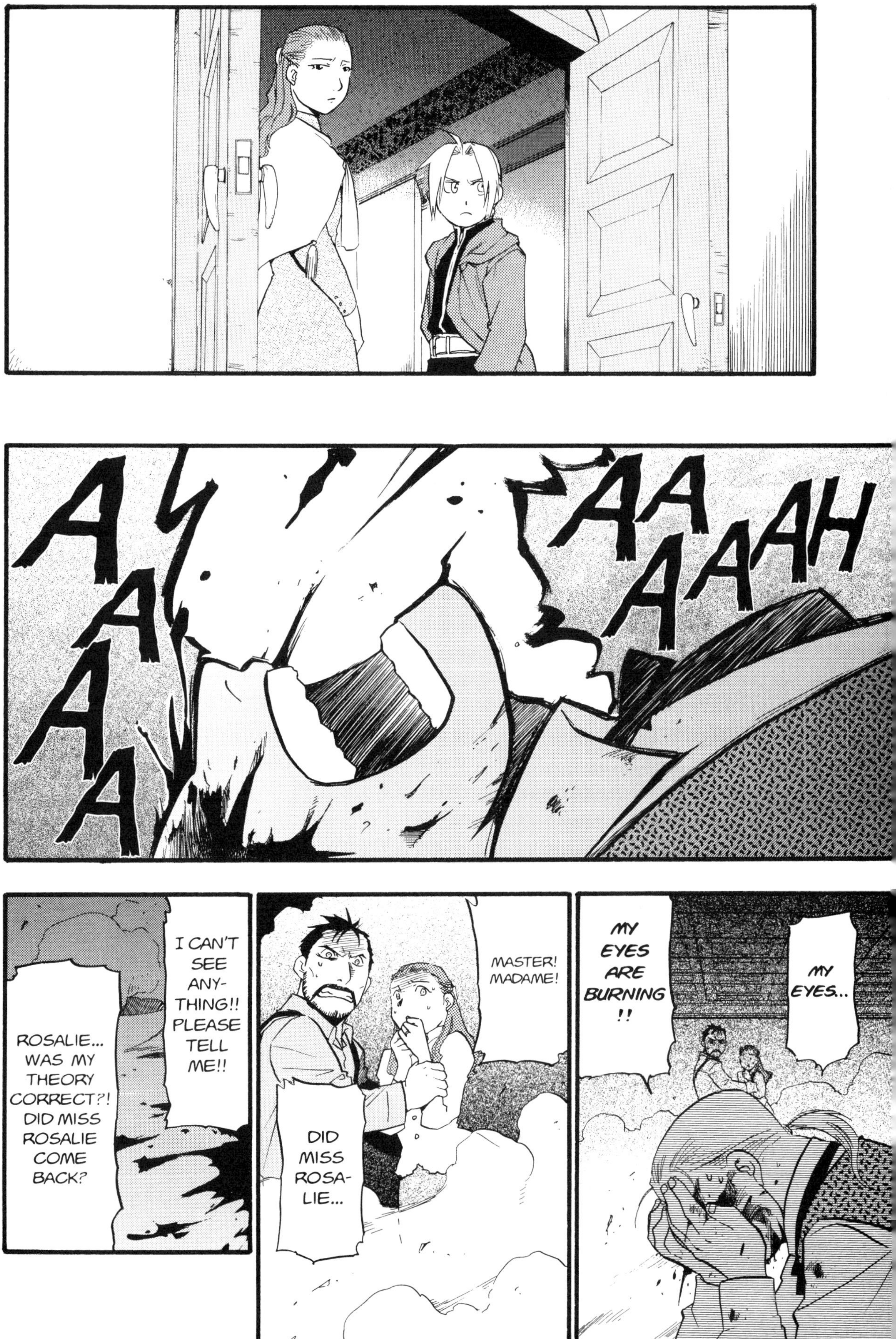
AAAAA
AAAAAAH
MY EYES...
MY EYES ARE BURNING!!
MASTER! MADAME!
DID MISS ROSALIE...
I CAN'T SEE ANYTHING!! PLEASE TELL ME!!
ROSALIE... WAS MY THEORY CORRECT?! DID MISS ROSALIE COME BACK?

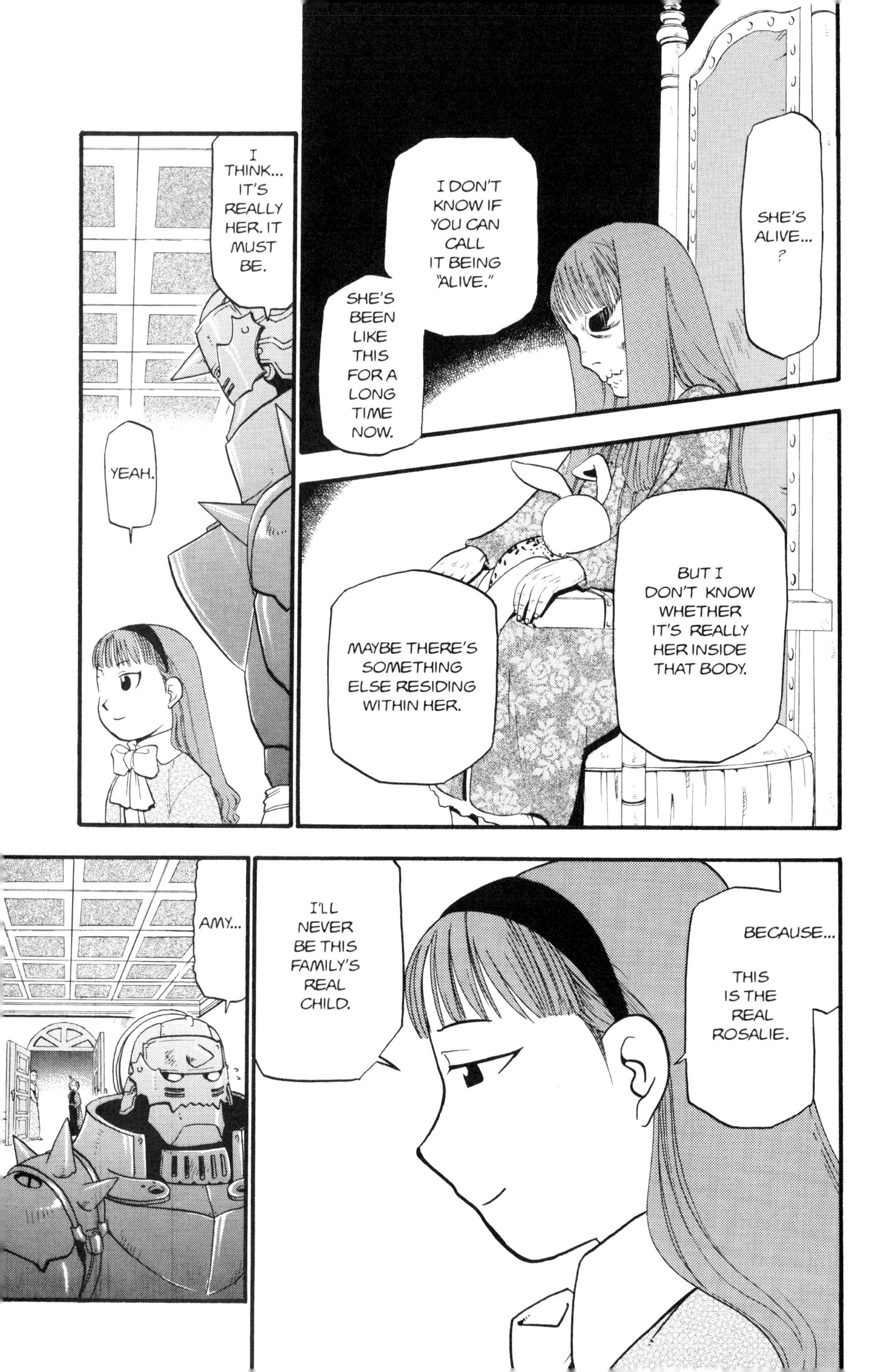
SHE'S ALIVE...?
I DON'T KNOW IF YOU CAN CALL IT BEING "ALIVE."
SHE'S BEEN LIKE THIS FOR A LONG TIME NOW.
BUT I DON'T KNOW WHETHER IT'S REALLY HER INSIDE THAT BODY.
MAYBE THERE'S SOMETHING ELSE RESIDING WITHIN HER.
I THINK... IT'S REALLY HER. IT MUST BE.
YEAH.
BECAUSE... THIS IS THE REAL ROSALIE.
I'LL NEVER BE THIS FAMILY'S REAL CHILD.
AMY...

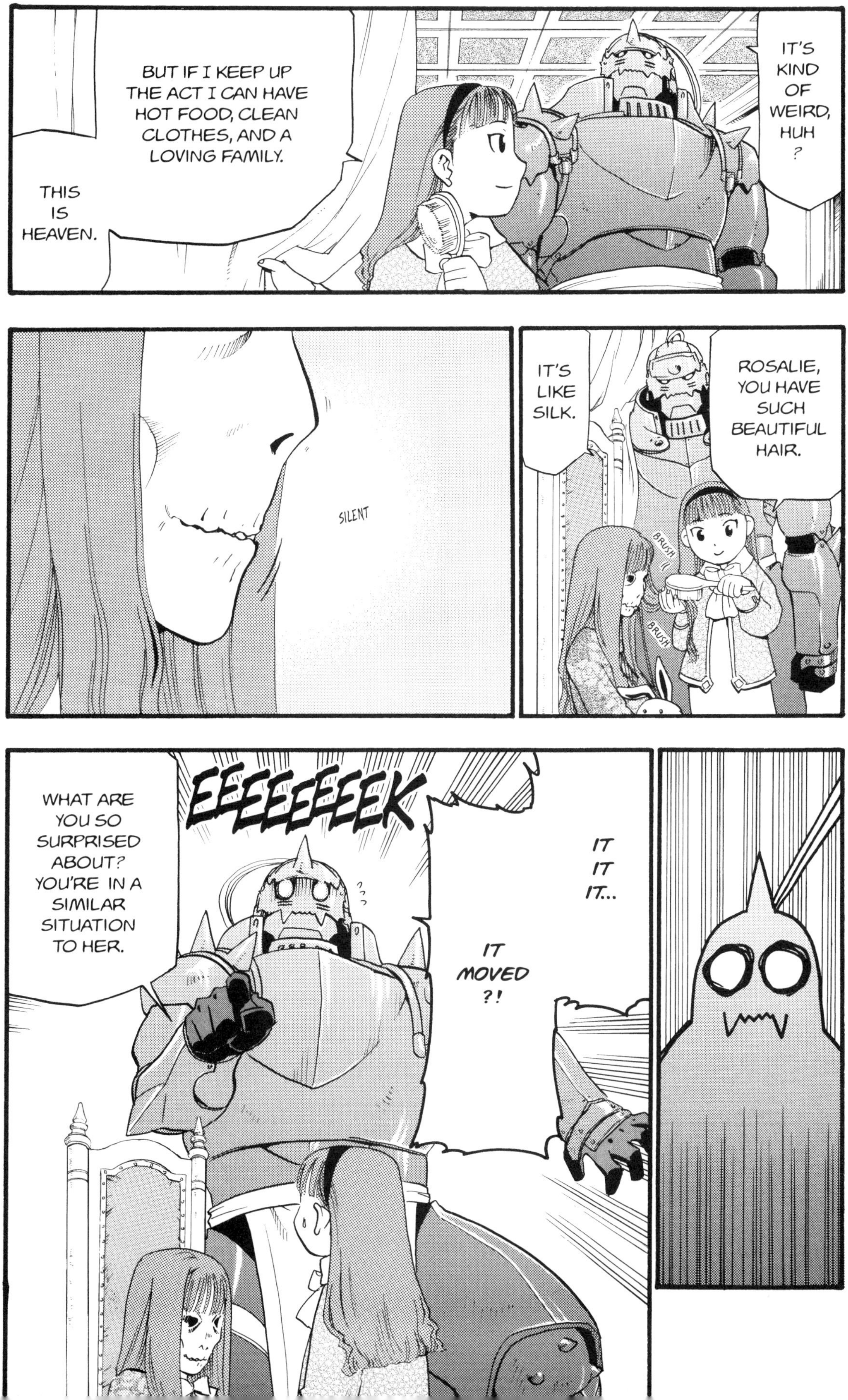
IT'S KIND OF WEIRD, HUH?
BUT IF I KEEP UP THE ACT I CAN HAVE HOT FOOD, CLEAN CLOTHES, AND A LOVING FAMILY.
THIS IS HEAVEN.
ROSALIE, YOU HAVE SUCH BEAUTIFUL HAIR.
IT'S LIKE SILK.
BRUSH
BRUSH
SILENT
EEEEEEEEK
IT IT IT...
IT MOVED?!
WHAT ARE YOU SO SURPRISED ABOUT? YOU'RE IN A SIMILAR SITUATION TO HER.

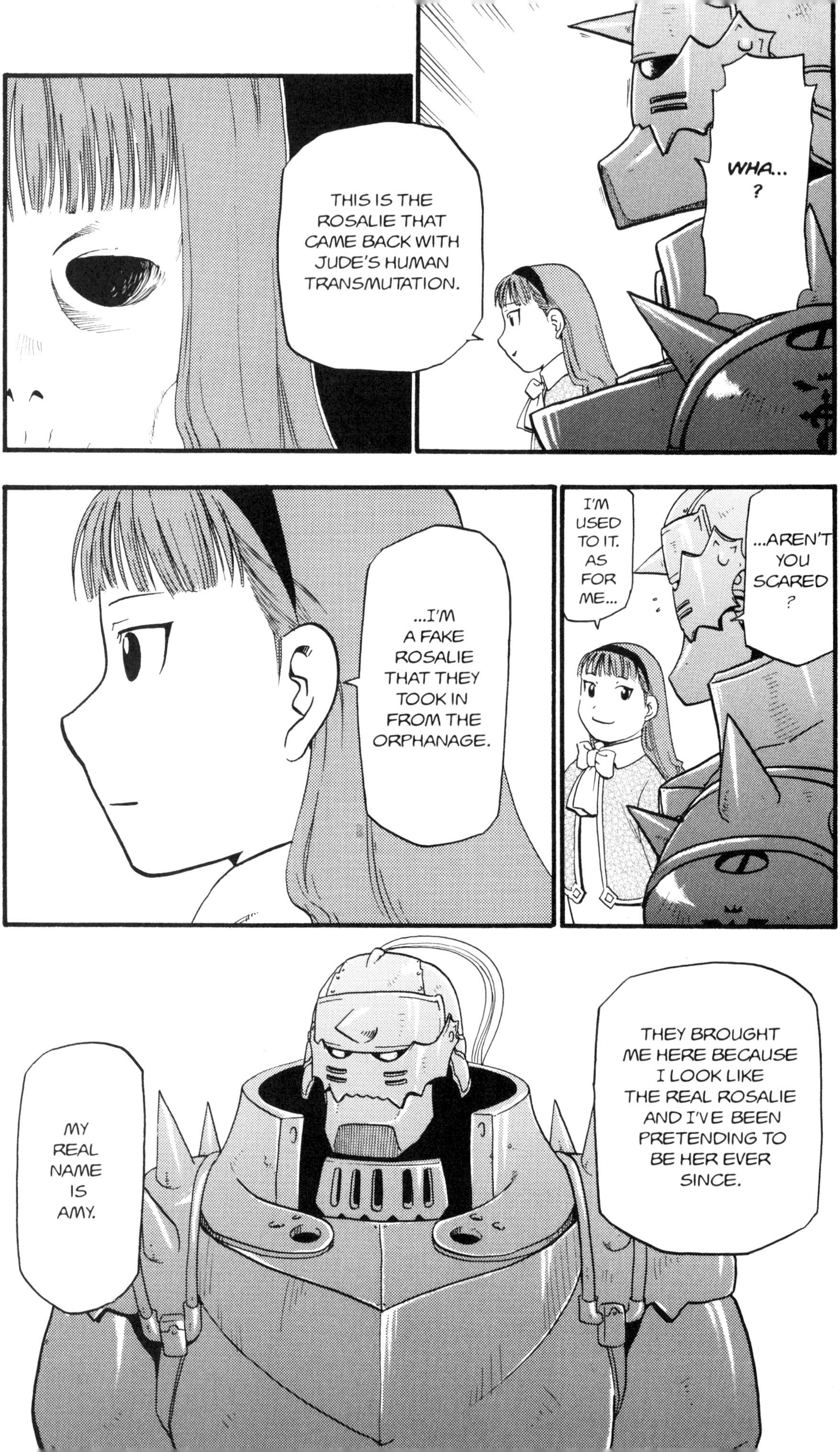
WHA...?
THIS IS THE ROSALIE THAT CAME BACK WITH JUDE'S HUMAN TRANSMUTATION.
...AREN'T YOU SCARED?
I'M USED TO IT. AS FOR ME...
...I'M A FAKE ROSALIE THAT THEY TOOK IN FROM THE ORPHANAGE.
THEY BROUGHT ME HERE BECAUSE I LOOK LIKE THE REAL ROSALIE AND I'VE BEEN PRETENDING TO BE HER EVER SINCE.
MY REAL NAME IS AMY.

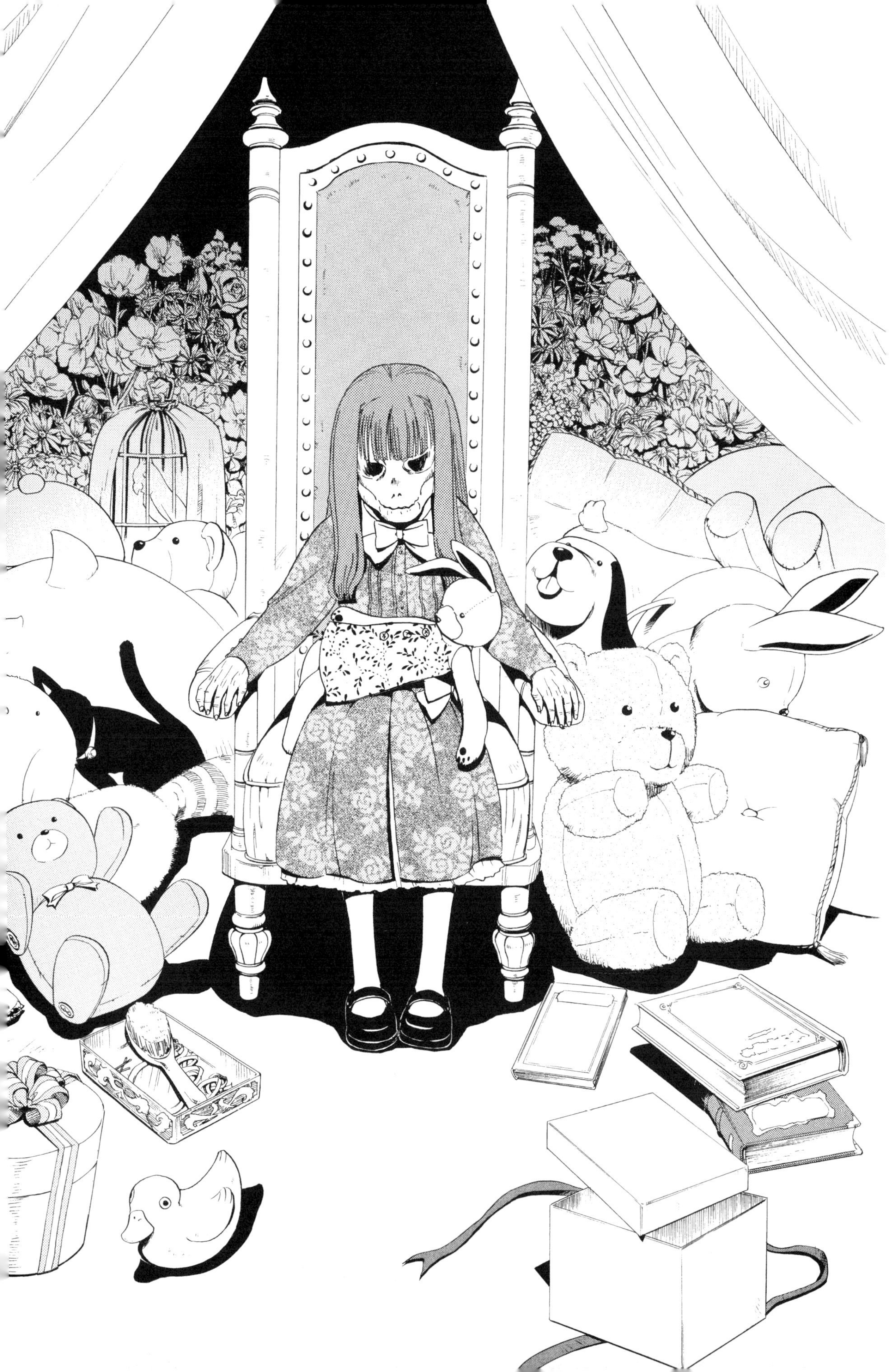

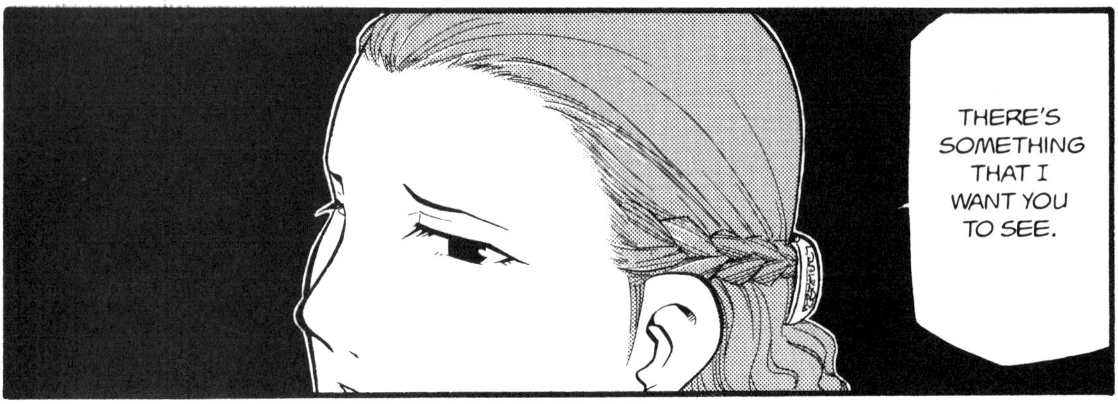
THERE'S SOMETHING THAT I WANT YOU TO SEE.

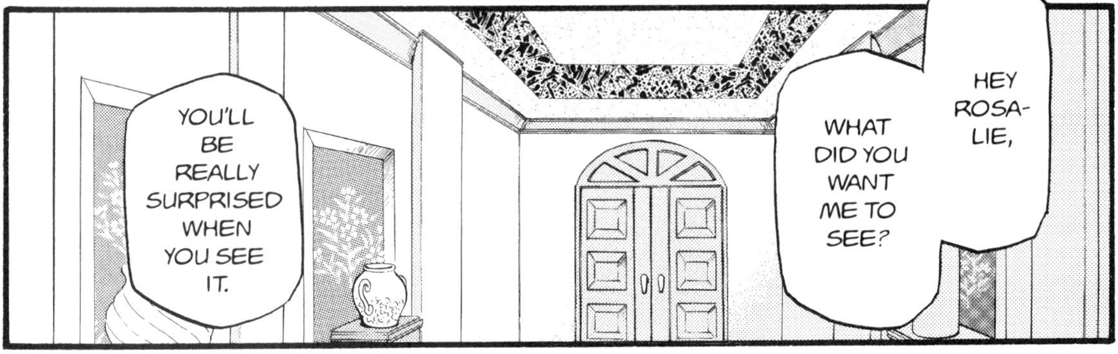
HEY ROSA-LIE,
WHAT DID YOU WANT ME TO SEE?
YOU'LL BE REALLY SURPRISED WHEN YOU SEE IT.

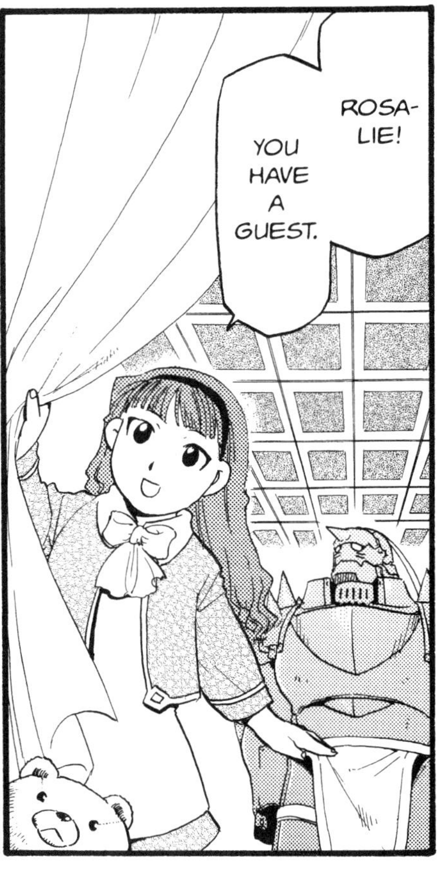
ROSA-LIE!
YOU HAVE A GUEST.

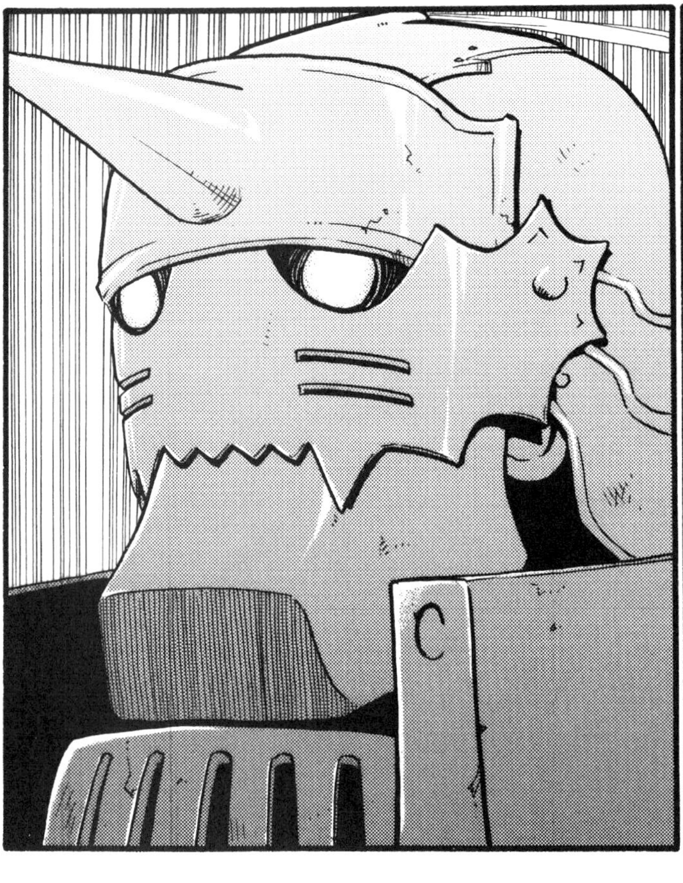

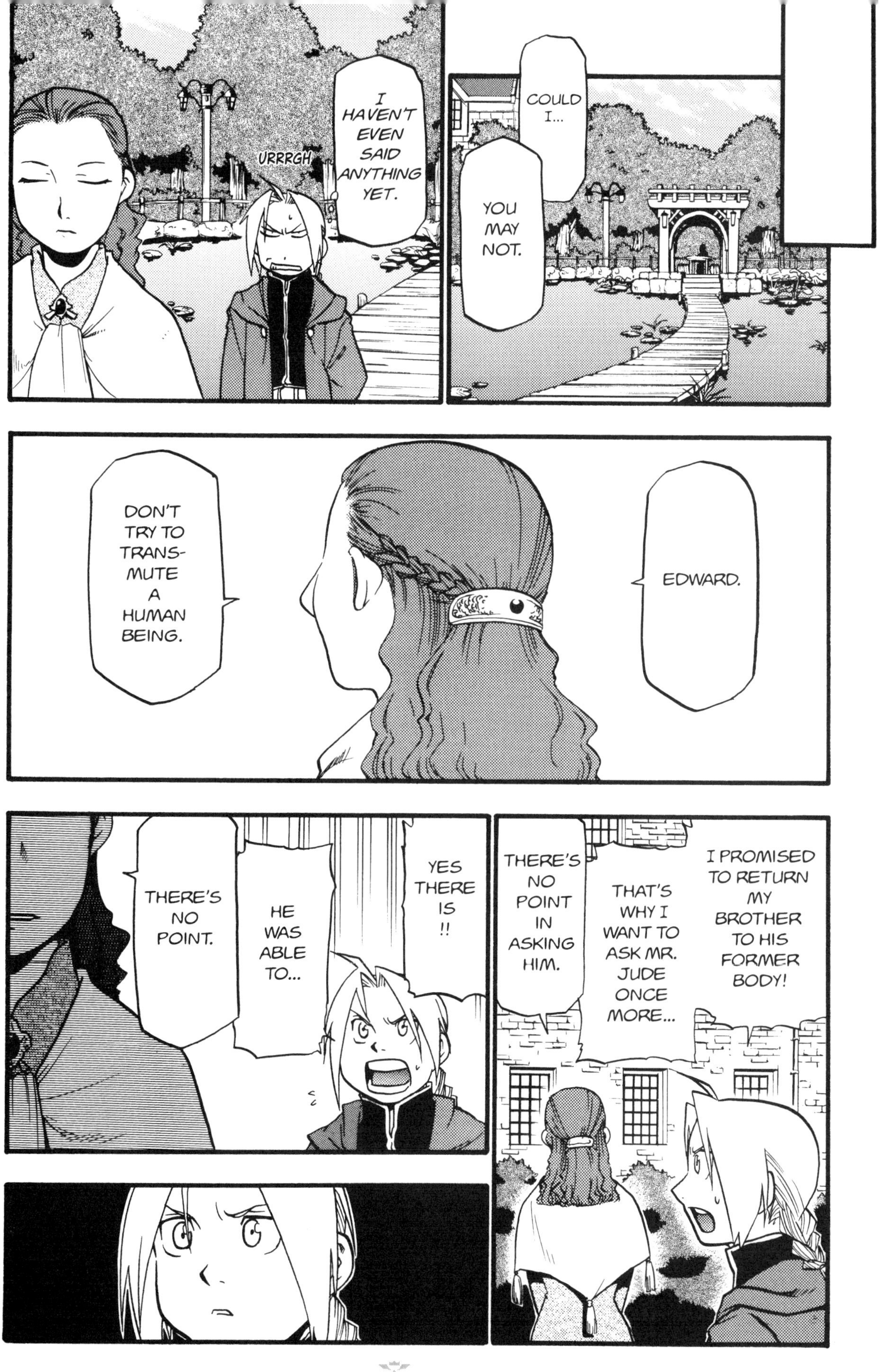
COULD I...
YOU MAY NOT.
I HAVEN'T EVEN SAID ANYTHING YET.
URRRGH
EDWARD.
DON'T TRY TO TRANS-MUTE A HUMAN BEING.
I PROMISED TO RETURN MY BROTHER TO HIS FORMER BODY!
THAT'S WHY I WANT TO ASK MR. JUDE ONCE MORE...
THERE'S NO POINT IN ASKING HIM.
YES THERE IS !!
HE WAS ABLE TO...
THERE'S NO POINT.

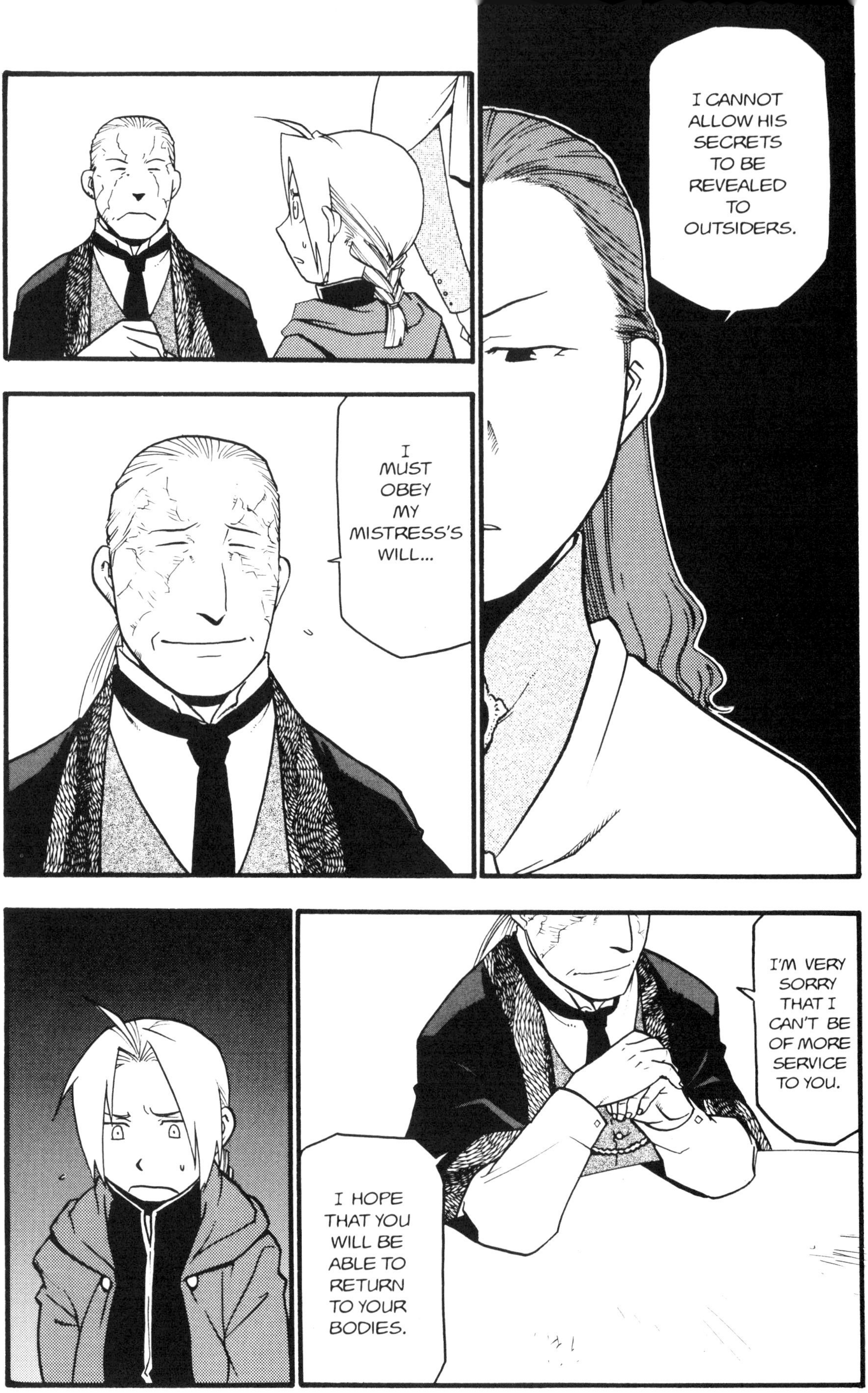
I CANNOT ALLOW HIS SECRETS TO BE REVEALED TO OUTSIDERS.
I MUST OBEY MY MISTRESS'S WILL...
I'M VERY SORRY THAT I CAN'T BE OF MORE SERVICE TO YOU.
I HOPE THAT YOU WILL BE ABLE TO RETURN TO YOUR BODIES.

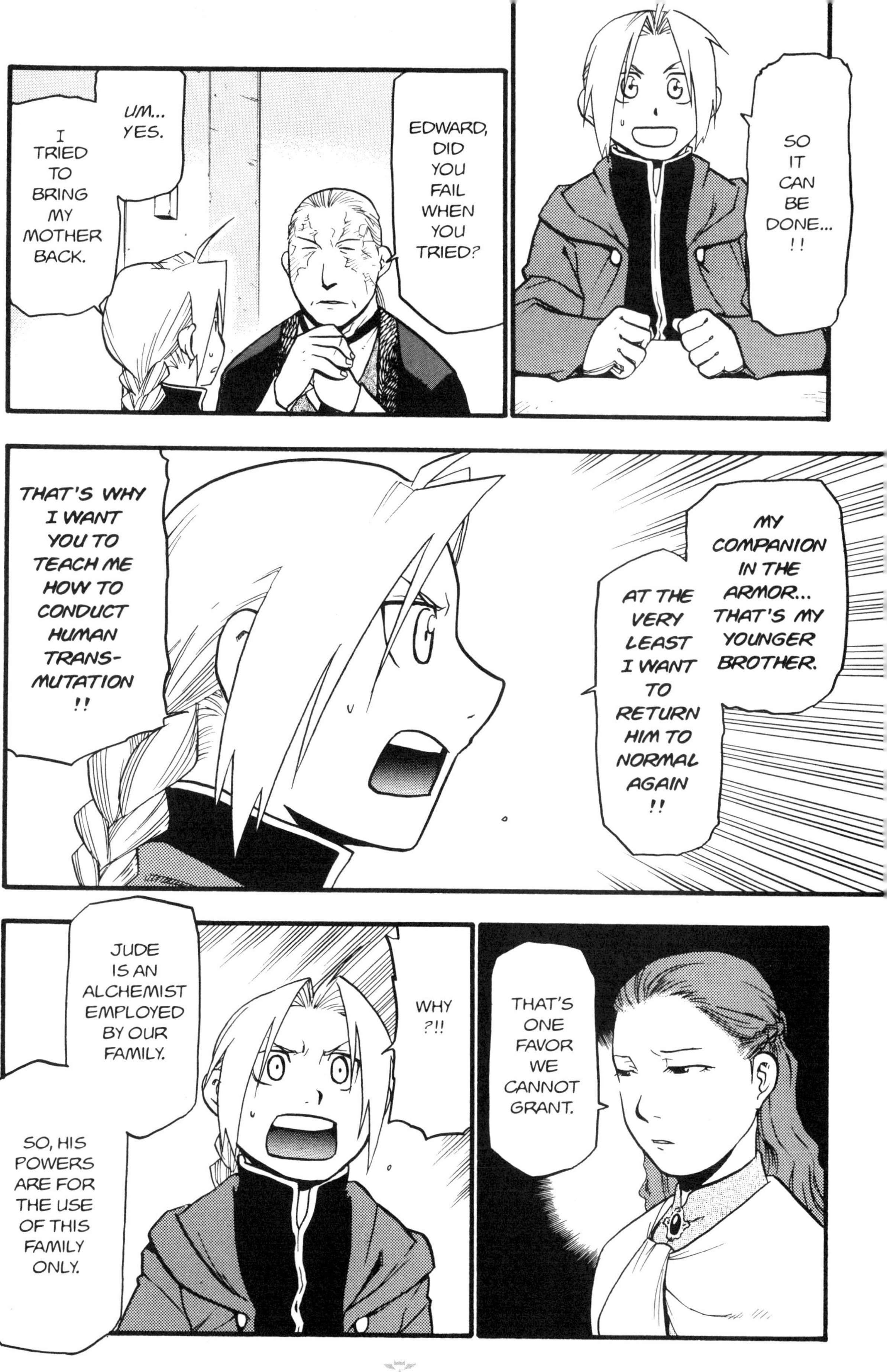
SO IT CAN BE DONE...!!
EDWARD, DID YOU FAIL WHEN YOU TRIED?
UM... YES.
I TRIED TO BRING MY MOTHER BACK.
MY COMPANION IN THE ARMOR... THAT'S MY YOUNGER BROTHER.
AT THE VERY LEAST I WANT TO RETURN HIM TO NORMAL AGAIN!!
THAT'S WHY I WANT YOU TO TEACH ME HOW TO CONDUCT HUMAN TRANS-MUTATION!!
THAT'S ONE FAVOR WE CANNOT GRANT.
WHY?!!
JUDE IS AN ALCHEMIST EMPLOYED BY OUR FAMILY.
SO, HIS POWERS ARE FOR THE USE OF THIS FAMILY ONLY.

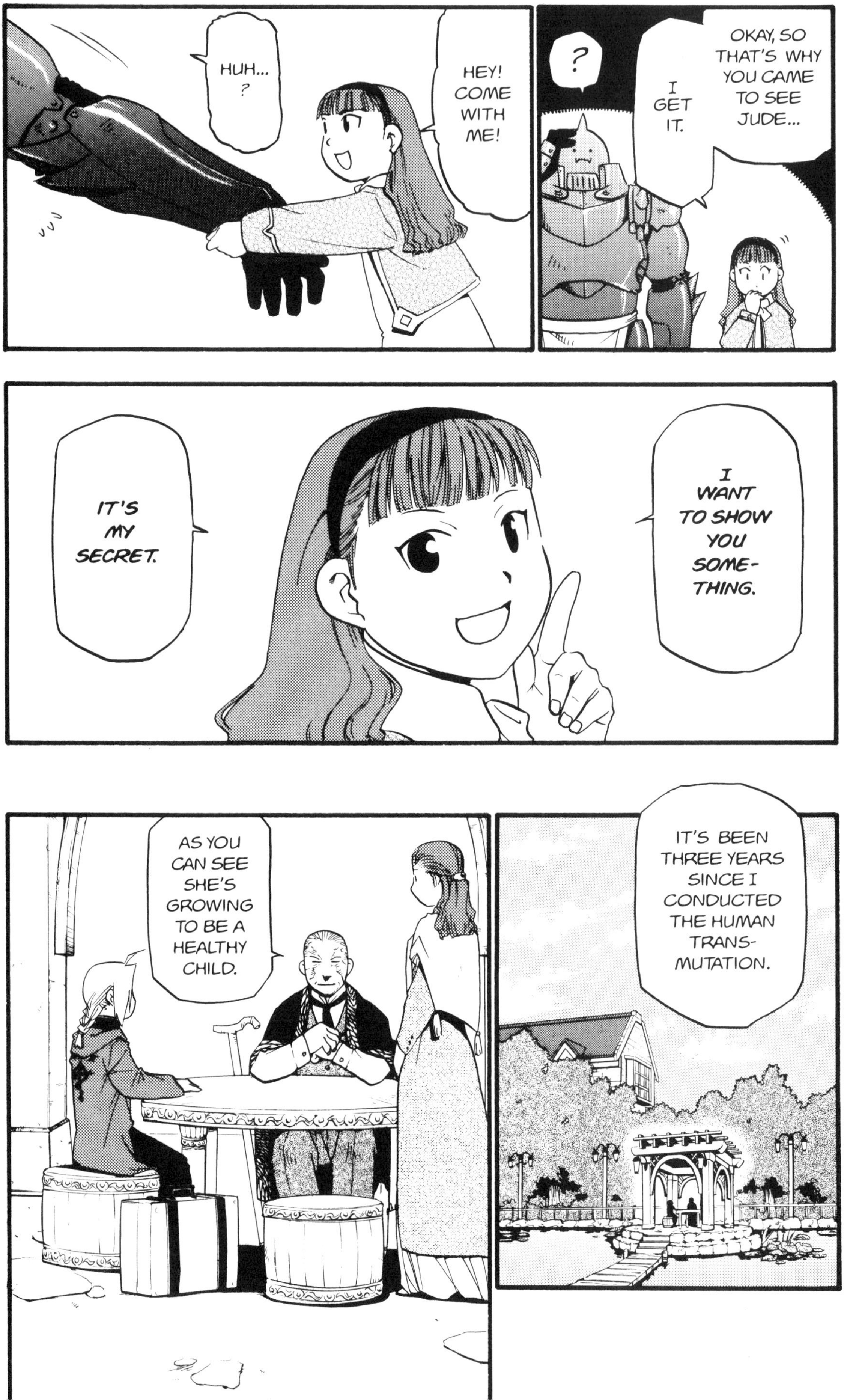
OKAY, SO THAT'S WHY YOU CAME TO SEE JUDE...
I GET IT.
?
HEY! COME WITH ME!
HUH... ?
I WANT TO SHOW YOU SOME-THING.
IT'S MY SECRET.
IT'S BEEN THREE YEARS SINCE I CONDUCTED THE HUMAN TRANS-MUTATION.
AS YOU CAN SEE SHE'S GROWING TO BE A HEALTHY CHILD.

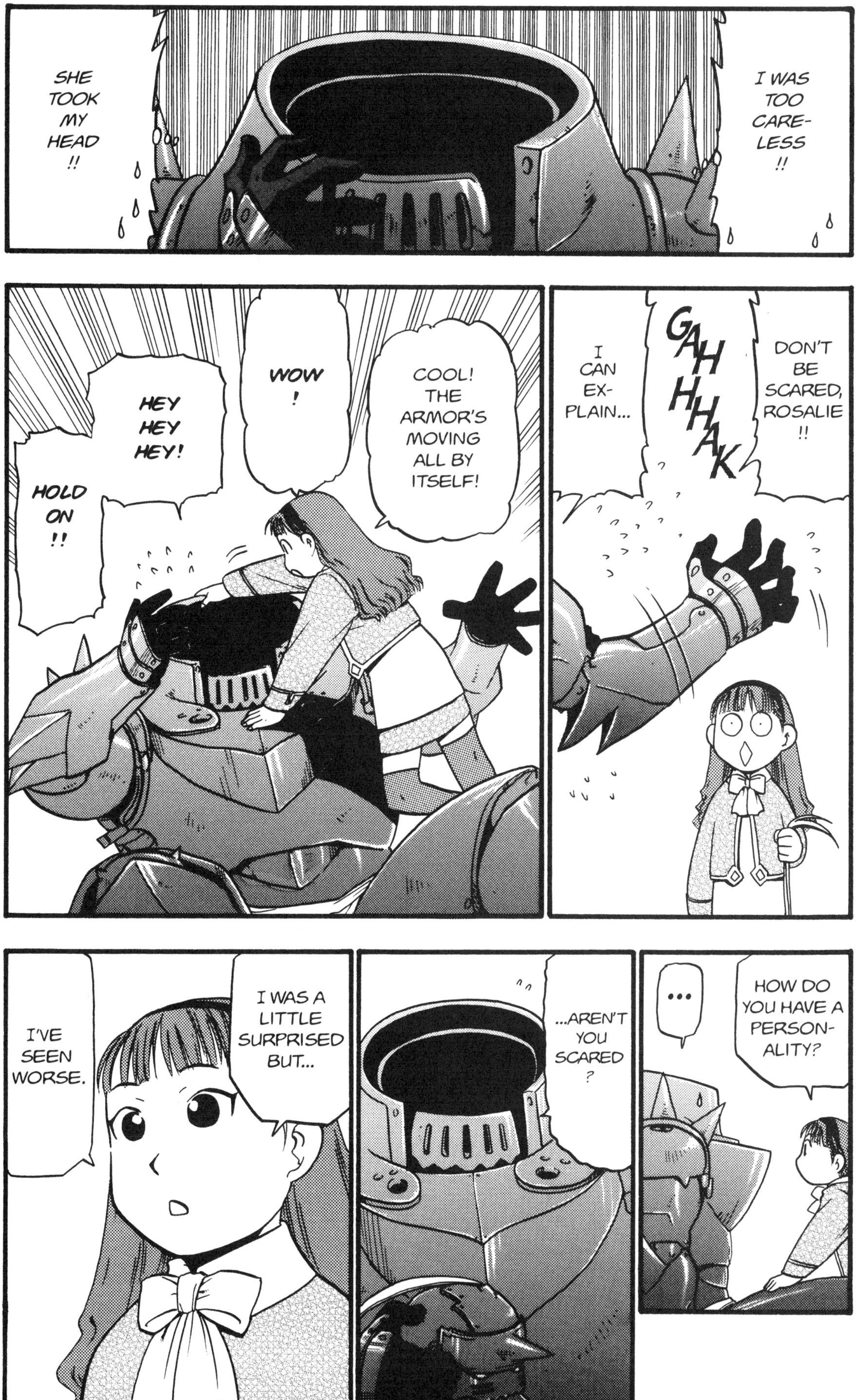
I WAS TOO CARE-LESS!!
SHE TOOK MY HEAD!!
DON'T BE SCARED, ROSALIE!!
GAHHHHAK
I CAN EX-PLAIN...
COOL! THE ARMOR'S MOVING ALL BY ITSELF!
WOW!
HEY HEY HEY!
HOLD ON!!
HOW DO YOU HAVE A PERSON-ALITY?
...
...AREN'T YOU SCARED?
I WAS A LITTLE SURPRISED BUT...
I'VE SEEN WORSE.

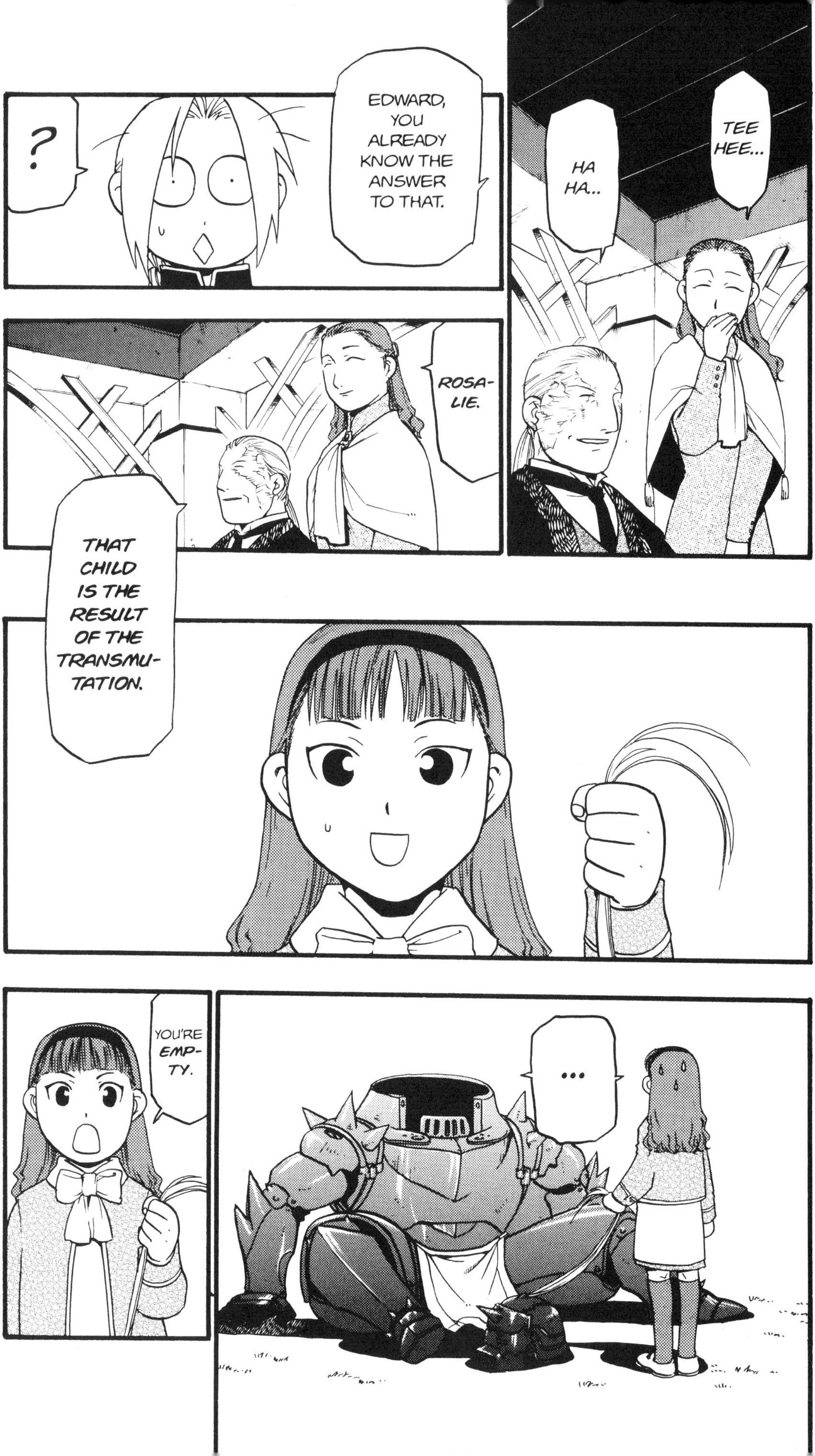
?
EDWARD, YOU ALREADY KNOW THE ANSWER TO THAT.
ROSA-LIE.
HA HA...
TEE HEE...
THAT CHILD IS THE RESULT OF THE TRANSMU-TATION.
YOU'RE EMP-TY.
...

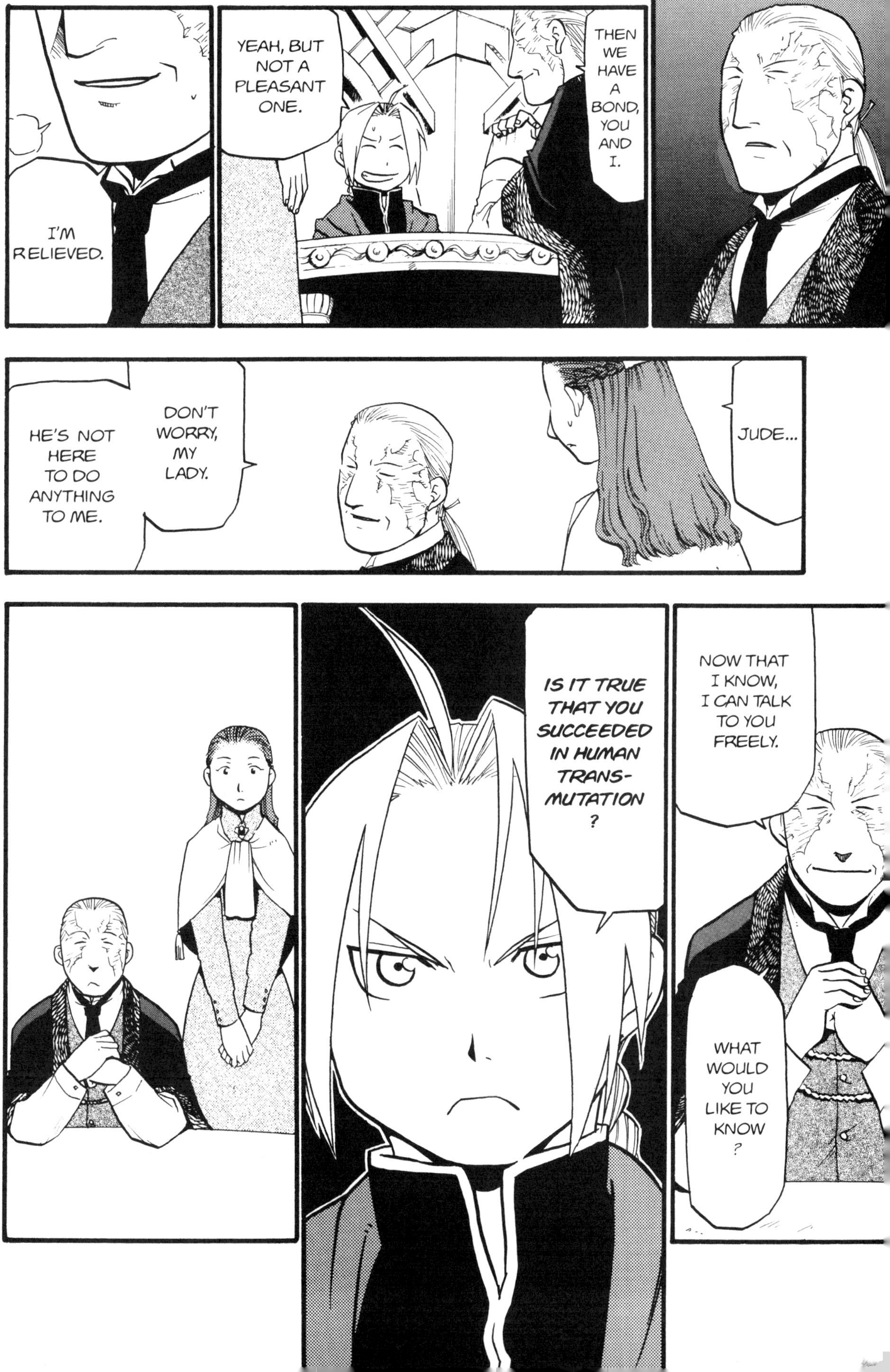
THEN WE HAVE A BOND, YOU AND I.
YEAH, BUT NOT A PLEASANT ONE.
I'M RELIEVED.
JUDE...
DON'T WORRY, MY LADY.
HE'S NOT HERE TO DO ANYTHING TO ME.
NOW THAT I KNOW, I CAN TALK TO YOU FREELY.
WHAT WOULD YOU LIKE TO KNOW?
IS IT TRUE THAT YOU SUCCEEDED IN HUMAN TRANS-MUTATION?

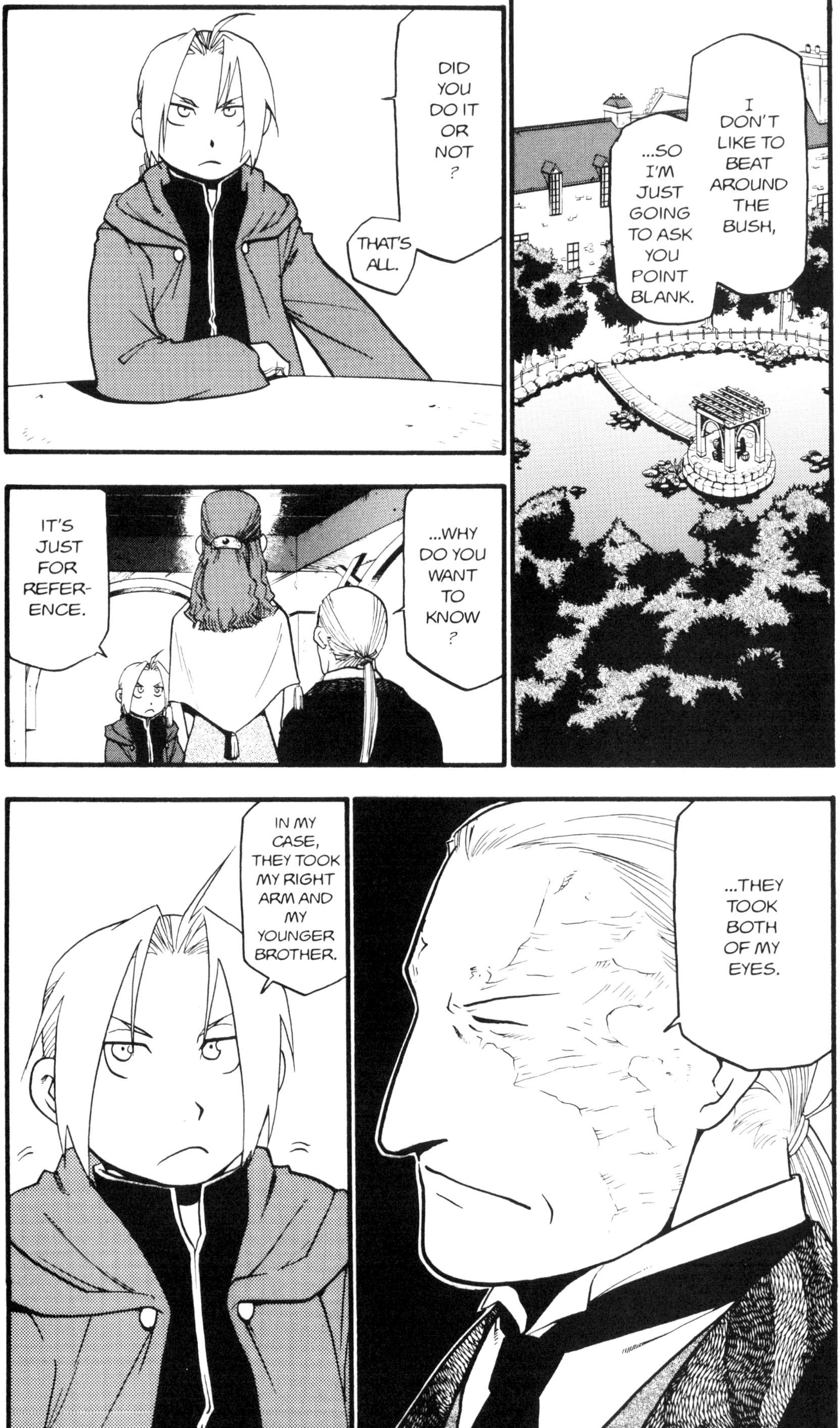
I DON'T LIKE TO BEAT AROUND THE BUSH,
...SO I'M JUST GOING TO ASK YOU POINT BLANK.
DID YOU DO IT OR NOT?
THAT'S ALL.
...WHY DO YOU WANT TO KNOW?
IT'S JUST FOR REFERENCE.
...THEY TOOK BOTH OF MY EYES.
IN MY CASE, THEY TOOK MY RIGHT ARM AND MY YOUNGER BROTHER.

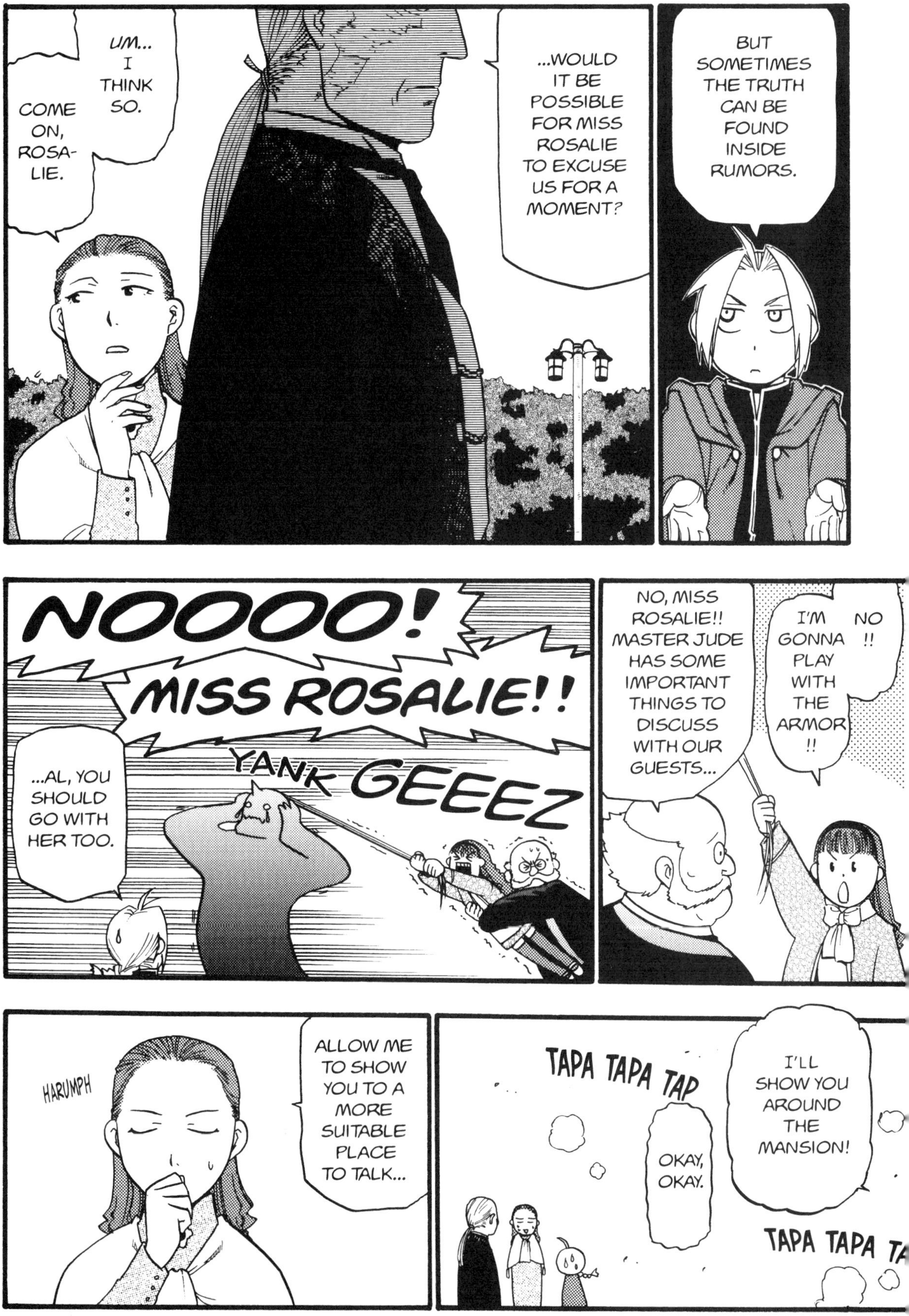
BUT SOMETIMES THE TRUTH CAN BE FOUND INSIDE RUMORS.
...WOULD IT BE POSSIBLE FOR MISS ROSALIE TO EXCUSE US FOR A MOMENT?
UM... I THINK SO.
COME ON, ROSALIE.
NO !!
I'M GONNA PLAY WITH THE ARMOR !!
NO, MISS ROSALIE!! MASTER JUDE HAS SOME IMPORTANT THINGS TO DISCUSS WITH OUR GUESTS...
NOOOO!
MISS ROSALIE!!
YANK
GEEEZ
...AL, YOU SHOULD GO WITH HER TOO.
I'LL SHOW YOU AROUND THE MANSION!
TAPA TAPA TAP
OKAY, OKAY.
TAPA TAPA TA
ALLOW ME TO SHOW YOU TO A MORE SUITABLE PLACE TO TALK...
HARUMPH

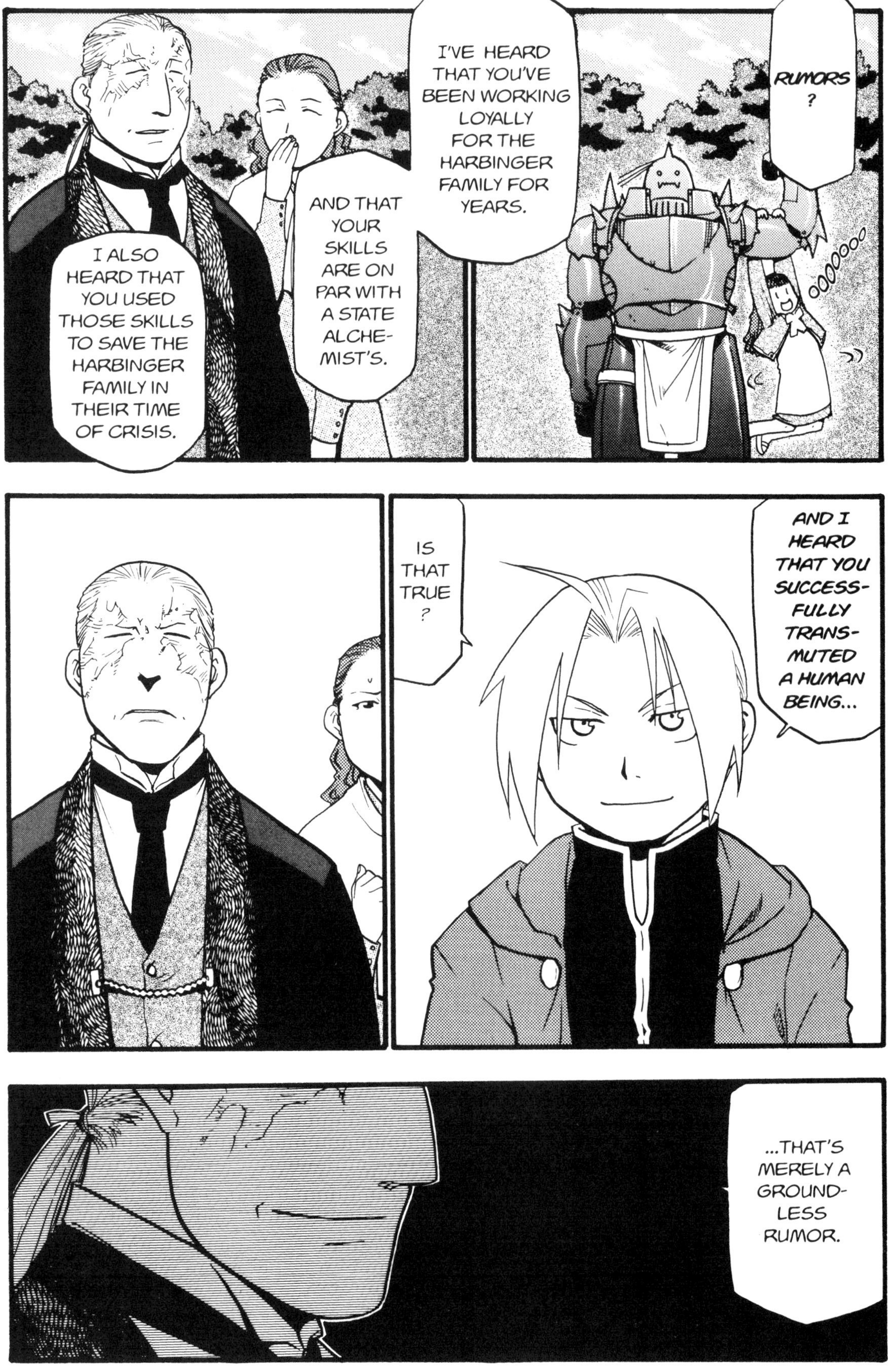
RUMORS ?
I'VE HEARD THAT YOU'VE BEEN WORKING LOYALLY FOR THE HARBINGER FAMILY FOR YEARS.
AND THAT YOUR SKILLS ARE ON PAR WITH A STATE ALCHEMIST'S.
I ALSO HEARD THAT YOU USED THOSE SKILLS TO SAVE THE HARBINGER FAMILY IN THEIR TIME OF CRISIS.
AND I HEARD THAT YOU SUCCESSFULLY TRANSMUTED A HUMAN BEING...
IS THAT TRUE ?
...THAT'S MERELY A GROUNDLESS RUMOR.

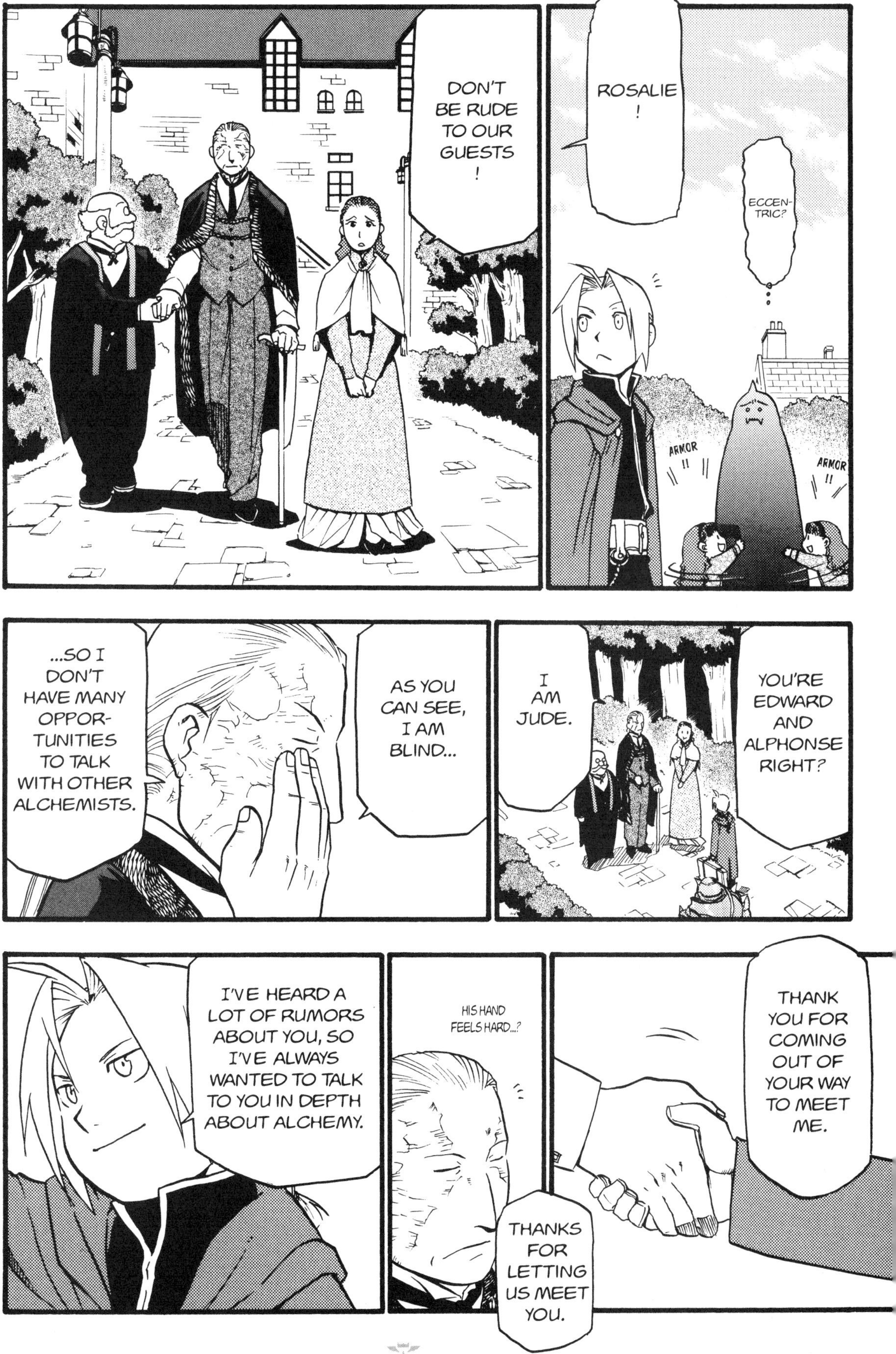
ROSALIE!
ECCENTRIC?
ARMOR!!
ARMOR!!
DON'T BE RUDE TO OUR GUESTS!
YOU'RE EDWARD AND ALPHONSE RIGHT?
I AM JUDE.
AS YOU CAN SEE, I AM BLIND...
...SO I DON'T HAVE MANY OPPORTUNITIES TO TALK WITH OTHER ALCHEMISTS.
THANK YOU FOR COMING OUT OF YOUR WAY TO MEET ME.
THANKS FOR LETTING US MEET YOU.
HIS HAND FEELS HARD...?
I'VE HEARD A LOT OF RUMORS ABOUT YOU, SO I'VE ALWAYS WANTED TO TALK TO YOU IN DEPTH ABOUT ALCHEMY.

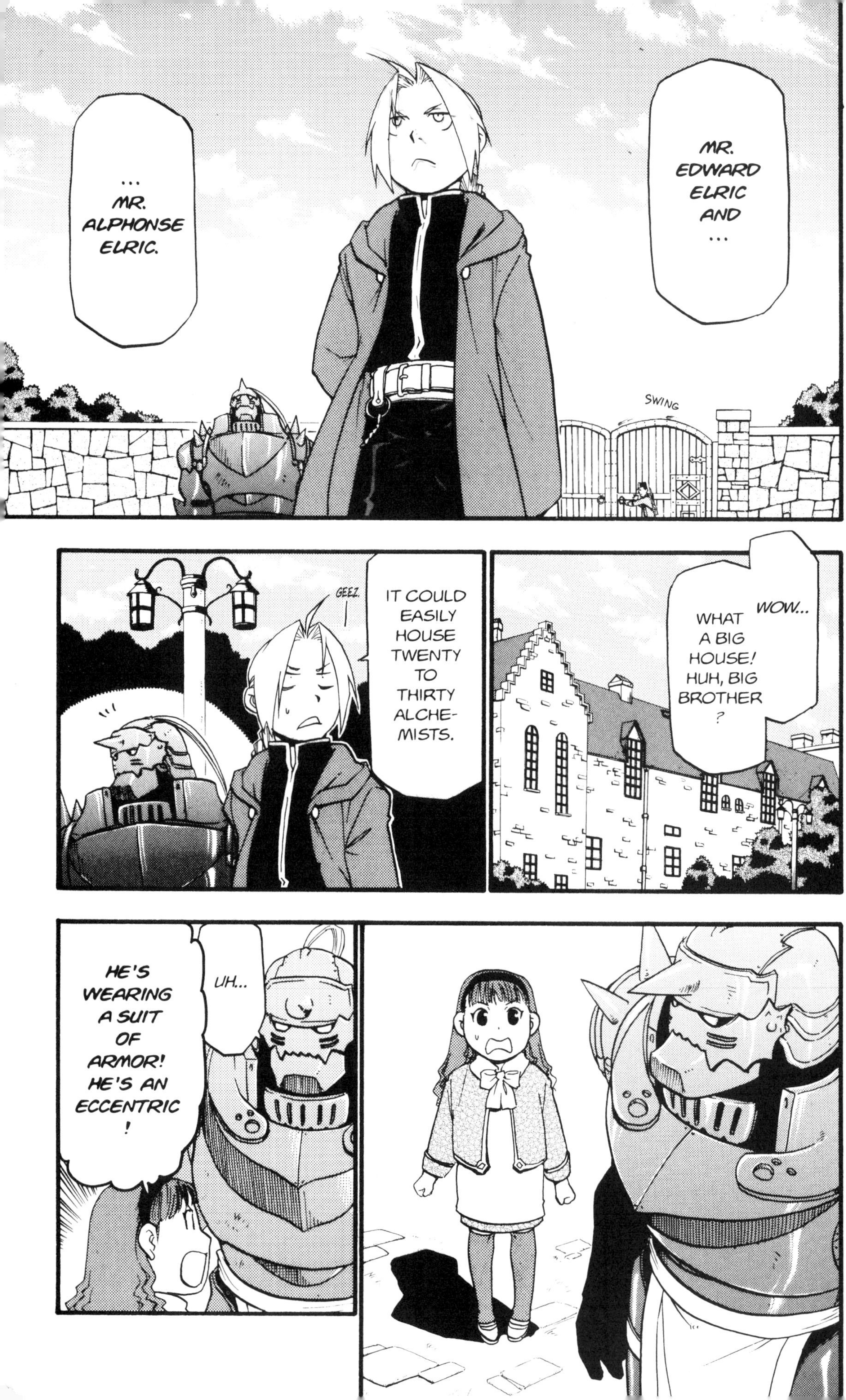
MR. EDWARD ELRIC AND ...
... MR. ALPHONSE ELRIC.
SWING
WOW... WHAT A BIG HOUSE! HUH, BIG BROTHER?
GEEZ.
IT COULD EASILY HOUSE TWENTY TO THIRTY ALCHE-MISTS.
UH...
HE'S WEARING A SUIT OF ARMOR! HE'S AN ECCENTRIC!

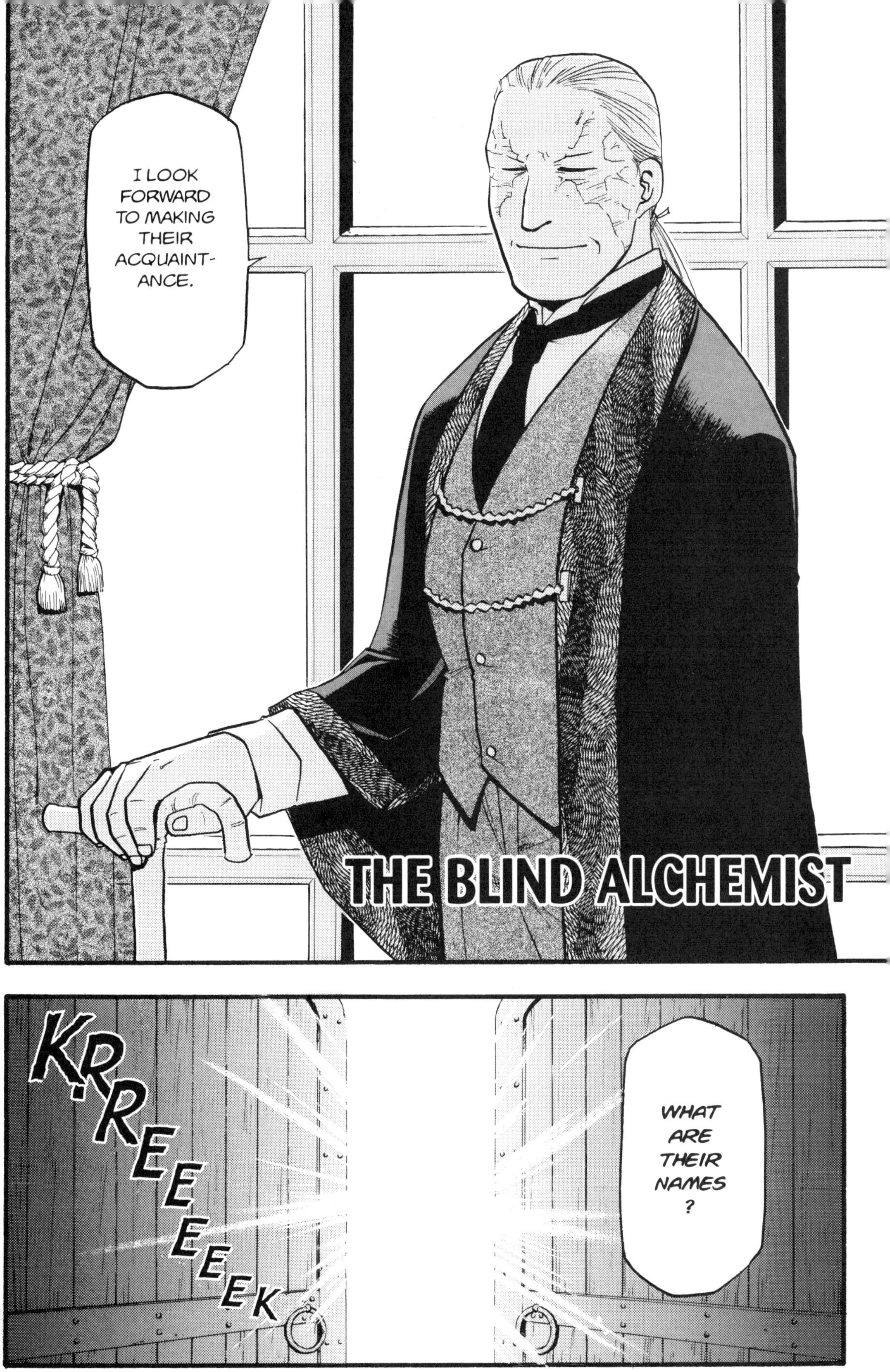
I LOOK FORWARD TO MAKING THEIR ACQUAINT-ANCE.
THE BLIND ALCHEMIST
WHAT ARE THEIR NAMES ?
KRREEEEEEK

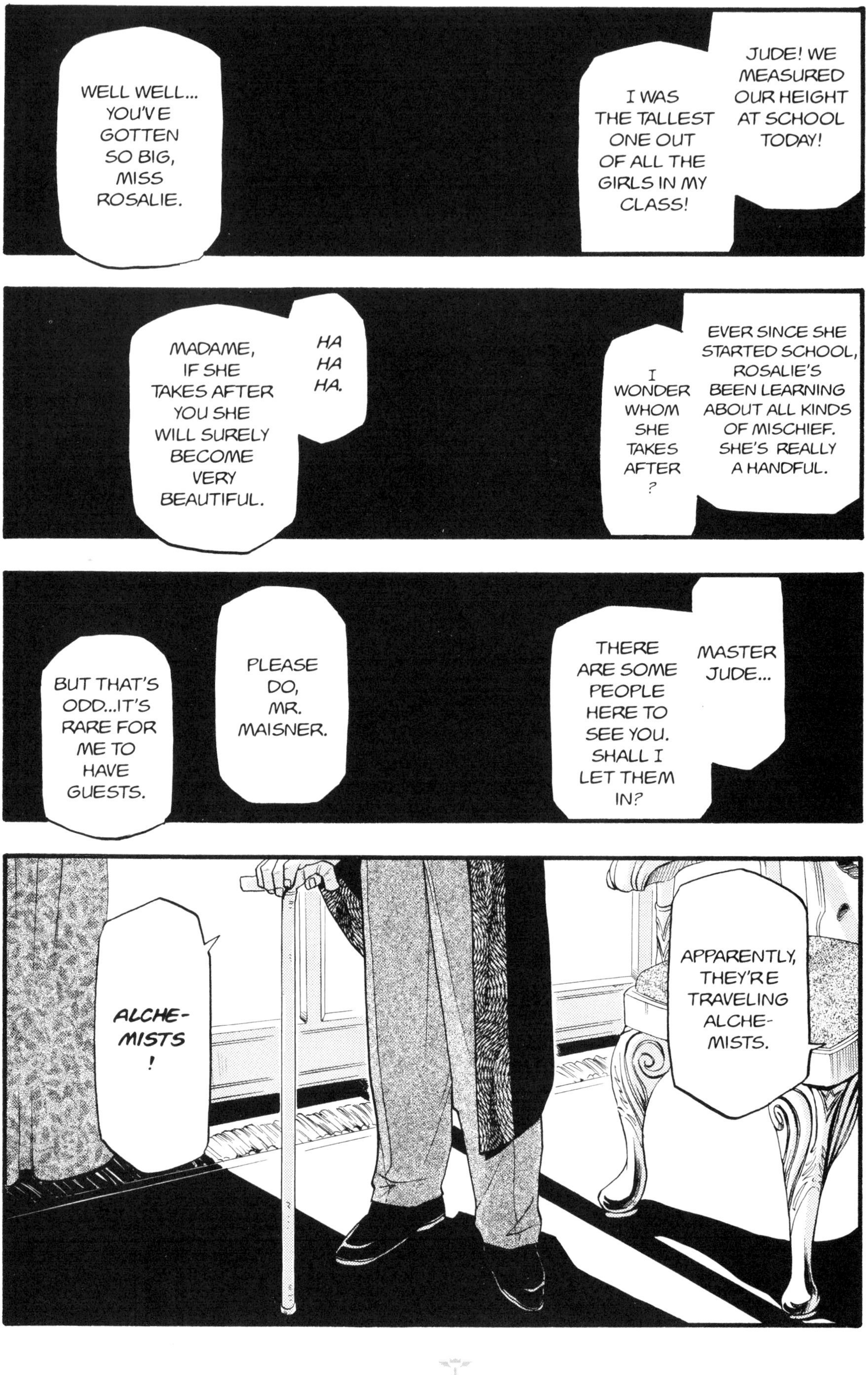
JUDE! WE MEASURED OUR HEIGHT AT SCHOOL TODAY!
I WAS THE TALLEST ONE OUT OF ALL THE GIRLS IN MY CLASS!
WELL WELL... YOU'VE GOTTEN SO BIG, MISS ROSALIE.
EVER SINCE SHE STARTED SCHOOL, ROSALIE'S BEEN LEARNING ABOUT ALL KINDS OF MISCHIEF. SHE'S REALLY A HANDFUL.
I WONDER WHOM SHE TAKES AFTER?
HA HA HA.
MADAME, IF SHE TAKES AFTER YOU SHE WILL SURELY BECOME VERY BEAUTIFUL.
MASTER JUDE...
THERE ARE SOME PEOPLE HERE TO SEE YOU. SHALL I LET THEM IN?
PLEASE DO, MR. MAISNER.
BUT THAT'S ODD...IT'S RARE FOR ME TO HAVE GUESTS.
APPARENTLY, THEY'RE TRAVELING ALCHE-MISTS.
ALCHE-MISTS!

FULLMETAL ALCHEMIST™

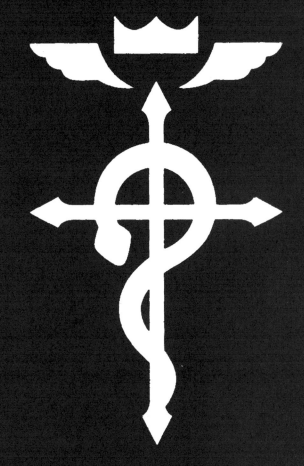

THE BLIND ALCHEMIST

THE BONUS MANGA STARTS HERE. BUT THE REST OF THE BOOK GOES THE OTHER DIRECTION. IF YOU WANT TO READ THE PROFILE GUIDE THE WAY WE INTENDED, YOU'LL HAVE TO FLIP IT AROUND. OR YOU CAN START THE MANGA NOW.

STOP!

WE LIKE TO KEEP YOU ON YOUR TOES.